ACUA
Underwater Archaeology
Proceedings
2016

edited by
Paul F. Johnston

AN ADVISORY COUNCIL ON UNDERWATER ARCHAEOLOGY PUBLICATION

2016 © Advisory Council on Underwater Archaeology

Library of Congress Control Number: 2016955454

Made possible in part through the support of
the Society for Historical Archaeology.

Cover Image: Walters, Samuel. *The* Queen of the Ocean *Going to the Rescue of the* Ocean Monarch, 1848.
Oil on canvas. Courtesy of the Smithsonian: NMAH Transportation, Washington, DC.

Contents

Foreword..vi

Contributed Papers

Bricks as Ballast: An Archaeological Investigation of a Shipwreck Site in Cahuita National Park, Costa Rica 8
    JEREMY BORRELLI, LYNN B. HARRIS

The South Carolina BOEM Cooperative Agreement: Geophysical Mapping and Identification of Paleolandscapes and Historic Shipwrecks Offshore South Carolina, Year One..17
    DANIEL MARK BROWN, JAMES D. SPIREK

Hidden in Plain Sight: Monitoring Shipwrecks in the Atlantic Waters of St. Augustine, Florida..25
    P. BRENDAN BURKE

Diving into the Past: F4U Corsair at Crystal Cove State Marine Conservation Area.....35
    TRICIA DODDS

Establishing an Integrated Conservation Priority for Artillery from Site 31CR314, *Queen Anne's Revenge* (1718)..40
    ERIK FARRELL

The 'Maritime Cultural Landscape' Approach as a Framework for Addressing Neglected Narratives: Point Pearce Aboriginal Mission/Burgiyana, South Australia......................48
    MADELINE FOWLER

A Model for Analyzing Wreck and Cargo Selective Salvage Using Economic and Utilitarian Values...58
    CHELSEA R. FREELAND

Results from the first excavation on the Saintes Bay's Shipwreck, Guadeloupe, FWI.....65
    JEAN-SÉBASTIEN GUIBERT

The Maritime Archaeology of Slave Ships: Overview, Assessment and Prospectus........71
    JESSICA IRWIN, DAVE CONLIN

Lake Tahoe Maritime Heritage Trail..75
    DENISE JAFFKE, TRICIA DODDS

The 2012 Field Season of the 1630-31 New Spain Fleet Archaeological Project in the Gulf of Mexico..79
    Roberto Junco, Flor Trejo

Prioritizing the Concretions from *Queen Anne's Revenge* for Conservation: A Case Study in Managing a Large Collection..84
    Kimberly P. Kenyon

Legacies of an Old Design: Reconstructing Rapid's Lines Using 3D Modelling Software..90
    Ivor Mollema, Jennifer F. McKinnon

Examining Golden Age Pirates as a Distinct Culture Through Artifact Patterning........95
    Courtney E. Page

A Maritime Context for Richmond, Virginia and Environs: Assessment and Recommendations for Future Study..102
    Bruce G. Terrell

An Initial Site Assessment of Submerged Naval Aircraft off the Coast of Pensacola, Florida..110
    Hunter W. Whitehead, Nicole Mauro

Shallow Water Hydrographic Surveys in Support of Archaeological Site Preservation: *Queen Anne's Revenge* Wreck Site, North Carolina..117
    Mark U. Wilde-Ramsing, David J. Bernstein, Christopher W. Freeman

The Storm Wreck

The Archaeology, Conservation, and Interpretation of the Storm Wreck, a Wartime Refugee Vessel Evacuating Charleston, South Carolina at the End of the American Revolution and Lost at St. Augustine, Florida on 31 December 1782..122
    Carolane Veilleux, Chuck Meide

Archival Research and the Historical Background of the 1782 Evacuation of Charleston and the Loss of the Storm Wreck..133
    Molly L. Trivelpiece, Chuck Meide

Bang Bang! Cannons, Carronades, and the Gun Carriage from the Storm Wreck.......142
    Chuck Meide

Pew Pew! Small Arms from the Storm Wreck, a Loyalist Evacuation Ship from the End of the American Revolutionary War..153
    Starr Cox

Ship's Equipment, Fittings, and Rigging Components from the Storm Wreck.............160
    Eden Andes

Navigational Instruments found on the Storm Wreck...164
    Mary Burkett

Household Artifacts from the Storm Wreck..169
    Christopher McCarron

An Archaeological Examination of Cookware from the Storm Wreck, 8SJ5459..........177
    Annie Elizabeth Carter

Have Tools Will Travel: An Examination of Tools found on the Storm Wreck, A Loyalist Evacuation Transport Wrecked on the St. Augustine Bar in 1782...............................182
    Sam Turner

Taking it Personally: Personal Items from the Storm Wreck..187
    Hunter Brendel

Weight, Weight…Don't Tell Me: Assemblage of Weights from the Storm Wreck.........194
    Andrew Thomson

Life Among the Wind and Waves: Examining Living Conditions on Sailing Vessels Through the Use of Microscopic Remains..202
    Jacob Shidner

Gone for a Soldier: An Archaeological Signature of a Military Presence aboard the Storm Wreck..209
    Brian McNamara

Archaeology for the Masses: Presenting the Storm Wreck through Public Archaeology..214
    Olivia McDaniel, Brenda Swann, Jill Titcomb, and Paul Zielinski

Wrecked! An Interactive Exhibition on a Revolutionary War Shipwreck in St. Augustine, Florida..220
    Brenda Swann, Olivia McDaniel

Foreword

The Past and Future

The East and West Coast meetings of the Society for Historical Archaeology usually attract the largest groups of attendees, and 2016 was no different. Mix in the 100th anniversary of the National Park Service and the 50th anniversary of the National Historic Preservation Act, and a truly large and diverse group of historical archaeologists emerged from their labors to get together and share their results.

We had 1,401 registrants and 927 papers—of which 204 were underwater. There were dozens of concurrent sessions, workshops, tours, roundtable luncheons, plenaries, a revival of the Underwater Film Festival, all combined into the second largest meetings in the long and venerable history of the SHA. Great stuff, and it all went very smoothly from our location at Washington's historic Omni Shoreham Hotel to the local weather.

It has been a pleasure to read and edit the 31 underwater *Proceedings* papers from the 2016 SHA meetings. Underwater chairs don't have much opportunity to attend papers or sessions, so this was a great way to see personally and in detail what our colleagues and their students are working on and learn the latest results. Fifteen of the papers are devoted to the 1781 Storm Wreck off St. Augustine, FL. Excavations on this important wreck site from the very end of the American Revolution have ended, and the papers in this volume present results of the preliminary studies of the many categories of artifacts found aboard this wreck.

The other half of the papers also contain a wealth of information about new techniques and methods, new sites, and new ways to investigate and interpret them. Some of the finds and theories presented here may find their way into future textbooks, and others will not. But that's the nature of the field, and it's just as important to learn from our side steps as from our successes. Hopefully these papers will buttress our shared past and build for our future, as reflected in their authors' words and perspectives, and provide fresh new insights for further reflection, discussion and investigation.

Our sincerest thanks to the staff of the PAST Foundation for their strong and lasting support of these *Proceedings*.

PAUL F. JOHNSTON
Smithsonian Institution

ACUA
Underwater Archaeology
Proceedings
2016

Bricks as Ballast: An Archaeological Investigation of a Shipwreck Site in Cahuita National Park, Costa Rica

Jeremy Borrelli and Lynn B. Harris

Wooden ships wrecked in Caribbean waters seldom preserve their structural integrity. Often only ferrous artifacts and ballast remain as cultural indicators. Recently ballast has been utilized more as a tool to interpret a wreck site. In 2015 an East Carolina University team investigated a wreck site in Costa Rica consisting of yellow bricks stacked in a concentrated, organized pile. This paper examines the potential function of brick as ballast cargo in the historical record of the Afro-Caribbean region. It argues that detailed documentation of commercial ballast patterns may yield important interpretive data regarding the identification and analysis of the site.

Introduction

Ballast is one of the most commonly found artifacts on shipwreck sites, especially those with minimal or no wooden hull remains. Several studies have argued that ballast material has potential to provide invaluable provenance information upon which to base historical research to find references of lost ships and for comparative artifact material to support observations made on a particular site (Keith and Simmons 1985; Lamb 1988; Garrison et al 1989; Buckland and Sadler 1990; Meide 1994:1; Conaghan et al. 1998; Smith et al 1998; Callahan et al. 2001; Keeping 2009; Gifford 2014). This research focuses on the use of bricks as ballast and the potential implications this has for the identification of a shipwreck site. The potential utility of an assemblage of brick as a contextual tool for identifying an unknown shipwreck site will be examined through a discussion of a Costa Rican shipwreck site located in the protected marine area of Cahuita National Park, Costa Rica.

Project Background

Cahuita is a small town located in the Talamanca Province on Costa Rica's southern Caribbean coastline. In 1970 the coral reefs surrounding Cahuita Point, the historic location for the town, were declared a national monument (Weitzner and Borrás 1999:133). In June 2015, East Carolina University's (ECU) Program in Maritime Studies conducted a field school in the Parque Nacional de Cahuita (Cahuita National Park). The primary focus of this fieldwork centered on two shipwreck sites investigated in 1981 by University of Florida archaeologist Steven Gluckman (now deceased) (Figure 1). In accordance with a permit issued by Systema Nacional De Áreas De Conservación (SINAC), the ultimate goal for the project was to conduct non-disturbance mapping and documentation of the underwater sites and examine the historical record of the area to investigate the claim that the wrecks were Danish slaving vessels.

Gluckman was the first archaeologist to visit Cahuita by invitation from Costa Rican officials. Due to time constraints and lack of sufficient tools, he was only able to provide general observations and interpretations of what will be referred to as the "Brick Site." Gluckman described the wreck as a large pile of bricks 19 m long and 9.5 m wide, oriented 30° west of north and about 2 m high at its midpoint (Gluckman 1992:460). He noted that the bricks were approximately the same size and shape as traditional 18th century Dutch bricks, but the quality was significantly lower than common bricks of this type. The brick showed evidence of inconsistent firing at lower temperatures, with sloppy molding and incompletely ground clay (Gluckman 1992:465). No

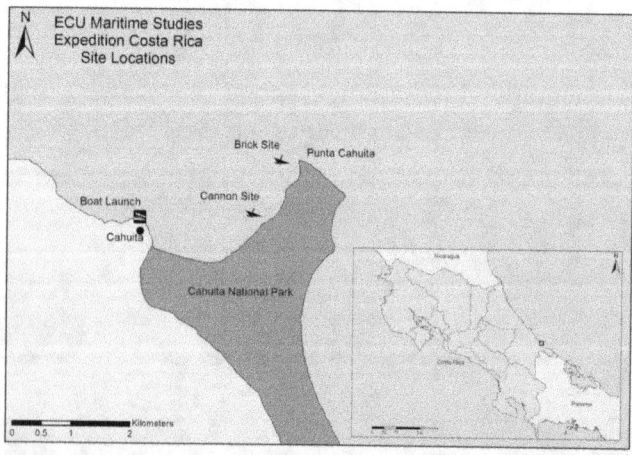

Figure 1. Map depicting the study area in Cahuita and Cahuita National Park, Costa Rica. The locations of the Brick Site and nearby Cannon Site are shown in relation to the town of Cahuita (Map by J. Borrelli, 2015).

evidence of ballast stones or other heavy cargo, aside from two cannon, was found on the site.

In addition to the brick, Gluckman (1992:460) discovered hull planking that ran immediately below the brick near its eastern edge. Of the two cannons found on the site, one was found in association with the hull remains. Local divers and fishermen described an anchor observed on the site, but during the fieldwork the anchor was never found. Gluckman (1992:461) also recounted how possibly ten manillas, or items used as a medium of exchange in the slave trade, had reputedly been recovered from the site. Due to the significance of manillas in historical literature of the slave trade, Gluckman suggested that the wreck might have been involved with the Atlantic slave trade (Alpern 1995:13).

Fieldwork

ECU mapping operations began on the Brick Site first to determine the extent of the artifact scatter relative to the brick pile. Based on the relatively unobstructed flat topography over the site, researchers selected a baseline method to map the wreck. The baseline measured 54 m, with the line oriented at 335° along the north-south axis of the estimated shipwreck area and main concentration of brick. The team divided the site into 22 units measuring 5 m on either side of the baseline, and mapped individual units using 90° offset measurements (Figure 2).

The main feature of the Brick Site was a large, organized mound of stacked yellow bricks. The bricks seemed to be deliberately stacked along their longitudinal edge, with the face of the bricks pointing east and west. Clear edges of the brick stack were found at 17 m and 30 m on the baseline, which defined the pile's north-south axis. A sample of 30 bricks taken from this central area measured an average of 21.82 cm x 10.79 cm x 4.39 cm in dimension. The western side of the pile was partially exposed, while the easternmost extent of the pile could not be defined due to sand overburden. This difference could be due to the dominant currents in the area, which would have created a scouring effect on the

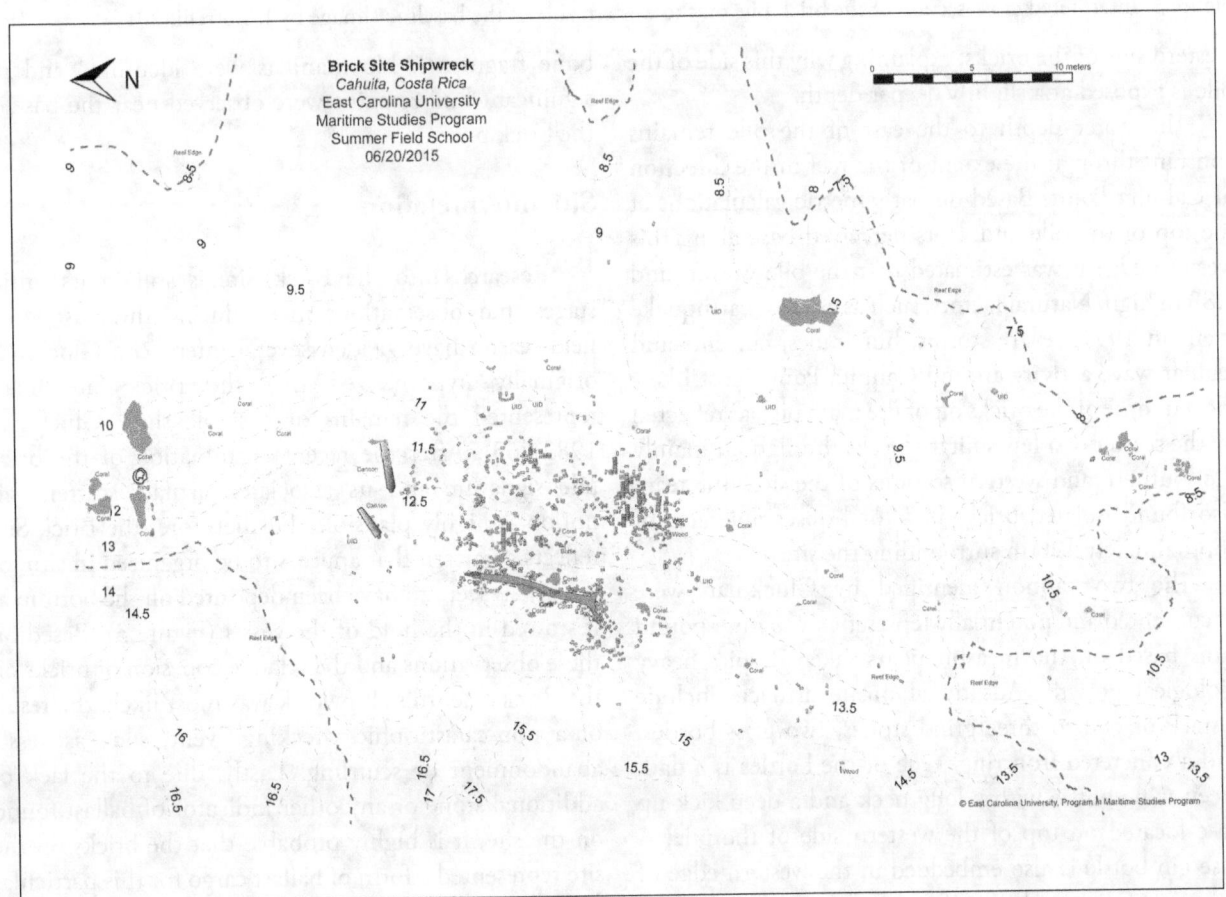

Figure 2. Site plan for the Brick Site with bathymetric contours to demonstrate bottom topography (Image by N. Richards, 2015).

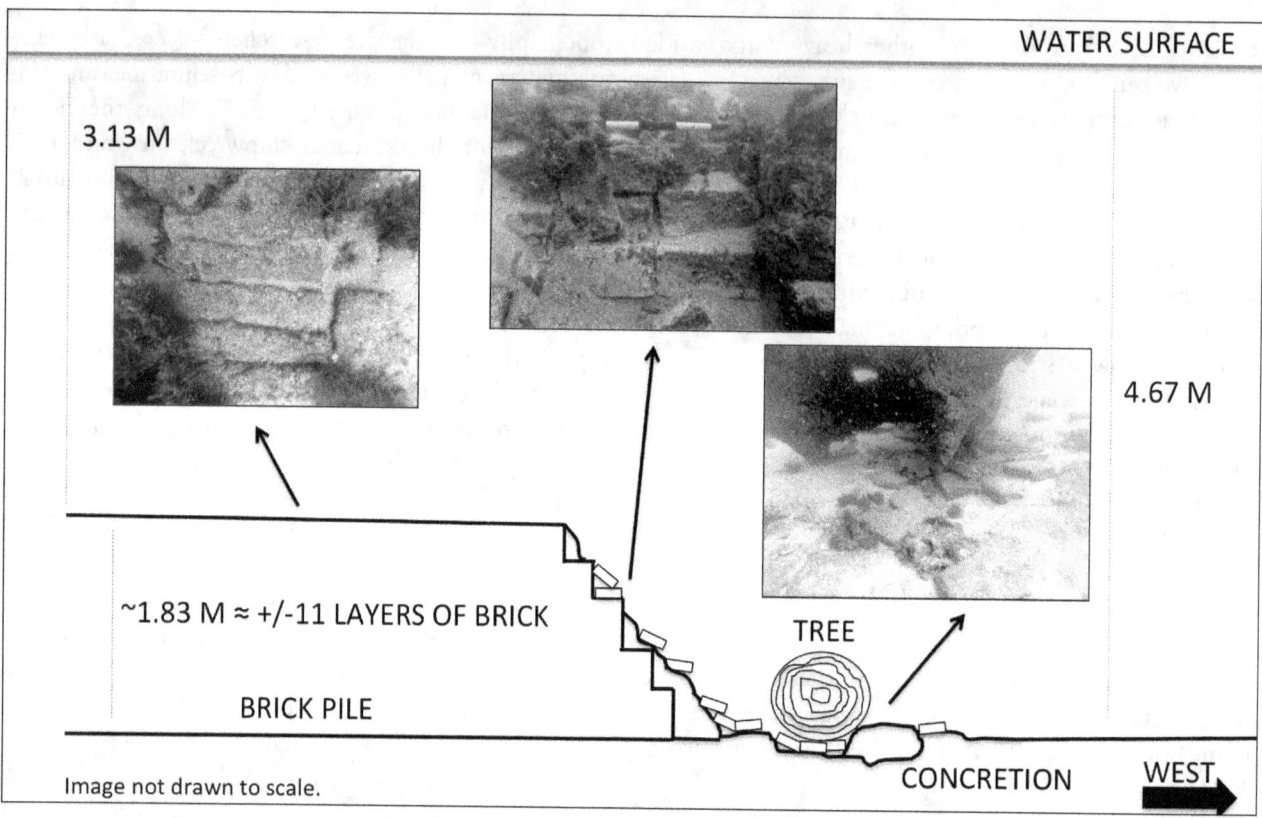

Figure 3. Interpreted cross-section of the brick pile on the western side of the baseline (Image by J. Borrelli, 2015).

western side of the bricks, explaining why this side of the pile is exposed at a slightly deeper depth.

The water depth to the east of the pile remains constant through the extent of the reef in the direction of Cahuita Point. Based on bathymetric calculations at the top of the pile and at its perceived base along this western edge it was estimated that the pile was around 1.83 m high. Natural factors, such as a major earthquake event in 1991, severe storms, hurricanes, currents and regular wave activity around Cahuita Point most likely moved some of the bricks off of the main pile, as reflected by the scatter of a few solitary bricks throughout mainly the southern and western sections of the site. The team also found isolated bricks in a total observable area of approximately 120 m surrounding the site.

The two cannon identified by Gluckman were documented and potentially represent six to nine-pound guns based on the measurements taken despite heavy biological growth. Additional onsite artifacts include a stack of two to three grind stones, two glass bottles, and a concreted iron ring. One of the bottles is a dark green wine bottle with a long neck and a deep kick-up base located on top of the western side of the pile. A case gin bottle is also embedded in the western edge of the brick. Several other artifacts were mapped, including multiple unidentified concretions and a few wood and bone fragments. No manillas were identified and no significant hull remains were observed near the base of the brick pile.

Site Interpretation

Research into the Brick Site is still in its initial stages, but observations made during this past year's field season have yielded several inferences. Gluckman originally hypothesized that the Brick Site likely represented the remains of a single ship (Gluckman 1982:463). After the recent examination of the brick pile signature and its associated artifact scatter, this notion is highly plausible. Furthermore, the Brick Site reflects a pattern that appears to be organized in situ, or the bricks seem to have been deposited on the bottom as if stowed in the hold of the vessel (Figure 3). Based on these observations and the relative cohesion of bricks on the Brick Site, this shipwreck was most likely the result of a non-catastrophic wrecking event, such as vessel abandonment or scuttling. Lastly, due to the lack of additional stone or any other indicator of ballast found on the site, it is highly probable that the bricks on the site represented a form of ballast cargo for this particular vessel.

Bricks as Ballast

Ballast refers to any additional material placed in the bottommost portion of a ship to lower the vessel's center of gravity, improve ship handling and sailing balance (Gifford 2014:26-27). Historically, ballast has taken several forms including stone, gravel, dirt, sand, brick, metal ingots or bars, cement, and the recent introduction of water tank ballasting. There have been several previous studies, which have arranged the various forms of ballast into different types (Lamb 1988; McGrail 1989).

Sean McGrail (1989:357) developed a classification for ballast in which material fell into two groupings: "saleable" or commercial ballast and "unsaleable" or non-commercial ballast. In order to frame his grouping, McGrail (1989:356-357) outlined the concepts of cargo density and stowage factors. Examples of low stowage factor cargo are high density, heavy items that take up less comparative space per individual unit, such as bricks, lead, iron, or marble, while high stowage factor goods consist of objects of typically greater quantity and bulk, but lesser weight and cargo density such as wine, firearms, or fabrics.

Using these modern concepts, McGrail posited that if a vessel embarked with a cargo of low stowage factor goods, these items could not only be sold as profitable commercial objects but also could fill optimal space in the hold and effectively serve as ballast (McGrail 1989:357). Ideally, this heavier cargo would be coupled with smaller, high stowage factor goods, all of which could be sold upon arrival to multiply a ship's potential profitability from a single voyage (Keeping 2006:10; Gifford 2014:27). The underlying premise of this idea is that a single cargo item, such as brick, may hold multiple functions on a vessel. Commercial ballast can therefore be defined as any consignment of cargo placed in the hold of a vessel with the intent to bring in profit of some form at the port of arrival, which also contributes a significant ballasting effect. One of the most archaeologically documented forms of commercial ballast was brick.

Historically, bricks were used for general building purposes, in major engineering projects, to pave streets or floors and due to their resistance to heat, firebricks were used to line fireplaces, hearths or kilns (Meide 1994:1-7). In a maritime context, the majority of bricks found on shipwreck sites have been associated with either the ballasting of the vessel or the galley or hearth area (e.g. Skelton 2010:249). There is early evidence for the shipment of ballast bricks and tiles from northern Italy to Dalmatia in the first century AD. These bricks appeared almost exclusively among coastal regions along the Adriatic and northern Africa and were likely transported as cargoes of profitable ballast for specific projects or as general roofing material (Glicksman 2005:194-195).

Brickmaking and the exportation of large quantities of brick spread to other parts of northern Europe as early as the 12th century (Bernotas 2013:140). This practice continued well into the late 19th century, with many Spanish and English bricks making their way to the Americas as commercial ballast (Meide 1994:7-8). There is an abundance of archaeological evidence to further support the shipment of commercial ballast bricks, which is mainly demonstrated by the presence of large caches of such bricks on 16th and 17th century colonial and shipwreck sites (Forster and Higgs 1973:29; Becker 1977:112; Green 1977:169-172, 1986:103, 1989:190; Stenuit 1974:235; Pietruzska 2011:149; Gifford 2013:32).

The Brick Site is distinctive due to the fact that the original integrity of the brick pile appears to be mostly undamaged. In comparison, the Dutch East India Company vessel *Vergulde Draeck* struck a reef in 1655 and subsequently broke up in the wave activity along with its cargo of ballast brick. The violent nature of the wrecking event resulted in a dispersed pattern of jumbled bricks and artifacts throughout the wreckage area (Green 1973:267, 1977:91). Therefore, the Brick Site presents a unique opportunity to examine the nature of brick cargo and commercial ballast in regards to stowage patterns and potential utility of ballast brick as an identifying feature on a shipwreck site.

Yellow Brick

The transportation of bricks as ballast was most extensively recorded during the 17th century, when small yellow bricks were widely produced and distributed throughout Holland and Northern Europe. There was an increase in the manufacture of yellow bricks from the 16th to the 17th century, when population growth in the region necessitated the construction of newer buildings, paved streets, an increase in large-scale engineering projects, and a need to reinforce fortifications domestically and abroad (De Vries and Van der Woude 1997:304). Architects from these areas utilized yellow bricks in the Netherlands, Denmark, Sweden, and Germany, which created a common aesthetic between the urban centers of these countries. This aesthetic was transferred to various colonial settlements primarily via bricks manufactured in the Old World and shipped as ballast to various holdings worldwide. This technique was later named the "Copenhagen style" by architectural historian Hans Henrik Engquist due to its prevalence in the Danish West Indies (Chapman 1995:139).

As a result of the demand for bricks in colonial outposts, yellow bricks frequently appeared in outbound shipping records as ballast (Becker 1977:112-113). Danish ships, for example, were known to carry up to 10,000 yellow bricks as ballast to augment the architectural need for brick in the West Indies (Lunn et al 2016:4). Historical sources for *Vergulde Draeck* have shown that the vessel carried approximately 26,000 *Vries clijnkert*, or Friesland bricks, in its initial 1653 voyage to Batavia (Green 1977:170). When *Vergulde Draeck* called at Table Bay, South Africa to unload cargo for the new settlement at the Cape, the ship's records note:

There are plenty of such bricks in the cargo of the two ships…but as they are lying on the keel and under all the cargo [the crew] did not proceed to unload them. The ships would then need to have other ballast instead and to be completely unloaded which would cause considerable delay (Green 1977:32).

It is important to note the manner in which the low stowage factor bricks were packed deeper in the hull in relation to the other cargo items during their voyage. Such shipments of commercial ballast bricks were a part of a larger system whereby local governors would submit specific requests that were filled by the VOC in the Netherlands and distributed on a limited number of vessels annually (Green 1977:170). The employment of certain vessels to carry a large amount of bricks demonstrates a cognitive willingness to sacrifice an allotment of cargo space for the transportation of construction materials to aid various global holdings (Pietruszka 2011:151). This implies that ballast bricks were not shipped arbitrarily, but rather explicitly as commercial ballast cargo that should be reflected in the historical record for a particular vessel. Through an examination of the physical characteristics of the types of yellow commercial ballast bricks, a possible origin upon which to base further historical research on the Brick Site can be determined.

Identifying the Yellow Brick

The most obvious physical characteristics of the brick are color, shape, size and quality. Color, however, is troublesome when used as an identifying factor for brick since there are aspects of both composition as well as the firing process that impacts the color of brick. The shape of bricks is also problematic since the shape of the brick is largely dependent on its intended use (Meide 1994:10-11). South, however, notes that brick size, while not necessarily useful for dating purposes, can add functional, temporal, or areal significance when wide variations in size and form are equated with one another (South 1964:73). Without compositional analysis, a comparison between the sizes of known brick assemblages can be the most reliable method for potentially identifying an unknown type of brick.

There are various types of yellow-bodied bricks found in the archaeological literature that potentially match those found on the Brick Site. Gluckman originally identified the bricks on the site as 18th century Dutch yellow brick. The known size range for 8,000 yellow bricks found on *Vergulde Draeck*, for example, varied between 17-18 cm in length, 7-8 cm in width, and 3-3.8 cm in thickness (Green 1977:170). Similar to the Brick Site, these bricks also appeared to be crudely made. Ballast bricks found on the Dutch fluit *Risdam* averaged a dimension of 17.6 cm x 7.6 cm x 3.4 cm (Green 1985:28). At the colonial Pintzhof Site in Pennsylvania, the majority of whole yellow bricks conformed to the average size for Dutch bricks (Becker 1977:116-118).

During the 17th and 18th centuries, Danish vessels would typically carry the modern *flensburger*, a type of brick that was produced at brick works near Flensborg Fjord and on Sjælland in Denmark (Lunn et al 2016:4). The Danish brickmaking tradition began in medieval times, and the typical Flensburg brick found on St. Thomas is typically larger than the Dutch style at an average of 22.8 cm in length, 10.8 cm in width and 4 cm in thickness. The 1786 wreck of the Danish brigantine *Die Frau Metta Catharina von Flensburg* had several Flensburg bricks found in association with the ship's galley area, which measured an average of 22.2 cm x 11.1 cm x 4.1 cm (Skelton 2010:249).

Another type of yellow brick found on early Spanish colonial sites in the Americas and Caribbean are called *ladrillos*. *Ladrillos* are flat, wide, tile-like bricks made of unglazed coarse earthenware and were among the first to be produced in the New World (Meide 1994:18). Of the 89 yellow *ladrillos* found on the 1766 Spanish wreck, *El Nuevo Constante* for example, the average measurement for these bricks were 23 cm x 11 cm x 3.3 cm (Gifford 2013:33). *Ladrillos* found on both shipwreck and colonial sites range from approximately

19-37 cm in length, 9-15 cm in width, and 3-5 cm in thickness (Meide 1994:22).

Based on the above descriptions, it is possible to speculate about the style of brick discovered on the Brick Site. For each type found in different geographical areas and on multiple shipwreck sites, the average dimensions are compared in Table 1. The initial appearance of the yellow brick appeared identical to the Dutch style, which has been extensively researched within archaeological literature, but is typically much smaller in size than those found on the Brick Site. Furthermore, unlike the *ladrillos*, which vary anywhere between 19-37 cm in length, the bricks found on the Brick Site only range from about 21 to 23 cm. Instead, the bricks most closely resemble the Danish *flensburger* type (Figure 4). Each brick is crudely made, the same general color, and most importantly, within the same average size range from other artifact assemblages. Further compositional analyses are needed to corroborate this claim. Two shipwrecks that are historically known to have wrecked near the present research location at Punta Cahuita, however, were the Danish slave ships *Fredericus Quartus* and *Christianus Quintus*.

Shipwreck Candidates

In December 1708, *Christianus Quintus* and *Fredericus Quartus* embarked from Copenhagen, Denmark on a slaving voyage to St. Thomas via the African Gold Coast. After arriving at Danish-held Christiansborg Castle on the Gold Coast, both vessels learned that the number of slaves available were severely limited due to local conflicts. Ultimately, *Fredericus Quartus* was able to acquire about 450 slaves, 51 marks, and 8,000 lbs. of elephant tusks and *Christianus Quintus* was able to obtain a total number of 373 slaves when the two ships finally left Africa in October 1709 (Holm 1978:183-184; Justesen 2005:223; Lohse 2005:43). Both ships endured multiple navigational errors on the voyage across the Atlantic, in addition to a heavy storm that ultimately landed them at what is now believed to be Punta Cahuita (Nørregård 1948:81; Holm 1978:185). Discontented with the harsh conditions and poor leadership, the crew mutinied and both vessels were burned to the waterline soon thereafter (Holm 1978:186). Many of the slaves were released in the local area, and the crew bartered passage to Panama,

Yellow Brick Type	Site / Region	Length (cm)	Width (cm)	Thickness (cm)
Dutch Yellow Brick	Virginia (Nöel Hume 1969)	18.10	8.30	3.50
	West Netherlands (Becker 1977)	17.20	7.30	3.20
	Pintzhof Site, 36DE3 (Becker 1977)	17.20	8.00	3.60
	Batavia (Green 1989)	18.20	8.40	3.70
	Risdam (Green 1986)	17.60	7.60	3.40
	Vergulde Draeck (Green 1977)	17.60	7.60	3.40
	Lastdrager (Stenuit 1974)	17.40	7.60	3.50
	Elmina Wreck (Pietruszka 2011)	16.40	8.13	3.13
	Average	**17.46**	**7.87**	**3.43**
Danish Flensburger	St. Thomas (Lunn 2016)	22.80	10.80	4.00
	Die Frau Metta Catharina von Flensburg (Skelton 2010)	22.20	11.10	4.10
	Average	**22.50**	**10.95**	**4.05**
Spanish *Ladrillos*	*La Isabela* (Meide 1994)		11.00	5.00
	Concepcion de la Vega (Meide 1994)	29.00	13.00	4.50
	Puerto Real (Meide 1994)	28.00	13.60	4.00
	Nuestra Senorita de Rosario (Meide 1994)	30.00	14.00	
	Santa Rosa (Meide 1994)	23.00	11.00	3.60
	San José (Meide 1994)	28.00	13.00	3.00
	El Nuevo Constante (Meide 1994)	23.00	11.00	3.30
	Bateria de San Antonio (Meide 1994)	28.00	12.30	4.75
	Average	**27.00**	**12.36**	**4.02**
Brick Site	**Average**	**21.82**	**10.79**	**4.39**

Table 1. Table comparing the different dimensions of yellow-bodied brick found within archaeological literature. The total average measurements are displayed in bold for each type.

while the two captains returned back to Denmark empty-handed.

Both of these slave ships were bound for St. Thomas, a Danish port in the West Indies at the time. During this time, northern European building traditions heavily utilized brick, and this style of construction dominated the built heritage exhibited in the Danish West Indies. Initial research into the historical record for these vessels revealed that *Christianus Quintus* contained an outbound cargo intended for Africa such as cloth, metal goods, and weapons all to be traded with the Africans, as well as building materials, bricks, and boards to repair and enlarge Danish forts on the African coast (Nørregård 1948:70). The initial cargo of *Fredericus Quartus* included 30 chests of sheets, eight chests of guns, two casks of knives, 522 bars of Norwegian iron, 648 bars of Swedish iron, and nineteen cases of gifts to sell and trade in Africa (Holm 1978:183).

Pietruszka (2011:151) has argued that vessels traveling to the Gold Coast likely decreased the potential profitability of the voyage by including building supplies within the initial cargo space since it does not allow for the maximum trading material for which to acquire slaves. However, the practice of stocking the hold with heavier, low stowage factor ballast bricks may have been a predetermined sacrifice since human cargo would have been much lighter than the original outbound cargo. The bricks, while not part of the cargo traded for slaves at the Gold Coast, would have provided some profit upon arriving at the final destination of St. Thomas in the form of building material for the growing colony (Lunn 2016:4).

To conclude, based on the consignment of ballast bricks, *Fredericus Quartus* and *Christianus Quintus* are the strongest candidates for the Brick Site shipwreck. This preliminary research has revealed a new avenue of research into these potential ships from their possible ballast signature in the archaeological record. These interpretations are not conclusive, but rather establish a foundation for further inquiry. Therefore, additional research is needed within the Danish archives for each vessel to substantiate the tangible evidence presented above. It is ultimately hoped that this study of commercial ballast brick will promote the potential for future research on bricks and ballast in order to further our understanding of these often neglected artifact assemblages and more importantly, how they may contribute to a holistic interpretation of a shipwreck site.

Figure 4. Example of typical yellow brick found on the Brick Site (Photo by J. Borrelli).

Acknowledgments

First, we would like to thank Jorge Martinez Mojica of Willie's Tours in Costa Rica for organizing the day-to-day requirements for the field project. Also David and Toni Van Zandt for collaborating on the permit application, and Jorge Gonzalez of SINAC for processing the necessary paperwork and scientific passports. We would also like to thank all ECU faculty and graduate students for contributing to the fieldwork on the Brick Site, specifically Dr. Nathan Richards who was co-primary investigator for the project. Lastly we recognize Dom Manuel, Luis, Minor, and Chul, our boat captains, who were invaluable assets throughout the fieldwork.

References

ALPERN, STANLEY B.
1995 What Africans Got for Their Slaves: A master list of European trade goods. *History in Africa* 22:5-43.

BECKER, MICHAEL J.
1977 "Swedish" Colonial Yellow Bricks: Notes on their uses and possible origins in 17th century America. *Historical Archaeology* 11:112-118.

BERNOTAS, RIVO
2013 Brick-making in Medieval Livonia – The Estonian Example. *Estonian Journal of Archaeology* 17(2):139-156.

BUCKLAND, P.C., AND JON SADLER
2010 Ballast and Building Stone: A Discussion. In *Stone: Quarrying and building in England AD 43-1525*, David Parsons, editor, pp. 114-125. Phillimore, Royal Archaeological Institute, Chichester, United Kingdom.

CALLAHAN, JOHN, E., J. WILLIAM MILLER, AND JAMES R. CRAIG
2001 Ballast Stone Studies From North Carolina Shipwreck 0003BUI, The *Queen Anne's Revenge*: Hand Specimen, X-Ray, Petrographic, Chemical, Paramagnetic, and 40K-40AR Age Results. *Southeastern Geology* 40(1):49-57.

CHAPMAN, WILLIAM
1995 Irreconcilable Differences: Urban residences in the Danish West Indies, 1700-1900. *Winterthur Portfolio* 30(2/3):129-172.

CONAGHAN, P.J., W. DELANEY, AND H.M. HAWLANDER
1998 Geoarchaeological Confirmation of Shipwreck Identity, Cockburn Reef, Far-North Queensland, Australia. *Geoarchaeology: An International Journal* 13(2):161-199.

DE VRIES, JAN AND AD VAN DER WOUDE
1997 *The First Modern Economy: Success, Failure, and Perseverance of the Dutch Economy, 1500-1815*. Cambridge University Press, Cambridge, United Kingdom.

FORSTER, WILLIAM A. AND KENNETH B. HIGGS
1973 The Kennemerland, 1971: An Interim Report. *IJNA* 2:291-300.

GARRISON, ERVAN G., CHARLES P. GIAMMONA, JAMES JOBLING, ANTHONY R. TRIPP, ERI N. WEINSTEIN, AND GARY A. WOLFF
1989 An Eighteenth-Century Ballast Pile, Chandeleur Islands, Louisiana: An instrumental and archaeological study. OCS Study/MMS 890092 U.S. Dept. of the Interior, Minerals Mgmt. Service, Gulf of Mexico OCS Regional Office, New Orleans, Louisiana.

GIFFORD, ERICA K
2013 Organic and Inorganic Chemical Characterization of Artifacts from the Emanuel Point Shipwrecks. Master's thesis, Department of Anthropology, The University of West Florida, Pensacola, Florida.

GIFFORD, MATTHEW J
2014 Everything is Ballast: An examination of ballast related practices and ballast stones from the Emanuel Point Shipwrecks. Master's thesis, Department of Anthropology, The University of West Florida, Pensacola, Florida.

GLICKSMAN, KRISTINA
2005 Internal and External Trade in the Roman Province of Dalmatia. *Opsvcula Archaeologica* 29:189-230.

GLUCKMAN, STEPHEN
1992 Preliminary Investigation of a Shipwreck, Pumpata Cahuita National Park, Costa Rica. In *Maritime Archaeology: A Reader of Substantive and Theoretical Contributions*, Lawrence E. Babits and Hans Van Tilberg, editors, pp. 453-469. Plenum Press, New York.

GREEN, JEREMY N.
1973 The Wreck of the Dutch East Indiaman the Vergulde Draeck, 1656. *IJNA* 2(2): 267-289.

1977 The Loss of the Vereenigde Oostindische Compagnie Jacht Vergulde Draek, Western Australia 1656: An historical background and excavation report with an appendix on similar loss of the fluit Lastdrager, Part 1. *British Archaeological Reports*, Supplementary Series 36, Oxford, UK.

1986 The Survey of the VOC fluit Risdam (1727), Malaysia. *IJNA* 15(2):93-104.

1989 The Loss of the Vereenigde Oostindische Compagnie retourschip Batavia, Western Australia 1629 an Excavation Report and Catalogue of Artefacts. *British Archaeological Reports*, International Series 489, Oxford, United Kingdom.

GURKE, KARL
1987 *Bricks and Brickmaking: A handbook for historical archaeology*. University of Idaho Press, Moscow, Idaho.

HOLM, JOHN ALEXANDER
1978 The Creole English of Nicaragua's Miskito Coast: Its Sociolinguistic History and a Comparative Study of its Lexicon and Syntax. Doctoral Dissertation, University College of London. University Microfilms International, Ann Arbor, Michigan.

JUSTESEN, OLE (EDITOR)
2005 *Danish Sources for the History of Ghana, Vol. 1: 1657-1735*. The Royal Danish Academy of Sciences and Letters, Copenhagen, Denmark.

Keeping, Kenneth
2009 Ballast: An Archaeological Perspective on the Provenance of Stone Material and the Comparison of Isolated Deposits. Master's thesis, Department of Archaeology, Flinders University, South Australia.

Keith, Donald H., and Joe J. Simmons III
1985 Analysis of Hull Remains, Ballast and Artifact Distribution of a 16th-Century. Shipwreck, Molasses Reef, British West Indies. *Journal of Field Archaeology* 12(4):411-424.

Lamb, William R.
1988 The Provenance of the Stone Ballast from the Molasses Reef Wreck. Master's thesis, Department of Anthropology, Texas A&M University, College Station, Texas.

Lohse, Russel
2005 Africans and their Descendants in Colonial Costa Rica, 1600-1750. Dissertation, University of Texas, Austin, Texas.

Lunn, Ulla, Louise Sebro, and George Tyson
2016 Construction: Brick. The West Indian Heritage, National Museum of Denmark, Copenhagen http://den-vestindiske-arv.dk/en/the-project-and-the-website/construction/. Accessed 13 January 13, 2016.

McGrail, Sean
1989 The Shipment of Traded Goods and Ballast in Antiquity. *The Oxford Journal of Archaeology* 8(3):353-358.

Meide, Chuck
1994 Bricks: An overview of function, form and historical types. LAMP Artifact Study No. 1, Prepared for the Florida State University Department of Anthropology, Tallahassee, Florida. Lighthouse Archaeological Maritime Program, St. Augustine Lighthouse and Museum, St. Augustine, Florida.

Noel, Hume
1969 *A Guide to Artifacts of Colonial America*. Random House, New York.

Nørregård, Georg
1948 "Forliset ved Nicaragua 1710." Årbog 1948 (Handels Søfartsmuseet på Kronborg, Helsingør, Denmark), 67-98.

Pietruszka, Andrew T.
2011 Artifacts of Exchange: A multiscalar approach to maritime archaeology at Emina, Ghana. PhD dissertation, School of Philosophy, Anthropology, Syracuse University, Syracuse, New York.

Skelton, Ian
2010 Die Frau Metta Catharina von Flensburg: A Danish brigantine wrecked in 1786 in Plymouth Sound, England. *IJNA* 39(2):235-257.

Smith, Roger C., John R. Bratten, J. Cozzi, and Keith Plaskett
1998 The Emanuel Point Ship Archaeological Investigations 1997-1998. Report of Investigations 68, University of West Florida, Archaeology Institute, Pensacola, Forida.

South, Stanley
1964 Some Notes on Bricks. *Florida Anthropologist* 17(2):67-74.

Stenuit, Robert
1974 Early Relics of the VOC Trade from Shetland: The Wreck of the Flute Lastdrager Lost Off Yell, 1653. *IJNA* 3(2):213-156.

Weitzner, Viviane, and Marvin F. Borrás
1999 Cahuita, Límon, Costa Rica: From conflict to collaboration. In *Cultivating Peace: Conflict and Collaboration in Natural Resource Management*, Daniel Buckles, editor, pp. 129-150. International Development Research Centre, World Bank Institute, Washington, D.C.

Jeremy Borrelli
QAR Staff Archaeologist
North Carolina Department of Natural
 and Cultural Resources
1157 VOA Site C Rd.
Greenville, NC 27834

Lynn B. Harris, Ph.D.
Associate Professor
Program in Maritime Studies, History Department
East Carolina University
Admiral Eller House, #200
Greenville, NC 27858--4353

The South Carolina BOEM Cooperative Agreement: Geophysical Mapping and Identification of Paleolandscapes and Historic Shipwrecks Offshore South Carolina, Year One

Daniel Mark Brown and James D. Spirek

In 2014, the Bureau of Ocean Energy Management's Office of Renewable Energy Program (BOEM) signed a Cooperative Agreement with the South Carolina Sea Grant Consortium to explore potential Wind Energy Areas (WEA) off South Carolina's portion of the Outer Continental Shelf (OCS). The aim of the project is to conduct geophysical and archaeological survey of seafloor to explore the possibility of developing future WEAs. The project consists of a remote sensing survey: certain areas of the survey will be refined for paleolandscapes, shipwrecks, and objects of significance to be ground-truthed later. This paper provides a summary of preliminary results.

Introduction

Created in 2010, the Bureau of Ocean Energy Management (BOEM) is responsible for managing all offshore energy. As a federal agency, it is subject to the requirements of the National Historic Preservation Act and Executive Order 11593 to maintain Section 106 compliance. With the development of interest in renewable energy specific to archaeology, an updated Notice To Lessee issued in 2005 (updated in 2011) outlines the current requirements for surveys and reports used to identify the two types of cultural resources most likely encountered on the OCS (BOEM 2011:2-3). On the Atlantic Coast, these are historic sites (generally shipwrecks, lighthouses, ballast piles), and drowned sites representing prehistoric occupation or exploitation dating from the Late Pleistocene, when sea-levels were lower than at present by more than 100 meters on average (Harris et al. 2013:6). With the growth of renewable energy and improved technologies, increased competition has reduced the price of the energy delivered. Simultaneously, multiple states, including South Carolina, have assessed the potential for offshore renewable energy resources. The data yield promising potential off South Carolina.

BOEM generally operates in conjunction with other federal agencies and local and state agencies in order to carry out its NHPA responsibilities. As such, in November 2014, BOEM's Office of Renewable Energy Program (OREP) signed a Cooperative Agreement with the South Carolina Sea Grant Consortium to explore potential WEA offshore of South Carolina's portion of the OCS. The result of this agreement is the Atlantic Offshore Wind Energy Development Project: Geophysical Mapping and Identification of Paleolandscapes and Historic Shipwrecks Offshore South Carolina (herein referred to as the SC-BOEM Cooperative Agreement).

This is a joint project with several SC state agencies and universities: South Carolina Sea Grant, South Carolina Energy Office, Coastal Carolina University (CCU), the College of Charleston (CofC), the University of South Carolina's (USC) Earth Sciences Institute (ESRI), and the South Carolina Institute for Archaeology and Anthropology's Maritime Research Division (SCIAA MRD). SCIAA is a principal member of the project, responsible for aiding remote sensing operations; ground truthing targets through dive operations; delivering analysis of cultural resources; and writing the archaeological report.

Thesis

As interest in WEAs has increased all along the east coast, BOEM seeks to explore the archaeological potential for prehistoric and historic sites submerged in the OCS. In carrying out its mission, BOEM has participated in and funded similar surveys off Massachusetts, Maryland, North Carolina, the Gulf of Mexico near Florida, and the Pacific coast. Since the 1970s, evidence of drastic prehistoric sea level change has fueled speculation on the existence of submerged prehistoric habitation and exploitation sites. Recent technological advances in remote sensing are beginning to make detection of those sites a reality. As a result, scientists, along with divers and fishermen, continue to discover evidence of prehistoric habitation along the now submerged Atlantic OCS before sea levels rose to modern levels around 6,000 years before present (YBP). The SC portion of the OCS has the potential to yield a wealth of archaeological information about the early peopling of North America and the historic seafaring traditions of exploration, trade, and warfare since the Spanish first reached North America in 1492 AD. From 16,000 to 3,000 YBP, the OCS was open for human habitation and exploitation of natural and geological resources (Harris et al. 2013:8). Terrestrial evidence at the Topper Site along the Savannah River in South Carolina suggests occupation as early as 13,500 YBP (Goodyear 2005:107).

Rising sea levels, or transgressions, of the Atlantic Ocean covered areas once occupied by two cultural groups: Paleoindian (13,000-9,000 YBP) and Early to Middle Archaic (9,000-3,000 YBP). Potential inundated archaeological sites include habitation or exploitation sites containing evidence of lithic technology,(points) and organics (bone, antlers, wood and other cultural features). A key research component associated with seeking evidence of early human occupation in the SC-OCS is the geophysical identification of relict waterways, e.g., rivers, bays, and estuaries that have a high potential to preserve prehistoric archaeological sites (Harris et al. 2013:12). Concomitantly, remote sensing and underwater survey off South Carolina has revealed potential for evidence of habitation, including an 11,000-year-old drowned cypress forest located 19 miles off Georgetown, and a Paleolithic stone blade dated to the Early Archaic Period around 9,000 YPB (Powell 1990; Goodyear pers. comm. 2015).

Recent re-nourishment of Folly Beach in Charleston, SC resulted in the finding of a prehistoric stone artifact by local residents, and reportedly other points as well. The sands were dredged from a borrow eight km (5 miles) offshore, and the borrow site apparently included an Early Archaic site. The OCS off South Carolina was a terrestrial landscape for almost 40,000 years eventually covered around 6,000 YBP; it was a landscape that witnessed the arrival of Paleoamericans sometime before 14,000 YBP (Harris et al. 2013:6). All this supports the exciting possibility of discovering evidence of peoples who occupied areas of the OCS as far back as 13,500 YBP or earlier.

Important historical archeological resources lying on the SC-OCS include shipwrecks and historic artifacts. From the earliest European explorations to World War II, the Atlantic Ocean contains shipwrecks associated with these endeavors, along with isolated objects, such as anchors, cannons, and other artifacts of historical significance. Other cultural features of a more hazardous nature—Munitions of Explosive Concern (MEC) or Unexploded Ordnance (UXO) related to bombing areas or to defensive barriers—also are present in the SC-OCS.

More recent cultural objects in the form of artificial reefs also occupy the OCS. Purposefully sunk vessels, subway cars, decommissioned army APCs, and large concrete and steel structures have all been deposited by the SC National Guard and the SC Department of Natural Resources (SCDNR) and are monitored by SCDNR Marine Resources Division. As these objects are part of the marine habitat of the WEA, location of the reefs is significant to the placement and construction of future wind turbines. Embarking on an archaeological assessment consisting of research and geophysical survey will provide baseline information concerning the potential to identify prehistoric and relict landforms, historic shipwrecks and objects, and hazardous MEC/UXO lying in the SC-OCS. The survey will assist BOEM in meeting its management responsibilities under NHPA to identify and mitigate potential adverse impacts to historical and archaeological sites from energy-related activities.

Objectives

The aim of the project was to conduct geophysical and archaeological survey of the seafloor 17 to 26 kilometers (11-16 miles) offshore of North Myrtle Beach and Georgetown, SC, to explore the possibility of developing future WEAs (Figure 1). The first year of the project consisted of a remote sensing survey utilizing a suite of electronic instruments including a side-scan sonar, multi-beam/backscatter, sub-bottom profiler, and magnetometer. Certain areas of the survey will be refined for paleolandscapes, shipwrecks, and objects of archaeological and or historical significance to be ground-truthed later by MRD and BOEM archaeologists.

Methodology

The SC-BOEM Cooperative Agreement divides fieldwork into three Phases: Phase 1; geophysical survey of four Survey Blocks with 75-meter lanes; Phase 2, refined survey of potential targets with 20-meter or less lanes; Phase 3, ground truthing operations by dive teams and ROVs of potential submerged cultural resources. Concomitantly during the geophysical survey, the project underwater archaeologist hired by MRD undertook a compilation of archaeological and historical records of potential cultural resources with consultation of experts in paleo landscapes. The data acquired by the geophysical survey were processed by the USC ESRI and then analyzed by the project underwater archaeologist.

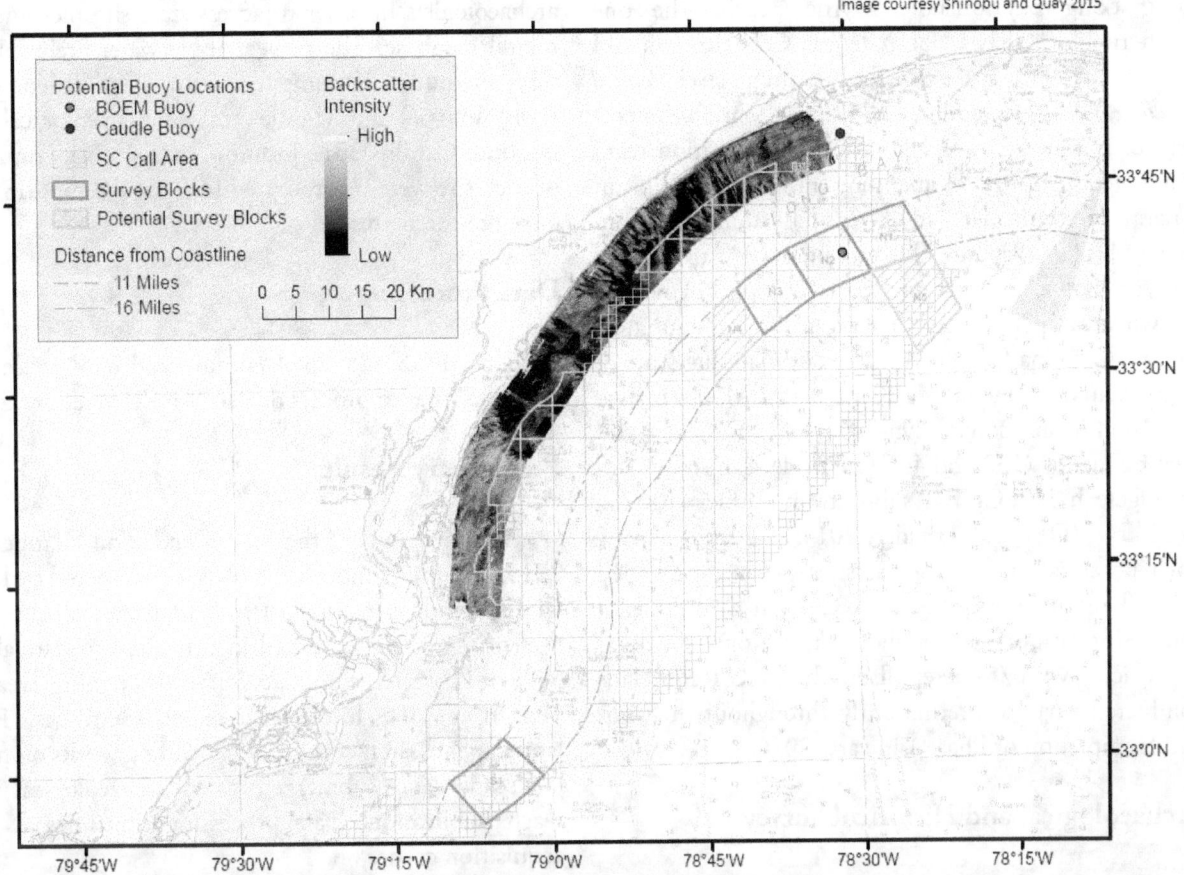

Figure 1. Research Area and four priority Survey Blocks (Image courtesy Shinobu and Quay, 2015).

RE: Conditions Favorable to Prehistoric Preservation

For a submerged prehistoric site to be found *in situ*, it must first survive terrestrial burial, then one or multiple transgression episodes of inundation (Bailey & Flemming 2008 in Evans et al. 2014:18). The site of greatest impact on archaeological preservation is in the surf zone, with obvious high-energy conditions. Although constant exposure to these forces results in deposit disturbance, it is rare events, such as extreme storm systems, tsunamis, iceberg grounding, and peak tides and currents that result in the most damage to archaeological sites undergoing or even having completed transgression (Lacroix et al. 2014:18). An exception can be topographical features such as sediments stabilized by sea grasses (Kellter, et al. 2014:18). Medium-energy conditions mostly affect fine-grained sediments, often leaving larger objects in place.

The most likely environ to find *in situ* archaeological deposits is in *low-energy settings*. Such low-energy conditions can occur on a local scale, depending on the particular geomorphology of a given location. Freshwater lakes close to the shoreline can offer spits, barrier beaches, and lagoons, which if inundated suddenly, can provide good potential for preservation. Similarly, fluvial systems preserved near the modern coast might offer similar preservation; river delta systems could also provide ample sediment deposit during transgression, and thus can potentially offer stabilized conditions. These buried fluvial systems are also referred to as Paleochannels. Specific to the Upper Coastal Plain of SC, Carolina bays and other shallow ponds offer good preservation potential. Similar geographic features might exist preserved under sediment on the OCS as well (Brooks et al. 1996:2; Goodyear pers. comm 2015).

Geophysical Survey

After reviewing data on wind speeds offshore South Carolina, researchers dedicated four Survey Blocks from the SC Call Area along with two Potential Survey Blocks based on greatest energy yield potential. The three northern blocks, N1, N2, and N3, are located along Long Bay offshore Myrtle Beach. The one southern block, S1, is located near Cape Romain off Georgetown. Using their 54-foot research vessel *Coastal Explorer*, CCU's School of Coastal and Marine Systems Science initiated the survey. The data acquisition team conducted geophysical mapping utilizing multibeam sonar, side scan sonar and chirp subbottom profiler in Survey Blocks N1 and N2, targeting 10% overlap of side scan sonar coverage and 50% multibeam coverage of two areas per BOEM habitat mapping standards. Coastal Carolina University's sea floor mapping suite of instrumentation includes a Kongsberg EM3002b dual head multibeam sonar (293-307 kHz), a Klein 3000 dual frequency (132 and 445 kHz) side scan sonar, and an Edgetech 512i CHIRP sub-bottom profiler (500 Hz to 12 kHz) (DeVoe and Bradley 2014:11-14). To narrow down potential cultural resource sites warranting detailed cultural resource site surveys, CCU ran a multibeam and cesium vapor magnetometer survey on 150-meter line spacing with 75-meter offset. The CCU technicians conducted surveys intermittently throughout the year, with completion of Phase 1 in early 2016.

Archaeological and Historical Survey

The project underwater archaeologist conducted an exhaustive literature review of all relevant reports on comparative submerged Paleolithic sites, as well as critical archaeological publications, totalling more than 40 sources. This occurred in conjunction with historic research on potential historic wrecks that might exist within the survey area. The project underwater archaeologist created a GIS map with all known historic shipwrecks from the Atlantic Shipwreck Database (ASD) and the Automated Wreck and Obstruction Information System (AWOIS), as well as artificial reefs managed by SCDNR Marine Resources Division. After cataloging, the project archaeologist constructed a predictive model based on submerged paleolandscape features that revealed evidence of occupation and exploitation, as well as a review of what types of artifacts may survive discovered on the OCS. The model draws on a review of global trends, hemispheric differences, and Atlantic surveys, in order to provide a regional model for the offshore area between North Myrtle Beach and Cape Romain, South Carolina. The co-PI and project underwater archaeologists consulted with SCIAA prehistoric archaeologists to discuss what kind of paleo land features to look for in the data acquired through the geophysical survey. They also met with SCIAA archaeologists in order to access state site files and the digital database. The project underwater archaeologist then methodically compiled a list of all Paleoindian, Early Archaic, and Middle Archaic archaeological sites in South Carolina. The location, date, and site numbers of each site were incorporated into the master GIS map of the research area.

Data Processing

USC-EOS and ESRI commenced data processing and continues to process data as it is delivered by CCU.

Preliminary Results

Year One (Y1) of the project ended on October 31, 2015. The initial months of Y1 were hampered by harsh winter weather in 2014-2015 and technical delays in the spring. Survey resumed in June, and to date about 50% of Phase 1 is complete. Survey is ongoing, weather permitting, and historical research continues. Paleo landscape research continues as pending works on paleo landscapes and submerged paleo archaeological sites reach publication. Data processing continues as data acquisition carries on.

Geophysical Survey

With 50% of the Survey Blocks completed (Figure 2), thus far two anomalies exist in N1 with an additional anomaly in N2. Closer examination of the bathymetric data reflects possible ballast pile and two additional targets. Further analysis is pending completion of the Survey Blocks and interpretation of any potential paleo

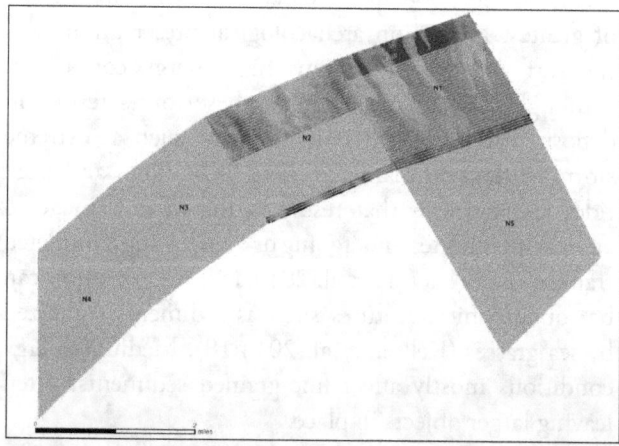

Figure 2. Survey Blocks N1-N5 with data acquisition as of December 2015 (Image courtesy USC ESRI 2015).

landforms by the project geo-archaeologist, M. Scott Harris. For the most part, archaeologists agree that there are three basic criteria for a submerged archaeological landscape to exist:
1. The sea level must have been lower at some point in the past.
2. Prehistoric humans must have been present and occupied the exposed land.
3. Most importantly, sedimentary processes during transgression must have preserved rather than eroded the landscape (Westley et al. 2011:99).

Presently, the survey is ongoing and data continue to come in. The second year of the project will involve refining survey areas and ground truthing potential historic and prehistoric sites.

Archaeological and Historical Survey

In total, there are almost 3,000 Paleo-Archaic sites across the state. About half fall within the Paleo, Early and Middle Archaic habitation periods. That fact that Late Archaic sites, dated to modern sea-level rise and later, make up the other half suggests great potential for additional Paleo-Archaic sites offshore. The oldest of these are 469 Paleoindian fluted stone points recorded by archaeologists in South Carolina (CGM 2005). Of these, 261 are thought to be Early Paleoindian, or Pre-Clovis, dating prior to 13,250 YBP. Regionally, more than half of the fluted stone points were found on the Coastal Plain (221), the others found on the Piedmont (116) or the Fall Line (93), with a fraction of them found in the Blue Ridge (Figure 3). This suggests that any surviving paleo landforms that resemble the modern geography from the fall line to the coastal plain would offer the greatest potential for an inundated Paleo-Archaic habitation site.

Within the broader Call Areas established by BOEM off SC are 401 potential targets occupying the OCS. Within the six Survey Blocks are 40 known targets. Historical research revealed a list of 27 historic shipwreck events that occurred between 1745 and 1863 in the broader vicinity of the research area. Some of the known historic wrecks are clustered with modern wrecks, purposely sunk vessels, and other objects compiling 35

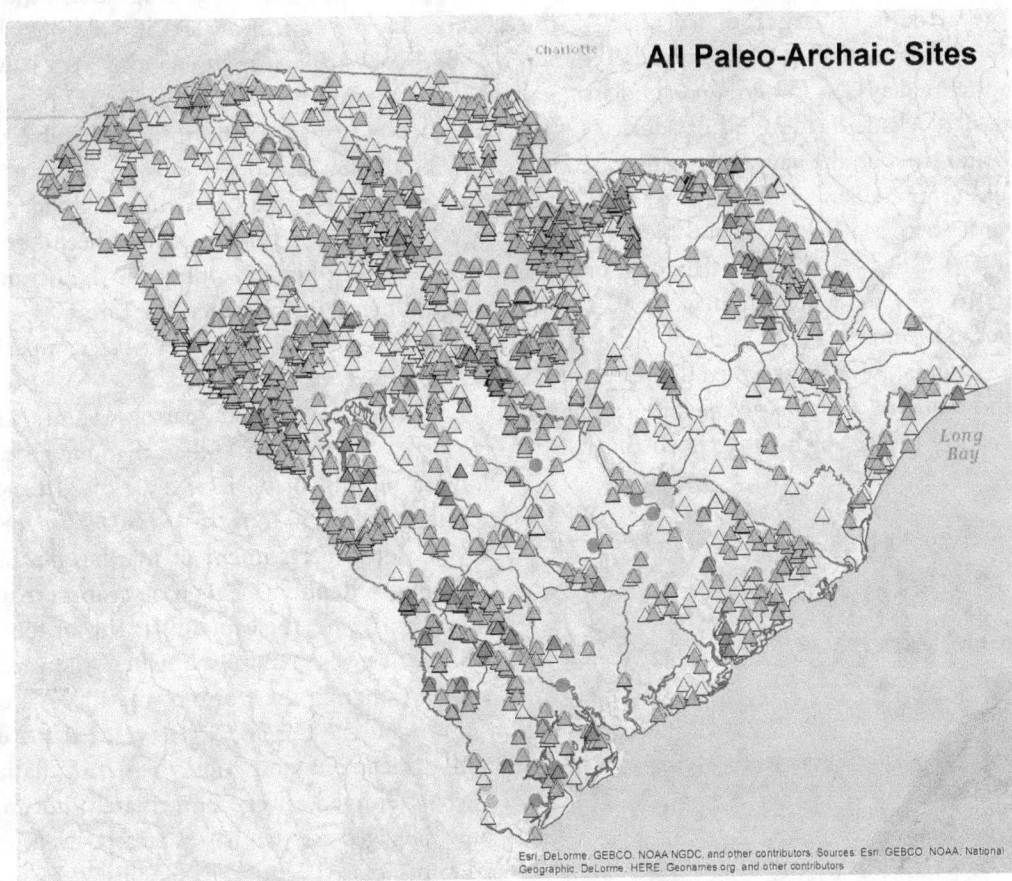

Figure 3. All Paleo-Archaic Sites recorded in South Carolina (Image by Brown 2015).

total artificial reefs in the Survey Blocks. As part of the marine habitat, it is as significant to protect those natural resources, some of which are also cultural resources.

Utilizing the ASD, AWOIS, and historical sources, five known historic wrecks fall within the Survey Blocks (with a sixth just north of N1). They are *North Carolina*, wrecked 1840; *Sherman*, wrecked 1874; *William Richard*, wrecked 1884; *Hector*, lost 1916; and *Torungen*, listed as lost 1943. Built in 1838, *North Carolina* operated on the Wilmington-Charleston mail route. The packet steamer sank after colliding with its sister ship *Governor Dudley* on a clear night in July 1840. The collision damaged *Dudley*'s bow, but the vessel managed to take on the crew and passengers. *North Carolina* reportedly sank in 15 minutes. All crew and passengers survived, but up to $20,000 went down with the vessel. A diver discovered the vessel remains in the 1980s and in the mid 1990s treasure salvors salvaged the remains (Gentile 2003:83).

Built in Glasgow, Scotland, in 1861, *Sherman* was originally a two-cylinder single prop screw steamer named *Princess Royal*. The third vessel by this name, it served as a packet steamer between Glasgow and Liverpool until a Charleston blockade running firm purchased it in 1862. In a relatively short career as a blockade runner, *Princess Royal* was captured in January 1863 (Figure 4). The vessel was then taken to Philadelphia, purchased by the US Navy and refitted as USS *Princess Royal* and assigned to the Western Blockade in the Gulf of Mexico (Wise 1988:317). After the war, the navy decommissioned the vessel and sold it for civilian use. It finished its career as a packet steamer between Baltimore and New Orleans. An 1873 survey lists the vessel at 196 feet long, breadth 27 feet, draft 16 feet, and a gross tonnage of 973 tons. *Sherman* wrecked January 1874 just off Little River Inlet, South Carolina. Divers discovered the vessel in the late 1970s and the wreck remains a popular location for divers; its location is just north of Research Block N2.

Figure 4. A sketch of the captured *Princess Royal*.

There is another wreck south of Block S1 identified as *General Sherman*, at one point thought to be the *Princess Royal*, but its location off Georgetown and the erroneous addition of *General* suggest it is some other unknown steamer.

The schooner *William Richard* was built at the Schellinger's Landing shipyard, launched in 1869. Dimension are listed as 60.7 feet long, breadth 21 feet, draft 4.8 feet, owned by Boston merchant L.B. Smith. In December 1887, the schooner was shipping a load of timber to Martinique when it sprang a leak off Frying Pan Lightship off North Carolina. Along with four crew, the captain's wife and two daughters were onboard. When the cabin filled with water, the 16- and 10-year-old girls were lashed to the mainmast. The mast soon gave way and went overboard with the girls. Two sailors of color leapt into the water and rescued the girls. The crew worked to keep the vessel afloat until they were rescued by the British steam ship *Timor* bound for Liverpool. The dramatic story made headlines until March, when the captain and mate of *Timor* were awarded medals by the United States government. Ironically, and reflective of the time, there is no record of the two sailors that risked their lives receiving recognition other than their names in *The Sun* in an article published February 2, 1888. Newspapers reported the vessel wrecked 60 miles of Frying Pan Shoals. The ASD puts its location in Block N2 (Figure 10), but it is possible target N2-1 may be the remains of *William Richard* since the vessel was reported as waterlogged but still afloat on January 3, 1888. Waterlogged vessels have been known to float great distances before settling on the ocean floor. The rough dimensions of target N2-1are 50 feet by 16 feet (15 by 5 meters), putting it in the comparable size of *William Richard*.

Built for the Navy at Sparrow's Point, MD in 1909, *Hector* was a modern collier that measured 403 feet long, a breadth of 53 feet, draft of 24 feet, and gross tonnage of 11,250 tons. In 1916 *Hector* received orders to pick up a detachment of marines destined for the Dominican Republic. Caught in a storm that developed into a hurricane, the captain battled for four days until being driven onto a sandbar where the vessel broke in two. Weathering the storm until 1:00AM, two vessels, *Cyprus* and the tug *Wellington* rescued the entire crew and detachment and took them to Charleston. The Navy attempted salvage immediately, but foul weather only damaged the two halves greatly. Eventually salvage attempts ceased, and the remains were marked as a navigation hazard. SCDNR considers the wreck an artificial reef; little cohesive structure remains according to divers who visited the site.

The last vessel lay within Block N1 and is associated with the Little River Artificial Reef. It is identified in ASD as the Norwegian freighter *Torungen*; however, historical research suggests this is a misidentification. Built by Trondhjems Mekaniske Verksted, Trondheim in 1931, the vessel was 1,948 gross tons. There are multiple sources and accounts of *Torungen* having been suck by a German U-boat off Halifax in 1942; that event included eyewitnesses. The date of 1943, the highly unlikely probability of a torpedoed vessel drifting all the way to South Carolina, and the dimensions of the wreck remains in N1 are too small to be the same cargo vessel. Completion of Phase 1 may yield additional wrecks or confirm the location of known wrecks as well as artificial reefs.

Anomalies

Upon completion of Phase 1, Dr. Scott Harris, the project geo-archaeologist from CofC, will complete geological analysis and make recommendations for Phase 2: refined high-resolution scanning of potential paleo landforms that may reveal inundated Paleolithic sites of habitation or exploitation. To date, the survey has revealed three possible historic wrecks with magnetic signatures and significant relief that should be included in Phase 2 refinement. The first anomaly, target N1-1, measures approximately 22.86 meters by 15.24 meters (75 by 50 feet), is oval and has the characteristics of a ballast pile. The second anomaly, target N1-2, is located near an artificial reef; the object is boat-like in shape and measures approximately 21.336 meters by 7 meters (70 by 23 feet). The third anomaly, target N2-1, measures approximately 15.24 meters by 4.8768 meters (50 by 16 feet), also boat-like in its dimensions and relief. It may be possible this target is the remains of the vessel *William Richard*, noted as 18.5 meters (60.7 feet) long, breadth of 6.4 meters (21 feet), and a draft of 1.46 meters (4.8 feet) (Record 1887:890). The vessel foundered December 29, 1887, according to contemporary newspaper accounts. All hands were saved, though the vessel and her cargo of lumber were a complete loss (ASD 2015, NYT Jan. 4, 1888). The ASD location of *William Richard* is almost 4.95 kilometers (5,421 yards) north of target N2-1. However, as noted above, waterlogged vessels have been reported to drift great distances before settling on the seafloor. Phase 2 survey and Phase 3 ground truthing may confirm or discount this target as the remains of *William Richard*.

Future Work (Conclusion)

Despite weather and equipment delays, progress continues with CCU's data acquisition. Geo-archaeological analysis of the WEA and its potential for inundated prehistoric habitation and exploitation sites are pending completion of the geophysical survey. As data are processed by USC ESRI and passed on to MRD, historical research continues as anomalies are identified and assessed. Completion of Phase 1 is expected in early 2016, with Phase 2 refinement and Phase 3 ground truthing anticipated this spring and summer. MRD is responsible for coordinating ground truthing with CCU crew and dive safety officer along with BOEM marine archaeologists. With the increased interest and research into submerged prehistoric archaeological sites, the archaeological potential for cultural resources in South Carolina's OCS has increased exponentially, from one measured in centuries to the time of European contact to one stretching back millennia to the peopling of North America sometime before 13,500 YBP. Contributing to BOEM's ongoing responsibility to protect submerged cultural resources in federal waters, this project adds to the growing list of studies undertaken with the aim of reconstructing both the more recent past and unraveling the mystery of when and how the first people set foot in South Carolina, even if that footprint is now underwater.

Acknowledgements

No project is accomplished alone. The authors would like to thank the following people: Amanda Evans, Tesla; Scott Harris, College of Charleston; Al Goodyear, Christopher Moore, Mark Brooks, Keith Derting, Tamara Wilson, and Joe Beatty of SCIAA; David Robinson, University of Rhode Island, Camelia Knapp, Bradley Battista, and Duke Brantley of U of SC ESRI; Capt. Jamie Phillips, Capt. Brian Johnson, Robbie Moorer, and Shinobu Okano of Coastal Carolina University. Many of the above people contributed resources and shared insight, whereas others provided countless hours of data acquisition and processing. Their tireless efforts are very much appreciated.

References

BOEM
2011 *Notice to Lessees and Operators (NTL) of Federal Oil and Gas Leases and Pipeline Right-of-Way (ROW) Holders and the Outer Continental Shelf (OCS).* Notice to Lessees, Washington, D.C.: Bureau of Ocean Energy Management.

BROOKS, MARK, BARBARA E. TAYLOR, AND JOHN A. GRANT
1996 "Carolina Bay Geoarchaeology and Holocene Landscape Evolution on the Upper Coastal Plain of South Carolina." *Geoarchaeology* 481-504.

DEVOE, M. RICHARD, AND RYAN C. BRADLEY
2014 *Atlantic Offshore Wind Energy Development: Geophysical Mapping and Identification of Paleolandscapes and Historic Shipwrecks Offshore South Carolina.* Proposal, Charleston, South Carolina: The South Carolina Sea Grant Consortium.

EVANS, A. M.
2014 *Examining and Testing Potential Prehistoric Archaeological Features on the Gulf of Mexico Outer Continental Shelf.* Draft, New Orleans: U.S. Department of the Interior, Bureau of Ocean Energy Management, Gulf of Mexico OCS Region.

GENTILE, GARY
2003 *Shipwrecks of South Carolina and Georgia.* Philadelphia, Pennsylvania: Gary Gentile Productions.

GOODYEAR, ALBERT C.
2013 "Evidence for Pre-Clovis Sites in the Eastern United States." In *Paleoamerican Origins: Beyond Clovis*, by Bradley T. Lepper, Michael R. Waters, Dennis Stanford Robson Bonnichsen, 103-112. College Station: Texas A&M University.

HARRIS, M. SCOTT, LESLIE REYNOLDS SAUTTER, KACEY L. JOHNSON, KATHERINE E. LUCIANO, GEROGE R. SEDBERRY, ERIC E. WRIGHT, AND AMY N.S. SIUDA
2013 "Continental shelf landscapes of the southeastern United States since the last interglacia." *Geomorphology* 6-24.

HOUSE, JOHN H., AND RONALD W. WOGAMAN
1978 *Windy Ridge: A Prehistoric Site in the Inter-Riverine Piedmont in South Carolina.* Columbia: Archaeology and Anthropology, South Carolina Institute at Scholar Commons.

KELLER, JESSICA A., CHRISTOPHER R. SHERWOOD, JOSH MARANO, CHARLES LAWSON, AND REBECCA BEAVERS
2014 *Biscayne National Park HMS Fowey PRE-Stabilization Report.* Technical, Lakewood, Colorado: National Park Service Submerged Resources Center.

KVAMME, KENNETH L.
2003 "Archaeology Geophysical Surveys as Landscape Archaeology." *American Antiquity* (Society for American Archaeology) 68 (3): 435-457.

LACROIX, DOMINIC, TREVOR BELL, JOHN SHAW, AND KIERAN WESTLEY
2014 "Submerged Archaeological Landscapes and the Recording of Contact History: Examples rom Atlantic Canada." In *Prehistoric Archaeology on the Continental Shelf: A Global Review*, by Amanda M. Evans, Joseph C. Flatman and Nicholas C. Flemming, 13-36. New York, New York: Springer.

POWELL, JOHN
1990 *Points and Blades of the Coastal Plain: A Guide to the Classification of Native American Hafted Implements in the Southeastern Coastal Plain Region.* West Columbia: American Systems of the Carolinas, Inc.

WISE, STEPHEN R.
1988 *Lifeline of the Confederacy: Blockade Running During the Civil War.* Columbia, South Carolina: University of South Carolina Press.

Daniel M. Brown, MA, RPA
Data Exploitation Analyst
Oceaneering International Inc.
7001 Dorsey Road
Hanover, MD 21076
Office: (443) 459-3920
Fax: (443) 459-3980
Brown.daniel.mark@gmail.com

James D. Spirek
State Underwater Archaeologist
Maritime Research Division
South Carolina Institute of Archaeology and
    Anthropology, College of Arts and Sciences
University of South Carolina
1321 Pendleton Street
Columbia SC 29208 USA
Bus: (803) 576-6566
Fax: (803) 254-1338
spirek@sc.edu

Hidden in Plain Sight: Monitoring Shipwrecks in the Atlantic Waters of St. Augustine, Florida

P. Brendan Burke

The Lighthouse Archaeological Maritime Program (LAMP), research division of the St. Augustine Lighthouse & Maritime Museum, has actively engaged in the discovery and preservation of submerged cultural sites in northeast Florida. Among its research agendas is the continual monitoring of offshore shipwreck sites to better understand their interaction with the ocean and humans. Much of the monitoring has used sidescan sonar to generate a database of site images. This paper explores some of the inferences drawn from the sonar record. It also presents some new challenges faced by maritime archaeologists as the underwater world becomes more accessible to the public.

Introduction

Since 1999, archaeologists from LAMP have worked to discover, present, and preserve maritime archaeological resources of the First Coast region. Research expeditions have included much of northeast Florida, and monitoring has taken place in the nearshore waters of St. Augustine. In 2015, the city commemorated its 450th birthday, making it the oldest continually-occupied port in the United States. St. Augustine has long been connected to an Atlantic world and until the 20th century, its front door faced the sea. Linking the city's port to the ocean and the world beyond is an inlet that until recently was a wild and wandering part of the region's geomorphology. Within its shifting sands, a library of shipwrecks tragically assembled, today a laboratory for archaeological study.

LAMP archaeologists have worked to plot where the St. Augustine inlet has moved, from the 16th century to 1939. By World War II, St. Augustine had grown weary of an inlet that, over three centuries, wandered over a two-mile-long stretch of the coast. With assistance from the U.S. Army Corps of Engineers (USACE), the port constructed a jetty and dredged a straight channel in an effort to tame nature (Shabica et al 1993: 8). In its natural state, the inlet's beguiling location was a notorious ship trap, feared by competent mariners who knew how suddenly the channel's location could change. Thus, from 1565 until the second quarter of the 20th century, vessels of all types came to grief along Anastasia Island, St. Augustine's barrier to the Atlantic. Through documentary research, remote sensing survey, target-testing and excavation, LAMP has relocated several wreck sites. This inventory of wrecks has provided the research program an 'ocean laboratory' to study, generating a unique body of knowledge concerning the history of the region, inlet dynamics, human interaction with wreck sites, and ongoing site formation processes. Since the goals of this paper are to highlight what has been observed through LAMP's monitoring experience, the human story of each wreck has been omitted here, an intentional void addressed elsewhere (Meide et al 2009; Morris et al 1998).

The Inlet

The modern, dredged St. Augustine Inlet is a central node in an inlet complex spreading north and south of a federally maintained channel. Numerous studies have examined longshore sediment transport in the vicinity of the inlet and generally agree that net accretion of sediment occurs on the southern lobe of the inlet's ebb shoal (Walton 1973; USACE 1979; Fields et al 1988; USACE 1991; Srinivas et al 1996; PBS&J 2009; Walton et al 2011; and Florida Department of Environmental Protection [FDEP] 2012). If this is indeed a trend induced by jettying the modern inlet, then it may be assumed that areas of St. Augustine's historic inlet locations have experienced the addition of sediments. However, more nuanced hydrologic study of the inlet bypassing nature from 1998 to 2010 demonstrates that while the southern inlet area is a net recipient of sediments, certain areas appear to sustain a net loss, as much as two to four meters of sediment loss (USACE 2012). Figure 1 depicts the southern ebb shoal lobe net gain, as well as sediment change observed during the 2012 study.

Coastline surrounding the St. Augustine Beach pier has undergone a net loss cycle as a result of the modern location of the inlet. In response, the USACE, together with state and local management entities, undertook three separate beach 'renourishment' projects to pump sand onto the beach, an area on which the local economy is dependent for tourism dollars. Total volume for the

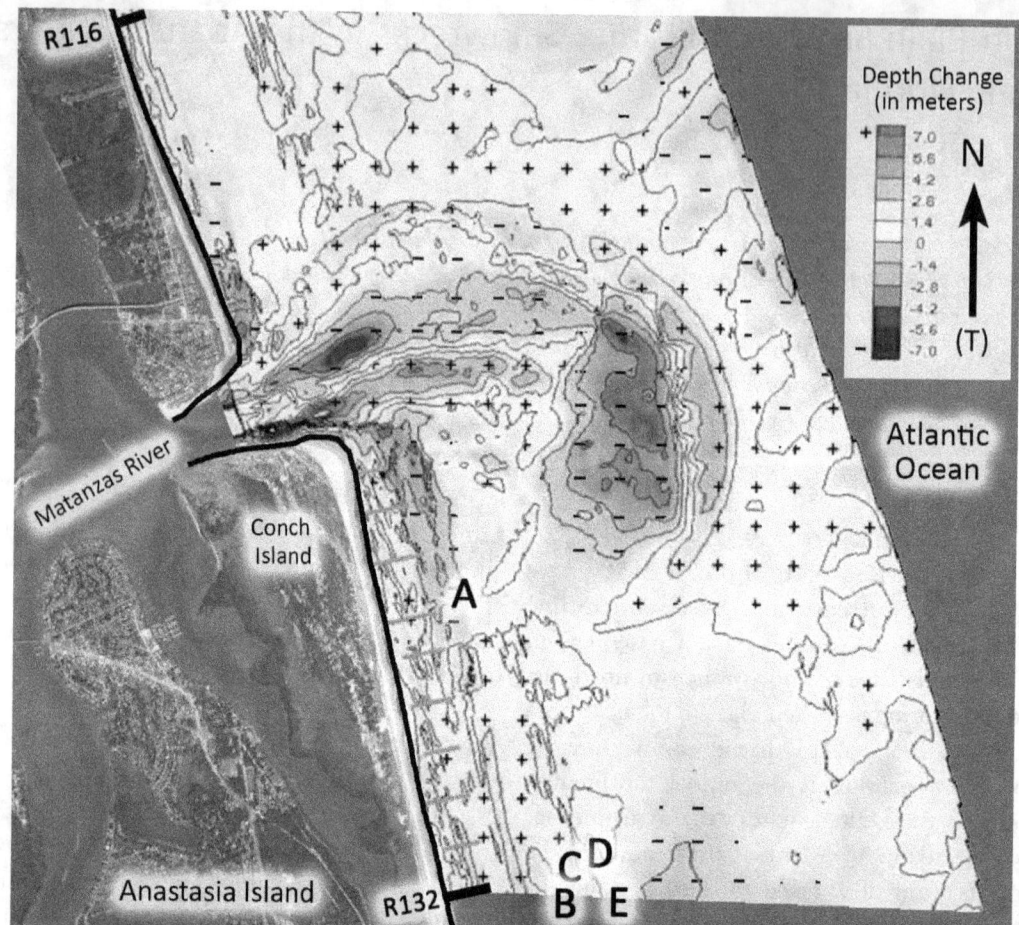

Figure 1. The St. Augustine Inlet shown with net sediment change from 1998-2010 (sediment data courtesy of U. S. Army Corps of Engineers). Selected shipwreck sites are generally plotted to give an idea of wreck locations in relation to sediment loss/gain. 'A' is a shipwreck likely dating to the 18th century, 'B' is the Industry Site (8SJ3478), 'C' is the 19th century Steamship/Ballast Pile site (8SJ3310), 'D' is the 19th century Centerboard Schooner (8SJ3309) site, and 'E' is the 1782 Storm Wreck site (8SJ5459).

three restoration attempts (in 2003, 2005 and 2012) equaled 9.2 million cubic yards (7.03 m³), enough to cover 475 acres with twelve feet (3.65 m) of sand. This is in comparison to the 1.4 million cubic yards of sand removed from the St. Augustine Inlet between 1940-1986 for navigational dredging, all deposited nearby in spoil dump zones (FDEP 2012:5). While all project activities were conducted within legal guidelines to protect natural and cultural resources, the massive movements of sand occurred within an established shipwreck preserve and straddled a zone with a high density of wreck sites (U.S. Department of Commerce, Coastal Resources Center [USDCCRC] 1994: 26-27). Figure 2 depicts the principal area of shipwrecks situated in context to the inlet, areas of coastal erosion, and areas of net sediment gain/loss.

What makes these data salient to archaeologists? Understanding site formation processes is guided by understanding the environment in which a wreck has come to exist (Ford et al 2015; Keith et al 2015; Schiffer 1987). Moreover, regional and micro-regional forces shape and reshape the environment of a wreck. In the case of coastal shipwrecks, especially those near an inlet, these forces are always at play with varying levels of intensity. Thus, few offshore littoral sites are in true stasis as sediments of varying types are constantly added and subtracted. Similarly, different sediment grain sizes may filter their way into, and onto, sites as site structure changes, affecting the hydrodynamic micro-environment of the site. During periods of dramatic exposure, site materials, from hull fragments, to ordnance and buttons, may be moved laterally or even buried deeper. Through sidescan sonar monitoring, we hope to better understand the natural and anthropogenic forces affecting St. Augustine's nearshore shipwrecks—forces which affect our ability to locate and document submerged culture successfully.

LAMP Shipwreck Monitoring

LAMP's preferred monitoring tool is sidescan sonar. Water clarity is persistently poor, especially during summer months, in the nearshore waters of northeast Florida. While diver observation has its merits, and may often be the best (sometimes only) method for data collection, sidescan sonography collects large-scale imagery rarely available to divers. Recorded imagery forms a comparative dataset; inferences may be constructed about sediment migration, formation processes, and site integrity.

Site monitoring was performed primarily during the summer field season, and before/after major storm events in two examples. The sidescan sonar unit deployed for monitoring was a Klein System 3900 with an operational frequency of 900khZ. Positioning was established with a Trimble DSM-232 DGPS. Files were recorded in .xtf format on a Dell Latitude E5500 hard drive. Control over the towfish was managed through SonarPro, versions 11 and 12, and postprocessing of sidescan sonar data was performed using Chesapeake Technology's SonarWiz.

Industry

On May 6th, 1764, Daniel Lawrence, master of the transport sloop *Industry*, found himself in a position envied by no sea captain. His command was firmly aground on the St. Augustine bar. Waves passed by the ship without effect, their tops foaming as crests formed and broke under the ship's bows. With a hold full of government supplies, the *Industry* meant infrastructure to East Florida, the newest possession in the British Empire. Cannon and ammunition carried in the orlop were to defend the colony; grindstones, mooring anchors, and boxes of tools were to help build it back up after Spain's departure literally stripped the doors of their hinges. But Lawrence stood on the deck of a doomed vessel, stranded less than two miles from his destination after a voyage of over eight hundred. Like many ships cast upon St. Augustine's bar, the *Industry's* wooden bones cracked under a pounding sea, and she came apart. Portions of her hull ripped free and rode tidal currents until beached. Her heavy cargo settled into the sand, lost to history for the next 233 years.

Archaeologists from Southern Oceans Archaeological Research, Inc., working with the St. Augustine Lighthouse & Museum, discovered the *Industry* wreck (8SJ3478) in 1997. The site was first identified only by an exposed fluke of a single-arm mooring anchor. In 1998, excavations uncovered a row of eight 6-pdr cannon, iron bar stock, two mooring anchors, and associated concretions (Meide 2015: 360). One of the guns was raised, with the hope of finding identifying markings on the gun that would shed light on the wreck's identity. This goal was realized during the conservation process. At the end of the field season, the site was backfilled. *Industry's* second darkest chapter since her foundering unfolded during the spring of 1999. Using a propwash deflector, looters exposed a neat row of seven 6-pdr cannon, laid end to end. Each gun was tested for its material by having concretion chiseled off to apply a magnet to the original surface. Determining each gun to be iron, the looters stole two. It is quite likely that other artifacts exposed by the large blown hole in the sand were also stolen. The mass of cannon created a 'pocket' of artifacts ripe for looting, artifacts now lost to the public, to history, and to science.

The incident was a clarion call to LAMP

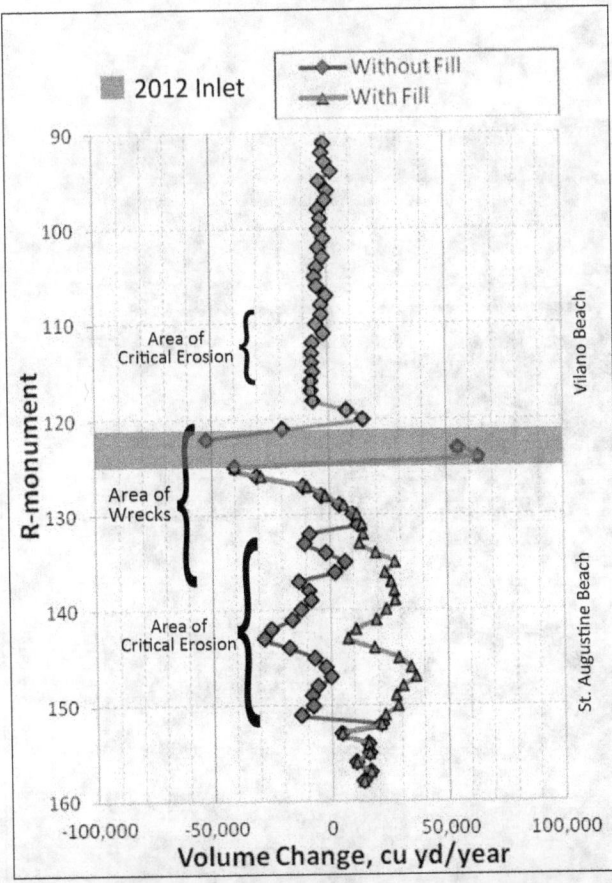

Figure 2. Data from a 2012 U.S. Army Corps of Engineers study depicts areas of sediment volume change, with the St. Augustine Inlet, areas of coastal erosion, and a concentration of known shipwrecks. Note that the shipwrecks are located in the areas of highest flux.

archaeologists, and an emergency salvage excavation was undertaken in July of 1999. Dozens of delicate artifacts were found exposed in the blower hole, including wooden shipping crates with ink labeling still legible. With the exception of iron rod-stock, mooring anchors, and remaining cannon, the exposed artifacts were recorded and recovered for conservation. For the next 15 years, these artifacts were the backbone of an exhibit on the British period at the St. Augustine Lighthouse & Museum. At the same time, LAMP worked to enhance their relationship with local law enforcement to raise awareness about the fragile historic resources in offshore waters. In tandem, the museum increased its public archaeology presence in the community to educate people about the importance of archaeological research and preservation. In 2007, LAMP was able to add sidescan sonar monitoring to its toolkit of monitoring techniques, previously limited to diving and vessel availability.

Since 2007, LAMP has monitored *Industry* 11 times. Observations from monitoring include regular covering/uncovering sequences. The central cannon pile acts as a bellwether for the site, and has been exposed to greater or lesser degrees in each monitoring exercise since

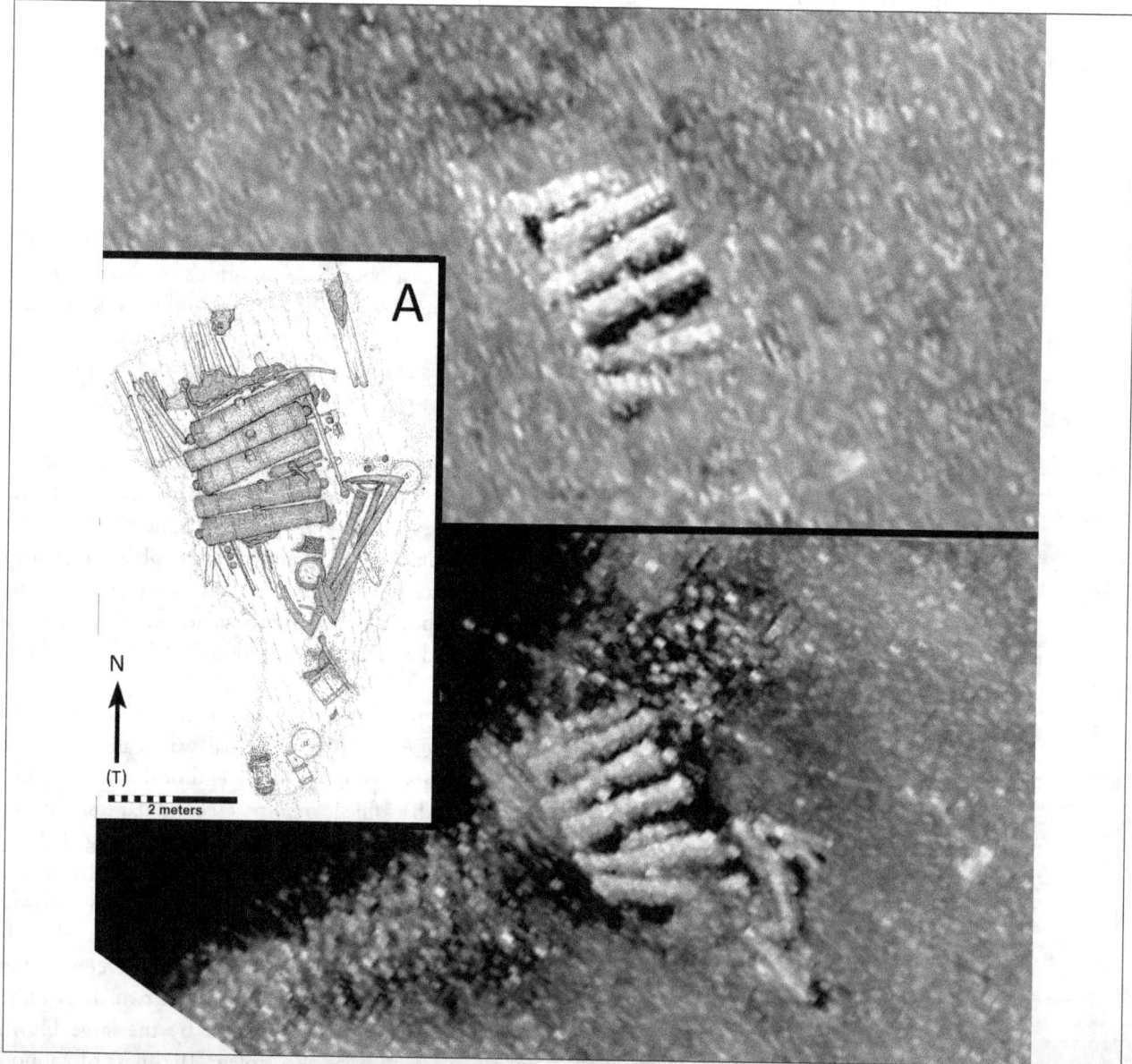

Figure 3. The *Industry* Site (8SJ3478) is depicted here before (top), and after (bottom) Tropical Storm Fay. Taken only days after the departure of the storm, during the summer of 2008, this was the most exposed the *Industry* Site had been recorded since its excavation, and subsequent looting, in 1999. The 1999 site plan is shown (A), as recorded by LAMP after the looting incident. (Site plan by John W. Morris, courtesy of the St. Augustine Lighthouse & Maritime Museum)

2000. Interestingly, this site is located less than 1,500 ft. (457 m) away from the Storm Wreck (8SJ5459), another 18th century shipwreck with a cannon pile that, having been exposed through archaeological excavation, has quickly reburied itself. The water depth (mean low water) over the *Industry* site is approximately 20 ft. (6 m), compared to the 27 ft. (8 m) of water over the Storm Wreck. Morris noted that a crater left by the illegal blower created a scour pattern that kept *Industry's* cannon pile uncovered (Morris et al. 2000:9). Since then, the site has remained uncovered, an attribute that is not completely understood. However, the exposure does permit observation of the cannon pile, and periodic exposure of nearby associated artifacts such as iron stock and mooring anchors. To date, the exposure has been observed to be somewhat consistent. From time to time, the site's scour hole has partially filled with mud, evidenced in the sonar as a dark, almost anechoic lens.

In August 2008, tropical storm Fay passed over northeast Florida, taking a full three days to blow through. Seas were whipped up by sustained winds in excess of 30 knots, often gusting much higher. Seven days after the storm, sonar was deployed to record local wreck sites. The storm had scoured more sediments from the cannon pile and immediate vicinity than had been previously recorded (Figure 3). In 2011, hurricane Irene passed approximately 275 nautical miles (509 km) offshore of St. Augustine. While the storm did not damage the city, it generated a large swell that pounded Florida's Atlantic coast. A sidescan sonar record was generated before and after the swell, just as a record had been created for tropical storm Fay. While significant

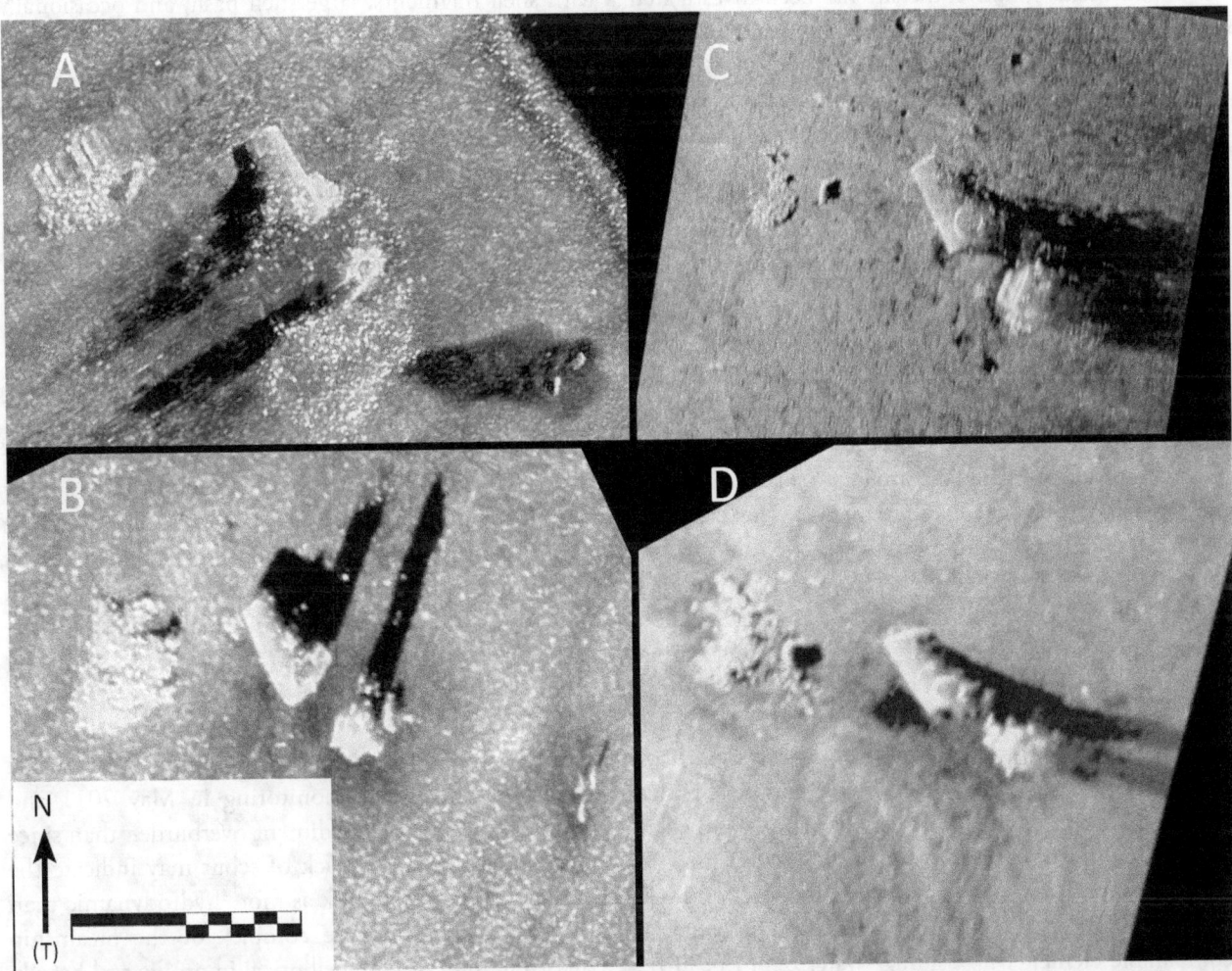

Figure 4. The Steamship/Ballast Pile Site (8SJ3310), seen in 'A,' before Tropical Storm Fay in June of 2008. Note a dark area of old scouring between the propeller and engine in the lower-right quarter of the image. Diver inspection revealed the scour hole to have filled with an anechoic mud. In 'B,' note the increased amount of ballast stone, compared to 'A.' Additionally, the area around the boiler and engine has received substantial scouring. In 'C,' the site was recorded prior to large swell from distant Hurricane Irene during the summer of 2011. Note sediment coverage over the ballast pile, compared to 'D,' showing a much-exposed site, including major scouring around the engine/boiler complex.

wave action was noted on the beach with wave height exceeding 10 ft. (3 m), no major sediment shift was noted on the *Industry* site.

Steamship/Ballast Pile Site

First excavated by LAMP in 1997, this site (8SJ3310) represents a ballast pile adjacent to a boiler/steam engine/shaft-screw assemblage. Whether or not the site is one or two wrecked vessels remains a mystery. All site remains and artifacts date to the mid to late 19th century. In 2007, LAMP resumed excavations, which continued in 2009 (Meide et al. 2010: 302). This site is unique among St. Augustine's coastal shipwreck sites for its profile. The vessel's steam engine stands proud above the seafloor, reaching halfway to the water surface at low tide. Like *Industry*, the site has been investigated periodically for over a decade and serves as a benchmark for sediment shift.

Figure 4 depicts the steamship ballast pile before and after tropical storm Fay and the Hurricane Irene swell. The site exhibited net sediment loss after both events—the only site to lose sand during both storms. The heights of the steam engine and boiler may contribute to sediment movement, by causing turbulence in bottom surge that lifts and transports materials away from the site. Diver observation has frequently noted an area of maximum scouring between the steam engine and boiler, where surge and tidal currents are compressed and velocity increased.

In both storm-related disturbances, substantial areas of the ballast pile, even hull remains, were exposed. Diver observation, mainly from 2007-2009, led to the tentative conclusion that the site appears to undergo cyclical, but irregular, exposure. Diver analysis in 2013 during a period of good visibility noted broad uncovering of the ballast pile. With both high and low profile areas, it is unique among St. Augustine wreck sites. A similar type of site exists near Egmont Key, at the mouth of Tampa Bay. The USS *Narcissus* site contains boiler remains, a steam engine of similar size and a propeller, making it almost identical to the Steamship/Ballast Pile site. However, *Narcissus*'s engine has fallen over and her boiler is no longer intact. Nonetheless, the site contains comparable elements in a similar water depth (<30 ft. [9.1 m]). While exposed to more powerful tidal currents, as observed by the author in 2012, the site would make an excellent study candidate, especially since achieving Florida Underwater Preserve status in 2015 (Roger C. Smith 2015 pers. comm.).

Storm Wreck

Discovered in 2009 by LAMP archaeologists, the Storm Wreck (8SJ5459) is a British transport, ferrying Loyalists out of Charleston in 1782 at the end of the American Revolution. Excavations have revealed a cross section of 18th century life, including civilian and military passengers. Unlike previously discussed wrecks, this site is routinely buried. Only once was the site observed as naturally exposed (December 17, 2010). In profile it is most similar to the *Industry* site, having a low profile, cannon pile, and numerous concreted artifacts.

Excavations carried out on the site from 2009 until 2015 have revealed numerous types of sediment sizes. Sediment types encountered throughout the wreck include fine sand, hard-packed clay, coarse sand with shell fragments, large shell hash, and occasionally an overlay of plough mud. From modern artifacts encountered within the Storm Wreck, the site has been periodically uncovered, evidenced by such items as a mid-20th century cola bottle from within a central node of concretions (Meide et al 2011: 155-156). Modern debris such as this acts as an indicator of the site's self-excavation, discussed in Ford et al (2015: 17-43), and the 2010 exposure may indicate that the site has not entered into a completely buried phase.

Centerboard Schooner Wreck

With a cargo of cement casks, the vessel at site (8SJ3309) was likely inbound to St. Augustine to supply a late 19th century building boom associated with Henry Flagler. Consisting of a concretized-cask pile, a buried centerboard trunk, and an assortment of heavy iron concretions, the site is the second tallest wreck in the area and the longest and widest at 130 ft. (39.55 m) by 28 ft. (8.79 m) (Meide et al 2010: 219).

While scouring has been noted, especially after tropical storm Fay, the site is usually without considerable erosion. During sonar monitoring in May 2011 and July 2015, it had more sediment overburden than since monitoring began. The lack of scour may indicate the general shape of the wreck as more hydrodynamic than that of the boiler/engine complex of the Steamship Ballast Pile site. Roughly elliptical in profile and heavily dimpled by the presence of several dozen casks, scouring currents may be foiled by the nature of the wreck site.

Coastal Population Pressure

By 2040, Florida is projected to be home to over 26 million people (Florida Office of Economic and Demographic Research 2015: 8). St. Johns County, home to St. Augustine, will contain an estimated 382,701 of the state's population by then. When compared to the roughly 53,000 inhabitants in 1980, the result is dramatic. Increased pressure on marine resources from coastal population growth is, however, certainly not limited to Florida. In response, establishing regional and local baselines for maritime heritage is critical. Sidescan sonar monitoring, supported by periodic diver investigation, provides one of the most efficient methods of baseline establishment.

Through outreach, increased public site awareness is a basic step towards shared stewardship. In St. Augustine, LAMP has worked locally to showcase diversity and the importance of local shipwrecks and submerged heritage. We continue to find that as more and more people learn about archaeology and understand its tools to connect with the past, a sense of investment and civic stewardship is often the most powerful byproduct. As a locale, St. Augustine has a vibrant archaeological community, including avocational archaeologists working with professional practitioners. Consistent public programming offers a stream of information to the public that brings archaeology out of the laboratory and into the minds and hands of citizens.

Part of LAMP's outreach programming includes sharing sidescan sonar imagery of local wreck sites. With consideration of the protection of site location, LAMP outreach has meshed positively with the local community for investment in the shared resource. During the past several years, fishermen have approached us when they have seen or heard something suspicious regarding shipwrecks in the area. Moreover, LAMP has worked consistently with state and local law enforcement to develop better methods of protecting marine resources. Area law enforcement has dived with LAMP's research team and site information is shared, so resource officers know where and what to protect.

Better Eyes, Fewer Secrets

The 20th century compressed the world into a smaller place, with more and cheaper access to more remote places. The introduction of SCUBA exposed great areas of coastline and interior waters to those eager to find shipwrecks. Continued innovation in underwater breathing apparatus pushed the limits of accessibility farther and deeper. By the 1990s, it was not uncommon for sport divers to access wrecks deeper than 200 ft. (60.96 m), too often in the familiar plunder for portholes and binnacles.

With the 1990s advent of cheaply printed microprocessors, marine electronics underwent a revolution. Along with chart plotters that could contain an entire coastline of electronic nautical charts, thousands of waypoints, and hundreds of miles of vessel tracks, boaters entering the new millennia had side imaging sonar at their fingertips. Not only could new electronics deliver more and better data, but at increasingly more affordable rates. Moreover, technology became more portable. Electronics packages with side imaging took on the portability of a lead line, easily moved from boat to boat. By 2010, a chart plotter with side imaging sonar, as well as a single beam fathometer, water temperature sensor, and GPS, could be purchased for under $2,000– at the time a fraction of the cost of commercial sidescan

Site Name	Period	Type I - TS Fay	Type II - Hurr. Irene	Wreck Characteristics
Industry	18th C.	decrease	none	low-profile, cannon pile with associated anchors and iron bar stock
Steamship/Ballast	19th C.	decrease	decrease	high profile, steam engine/boiler complex with associated nearby ballast pile
Centerboard Wreck	19th C.	decrease	increase	moderate profile consisting of cargo pile (cement barrels)
Storm Wreck	18th C.	not observed	increase	low, typically buried

Table 1. Event types versus event effects on shipwreck sites near St. Augustine, FL. Effect is measured in sediment increase/decrease over known wreck debris. A Type I event is considered one in which localized strong wind (>35 knots) generates large swell (>6 ft. [2 m]). A Type II event is limited to large swell emanating from a distant storm, without strong localized winds.

sonar.

While side imaging plotters did not replace commercial sidescan sonar, the accessibility of side imaging sonar brought not just the bass to the creel, but historic wrecks to the public. Inland rivers, lakes, and canals, often typified by low visibility were 'exposed' to the side imaging sonar. Instantly, southern rivers became infested with 'Confederate' wrecks. Coastlines similarly thickened with the wreckage of 'pirate ships'. The technology to discover has been more widely dispersed.

An additional side effect of more portable sonar units is an enhanced avocational community. Avocational groups, seeking to fill in where public budgets leave off, can act as effective sentries to submerged heritage, and whom James Delgado correctly refers to as 'citizen scientists' (2015: 18). Affordable side imaging sonar is a powerful tool for such entities, helping record new sites as well as monitor known sites for looting activities. In the case of the SHIP Project, the Institute for Maritime History monitored dozens of wreck sites throughout the Chesapeake Bay region, reporting site assessments to the Maryland Historic Trust and the Virginia Department of Historic Resources (David P. Howe 2015, pers. comm.). The result was a strengthened resource inventory, positive public-private partnership, and increased public protection of delicate submerged heritage.

Still, side imaging sonar is new, and its true implications not fully understood. Affordable side imaging sonar may prove to be one of the biggest challenges to resource managers and maritime archaeologists since the invention of SCUBA. With it, more of the submerged world is more accessible. Just how we deal with this is one challenge left to us.

Conclusions and Recommendations

Site monitoring has much to teach us and the process should never be approached as 'just another site visit.' While the push for new knowledge and the discovery of new wrecks should never cease, revisiting sites often influences how we develop theories of site formation, involves the incidental discovery of new data, and of increasing importance, reveals information about the changing oceans of the 21st century. Information from site monitoring in St. Augustine has revealed information about sediment transport; influenced our field work; and demonstrated a commitment to the resource by a private non-profit with strong community ties and sense of ownership.

As shown in Table 1, three sites in St. Augustine's littoral waters, all within 2.5 nautical miles (4.63 k) of the inlet, were monitored in 2008 and 2011, a period during which two storm events impacted local waters. The Storm Wreck site, not yet discovered in 2008, is only shown for its change during Hurricane Irene's swell. While the results are preliminary and in need of further substantiation from continued monitoring before and after storm effect, sediment net loss in the area occurs when significant wave action is joined by strong winds. Without wind to drive and create new currents, swell generates powerful surge in shallow waters but does not transport sediments laterally and move them offsite.

St. Augustine's Inlet Management Plan calls for the management of sediments in and around the inlet for safe navigation and beach renourishment. It also notes a sediment bypassing scheme that has averaged 651,000 cubic yards of sediment per year from 1999-2012 (FDEP 2013: 8). Persistent navigational and shoreline protection dredging, combined with natural forces, have dynamic implications for St. Augustine. The relatively recent dredging may not yet be fully understood, but it is consistent with an increase in coastal dredging projects to meet political pressures associated with increased coastal populations, and response to rising ocean levels and more frequent, and more powerful storms. With this trend, monitoring coastal heritage is increasingly important.

Often the best and most vigilant monitors are our neighbors. It is natural that an archaeologist's time is split between field and lab. From sea turtle patrols to commercial fishermen, the local populace is often a willing and capable monitoring entity, filling gaps and gathering data over a more comprehensive period. Groups such as LAMP, the Florida Public Archaeology Network (FPAN) and many others consistently strive to develop and implement outreach programming that try to link local communities back to their heritage and buttress existing ties. While program success can be difficult to measure (Della Scott-Ireton 2016 elec. comm.), basic goals include: teaching the value of archaeological resources; how to identify artifacts and archaeological sites; monitoring for illegal site disturbance; benefits of in-situ preservation versus excavation; and using volunteer effort to broaden outreach potential.

Site monitoring may lack the appeal of searching for and discovering new sites, but it is critical to archaeology. For one, it demonstrates a public commitment to the resource. Second, monitoring is never without results and new data. As seen from these examples, monitoring St. Augustine's Atlantic waters has increased not only professional awareness of site integrity, but has enhanced knowledge of the surrounding environment. Recognizing that our world is changing with increasing rapidity; undergoing increased stresses from population pressures, dredging regimes, and even a changing climate, site monitoring certainly retains, if not increases, its value.

Acknowledgements

David Howe, Evelyn Jaynes, the Valdes family, and Maury Keiser have each contributed their time, resources, and vessels to LAMP for field research. Additionally, the Florida Bureau of Historic Preservation, Division of Historical Resources, provided historic preservation grants that assisted in the completion of the fieldwork. To each, we owe a debt of gratitude.

References

Conlin, David L., Melvin Bell, Nancy T. DeWitt, Mark Hansen, Charles Holmes, William K. Johnson, Jr., Shea McLean, Marci Marot, Robert Martore, Claire P. Peachey, Suzanne Stroh, and Dana Weise
2005 *USS Housatonic Site Assessment*. Submerged Resources Center, Professional Papers Number 19/ Naval Historical Center, Underwater Archaeology Branch, Professional Papers Number 4. Washington D.C.

Delgado, James P.
2015 Maritime Archaeology in the 21st Century. *Sea History* 153 (Winter 2015-2016): 8-22.

Florida Department of Environmental Protection
2013 St. Augustine Inlet Management Plan, draft. Division of Water Resources Management. Submitted to St. Augustine Port, Waterway, and Beach District, St. Augustine, FL.

Florida Department of State, Division of Historic Resources, Bureau of Archaeological Research
1994 *Management Plan for Florida's Submerged Cultural Resources*. submitted to U.S. Department of Commerce, Coastal Resources Center. Charleston, SC.

Ford, Ben, Carrie Sowden, Katherine Farnsworth, and M. Scott Harris
2015 "Coastal and Inland Geologic and Geomorphic Processes". In *Site Formation Processes of Submerged Shipwrecks*. edited by Matthew E. Keith, 17-43. University Press of Florida. Gainesville, FL.

Keith, Matthew, Amanda Evan, and Tesla Offshore, LLC
2015 "Sediment and Site Formation in the Marine Environment". In *Site Formation Processes of Submerged Shipwrecks*. edited by Matthew E. Keith, 44-69. University Press of Florida. Gainesville, FL.

Meide, Chuck, Samuel P. Turner and P. Brendan Burke
2010 First Coast Maritime Archaeology Project 2007-2009: Report on Archaeological and Historical Investigations and Other Project Activities. Lighthouse Archaeological Maritime Program, St. Augustine Lighthouse & Museum, First Light Maritime Society, St. Augustine, FL.

Meide, Chuck, Samuel P. Turner, P. Brendan Burke and Starr Cox
2011 First Coast Maritime Archaeology Project 2010: Report on Archaeological Investigations. Lighthouse Archaeological Maritime Program, St. Augustine Lighthouse & Maritime Museum, St. Augustine, FL.

Meide, Chuck
2015 "Cast Away off the Bar": The Archaeological Investigation of British Period Shipwrekcs in St. Augustine. *The Florida Historical Quarterly* 23(3) 354-386.

Morris, John W. III, Marianne Franklin, Norine Carroll, Kelly Bumpass and Andrea P. White
1998 The St. Augustine Maritime Survey: 1998 Report on the Tube Gun Site 8SJ3478. Southern Oceans Archaeological Research, Inc. Site Report No. 2. Report 5489 on file at the Bureau of Archaeological Research, Division of Historical Resources, Tallahassee, FL.

Morris, John W. III
2000 Site 8SJ3478 The Tube Gun Site 1999 Field Season Report. Lighthouse Archaeological Maritime Program (LAMP), St. Augustine Lighthouse and Museum, St. Augustine, FL.

Schiffer, Michael B.
1987 *Formation Processes of the Archaeological Record*. University of Arizona Press. Tucson, AZ.

Shabica, Charles W., Stephan Cofer-Shabica, Stephen L. Bloom, and David E. Anderson
1993 *Inlets of the Southeast Region National Seashore Units: Effects of Inlet Maintenance and Recommended Action*. U.S. Department of the Interior National Park Service. Washington D.C.

Srinivas, R., S. J. Schropp, and R. B. Taylor
1996 *St. Augustine Inlet Management Plan – Part 2*. Taylor Engineering, Inc. Jacksonville, FL.

UNITED STATES ARMY CORPS OF ENGINEERS
1979   *Feasibility Report for Beach Erosion Control, St. Johns County, FL.* Jacksonville District (CESAJ). Jacksonville, FL.

UNITED STATES ARMY CORPS OF ENGINEERS
1991   St. Johns County, FL, Beach Erosion Control Project. Special Report. Jacksonville District (CESAJ). Jacksonville, FL.

UNITED STATES ARMY CORPS OF ENGINEERS
2012   *Regional Sediment Budget for St. Augustine Inlet and St. Johns County, FL. 1998/1999-2010.* Jacksonville District (CESAJ/ERDC/CHL) Letter Report. Jacksonville District (CESAJ). Jacksonville, FL.

WALTON, T. L.
1973   Littoral Drift Computations along the Coast of Florida by Means of Ship Wave Observations. Coastal Engineering Laboratory Report No. 15. University of Florida, Gainesville, FL.

WALTON, T. L., R.G. DEAN, J. GAY, M. MANUSA, AND R. WANG
2011   Inlet Management Restudy for St. Augustine Inlet, St. Johns County, Florida. Manuscript, Beaches and Shores Resource Center, Florida State University, Tallahassee, FL.

P. Brendan Burke
Lighthouse Archaeological Maritime Program (LAMP)
81 Lighthouse Avenue
St Augustine, FL 32080
904-829-0745
bburke@staugustinelighthouse.org

Diving into the Past: The F4U Corsair at Crystal Cove State Marine Conservation Area

Tricia Dodds

Crystal Cove State Park is home to many unique cultural resources that tell the story of California's fascinating past. Its marine conservation area is no less extraordinary. In 1949, a Navy F4U Corsair airplane met its watery grave off the coast of Crystal Cove. Since its rediscovery, this underwater site has been studied and recorded by California State Parks with the assistance of other institutions. In 2014, the California State Parks Dive Team revisited the Corsair to evaluate its current physical condition and to make future recommendations on this part of California's military history.

Crystal Cove is located in southern California on the Pacific Coast Highway between Laguna Beach and Newport Beach. The nearly 3,000-acre park offers some of the last remaining undeveloped coastal land in all of southern California and remains one of Orange County's largest examples of open space and natural seashore (Smith and Breece 2002; California Department of Parks and Recreation 2003). Archaeological evidence suggests that the earliest human presence occurred 7,500 years ago within the area. Sporadic European contact occurred as early as the mid-1500s, but extended contact did not occur until 1776 when the Spanish established the Mission of San Juan Capistrano (Smith and Breece 2002). Eventually, San Francisco merchant James Irvine bought the property in 1864 (Allan et al. 1981).

After coastal road development made the area more accessible, what would become Crystal Cove became a coastal community (California Department of Parks and Recreation 2001). Today, the historic cottages are the last beach community in Southern California relatively unchanged since World War II. The cottages are listed on the National Register of Historic Places (Allan et al. 1981). California Department of Parks and Recreation began acquiring land from the Irvine Company in 1979 and classified it as a State Park in 1980 (California Department of Parks and Recreation 2001). In 1982, Parks designated the offshore area out to the 120-foot contour a Marine Managed Area containing significant ecological and historical resources. Six historic vessels have been reported lost within the area (Smith and Breece 2002). The Corsair airplane rests in what is now designated as the Crystal Cove State Marine Conservation Area and is the only airplane to be documented in State Parks' waters (Tricia Dodds, personal communication 2015).

Model F4U-4 Corsairs were first built and delivered to the Navy in 1944. This model was characterized by an inverted gull wing, in which the wings were bent on both sides of the fuselage; a streamlined fuselage; and a large four-bladed propeller that replaced the previous three-bladed propeller of earlier models. This improved the speed and climb rate. These planes could reach speeds of up to 451 mph. Corsairs were among the most successful fighters in World War II, although this model arrived late in World War II and mainly served during the last four months of conflict. It was used substantially during the Korean War. The Japanese ground troops nicknamed the formidable Corsair "Whistling Death" from the whistling sounds it made from the airflow through the engine vents (National Naval Aviation Museum 2015; Fighter Planes and Military Aircraft 2015). The Corsair, including the F4U-4 model at Crystal Cove, proved to be a very effective fighter plane, which is why it continued to be used after World War II.

In 1949, Navy reserve pilot William H. Anderson of Los Angeles was assigned to Los Alamitos Naval Air Station near Long Beach for two weeks training duty (Orange County Register [OCR] 5 July 1949; Long Beach Independent [LBI] 6 July 1949 page 1). At 26, Lieutenant Anderson was no longer a rookie pilot, with over 1500 hours of flying time. On July 5, 1949, he left for San Diego in a Chance Vought F4U-4 Corsair on a routine navigational training flight with three other Corsairs (OCR 5 July 1949; U.S. Navy 1949; Anderson 1949). His particular Corsair had been built and delivered to the Navy in September 1945, although it did not see action in World War II (U.S. Navy Aircraft Data 1949). On Anderson's return trip to the naval air station around 1030 in the morning, his engine began to have trouble about two miles offshore of Laguna Beach (U.S. Navy 1949; Anderson 1949). On the previous flight in that aircraft, the pilot had reported the engine running rough, and the maintenance officer had replaced the spark plugs as a result. Before Anderson's flight, the plane had satisfactorily checked out on the ground (U.S. Naval Air Station 1949). Anderson was 43 minutes into his flight when he began to experience trouble. He moved his mixture control to full rich position to get enough fuel into the engine, but he could not get it to function well enough to continue the flight. He notified his flight leader that he would have to ditch his plane since he could not make it back to the air station. He unfastened his parachute, locked his shoulder straps, and locked his hood in the open position. He noticed a small fishing boat nearby and directed his plane that way. He readied the plane for a water landing near the fishing boat near Crystal Cove. He came in low, eased down, and made a perfect ditching, although the impact was still strong considering that the plane hit the water flat at about 90 mph. The Corsair skidded to the left, and water began to pour over Anderson. The plane began to sink immediately after it hit the water, but Anderson was able to unlock his safety belt and escape the Corsair. He stepped out onto the water-covered wing and noticed that the tail was already rising rapidly. Anderson jumped into the water and watched the plane disappear below the surface. Since he had unfastened his parachute, he left the pararaft inside his chute in the plane. He managed to inflate his Mae West lifevest, but he forgot to unfasten the harness attached to the parachute that was still inside the sinking plane. The pressure intensified as Anderson could not easily breathe while still attached to the parachute, and he struggled to unfasten the harness as the plane continued to sink to the bottom. Eventually, Anderson managed to deflate one side of his lifevest enough to release the parachute harness, and he was freed from the plane. The other three Corsairs were circling Anderson by now, and he waved to assure them that he was all right. Anderson kept on his shoes and clothes to protect himself from the rocky shoreline and began to swim on his back towards shore. After about 20 minutes, Anderson noticed the small fishing boat and waved at it frantically. The craft picked up a tired Anderson who noted that he had difficulty climbing into the boat. The fishermen took Anderson to Laguna Beach, where he was taken to the local police station to be transferred back to Los Alamitos Naval Air Station. He was debriefed back at the station, and it was recommended that the Navy review proper ditching procedure since he should not have inflated his lifevest before releasing himself from the parachute. Anderson did do everything else according to protocol. He was not injured by the crash, and the plane sat on the ocean floor, forgotten for years (U.S. Navy Accident Report 1949; Anderson, 1949).

The Corsair was rediscovered in 1961. A skin diver named Marine Corporal Thomas B. Fuller of El Toro Marine Corps Air Station was searching for the body of a fellow diver who had drowned, and he encountered the barnacle-encrusted plane. Fuller reported the plane to the Navy and mentioned that there was a body inside the plane (OCR January 1961). The Navy assigned Lt. Commander Tommy Thompson and divers from the Long Beach Naval Station Explosive Ordinance Disposal to investigate. After three weeks of searching with the most advanced technology of the day, the plane was located offshore in 75 feet of water. Navy divers observed that the plane was an intact Corsair, looking as if it had just landed on the ocean floor. The machine guns were in the wings, and the "body" turned out to be seat padding that was slowly deteriorating. A parachute was entangled in the wreckage. They returned to port and considered the task a success. Shortly afterwards, Thompson was ordered to return to the Corsair to remove the engine and machine guns to identify the plane and evaluate the effects of prolonged submersion in saltwater on the parts. The Navy's diving unit salvaged the Pratt & Whitney engine with a cable and salvage tug, and they positively identified the plane using the plates attached to the salvaged engine as ID #82097, Lt. Anderson's plane. The Navy left the remainder of the plane on the ocean floor (Miller 1991; Los Angeles Time [LAT] 24 January 1961; Samuel Miller, personal communication 2015; U.S. Navy Accident Report 1949).

In 1974, the plane was accidentally rediscovered by Dave Bewley and Mike Curtis when they were diving for deep reefs and noticed an abnormal reading on their depth sounder (Miller 1991). They dove down to investigate and discovered the plane, which "looked as though it made a near perfect landing." Bewley found a single propeller blade stuck upright in the sand, and

Figure 1. Front part of Corsair with engine compartment, cockpit, and one propeller blade, approximately early 1970s.

ten feet behind that was the plane. They noted that the tail section was broken off and the cockpit canopy was open (Figure 1). A tangle of nylon cloth—the parachute—was underneath the fuselage. The wing, body, and instrument panels were missing. The wings were half-buried in the sand, and the rear edge of the fuselage was supported by the tail landing gear. The pair observed that the wreck was overgrown with marine life. They noted the missing engine and bits of machinery still in the compartment. They decided to keep the plane wreck a secret and adopted a "look but don't take" policy to preserve the site (Hanauer 1977; Samuel Miller, personal communication 2015).

A 1977 *Skin Diver* magazine article by Eric Hanauer reported the condition of the Corsair, noting that overall it was largely intact, with some damage to the tail section (Figure 2). After the publication, more divers began to visit the wreck site and take souvenirs (Samuel Miller, personal communication 2015; Hanauer 1977). In 1979, California encountered one of its worst storms in years. Hanauer dove on the wreck afterwards and discovered that underwater wave action had tumbled the airplane along the ocean floor, damaging it. It also appeared that a fishing boat had entangled its anchor on the plane behind the cockpit and pulled the plane apart trying to retrieve the anchor (Miller 1991). From the windscreen to the tail, the fuselage had been reduced to twisted wreckage strewn over a 30-foot area. Hanauer later wrote an article for *Skin Diver* magazine observing that the wreck had greatly deteriorated (Hanauer 1981). In 1990, those who had recently dived on the Corsair noted that they could not even recognize it as an airplane anymore because the ocean had dispersed so much of the wreckage (Miller 1991).

In 2005, Sheli Smith and Annalies Corbin of the Partnering Anthropology with Science and Technology (PAST) Foundation along with Charlie Beeker of Indiana University conducted a study to map the Corsair site. The study identified the instrument panel outlets, rudder controls, and cockpit wiring of the Corsair. The fuselage was missing aft of the firewall, and only about eight feet was left of the fuselage. The cockpit and tail section were also missing, although the top of the rudder of the tail section was still present (Figure 3). Archaeologists were able to record general measurements of the forward engine housing and both gull-shaped wings. They noted pieces of the rear rudder and elevator flaps along with other mechanisms within the debris field. Observations of the remaining airplane suggest that the plane touched down on its left wing first and

Figure 3. Engine compartment of the Corsair during the 2005 dive.

then settled to the bottom in an upright position. The left wing was severely damaged or completely missing from the halfway point, and the right wing of the plane was just short of being completely intact (Beeker and Smith 2005; Smith 2005).

In the fall of 2014, the State Parks Dive Team returned to the Corsair as part of their training to complete a condition survey of the site. The divers

Figure 2. The cockpit of the Corsair, approximately 1977.

relocated the wreck in 70 feet of water. They conducted site maintenance, took measurements, and recorded its current condition to update the site records. Observation of the wreck indicates that it is rapidly deteriorating from underwater currents that continually move the wreckage around on the ocean floor. The cowling has disengaged and the fuselage has deteriorated (Figure 4). In addition, the wings have devolved to their cross structures (Dodds 2014).

As a result, the different forces acting on the Corsair such as surge, currents, marine organisms, saltwater corrosion, and divers removing pieces of the plane have all taken their toll on the site. Essentially, the wreck site is now a debris field with most of the pieces unidentifiable. Only a skeleton remains of the Corsair. It is beneficial that State Parks already recorded the Corsair because, at this rate, the plane will most likely be lost to the ocean (Dodds 2014).

Acknowledgements

Many individuals contributed to the successful research of the Corsair at Crystal Cove State Marine Conservation Area. I wish to thank the following individuals: Ken Kramer, the members of the State Parks Dive Team who participated in the 2014 recording (Todd Lewis, John Regan, Chris Gallina, Schuyler Kirby, Brian Lane, Sean Briscoe, Mark Allen, Paul Andrus, Phil Hauck, Ryan Gates, Bill Pfeiffer, Ryan Steele, Joel Nunn, John Rowe, Dick DeBoer, John Anderson, and Eric Dymmel), Alex Bevil, Steve Lawson, Pat Macha, Randy Biddle, George Schwarz, Samuel Miller, Sheli Smith, Annalies Corbin, Jeffrey Wedding, Megan Lickliter-Mundon, Craig Fuller, and others. Your assistance with my research is very much appreciated!

Figure 4. Forward fuselage of the Corsair during 2014 dive.

References

ALLAN, DAVID L., ALAN K. TANG, COURT TONOUYE, EILEEN HOOK, JOHN KELLY, JOHN MCALEER, JAMES M. TRUMBLEY, CLARK W. WOY, LARRY MARTZ, AND GARY CAPLENER
1981   *Crystal Cove State Park General Plan.* Draft of Preliminary. California State Parks. On file at California Department of Parks and Recreation, Southern Service Center, San Diego, California.

ANDERSON, WILLIAM H.
1949   Statement of Lieutenant William H. Anderson, A3 0263869 USNR-O VA-71A. Manuscript on file, United States Naval Air Station, Los Alamitos, California.

BEEKER, CHARLES, AND SHELI SMITH
2005   Crystal Cove F4U Corsair Airplane Wreck Scuba Maintenance and Survey Dive Close of Field Work Interim Report. On file at California Department of Parks and Recreation, Sacramento, California.

CALIFORNIA DEPARTMENT OF PARKS AND RECREATION
2001   *Crystal Cove Historic District Investigations and Interim Protection Plan.* Final Environmental Impact Report, SCH #2001031001. On file at California Department of Parks and Recreation, Southern Service Center, San Diego, California.

CALIFORNIA DEPARTMENT OF PARKS AND RECREATION
2003   *Crystal Cove Historic District Preservation and Public Use Plan Including Crystal Cove State Park General Plan Amendment.* On file at California Department of Parks and Recreation, Southern Service Center, San Diego, California.

DODDS, TRICIA
2014   Original unpublished fieldnotes from Crystal Cove State Marine Conservation Area and the Corsair. Manuscript on file, California State Parks, California.

FIGHTER PLANES AND MILITARY AIRCRAFT
2015   F4U Corsair, Chance-Vought. Electronic document, http://www.fighter-planes.com/, accessed May 3, 2005.

HANAUER, ERIC
1977   Laguna's Secret Plane Wreck. *Skin Diver* December pages 33, 94.

1981   Scotchman's Cove. *Skin Diver* February pages 24, 28.

LONG BEACH INDEPENDENT (LBI) [LONG BEACH, CALIFORNIA]
1949   "Pilot Rescued After Sea Crash." 6 July: page 1. Long Beach, California.

LOS ANGELES TIMES (LAT) [LOS ANGELES, CALIFORNIA]
1961   "Old Plane Wreckage in Ocean Identified." 24 January. Los Angeles, California.

MILLER, DR. SAMUEL
1991   The Discovery and Demise of the Mystery of the Plane of Scotsman's Cove. *Discover Diving* January/February, pages 63-64.

NATIONAL NAVAL AVIATION MUSEUM
2015   F4U-4 Corsair. Electronic document, http://www.navalaviationmuseum.org/attractions/aircraft-exhibits/item/?item=f4u-4_corsair, accessed April 24, 2015.

ORANGE COUNTY REGISTER (OCR) [ORANGE, CALIFORNIA]
1949   "Pilot Escapes Injury in Crash." 5 July. Orange, California.

1961   "Skindiver Continues Search." January. Orange, California.

SMITH, SHELI O.
2005   Project Corsair: Underwater Expedition at Crystal Cove, California Powerpoint Presentation. On file at California State Parks, Sacramento, California.

SMITH, SHELI O., AND LAUREL H. BREECE
2002   *California State Marine Managed Areas: Cultural Resource Survey 2001/2002.* Long Beach City College Maritime Archaeology Certificate Program, Long Beach, California.

UNITED STATES NAVAL AIR STATION
1949   Material Officer's Statement for incident on 5 July 1949. Manuscript on file, Department of the Navy, Underwater Archaeology Branch, Washington, D.C.

UNITED STATES NAVY
1949   Accident Report, Serial No. 14-49 for incident on 5 July 1949. Manuscript on file, Department of the Navy, Underwater Archaeology Branch, Washington D.C.

Tricia Dodds
California State Parks
5172 Highway 78 #10
Borrego Springs, CA 92004

Establishing an Integrated Conservation Priority for Artillery from Site 31CR314, *Queen Anne's Revenge* (1718)

Erik Farrell

Among the artifacts from the wreck of Queen Anne's Revenge (QAR), *the artillery represents a particularly evocative and informative subset. Conserving a cannon represents one of the largest single-object expenditures of time and materials of any subset of* QAR *artifacts, and this must be prioritized within the ongoing conservation of hundreds of thousands of individual objects. Conservators, archaeologists and museum staff associated with the* QAR *project were surveyed regarding preferences for cannon conservation, the results of which have been used to determine a priority order for the conservation of* QAR *cannon.*

Introduction

Queen Anne's Revenge (*QAR*) was the flagship of pirate Edward Teach, widely known as 'Blackbeard'. The vessel began as *La Concorde*, a French-built slaver, captured and renamed by Teach in 1717. By late 1718, *QAR* was lost, and Blackbeard himself was killed in battle shortly thereafter (Wilde-Ramsing and Ewen 2012:113; Lawrence and Wilde-Ramsing 2001:2.)

As a part of North Carolina's cultural heritage, the *QAR* Project falls under the mandate of the NC Department of Natural and Cultural Resources, Office of Archives and History: "to collect, preserve, and utilize the state's historic resources so that present and future residents may better understand their history" (NCOAH 2013). All *QAR* Project activities must contribute towards the education and improvement of state residents, present and future.

The *QAR* wreck has been mandated by the state of North Carolina for complete excavation due to its historical significance and vulnerability to damage and loss (Wilde-Ramsing and Lusardi 1999). Because of the quantity of material recovered and projected for future recovery (See Watkins-Kenney 2010; Kenyon 2016), it has become necessary to prioritize artifact conservation to best achieve the goals of the project. Within the overall collection, the artillery represents a particularly informative and evocative subset, but one with significant conservation costs and challenges.

Problems of Scale

At present, the *Queen Anne's Revenge* Conservation Laboratory (*QAR* Lab) in Greenville, NC employs the full-time equivalent of 2.5 conservators. Among more than 400,000 individual artifacts recovered thus far are 18 cast iron cannon currently in the lab. An additional five cast iron cannon have been conserved and transferred to the North Carolina Maritime Museum at Beaufort (NCMM), and at least six additional cannon are present at the wreck site. Through full recovery, a total artifact count up to 1,000,000 objects is expected.

With limited staff, space, time, equipment, and budget, it is impossible to conserve everything simultaneously. As a result, a cohesive plan for the prioritization of conservation treatments has become necessary. The prioritization of small finds in concretion was planned by *QAR* Conservator Kimberly Kenyon (See Kenyon 2016, this volume). However, the artillery collection presents additional problems in scale, such that it could not readily be included in the general conservation priority order.

The time and resource commitment to a single cannon is exponentially greater than for the majority of smaller artifacts. Granting equal priority to a cannon and a small find results in far more time spent on the gun, delaying progression of small finds. Committing equal time results in extreme delays in the progression of a cannon. Creation of a separate priority for artillery was necessary to address this disparity, so the artillery could be integrated into the general order for long-term planning.

Cannon

QAR's primary armament consists of cast iron guns, of which 29 are known. One bronze signal gun [C25] has been recovered and conserved, but is not addressed here. It is possible that further cast iron guns will be discovered as excavation progresses; approximately 40% of the site remains unexcavated, and 1-pounders have been discovered during excavation previously.

Cannon represent a greater-than-average time commitment to recover and conserve, but provide greater media exposure and better enable the project to meet its educational mandate through increased museum visitation. *QAR* cannon have been placed on long-term loan by the NCMM to the NC Museum of History and the Museum of the Albemarle, with additional national and foreign museums requesting cannon loans as more are completed.

There are a number of interests in setting conservation priorities in general, and prioritizing the cannon in particular:

For public education and outreach, it is desirable to prioritize artifacts that NCMM can use for compelling displays and engaging educational programming. Cannon are large, eye-catching artifacts evocative of the Golden Age of Piracy.

For archaeological purposes, it is desirable to prioritize artifacts that have the greatest analytical value. Of the five cast iron cannon conserved so far, three have marks identifying date and/or location of manufacture. Two cannon currently in progress also possess identifying marks.

To preserve the collection, it is desirable to prioritize unstable or extremely fragile artifacts. Some cannon at the *QAR* Lab have been noted as corroding in storage, and other artifacts caught in concretion may be chemically attacked by the highly alkaline sodium carbonate solution used to help stabilize iron. Glass, glazed ceramics and wood are particularly vulnerable to such attack (Cronyn 1990:135, Florian 1987:45).

Defining knowns

In developing criteria for a priority sequence, there are a limited number of known variables for concreted cannon:

Size may be broadly determined, dividing into small guns of 2-pounders and lesser, 4-pounders, and 6-pounders.

The presence of identifying marks cannot be determined before cleaning. Thus far, 4-pounders and smaller have all been identifiable, but the sample size is insufficient to make predictions on this basis.

An approximate count of other artifacts caught in concretion with a cannon may be derived by counting unusual protrusions and partially exposed objects, but this number is almost always a low estimate.

Whether or not a gun is loaded (load status) may rarely be determined. As part of a documentary filmed in 2014, *QAR* Lab was able to work with industrial radiographers from Applied Technical Services, GE, and NewCo, Inc. to x-ray 6 cannon, determining four to be loaded. Discounting such unusual events, it is assumed that any gun which appears to have a tampion in place is loaded, but the absence of a tampion is not a reliable indication that a gun is unloaded.

For this survey, stability is determined by visual inspection; if a gun or concretion is growing 'rusticles' (small stalactites of orange-brown rust), it is assumed to be unstable. Electrochemical readings are taken periodically, but due to the lesser time burden visual inspection is carried out more often and is therefore of greater use for a continuously updated priority.

Partially exposed objects are assumed to be unstable if they are a material degraded by strong alkali.

Time requirements for full conservation vary widely. As baseline averages, a small cannon requires 90 conservator-days of active time, 130 for a 4-pounder, and 160 for a 6-pounder. For heavily concreted guns, this figure can be drastically higher. All cannon require 5-8 years of additional passive time for desalination and controlled drying.

Status and Condition Reports

The first step in determining a conservation order was to gather as much information regarding the above points of interest as possible. To that end, a status and condition survey was carried out on the artillery collection, the results of which are summarized in Table 1. Data were collected on cast iron cannon currently awaiting conservation—already conserved cannon and unexcavated examples are not included. Due to the limited scope (artillery only) and goals (condition audit leading to priorities assessment), all objects of this class were surveyed (Keene 2002:140-141; 152).

Cannon C22, C24, and C26 are fully cleaned and in desalination; they require minimal active conservation time to complete.

Any cannon displaying new corrosion and exposed iron surface as a corrosion risk factor is considered actively corroding in alkaline storage media (2.5% aqueous solution of sodium carbonate). For C15, new corrosion only appeared after partial cleaning occurred, likely due to increased oxygenation at the metal interface. Both C27 and C29 exhibited new corrosion prior to any concretion removal in the lab corrosion accelerated after surface cleaning began. For C29, partial concretion removal during excavation was necessary, which contributed to initial corrosion in storage.

C28 was likewise partially exposed during

C #	QAR #	Poundage	Load Status	Artifact Cover	New Corrosion	Damage and Corrosion Risks	Artifact Materials and Types
C1	3385	6		Major	No	Exposed wood	Ballast, wood, unknowns
C5	811	4		Full	No		Ballast
C6	3768	6		Major	No	No	Ballast, unknowns
C8	3891	4	Round, langrage (?)	Minor	Yes		Tampion(?), unknowns
C12	2100	6		Minor	No		Lead (?), unknowns
C13	3350	6		Major	No		Ballast, unknowns
C14	2005	6		Major	No	Exposed wood	Ballast, wood, unknowns
C15	636.001	4	Round	Few	Yes	Partial exposed iron surface, rope, wood	Tampion, rope
C16	2300	6		Full	No	Exposed pewter, wood, glass, other	Pewter, wood, glass, lead, unknowns
C17	2299	6		Full	No	Large concretion protrusion	Ballast, unknowns
C18	1875	6	Unloaded	Minor	No		Unknowns
C20	2004	6	Unloaded	Minor	No		Unknowns
C22	509.15	1	Round	None	No	In desalination	None
C24	637.05	6	Unloaded	None	No	In desalination	None
C26	3633	1	Round	None	No	In desalination	None
C27	3650	1	Round	Few	Yes	Exposed iron surface	Unknown
C28	4038	1/2(?)	Tampion (?)	Few	Yes	Exposed iron surface	Ballast
C29	3860	2		Few	Yes	Exposed iron surface	Ballast

TABLE 1: Status and Condition Summary

FIGURE 1: Cannon C22 from *QAR* (cast iron 1-pounder) prior to cleaning. Significant concretion is present, encapsulating numerous ballast stones and additional artifacts. (Photograph by DNCR staff, 2005. Image courtesy of North Carolina Department of Natural and Cultural Resources)

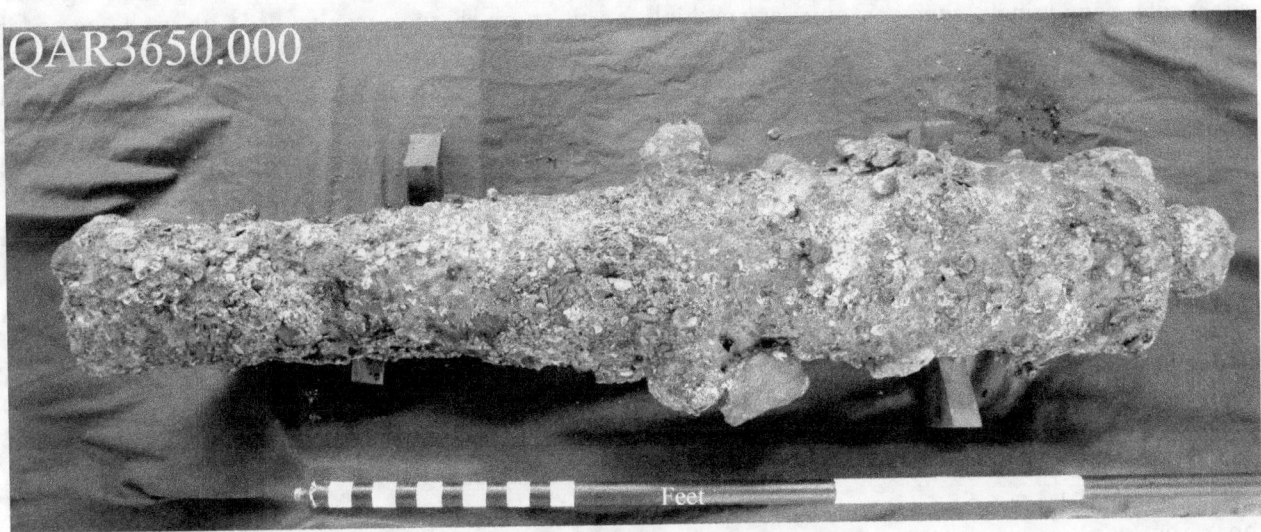

FIGURE 2: Cannon C27 from *QAR* (cast iron 1-pounder) prior to cleaning. Object exhibits thin, uniform concretion cover with few associated artifacts. (Photograph by DNCR staff, 2014. Image courtesy of North Carolina Department of Natural

excavation, but conservation cleaning in the lab has not begun. Other noted corrosion/damage risks (C1, C14, C15, C16, C17) apply to artifacts caught in concretion with cannon that are at risk of physical or chemical damage.

The category of "artifact cover" in Table 1 refers to the combined amount of artifacts and ferrous concretion encapsulating a cannon. This does not directly affect the stability of the cannon or associated objects, but heavily impacts the amount of time required to fully deconcrete the cannon. This variable is described in Table 1 as: None (No concretion); Few (0-5 small objects); Minor (5-10 small objects, 0-5 large); Major (10-15 small objects, 5-10 large); Full (15+ small objects, 10+ large). The degree of concretion cover tends to correlate positively with the number of artifacts contained. With greater artifact and concretion cover, more time is required to clean a cannon, and greater expense incurred. Differences in artifact and concretion cover between *QAR* artifacts can be substantial (Figures 1-2); of the definable variables, this has by far the greatest impact on time and resource requirements.

Personnel Survey

The condition survey was used to determine the conservation priorities without consideration of other interests. Overall prioritization must account for museum/educational and archaeological interests as components of the overall *QAR* Project, with the acknowledgement that the direct interests of the conservation team are not the sole interests of the project (Pye 2001:157-160). To this end, a survey was circulated among fourteen museum, archaeological, and conservation staff affiliated with the *QAR* Project at NCMM, *QAR* Lab, the Office of State Archaeology (OSA) and Underwater Archaeology Branch (UAB). Eight full or partial responses were received.

Project staff were questioned on a range of topics, including exposing particular diagnostic components on a cannon, size of cannon, location of cannon on site, number and nature of objects caught in concretion with cannon, load status, and country of manufacture. Additionally, project staff were asked to choose between either conserving a single cannon or conserving multiple small finds.

Cleaning to expose diagnostic features was of low importance to respondents. The highest ranked options for partial cleaning were: cleaning the bore interior (specifically to accelerate desalination) and removal of associated artifacts from concretion (to prevent damage and conserve diagnostic artifacts). The next most desirable option was cleaning the entire surface of a cannon. Cleaning of diagnostic features (first reinforce, trunnion ends, or complete profile) were all ranked lower on average than completely cleaning the cannon. Additionally, incomplete cleaning would increase oxygenation at exposed areas and thereby increase risk of corrosion and loss of important features (Farrell 2014:192).

Onsite cannon location was a low priority. Both options (on central pile and not on central pile) were given the lowest level of importance on average. Load status was likewise assigned low importance by respondents, with 7 of 8 respondents specifying a lack of preference between loaded and unloaded cannon (Farrell 2014:193-194). Conservators have since found cleaning a cannon with a known load status to be easier than an unknown, but without bias towards that status being specifically loaded or unloaded.

Three of eight responses expressed the opinion that cannon of unknown origin should be given higher priority, while remaining responses expressed no opinion (Farrell 2014:194). Cleaning cannon of unknown manufacture may provide archaeologically significant information. However, as it is extremely rare to be able to determine country of manufacture before cleaning, the preference towards unknowns in this instance has little impact.

On average, large guns were ranked the third lowest priority (only ahead of location on site), while small cannon tied with fragile/diagnostic artifacts as the highest ranked priority (Farrell 2014:192). With respect to archaeological interests, small cannon – cast iron guns sized 4-pounder and smaller – thus far have all borne an identifying mark (maker's mark, proof marks, etc.) For the museum, the main interest expressed was in having guns completed quickly for display, and smaller sizes are faster to clean. Conservators did not express a direct size preference, but all of the actively corroding guns are currently 4-pounders and smaller. As a result, conservators have a functional preference for small cannon.

Cannon with fragile or archaeologically diagnostic artifacts caught in concretion tied with small cannon for the highest priority (Farrell 2014:193). More diagnostic artifacts aid site interpretation for archaeologists, and removing fragile or at-risk artifacts from damaging conditions is of principle concern to conservators. Museum staff prefer cannon with additional artifacts in concretion as a means of combining tasks, and theoretically increasing the number of artifacts conserved in a given time frame. Most of the cannon with a significant number of known objects in concretion, however, are 6-pounders; the preference for cannon with many associated artifacts runs contrary to the preference for smaller guns.

A majority (5 of 7 who answered) also expressed the opinion that – given limited time and resources – it is more important to conserve a variety of non-artillery artifacts than to spend equivalent time on a single cannon. Additional commentary outside of the formal survey agreed that cannon should be completed as quickly as possible, without detracting from the conservation of other materials (Farrell 2014:195).

Resulting Treatment Priorities

Working from the survey, it then became necessary to incorporate the expressed results into a working priority.

The preference for small guns conflicts with the preference for guns with multiple artifacts in concretion, simply because those guns with greatest exposed artifact count happen to be 6-pounders. It was decided that this issue could be managed by treating the removal of associated, exposed objects as a separate operation from cleaning a cannon's entire surface.

Once the contradictory preferences for small cannon and cannon with many associated artifacts were reconciled, only a few variables with direct effect on a cannon's conservation priority remained. These were used to form a ranked list for making decisions regarding the overall priority of any given cannon within the artillery collection: A set of five distinct priority categories is derived from the ranked criteria (Table 2).

1. Corrosion risk
    a. To the cannon – guns which are visibly corroding in alkaline storage media are given priority over stable guns.
    b. Artifact cover (exposed) – if all guns are stable, priority shifts to removing vulnerable, exposed artifacts from the concretion matrix around cannon.

2. Size – Small cannon (2-pounders and lesser) are given priority, followed by 4-pounders, and finally 6-pounders and greater.

3. Difficulty (Time required)
    a. Artifact and concretion cover – all other variables being equal, the gun with the least amount of concretion will be conserved first.
    b. Load status – all other variables being equal, a gun with known load status (loaded or unloaded) is prioritized over an unknown.

Integration of Priorities

In the personnel survey, a desire to conserve cannon without taking time away from other artifacts was strongly expressed; taken broadly, this was the purpose of integrating the artillery priority with the general objects/small finds priority.

Category	Description	Cannon (listed in order of priority within category)
Cat0	Desalination is in progress. Cannon are engaged in passive conservation processes; minimal additional input is required to complete conservation and produce a stable cannon for archaeological analysis and museum display.	C22, C24, C26
Cat1	Active conservation cleaning is ongoing. Surface cleaning is ongoing so that small, corroding guns may be progressed into desalination. This is the highest priority which is undergoing active conservation cleaning.	C27, C29
Cat2	Corroding in alkaline storage. Cleaning should be prioritized to allow conservation progression towards stabilization. This is the highest priority for cannon in storage awaiting cleaning.	C28, C15
Cat3	At-risk artifacts. Associated artifacts in concretion may be damaged by alkaline storage media, or are at risk of physical damage. Artifacts should be removed from concretion without full cleaning of the cannon.	C16, C14, C1, C17
Cat4	Stable. Stable cannon will be cleaned from smallest to largest, cleaning the least heavily concreted examples in a given size class first.	C8, C5, C12, C18, C20, C1, C6, C13, C14, C16, C17

TABLE 2: Priority Categories for Artillery

In order to achieve this, *QAR* conservators have improved efficiency in cleaning cannon by always having three to four people working on a cannon when it is out of storage. Removal from and replacement into storage tanks is accomplished with a manual chain hoist; this takes approximately one hour per working day. By ensuring multiple conservators are cleaning a cannon each time one is moved, the number of conservator/hours spent actively cleaning is maximized relative to time lost in moving cannon.

The impact of this on conservation of other artifact classes is mitigated by limiting cannon cleaning to 2-3 days/month. Remaining time is spent on other artifact classes, allowing conservation of small finds at a normal rate. At any given time, two cannon are actively progressing through cleaning (Cat1).

This schedule has allowed the integration of the artillery order into the general priority order. General objects in concretion are assigned a priority rating ranging from P1 (highest priority) to P5 (lowest priority) (Kenyon 2016). Rather than assign all cannon as P1 objects, the two cannon with the highest active priority at any given time (Cat1 in Table 2) are treated as P1 objects in the overall priority order. As a cannon is cleaned and enters desalination, the next-highest priority cannon will move up to replace it as a Cat1 in artillery priority, and functionally as a P1 in general priority.

Moving Forward

The priorities and specific conservation order as outlined above are not absolute; evaluation, feedback, and flexibility are necessary to ensure functionality (Keene 2002:202). Condition is continuously monitored, and if a cannon deteriorates, its priority may change accordingly. If museum/educational or archaeological priorities change with respect to the preference for smaller cannon, then the overall priority may change accordingly. Where compelling research interests exist for a specific cannon (e.g. cannon C12 with respect to Watkins-Kenney and Claggett 2015:47-48), that cannon may likewise have its priority altered. The artillery priority has not been established as a set of inalterable, absolute rules; it serves only as a general guideline for more efficient and considered cannon conservation. In following these guidelines, it is hoped to increase the overall efficiency of conservation work, and to steadily advance the conservation of both the artillery and the small finds towards completion.

Acknowledgements

I would like to acknowledge all *QAR* Project staff from *QAR* Lab, the NCMM, OSA, and UAB, without whom a priority determination could not have been made. In particular, Kimberly Kenyon and Sarah Watkins-Kenney, as this work builds on Kim's concreted small finds prioritization and Sarah's general management timeline. Additional thanks go to all the partner organizations whose support makes the excavation, conservation, and educational commitments of *QAR* Project possible. This paper is an updated version of one submitted to Durham University; many thanks to everyone who provided information and assistance for my M.A. portfolio.

References

Cronyn, J.M
1990   *The Elements of Archaeological Conservation.* Routledge, New York.

Farrell, Erik
2014   Detailed Conservation Survey and Conservation Priority Determination for Cannon from the Wreck of the *Queen Anne's Revenge* (1718). In *Portfolio of Professional Practice,* Masters Portfolio, Department of Archaeology, Durham University, Durham, UK. Pp. 167-206.

Florian, M-L. E.
1987   Deterioration of Organic Materials Other Than Wood. In *Conservation of Marine Archaeological Objects.* Colin Pearson, editor, pp.22-54. Butterworth & Co. (Publishers) Ltd., London.

Keene, Susan
2002   *Managing Conservation In Museums,* 2nd Edition Butterworth-Heinemann, Oxford.

Kenyon, Kimberly
2016   Prioritizing the Concretions from **Queen Anne's Revenge** for Conservation: A Case Study in Managing a Large Collection. *ACUA Proceedings 2016* (this volume).

Lawrence, Richard and Mark Wilde-Ramsing
2001   In Search of Blackbeard: Historical and Archaeological Research at Shipwreck Site 0003BUI, *Southeastern Geology,* 40(1):1-9.

NORTH CAROLINA OFFICE OF ARCHIVES AND HISTORY (NCOAH)
2013 Mission Statement, North Carolina Department of Natural and Cultural Resources: Office of Archives and History <http://www.history.ncdcr.gov/mission.htm> Accessed 20 February 2016).

PYE, ELIZABETH
2001 *Caring for the Past: Issues in Conservation for Archaeology and Museums.* James & James (Science Publishers) Ltd., London.

WATKINS-KENNEY, SARAH
2010 Conservation Provision for Beaufort Inlet Shipwreck 31CR314 *Queen Anne's Revenge* Shipwreck Project: 1996-2009. The Queen Anne's Revenge Shipwreck Project Research Report and Bulletin Series, QAR-R-10-01, North Carolina Department of Natural and Cultural Resources, Raleigh, NC.

WATKINS-KENNEY, SARAH AND STEVE CLAGGETT
2015 Developing a Corrosion Model for *Queen Anne's Revenge (QAR)* Shipwreck Site (31CR314) to Enhance the Management of Submerged Archaeological Remains. NC Sea Grant Project Number R/MG-1207 Final Report. Manuscript, QAR Lab, Greenville NC.

WILDE-RAMSING, MARK AND CHARLES EWEN
2012 Beyond Reasonable Doubt: A Case for *Queen Anne's Revenge. Historical Archaeology*, 46(2):110-133.

WILDE-RAMSING, MARK AND WAYNE LUSARDI
1999 Management Plan for North Carolina Shipwreck 31CR314, *Queen Anne's Revenge.* Manuscript, North Carolina Underwater Archaeology Branch, Kure Beach, NC.

Erik Farrell
North Carolina Department of Natural and Cultural Resources
1157 V O A Site C Road
Greenville, NC 27834
erik.farrell@ncdcr.gov

The 'Maritime Cultural Landscape' Approach as a Framework for Addressing Neglected Narratives: Point Pearce Aboriginal Mission/Burgiyana, South Australia

Madeline Fowler

Maritime activities at Point Pearce Aboriginal Mission/Burgiyana (1868–1966) in South Australia form the basis of an oral history, archaeological, and archival case study. This research assesses whether the maritime cultural landscape framework, a Western maritime archaeological concept, is applicable to Indigenous missions. The results of research at Point Pearce/Burgiyana indicate that care must be taken when applying maritime archaeological theories and associated attitudes to Indigenous archaeology ('with, for and by' Indigenous peoples). However, the application of a Western framework contributes towards the decolonization of maritime archaeology by accommodating the beliefs, knowledges, and lived experiences of Aboriginal peoples.

Big Fred the Great White Shark (Carcharodon carcharias)

Many years ago, when I was about 17, and his name was Big Fred, and he used to patrol the bay here and then down the bottom and go to Ardrossan and back. So one day me and my uncle and my brother was over here, Redbank, see there's Redbank. See straight out from Redbank, we was doing garfishing in the dinghy and I was standing up near the front of the boat. Now, are you going to believe this or not? And so when we looked we see Big Fred coming. We was in this dinghy and next minute the seat what I was standing on in the front of the dinghy broke. Arse-over-head I went in the water, Big Fred swimming past, this is true. And I come up on the boat, I had tobacco and matches in my shirt, when I was smoking and that, and my back got wet but my front never got wet. I come back into the boat, don't ask me how I done it. It was bloody frightening. Fell on my back in the water and then came straight back up. These things you can do when you're frightened, but try to do it normal times there's no way you can do it. Don't you reckon? You can do a lot of things when you frightened (Graham 2013).

"Now, are you going to believe this or not?" said Graham (2013), an Elder of the Narungga Aboriginal community, while on a boat off the coast of Yorke Peninsula/Guuranda, South Australia, in November of 2013 (Figure 1). It prefaced an anecdote that Graham (2013) recounted from an event that happened about 65 years previously, while he was fishing from the same spot. This quote, forming the title of the author's (Fowler 2015) doctoral research, represents a number of the key ideas and issues of the overall study, undertaken at the former Aboriginal mission, Point Pearce/Burgiyana.

First, it highlights the use of oral history in the wider research (Fowler et al. 2014, 2015). This approach complements the archaeological record and collaboration with the community throughout the research, particularly through on 'Country' recording, allowed the project to be more widely known and understood, as well as accepted and 'owned', by the broader Narungga and Point Pearce/Burgiyana communities (Roberts et al. 2014:27). Second, it speaks to the generally recent use of oral history in the archaeological discipline, certainly a method that has gained increasing acceptability over the past few decades (Bennett and Fowler 2016; Jones and Russell 2012:272–273; Nicholas and Watkins 2014:3782). Third, written text is a colonial practice, which has been used in the past to shape the colonial legacy and reinforce the assumptions, inequalities, and power relations of colonialism (Smith and Jackson 2006:313–314). While there is a historical paradox in

Figure 1. Graham recounting oral histories while at sea (J. Mushynsky, 26 November 2013).

situating Aboriginal oral history within a text produced in 'white' culture, oral history and written text need not be mutually exclusive (Dickinson 1994:320,326). As discussed below, Aboriginal peoples have been silenced in colonial archives and Western histories (Roberts et al. 2014:29). Maori academic Linda Tuhiwai Smith (Smith 2012:30–31), has also critiqued the role Western scholarly research played in the process of colonization of Indigenous cultures, and underlines the difficulties of discussing both 'research methodology' and 'Indigenous peoples' without acknowledging the entrenchment of colonial practices in the search for knowledge (Fox 2006:404).

This paper commences by deconstructing the title and introducing the research questions. An outline of the conclusions drawn from this study includes examples from the discussion of results collated through oral history, archaeological, and archival research.

Context

Maritime Cultural Landscapes

It must be recognized at the outset of course that maritime cultural landscapes are a Western construct—maritime culture as a concept is itself an archaeological construct, "rather than a means by which a society might define itself" (Charlton Christie 2013:155). H However, the framework is arguably one of the most popular in the maritime archaeology field, coming from a Nordic maritime archaeology tradition and first published in English in 1992 by Westerdahl (Meide 2013:12). A maritime cultural landscape comprises numerous elements, "material and immaterial remnants of maritime human life," which include shipwrecks, land remains, tradition of usage, natural topography, and place names (Westerdahl 1992:7–9). While the maritime cultural landscape concept draws on many ideas, the primary interpretive framework this study employs is that of 'facets.' The 11 facets of the maritime cultural landscape framework are: ritual/cultic, cognitive, topographic, outer resource, inner resource, transport, urban harbor, economic/subsistence/sustenance, social, territorial/power/resistance, and leisure maritime landscapes (Westerdahl 2008, 2011). Westerdahl (2006:8, 2008:215–216) devised these facets, intending to contrast, as well as combine, maritime and terrestrial components, and to allow for methodical cross-disciplinary analogies. Organizing the oral history, archaeological, and archival data collected within relevant facets provided a means of interpreting results thematically.

Neglected Narratives

'Neglected narratives' relate to the gap this research fills in the archaeological literature. Research in Australia has not previously employed the maritime cultural landscape framework, the conceptual approach used in this research, to explore maritime themes within Indigenous contexts. In Australia, maritime cultural landscape approaches have been confined to European heritage. Cross-cultural engagement themes within the maritime sphere, which have investigated Indigenous interaction with visiting mariners and shipwreck survivors (Mitchell 1996; Mulvaney and Kamminga 1999; Roberts 2004), Indigenous and shipwreck survivor interaction (Jeffery 2001; McCarthy 2008; Merry 2010; Morse 1988; Nash 2006), rock art representations of maritime contact (Bigourdan and McCarthy 2007; Burningham 1994; May et al. 2009; Taçon and May 2013; Wesley et al. 2012), impact of maritime contact on material culture and economy (Bowdler 1976; Gara 2013; MacKnight 1986; Mitchell 1996), and Indigenous labor forces in colonial maritime industries, such as whaling (Anderson in prep; Gibbs 2003; Staniforth et al. 2001), sealing (Clarke 1996; James 2002; Russell 2005; Taylor 2008), and pearling (McPhee 2001; Mullins 2012; O'Connor and Arrow 2008), have not adequately explored the context of missions. Mission studies, despite focusing on spatial arrangement, material culture, fringe camps, and built heritage, have largely ignored the maritime landscape (Ash et al. 2008; Birmingham 2000; Dalley and Memmott 2010; Griffin 2010; Jones 2009; Keating 2012; Smith and Beck 2003). This study aims to rectify

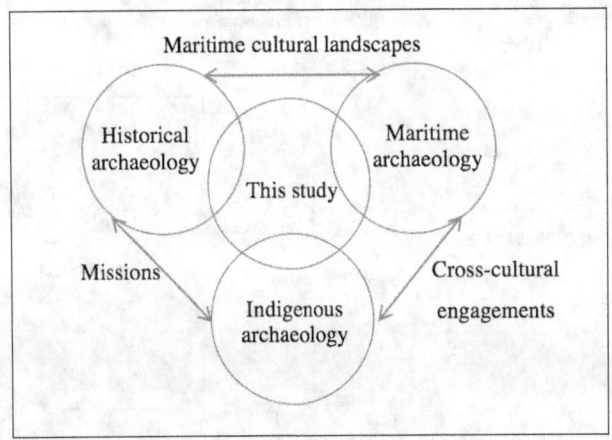

Figure 2. Illustration of the gap this research fills between three discrete subdisciplines (Author, 2015).

these gaps within the Australian archaeological literature (Figure 2).

Point Pearce Aboriginal Mission/Burgiyana

Point Pearce Mission/Burgiyana is located on Yorke Peninsula/Guuranda, South Australia—the traditional land of the Narungga people (Figure 3). The earliest interaction between Narungga and non-Indigenous peoples began with whalers and sealers in the 1830s, shortly followed by surveyors and pastoralists (Ball 1992:36; Krichauff 2008:51; Mattingley and Hampton 1992:195). Point Pearce Mission/Burgiyana was established in 1868, however during the late 1800s Narungga people were generally still mobile and were not restricted to the mission (Wanganeen 1987:25).

In 1915, following the 1913 Royal Commission into Aboriginal Affairs, Point Pearce/Burgiyana changed from operating as a mission by local trustees to being managed by the state government as a station. Aboriginal peoples' lives became increasingly regulated (Kartinyeri 2002:70; Krichauff 2013:59), although this is much more complicated and evidence of Aboriginal agency exists. Point Pearce/Burgiyana people were involved in all aspects of station life, including shearing, farming, and building (Mattingley and Hampton 1992:118; Wanganeen 1987:43,55). In 1966, the Point Pearce Aboriginal Reserve Land became vested in the Aboriginal Lands Trust—ending government control—and has since been self-managed (Kartinyeri 2002:70; Wanganeen 1987:75).

Methods

During prior research (Roberts et al. 2013), the inadequate documentation of aspects of Aboriginal peoples' involvement in maritime activities during the mission period became evident. As such, a collaborative project was developed to document past maritime activities at Point Pearce Mission/Burgiyana using a combination of oral history collection, archaeological surveys, and archival research methods.

Oral history collection included 13 interviews, both on 'Country'—including on boats—and off-site. Archaeology included non-disturbance surveys across terrestrial, coastal, and submerged environments at Point Pearce/Burgiyana. Finally, archival research featured a range of historical newspapers, photographs, children's crayon drawings, and other primary sources from the archives collected from the mission.

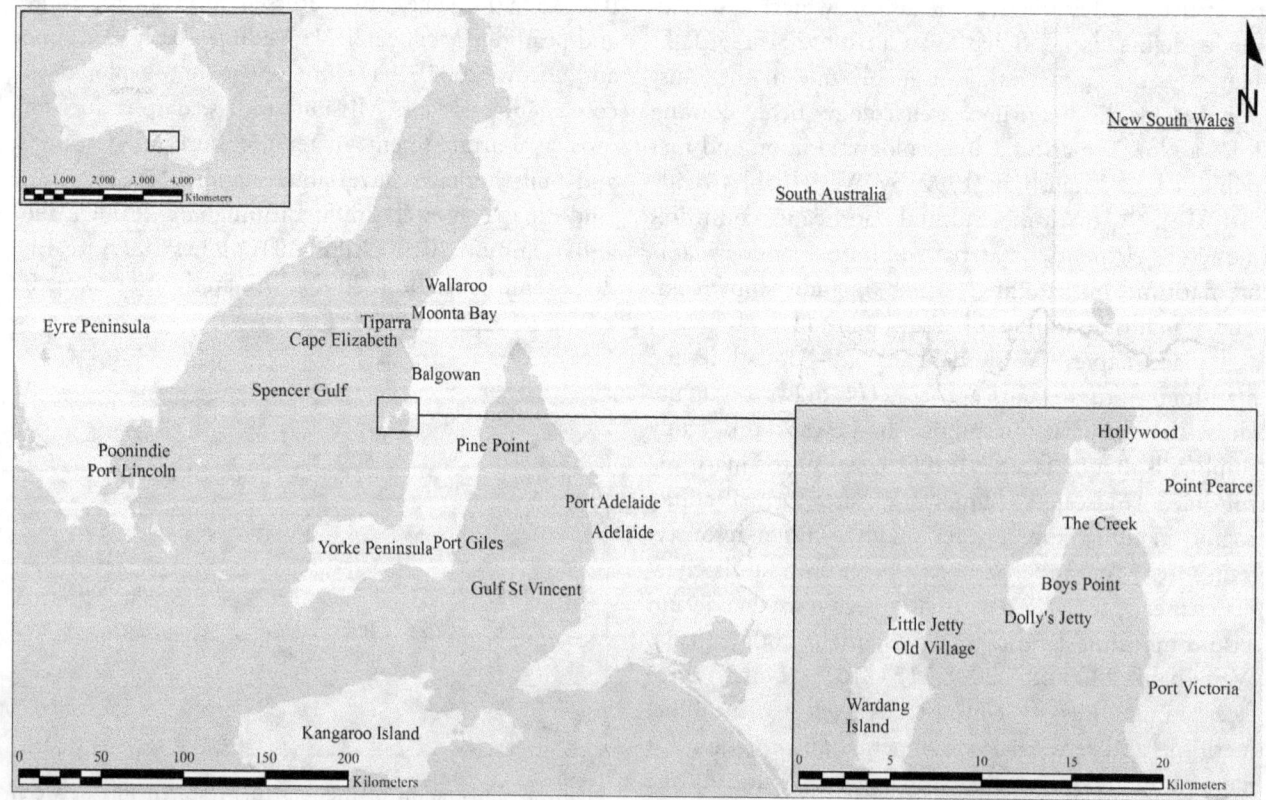

Figure 3. Map showing Point Pearce/Burgiyana in relation to South Australia and Australia (Author, 2015).

Research Questions

The research question is: Does a 'maritime cultural landscape' approach provide a useful or suitable framework for exploring and interpreting the cultural landscape of Point Pearce Mission/Burgiyana, South Australia? Further, what issues emerge (positive or negative) from the employment of a maritime cultural landscape framework in an Indigenous post-contact context?

In response to the first question, the maritime cultural landscape approach, with the following cautions and qualifications, may be useful for incorporating areas of importance to Indigenous Australian communities such as beliefs, knowledges, and lived experiences. Regarding the second question—and the cautions and qualifications—several issues emerge from this research. Of the five broad issues identified by the author (Fowler 2015:343–350), the following discussion of two of these issues includes some examples of oral history, archaeological, and archival research results. Fowler (2015) provides details of the other issues: Maritime archaeology discourse and underpinning attitudes need to be deconstructed; Maritime archaeology in Australia is generally Eurocentric; Oral histories are an integral source for exploring Indigenous maritime cultural landscapes.

Results and Discussion

Colonial Archives and Local Histories Often Silence Aboriginal Peoples

The first issue is that colonial archives and local histories often silence Aboriginal peoples (Fowler 2013). Lumping (the occupation of carrying heavy loads onto ships), an example from the urban harbor landscape facet, illustrates this. Lumping was just one part of the involvement of Aboriginal people in wider shipping activities (J. Newchurch 2013; Roberts et al. 2014:28–29). Many community members discussed people who lumped at a number of ports around South Australia. Graham (2013) described the transport of wheat and barley onto the sailing ships at Port Victoria/Dharldiwarldu:

> They used to bring wheat and barley, same as everyone else, on horse and buggy. Big thing on rails, put all the wheat on and pull it out to the end of the jetty with the horse, and put it in the boats and dinghies and that sort of thing, and take it out to the big ships.

When discussing stacking and lumping at Port Victoria/Dharldiwarldu, O'Loughlin stated, "Nhangga's [Aboriginal people] often had to do the low paid jobs anna [don't you think]?" (Roberts et al. 2014:28–29). In addition to oral histories, the missions' archives document Narungga people also working at ports at other places on Yorke Peninsula/Guuranda. In 1916 and 1919–1921, Point Pearce/Burgiyana men did most of the wheat lumping at Balgowan Jetty (Garnett 1920:10, 1921:10; South 1916:12, 1919:11).

Collaboration with Indigenous peoples can allow a glimpse of the invisible life of Aboriginal workers in the maritime industry which is largely undocumented in the colonial archive (Hemming 2002:55). The urban harbor facet highlights the importance to perceive wider landscapes when considering the maritime cultural landscape approach for Indigenous post-contact contexts. Aboriginal peoples have provided labor to Australia's maritime industry, lumping at a number of ports around Yorke Peninsula/Guuranda being a key area. Port Victoria/Dharldiwarldu may initially be considered a non-Indigenous maritime landscape, particularly given a lack of documentation of Aboriginal peoples' involvement in port work (such as lumping) in local non-Indigenous histories (Roberts et al. 2014:29). However, the results of this study indicate that it is equally important to the Aboriginal maritime landscape and reveals numerous insights into cross-cultural engagement. Indigenous employment is undocumented, for example published lists of lumpers (Moody 2012:66) do not contain any Aboriginal names (Roberts et al. 2014:29). The investigation of the urban harbor landscape has allowed for the reinsertion of "people and habitations made absent" and offers "a powerful antidote to colonising landscapes" (after Gill et al. 2005:3; Roberts et al. 2014:29).

Maritime Cultural Landscape Facets Need to Encompass Non-Western Systems of Knowledge

The second issue is that maritime cultural landscape facets need to encompass non-Western systems of knowledge. This will be illustrated using an example from the leisure landscape facet: tin canoes, which were recorded during this project through both oral histories and searching photographic collections. The construction of tin canoes by children at Point Pearce Mission/Burgiyana appears to have begun in the early 1950s. The canoes were carried by three kids on foot the 7 km to The Creek/Winggara, an open swampy area with a fairly big and deep creek (R. Newchurch 2013). R. Newchurch (2013) described their construction:

> *"We all made these tin canoes out of corrugated sheets of iron, we'd bend them over, at the end of it we'd put black tar, heat it up and seal the ends. We had great fun, made our own paddles."*

A piece of stick with a square of plywood at the ends, nailed on, formed paddles that were easily replaceable after breaking (R. Newchurch 2013).

The field walking survey that was conducted at Dead Man's Island/Mungari as part of the archaeological fieldwork for the project observed a paddle which was evidently home-made and could be similar to the type described by R. Newchurch (2013) (Figure 4). The canoes were only a one-person canoe but each child had one and sometimes up to 20 to 30 children would go and camp on the weekends, living off the land (R. Newchurch 2013). Mainly boys would go up and down The Creek/Winggara in the canoe, fishing line in the boat, catching fish (R. Newchurch 2013), although Weetra (2013) also remembered paddling in The Creek/Winggara in the tin canoes during an on 'Country' interview. In recent years, R. Newchurch (2013) has taught children at Point Pearce Aboriginal School what they used to do.

According to Westerdahl (2008:228), leisure is based around recent aspects of capitalism such as leisure sailing, seaside cottages, and marinas. The leisure landscape facet is conceptualized differently here, and this is attributed to the Aboriginal context of Point Pearce Mission/Burgiyana. The maritime cultural landscape framework does not acknowledge leisure practices that are part of long-term cultural structures. Leisure landscapes at Point Pearce Mission/Burgiyana include children making and playing in tin canoes, a practice which replicates the use of boats by the 'old people' and therefore transfers knowledge and skills from generation to generation. Cultural learning can take place through a variety of means—including 'fun', and it can also be seen in facets other than leisure, such as the economic/subsistence/sustenance and social facets. Therefore, it is difficult to separate leisure from culture in a Western sense and the distinct facets of the maritime cultural landscape may need to be blurred. There is a danger that the classification system of the maritime cultural landscape facets may confine Aboriginal worldviews, lived experiences, and cultural practices into rigid Western compartments (Fox 2006:405,407). Evidently, these frameworks within maritime cultural landscapes need to be broken down to some extent or a system needs to be devised to allow for complexity across facets.

Figure 4. Paddle or oar found at Dead Man's Island/Mungari (A. Berry, 25 January 2014).

Conclusions

In conclusion, this study evaluated the maritime cultural landscape framework and endeavoured to build upon this framework by applying it to an Indigenous Australian context. The interpretive framework of facets of a maritime cultural landscape was in most instances directly applicable and useful to the case study of Point Pearce Mission/Burgiyana. In other cases, subject to evaluation, the maritime cultural landscape approach needed to be adjusted and critiqued to enable it to become suitably applicable. For example, for the maritime cultural landscape framework to allow the incorporation of Indigenous worldviews and to blur the edges of the facets, such as leisure, specific deconstruction was required. Any attempt to fit Indigenous maritime cultural landscapes exclusively into the tradition of maritime archaeology ideas, which tend to value archaeological sites according to their connection to historical events, would be ineffective (after Richards 2013:13).

Thus, maritime archaeology needs to apply some of the 'with, for and by' attitudes that define Indigenous archaeology (as outlined by Nicholas and Andrews [1997]). Aboriginal achievements are being recognized on football fields and in art galleries, however—not at the playgrounds, workplaces, and dinner tables of the general public (Rigney 2015). The neglected narrative communicated here must become household history and reinsertion into local narratives is required to decolonize the past. "Now, are you going to believe this or not?"

Acknowledgments

The author is the grateful recipient of the Advisory Council on Underwater Archaeology 2016 George Fischer Student Travel Award. The author would like to thank the Narungga Aboriginal Corporation Regional Authority, Narungga Nation Aboriginal Corporation, Point Pearce Aboriginal Corporation, and Adjahdura Narungga Heritage Group for their involvement and support of this research. Also thanks to Point Pearce/Burgiyana Elders and community members who shared their knowledge during interviews recounted here. This research was approved by the Flinders University Social and Behavioural Research Ethics Committee (Project 5806).

References

Anderson, Ross
2016 Beneath the Colonial Gaze: Modelling Maritime Society and Cross Cultural Contact on Australia's Southern Ocean Frontier—the Archipelago of the Recherche, Western Australia. Doctor of Philosophy thesis draft, Department of Archaeology, University of Western Australia, Crawley, Western Australia.

Ash, Jeremy, Alasdair Brooks, Bruno David and Ian J. McNiven
2008 European Manufactured Objects from the 'Early Mission' Site at Totalai, Mua (Western Torres Strait). *Memoirs of the Queensland Museum Cultural Heritage Series* 4(2):473–492.

Anderson, Ross
2016 Beneath the Colonial Gaze: Modelling Maritime Society and Cross Cultural Contact on Australia's Southern Ocean Frontier—the Archipelago of the Recherche, Western Australia. Doctor of Philosophy thesis draft, Department of Archaeology, University of Western Australia, Crawley, Western Australia.

Ash, Jeremy, Alasdair Brooks, Bruno David and Ian J. McNiven
2008 European Manufactured Objects from the 'Early Mission' Site at Totalai, Mua (Western Torres Strait). *Memoirs of the Queensland Museum Cultural Heritage Series* 4(2):473–492.

Ball, Megan
1992 The Lesser of Two Evils: A Comparison of Government and Mission Policy at Raukkan and Point Pearce, 1890–1940. *Cabbages and Kings: Selected Essays in History and Australian Studies* 20:36–45.

Bennett, Kurt and Madeline Fowler
2016 'In my Memory, it says Rarawa': Abandoned Vessel Material Salvage and Reuse at Rangitoto Island, Aotearoa / New Zealand. *International Journal of Historical Archaeology* DOI 10.1007/s10761-016-0328-7.

Bigourdan, Nicolas and Michael McCarthy
2007 Aboriginal Watercraft Depictions in Western Australia: On Land, and Underwater? *Bulletin of the Australasian Institute for Maritime Archaeology* 31:1–10.

BIRMINGHAM, JUDY
2000 Resistance, Creolization or Optimal Foraging at Killalpaninna Mission, South Australia. In The Archaeology of Difference: Negotiating Cross-Cultural Engagements in *Oceania*, Robin Torrence and Anne Clarke, editors, pp. 361–405. Routledge, London, United Kingdom.

BOWDLER, SANDRA
1976 Hook, Line and Dilly Bag: An Interpretation of an Australian Coastal Shell Midden. *Mankind* 10(4):248–258.

BURNINGHAM, NICK
1994 Aboriginal Nautical Art: A Record of the Macassans and the Pearling Industry in Northern Australia. *The Great Circle* 16(2):139–151.

CHARLTON CHRISTIE, ANNALISA
2013 Were the Communities Living on the East African Coast also 'Maritime' Communities? An Archaeological Perspective. In *Perspectives from Historical Archaeology and ACUA Proceedings No. 7: Maritime Archaeology*, Ben Ford and Wendy van Duivenvoorde, editors, pp.162–172. Society for Historical Archaeology, Germantown, Maryland.

CLARKE, PHILIP A.
1996 Early European Interaction with Aboriginal Hunters and Gatherers on Kangaroo Island, South Australia. *Aboriginal History* 20:51–81.

DALLEY, CAMEO AND PAUL MEMMOTT
2010 Domains and the Intercultural: Understanding Aboriginal and Missionary Engagement at the Mornington Island Mission, Gulf of Carpentaria, Australia from 1914 to 1942. *International Journal of Historical Archaeology* 14:112–135.

DICKINSON, PETER
1994 "Orality in Literacy": Listening to Indigenous Writing. *The Canadian Journal of Native Studies* 14(2):319–340

FOWLER, MADELINE
2013 Aboriginal Missions and Post-Contact Maritime Archaeology: A South Australian Synthesis. *Journal of the Anthropological Society of South Australia* 37:73–89.

2015 "Now, are you going to believe this or not?" Addressing Neglected Narratives through the Maritime Cultural Landscape of Point Pearce Aboriginal Mission/Burgiyana, South Australia. Doctor of Philosophy thesis, Department of Archaeology, Flinders University, Adelaide, South Australia.

FOWLER, MADELINE, AMY ROBERTS, JENNIFER MCKINNON, CLEM O'LOUGHLIN AND FRED GRAHAM
2014 'They Camped Here Always': Archaeologies of Attachment to Seascapes Via a Case Study at Wardang Island (Waraldi/Wara-dharldhi), South Australia. *Australasian Historical Archaeology* 32:14–22.

FOWLER, MADELINE, AMY ROBERTS, FRED GRAHAM, LINDSAY SANSBURY AND CARLO SANSBURY
2015 Seeing Narungga (Aboriginal) Land from the Sea: A Case Study from Point Pearce/Burgiyana, South Australia. *Bulletin of the Australasian Institute for Maritime Archaeology* 39:60–70.

FOX, KAREN
2006 Leisure and Indigenous Peoples. *Leisure Studies* 25(4):403–409.

GARA, TOM
2013 Indigenous Bark Canoes in South Australia. Paper presented at the Flinders University Department of Archaeology Public Seminar, Adelaide, South Australia.

GARNETT, FRANCIS
1920 Report of the Chief Protector of Aboriginals for the Year Ended June 30, 1920. R.E.E. Rogers, Adelaide, South Australia.

1921 Report of the Protector of Aboriginals for the Year Ended June 30, 1921. R.E.E. Rogers, Adelaide, South Australia.

GIBBS, MARTIN
2003 Nebinyan's Songs: An Aboriginal Whaler of South-West Western Australia. *Aboriginal History* 27:1–15.

GRAHAM, FRED
2013 Interview by Madeline Fowler. Digital recording. 28 January. Port Victoria, South Australia.

2014 Interview by Madeline Fowler. Digital recording. 26 November. Spencer Gulf, South Australia.

GILL, NICHOLAS, ALISTAIR PATERSON AND M.J. KENNEDY
2005 'Do You Want to Delete This?' Hidden Histories and Hidden Landscapes in the Murchison and Davenport Ranges, Northern Territory, Australia. In 'The Power of Knowledge, the Resonance of Tradition'. Electronic publication of papers from the AIATSIS Indigenous Studies conference, September 2001, Graeme K. Ward and Adrian Muckle, editors, pp. 125–137. Research Program, Australian Institute of Aboriginal and Torres Strait Islander Studies, Canberra, Australian Capital Territory.

GRIFFIN, DARREN
2010 Identifying Domination and Resistance through the Spatial Organization of Poonindie Mission, South Australia. *International Journal of Historical Archaeology* 14:156–169.

HEMMING, STEVE
2002 Taming the Colonial Archive: History, Native Title and Colonialism. In *Through a Smoky Mirror:*

History and Native Title, Mandy Paul and Geoffrey Gray, editors, pp. 49–64. Aboriginal Studies Press, Canberra, Australian Capital Territory.

JAMES, KERYN
2002 Wife or Slave? The Kidnapped Aboriginal Women Workers and Australian Sealing Slavery on Kangaroo Island and Bass Strait Islands. Honour's thesis, Department of Archaeology, Flinders University, Adelaide, South Australia.

JEFFERY, BILL
2001 Cultural Contact along the Coorong in South Australia. *Bulletin of the Australian Institute for Maritime Archaeology* 25:29–38.

JONES, SUSANNE MONTANA
2009 The Anatomy of a Relationship: Doing Archaeology with an Indigenous Community on a Former Mission—A Case Study at Point Pearce, South Australia. Honour's thesis, Department of Archaeology. Flinders University, Adelaide, South Australia.

JONES, SIÂN AND LYNETTE RUSSELL
2012 Archaeology, Memory and Oral Tradition: An Introduction. *International Journal of Historical Archaeology* 16:267–283.

KARTINYERI, DOREEN
2002 Narungga Nation. Doreen Kartinyeri, Adelaide, South Australia.

KEATING, CLAIRE
2012 "We Want Men Whose Hearts are … Full of Zeal": An Investigation of Cross-Cultural Engagement within the Weipa Mission Station (1898–1932). Master's thesis, Department of Archaeology, Flinders University, Adelaide, South Australia.

KRICHAUFF, SKYE
2008 The Narungga and Europeans: Cross-Cultural Relations on Yorke Peninsula in the Nineteenth Century. Master's thesis, School of History and Politics, University of Adelaide, Adelaide, South Australia.

2013 Narungga, the Townspeople and Julius Kuhn: The Establishment and Origins of the Point Pearce Mission, South Australia. *Journal of the Anthropological Society of South Australia* 37:57–72.

MACKNIGHT, C.C.
1986 Macassans and the Aboriginal Past. *Archaeology in Oceania* 21:69–75.

MATTINGLEY, CHRISTOBEL AND KEN HAMPTON (EDITORS)
1992 Survival in Our Own Land: 'Aboriginal' Experiences in 'South Australia' since 1936: Told by Nungas and Others. Hodder & Stoughton, Rydalmere, New South Wales.

MAY, SALLY K., JENNIFER MCKINNON AND JASON RAUPP
2009 Boats on Bark: An Analysis of Groote Eylandt Aboriginal Bark-Paintings Featuring Macassan Praus from the 1948 Arnhem Land Expedition, Northern Territory, Australia. *The International Journal of Nautical Archaeology* 38(2):369–385.

MCCARTHY, MICHAEL
2008 The Australian Contact Shipwrecks Program. In *Strangers on the Shore: Early Coastal Contacts in Australia*, Peter Veth, Peter Sutton and Margo Neale, editors, pp. 227–236. National Museum of Australia Press, Canberra, Australian Capital Territory.

MCPHEE, EWEN
2001 A Preliminary Examination of the History and Archaeology of the Pearl Shelling Industry in Torres Strait. *Bulletin of the Australasian Institute for Maritime Archaeology* 25:1–4.

MEIDE, CHUCK
2013 The Development of Maritime Archaeology as a Discipline and the Evolving Use of Theory by Maritime Archaeologists. Dissertation position paper no. 2. College of William & Mary, Williamsburg, Virginia.

MERRY, KAY
2010 Shipwrecks, Castaways and the Coorong Aborigines. In *Something Rich and Strange: Sea Changes, Beaches and the Littoral in the Antipodes*, Susan Hosking, Rick Hosking, Rebecca Pannell and Nena Bierbaum, editors, pp. 179–194. Wakefield Press, Kent Town, South Australia.

MITCHELL, SCOTT
1996 Dugongs and Dugouts, Sharptacks and Shellbacks: Macassan Contact and Aboriginal Marine Hunting on the Cobourg Peninsula, North Western Arnhem Land. *Indo-Pacific Prehistory Association Bulletin* 15:181–191.

MOODY, STUART M.
2012 *Port Victoria's Ships and Shipwrecks*. Stuart M. Moody, Maitland, South Australia.

MORSE, KATE
1988 An Archaeological Survey of Midden Sites near the Zuytdorp Wreck, Western Australia. *Bulletin of the Australian Institute for Maritime Archaeology* 12(1):37–40.

MULLINS, STEVE
2012 Company Boats, Sailing Dinghies and Passenger Fish: Fathoming Torres Strait Islander Participation in the Maritime Economy. *Labour History* (103):39–58.

MULVANEY, JOHN AND JOHAN KAMMINGA
1999 *Prehistory of Australia*. Allen & Unwin, St Leonards, New South Wales.

NASH, MICHAEL
2006   *The Sydney Cove Shipwreck Survivors Camp*. Maritime Archaeology Monograph Series 2, Department of Archaeology, Flinders University, Adelaide, South Australia.

NEWCHURCH, JEFFREY
2013   Interview by Madeline Fowler. Digital recording. 25 September. Adelaide, South Australia.

NEWCHURCH, RONALD, JR.
2013   Interview by Madeline Fowler. Digital recording. 29 November. Port Victoria, South Australia.

NICHOLAS, GEORGE P. AND THOMAS D. ANDREWS (EDITORS)
1997   *At a Crossroads: Archaeologists and First Peoples in Canada*. Archaeology Press, Simon Fraser University, Burnaby, British Columbia.

NICHOLAS, GEORGE P. AND JOE E. WATKINS
2014   Indigenous Archaeologies in Archaeological Theory. In *Encyclopedia of Global Archaeology*, Claire Smith, editor, pp. 3777–3786. Springer, New York.

O'CONNOR, SUE AND STEVE ARROW
2008   Boat Images in the Rock Art of Northern Australia with Particular Reference to the Kimberley, Western Australia. In *Islands of Inquiry: Colonisation, Seafaring and the Archaeology of Maritime Landscapes*, Geoffrey Clark, Foss Leach and Sue O'Connor, editors, pp. 397–409. Australian National University E Press, Canberra, Australian Capital Territory.

RICHARDS, NATHAN
2013   Abandoned Ships and Ship Graveyards: Exploring Site Significance and Research Potential. In *The Archaeology of Watercraft Abandonment*, Nathan Richards and Sami K. Seeb, editors, pp. 1–16. Springer, New York.

RIGNEY, LESTER-IRABINNA
2015   View from the Shore Must Be Part of the Constitution. *Herald Sun*. 3 March.

ROBERTS, AMY, JENNIFER MCKINNON, CLEM O'LOUGHLIN, KLYNTON WANGANEEN, LESTER-IRABINNA RIGNEY AND MADELINE FOWLER
2013   Combining Indigenous and Maritime Archaeological Approaches: Experiences and Insights from the '(Re)locating Narrunga Project', Yorke Peninsula, South Australia. *Journal of Maritime Archaeology* 8(1):77–99.

ROBERTS, AMY, MADELINE FOWLER AND TAUTO SANSBURY
2014   A Report on the Exhibition Entitled 'Children, Boats and 'Hidden Histories': Crayon Drawings by Aboriginal Children at Point Pearce Mission (SA), 1939'. *Bulletin of the Australasian Institute for Maritime Archaeology* 38:24–30.

ROBERTS, DAVID A.
2004   Nautical Themes in the Aboriginal Rock Paintings of Mount Borradaile, Western Arnhem Land. *The Great Circle* 26(1):19–50.

RUSSELL, LYNETTE
2005   Kangaroo Island Sealers and Their Descendants: Ethnic and Gender Ambiguities in the Archaeology of a Creolised Community. *Australian Archaeology* 60:1–5.

SMITH, ANITA AND WENDY BECK
2003   The Archaeology of No Man's Land: Indigenous Camps at Corindi Beach, Mid-North Coast New South Wales. *Archaeology of Oceania* 38(1):66–77.

SMITH, CLAIRE AND GARY JACKSON
2006   Decolonizing Indigenous Archaeology: Developments from Down Under. *American Indian Quarterly* 30(3&4):311–349.

SMITH, LINDA TUHIWAI
2012   *Decolonizing Methodologies: Research and Indigenous Peoples*, Second Edition. Zed Books, London, United Kingdom.

SOUTH, WILLIAM GARNET
1916   Report of the Protector of Aborigines for the Year Ended June 30, 1916. R.E.E. Rogers, Adelaide, South Australia.

1919   Report of the Chief Protector of Aboriginals for the Year Ended June 30, 1919. R.E.E. Rogers, Adelaide, South Australia.

STANIFORTH, MARK, SUSAN BRIGGS AND CHRIS LEWCZAK
2001   Archaeology Unearthing the Invisible People: European Women and Children and Aboriginal People at South Australian Shore-Based Whaling Stations. *Mains'l Haul: A Journal of Pacific Maritime History* 36(3):12–19.

TAÇON, PAUL S.C. AND SALLY K. MAY
2013   Special Issue: Maritime Rock Art. *The Great Circle* 35(2).

TAYLOR, REBE
2008   *Unearthed: The Aboriginal Tasmanians of Kangaroo Island*. Second Edition. Wakefield Press, Kent Town, South Australia.

WANGANEEN, EILEEN (EDITOR)
1987   *Point Pearce: Past and Present*. Aboriginal Studies and Teacher Education Centre, Underdale, South Australia.

WEETRA, PEGGY
2013 Interview by Madeline Fowler. Digital recording. 28 November. Point Pearce, South Australia.

WESLEY, DARYL, JENNIFER MCKINNON AND JASON RAUPP
2012 Sails Set in Stone: A Technological Analysis of Non-Indigenous Watercraft Rock Art Paintings in North Western Arnhem Land. *Journal of Maritime Archaeology* 7:245–269.

WESTERDAHL, CHRISTER
1992 The Maritime Cultural Landscape. *The International Journal of Nautical Archaeology* 21(1):5–14.

2006 Maritime Cosmology and Archaeology. *Deutsches Schiffahrtsarchiv* 28:7–54.

2008 Fish and Ships: Towards a Theory of Maritime Culture. *Deutsches Schiffahrtsarchiv* 30:191–236.

2011 Conclusion: The Maritime Cultural Landscape Revisited. In *The Archaeology of Maritime Landscapes*, Ben Ford, editor, pp. 331–344. Springer, New York, New York.

Madeline Fowler
Flinders University
12/28 Murphy Street
Scarborough, Queensland 4020
Australia
maddy.fowler@flinders.edu.au

A Model for Analyzing Wreck and Cargo Selective Salvage Using Economic and Utilitarian Values

Chelsea R. Freeland

The Civil War shipwreck Modern Greece *serves as an example in the development of a theoretical model to analyze value as a means of interpreting time-dependent selective salvage for shipwrecks and cargo abandonment. This model outlines a set of multiple hypotheses to test the economic and utilitarian values associated with the abandonment of a large volume of blockade-runner cargo from this vessel. This project identifies the possibilities for expanding this theoretical framework to address the abandonment of other shipwrecks, cargos, and maritime sites.*

Introduction

This study presents a theoretical model for evaluating maritime selective salvage and cargo abandonment under a time duress to determine why some materials are saved over others. The primary example for this is the Civil War shipwreck *Modern Greece*, but this study also addresses the use of this model on other types of shipwrecks and on additional maritime sites. By using a multiple-hypothesis model, it is possible to identify various dichotomies of value that can then be analyzed for their roles in the selective salvage process.

The example of *Modern Greece*

Modern Greece was an English-operated blockade runner that ran aground at the mouth of the Cape Fear River near Wilmington, North Carolina, during the American Civil War (Bright 1977:3–19). Wilmington's eventual prowess as a blockade-running hub had yet to be recognized when the ship attempted the run into port in the summer of 1862, but the merchant vessel was eventually salvaged to take advantage of the materials it brought to the struggling war effort in the Confederacy (Barrett 1963:244–246; Wise 1988:124; Bright 1977:12–19). A full salvage of the ship's cargo was attempted, but was unsuccessful as is apparent from the re-excavation of several tons of artifacts from the ship in the mid-1960s by the North Carolina Underwater Archaeology Branch. The material culture recovered from this series of excavations is still undergoing conservation treatment (Henry 2014). The ship's location, close to the workforce of Fort Fisher, and the wartime economic hub of Wilmington, North Carolina, makes it an ideal candidate for this analysis. Salvage on the shipwreck was completed in a distinctly time-dependent manner, given the circumstances of the need for cargo and the ship's continual submergence into the water.

A research project completed in 2014 (Freeland 2014) aimed to determine why Confederate leaders at Fort Fisher and Wilmington decided to only salvage part of the cargo, rather than its entirety, abandoning the rest of the material. This study addressed this question within the framework of value analysis, looking at both the exchange value (monetary value in 1862) and the utilitarian value (non-monetary value) of the cargo and individual artifacts to determine if either was the primary factor in the selective salvage.

Theoretical Framework

The main theoretical construct for this project came not from archaeology, but from economics. This study centered on the idea of "value" in a contemporary historical sense, that is, what value certain objects had at the time of their salvage from *Modern Greece* in 1862. In order to address this, it is important to define the terms used to differentiate the types of value associated with these objects.

In traditional Marxist economics, commodities (in this case, the pieces of cargo from *Modern Greece*) have an inherent value, an exchange value, and a use-value (Marx 1887). The inherent value refers to the raw materials and labor that went into producing that commodity. The exchange value refers to the amount of other goods, services, or money for which you could exchange that commodity. In this study, the exchange value refers to the price of these objects at auction or on an open market: their "dollar worth." The exchange value is not the same as the inherent value because transportation of the goods, advertising, profit margins, and inflated demand during wartime, are not calculated into the inherent value. They are all part of the exchange value—they drive up the price.

The use-value is the value that a consumer will get from using the product. This is not a calculated value, but is relative to the needs and services of the individual consumer. This is also referred to as a utilitarian value, or the idea that an object is valuable because of its practical use instead of its inherent or exchange value (Moholy-Nagy 2002:1–3). For example, a bottle of champagne had a very high exchange value during the Civil War. Its use-value, however, was very low for the Confederate government. A bottle of champagne had a lower utilitarian value than a rifle, though a rifle had a lower exchange value. For this project, the utilitarian value means the perceived value of *Modern Greece's* cargo by troops at Fort Fisher or civilian residents of Wilmington in 1862, and presumably the cost-benefit analysis associated with salvage. This is different from the exchange value because even items that could have been sold at a high price in Wilmington may have been too dangerous to retrieve from the wrecked ship, lowering their utilitarian values because of environment or human agency. This study will use the term "utilitarian value," rather than use-value in an effort to differentiate from the idea of use value in modern theoretical models for assessing archaeological site value and significance.

In the case of *Modern Greece's* cargo, the utilitarian was much higher than the original exchange value, due to shortages of war as well as the imposition of the blockade along the Atlantic. This provides a strong distinction between the exchange value and utilitarian value of the cargo. This distinction can be studied using historical and archaeological source material. The main question is: why did the soldiers at Fort Fisher fail to retrieve supplies with a supposedly high value, instead choosing only to salvage part of the cargo?

This question was answered with the development of a multiple hypothesis model. This model sought to present a variety of dichotomies of value that could then be analyzed for their role in the selective salvage. These are all presented as answers to the above question.

Hypothesis 1: Environmental concerns prevented this cargo from being salvaged.

-The function of this hypothesis is to determine whether salvage was necessary (worth the effort) given the environment in which the abandonment occurred.

Hypothesis 2: The cargo and/or material to be salvaged had a low exchange value as a whole.

Hypothesis 3: The cargo and/or material to be salvaged had a low utilitarian value as a whole.

Hypothesis 4: The cargo and/or material salvaged had a high exchange value, while the cargo and/or material abandoned had a low exchange value.

Hypothesis 5: The cargo and/or material salvaged had a high utilitarian value, while the cargo and/or material abandoned had a low utilitarian value.

-The function of this hypothesis is to address a variety of dichotomies of worth that are not related to the exchange value of the cargo and/or material.

To illustrate this model in a more concrete example, these hypotheses are presented for the case of *Modern Greece*:

Hypothesis 1: Wilmington was a boomtown in June 1862 due to high blockade-runner traffic. The goods were not salvaged because they were not needed in this thriving city.

Hypothesis 2: Blockade-runner cargo had a low exchange value. The goods were not salvaged because they would not have sold for high prices in Wilmington.

Hypothesis 3: Blockade-runner cargo had a low utilitarian value. The goods were not salvaged because a decision was made that did not directly relate to the exchange value of the goods.

Hypothesis 4: The objects salvaged were those with the highest exchange value.

Hypothesis 5: The objects salvaged were those with the highest utilitarian value, given a variety of possible concerns of worth.

A. Issues of Time

1. Inclement weather prevented a full salvage.

2. Approaching armies prevented a full salvage, due to redirection of time/energy/resources/decision-making personnel.

3. The continual submergence of the ship prevented a full salvage, due to inaccessibility as the goods sunk below the waterline.

B. Issues of Labor

1. Troop shortages prevented a full salvage, due to redirection of troops to other projects.

2. Safety concerns prevented a full salvage, due to the continual submergence of the ship/dangerous circumstances causing potential harm to human capital.

C. Issues of Resources

1. Undamaged goods were preferentially saved over damaged goods.

2. Light or easier to transport goods were saved preferentially over heavy or harder to transport goods.

3. Goods in short supply in Wilmington, due to pressing warfare concerns, were saved preferentially over goods in excess.

4. Only as many goods were saved as there was available warehouse space to house/dry them.

5. The lack of a cargo manifest led to a lack of information about the total number and type of

materials on the ship, leading to an incomplete salvage based on unclear selection criteria.

Hypothesis 5 served as a "catch-all" category for issues that were not directly related to the exchange value of the cargo. This was appropriate due to the nature of this specific research topic, which was concerned with the dichotomy of exchange value vs. utilitarian value. This hypothesis could be divided and treated as whole individual hypotheses if the project suggested it. Additionally, there are issues addressed in Hypothesis 5 that could easily transfer to Hypothesis 1, dealing with environment, in a topic that was not focused on the wartime economic landscape, but rather the physical one.

Hypothesis 1

As a port city with first access to many goods coming from blockade-runners, it has been suggested that Wilmington experienced a small boom during the Civil War due to its trade (McKean 2011:895). If this was the case, it could explain why some of the goods carried across the Atlantic on *Modern Greece* were not salvaged. The evidence, however, suggests that Wilmington was not wealthy enough in the summer of 1862 to abandon the amount and variety of goods on-board *Modern Greece* without cause. Wilmington had the potential for economic success even during wartime, with business interest, infrastructure, and a high civilian population (Wise 1988:233–234; Lebergott 1981:867; Fonvielle 1994:15–16). These factors contributed to its growth and success during the rise in 1863. In 1862, however, shortages in all major areas of wartime and civilian materials were felt heavily, even in the port (Boaz 1996:9; McKean 2011:301–302). Wilmington did not have enough business interest or ships entering the blockade during that year to relieve the pressures of war on its citizens. This contradicts the idea that Wilmington's status as a boomtown during the Civil War would have contributed to the decision to abandon goods on *Modern Greece*, as this was not the case in 1862. The primary reasons for this include: the Federal spring Outer Banks campaign of 1862 which saw Confederate loss of a significant amount of heavy artillery and other supplies (Goff 1969:54); Wilmington's lack of blockade-runner traffic that year from the continual operation of Charleston harbor and an outbreak of yellow fever in fall 1862 (Wise 1988:233, 242; Webster 2010:77); and North Carolina's late entry to the war effort, one of the last states to join, which prevented the state from having a surplus of arms, artillery, and civilian goods (Barrett 1963:3, 28–29).

Hypothesis 2

This hypothesis required examining *Modern Greece*'s cargo to determine the exchange value of the cargo had the ship made it safely into port. By examining documents from the owner, the insurance company responsible for the ship, the auction records for the cargo sale in Wilmington, and prize court records for other blockade-runners of similar size, it was possible to piece together a picture of the exchange value of the cargo. Without a full cargo manifest, Bill of Entry, sales receipts from England, or auction results from Wilmington, however, the value of *Modern Greece*'s cargo is lacking complete representation within the historical record. From information gathered about the value of the cargo, and by comparing the circumstances of its loss to similar blockade-runners, an estimate of about £30,000 ($167,000) seemed to be the most logical value (Daily News 1864; Officer and Williamson 2013). It is safe to say that *Modern Greece*'s cargo had a significant exchange value, enough to expect a full salvage of the materials on-board, if possible (Wilmington Daily Journal 1862).

Hypothesis 3

This hypothesis required attempts to piece together a more complete story from the blockaders' reports, as well as information from the crew of *Modern Greece* and the soldiers stationed at Fort Fisher involved in the defense and salvage of the ship to discover the nature and reasoning behind the salvage. There were found to be no primary indicators for the reasoning behind stopping the salvage, particularly any based on the utilitarian value of the cargo as a whole. Presumably the reason for the salvage effort was a combination of the cargo's high exchange value and the fact that the Confederacy needed supplies that it was not getting on a regular basis due to the blockade (Surdam 2001:85, Trotter 1989:274–275, Wise 1988:27). This difference between exchange value and utilitarian value may have determined the effort put forth to save some of the cargo, while the rest remained on the ship. The historical analysis of this salvage is incomplete, a product of lack of Confederate records from this area in 1862.

Hypothesis 4

This hypothesis states that the soldiers at Fort Fisher, and others involved in the salvage, saved the pieces of cargo with the highest exchange values from *Modern Greece*, abandoning the less valuable cargo. This includes both civilian goods and government/wartime supplies removed from the ship and distributed throughout the Wilmington/Cape Fear district and the Confederacy. These were compared to the goods found underwater during the excavations in 1962-1963, as those goods are definitively "non-retrieved cargo" (Henry 2014). The evidence compiled supports the hypothesis that the items removed had, on average, higher exchange values than those abandoned (Freeland 2014).

Comparing the two categories, it is clear from the historical record that luxury items and guns were the two important groups of goods that were removed from the ship. Alcohol, medicine, and clothing were among the most expensive single-item products imported through the blockade. Of the goods from the first group, spices and small clothing accessories are the cheapest commodities, but their prices hardly compare to thousands of nails measured in price by their weight, rather than number. Without statistically accurate sampling and analysis, this qualitative assessment stands on the relationships between these particular types of goods. This comparison exemplifies the stark contrast in blockade-runner imports: war materials and luxury items. The information gathered suggests that the majority of items recovered immediately after wrecking had higher individual exchange values than the goods recovered in 1962, supporting the hypothesis that these goods were retrieved because of their high exchange values, though this information is necessarily correlative rather than definitively causative.

Hypothesis 5

After looking at other individual hypotheses, this section served as a "catch-all" to examine a variety of other possibilities. These alternate possibilities are not directly related to the exchange value of the goods. Instead, they are based on other types of value in decision-making. They can be broken into three groups: issues of time, issues of labor, and issues of resources. Each of these suggests that time, labor, or resources, were more valuable than the goods abandoned during salvage. Issues of time include inclement weather, approaching armies, or the ship submerging. Each could have sped up the process of salvage, where time was more valuable than some of the goods. Issues of labor include too few troops available for the task or that some objects were too far down in the ship causing safety concerns. In these cases, the value of the labor force expended on *Modern Greece* is in question: either the importance of preserving it (safety), or using it for salvage rather than other tasks in the Wilmington area. Issues of resources include damage to the goods, weight and transportation concerns, shortages of war, lack of warehouse space to dry and store goods, and lack of a cargo manifest, which may have influenced the decision-making process. These issues present five different dichotomies for saving goods over abandoning goods: working over damaged, in need over surplus, light over heavy, dry over wet, known over unknown.

In issues related to time, neither the weather nor an approaching army was cause to stop the salvage early. The submergence of the ship was probably not a primary factor indicated by the fact that it stayed above water for approximately three weeks. It is extremely likely that the wrecking and submergence had an eventual impact outside of the first week of salvage, but without more documentation, the overall impact is unknown. In issues related to labor, there were low numbers of troops in Wilmington during the summer of 1862 (Keith 2011:133). Past that, decisions made based on labor availability or safety of the troops are unclear. Issues related to resources provide an interesting array of possibilities. Damage to goods was not a main deciding factor on which objects were salvaged, as evidenced by the transfer of damaged guns for restoration to the Confederate Arsenal and Armory at Fayetteville, North Carolina (The Chattanooga Daily Rebel 1862). Lack of a manifest or available storage space were probably not main factors in deciding to stop the salvage early, though little information is available on these hypotheses. Weight, while certainly not a primary factor, may have become more important as the salvage progressed, and when combined with access to lower parts of the ship, may have been a determining factor for what cargo was saved later in the salvage process. Shortages are tied so closely to economic value that it is hard to distinguish clearly between these two during the Civil War. It is obvious that military and government shortages played a large part in the salvage of *Modern Greece*. The removal of four Whitworth cannons, despite their weight and the logistics of removing them from the ship, proves this point (Keith 2011:137; Trotter 1989:279–280). The removal of luxury goods, however, indicates that government shortage and surplus was not the only factor in the decision-making process (Wilmington Daily Journal 1862).

Methodology

Primary historical documents were the main resource for filling in information in each part of the model. These included local and foreign newspapers, auction records, insurance claims, prize court documents, journals, memoirs, letters, and military reports. For the *Modern Greece* project, these were accessed via both online and print collections. Given the extensive range of primary source documents, including federal, state, local, and private records, this shipwreck proved to be extremely well documented with a few notable exceptions. Records were either not available or did not exist for the loading of cargo in England or its salvage in Wilmington by the soldiers at the fort. This included a missing cargo manifest. The salvage process was interpreted using newspaper accounts, sometimes sensationalized, and letters and memoirs from soldiers at the fort recounting their own actions in the process. There is no formal account from the Confederate side, though the reports from the Federal blockaders USS *Cambridge* and USS *Stars and Stripes* were used in creating a timeline for salvage (Official Records of the Navy 1[7]:514–518).

The main data sets necessary for a functional model, using this methodology, are as follows:
- Environment [Landscape/seascape]
- Exchange values:
    - Cargo and/or material overall
    - Individual pieces of cargo and/or material (for comparative analysis)
- Utilitarian values:
    - Cargo and/or material overall
    - Individual pieces of cargo and/or material (for comparative analysis)

In order to effectively determine which of the main five hypotheses in this model has more support, and thus make recommendations about the decision-making process of selective salvage, there needs to be enough available information in each of these categories to sustain clear and reasonable analysis. Using this information as a baseline, it is then plausible to start evaluating other sites for possible application of this model. The following section presents a brief outline of this process for other maritime wrecking events and sites.

Applications

One of the most functional applications of this model would be its application for use with ships that are older and/or less well documented–older and/or non-wartime. One of the advantages of building models based on well-documented ships, like *Modern Greece*, is that they can then be used to help complete lesser-documented sites. The main methodological problem with this application, however, is trying to assess different types of value without historical documentation related to the site or wrecking incident. Following the methodology data sets listed above, it is possible to determine which data sets might be available even with lesser-documented wrecks.

The environmental data, to whatever degree necessary for evaluation, is something that can be addressed without substantial historical documentation. Condition-reporting based on archaeological methods or physical science protocols could add a wealth of information to the theoretical model. While the exact nature of Hypothesis 1 will change from project to project (e.g., in the case of *Modern Greece*, environment actually referred to the economic landscape of Wilmington, rather than the physical one), this hypothesis is probably one of the easiest to support using data other than historical source material. Another possibility is that even without records devoted to the site and/or wreck in particular, historical resources may be available for the environment or landscape itself that could help explain conditions for a selective salvage at a given time.

Finding exchange values of either the entire cargo and/or set of material or individual pieces from an assemblage might prove to be more difficult. The entire cargo value would be almost impossible without some type of historical record unless a full excavation was completed and the vessel was extremely well preserved. Even the total cargo value for *Modern Greece* is an estimate calculated from similar vessels under the same owner. With a lack of manifest and purchasing documents, there is no way to absolutely define a total value. It may be possible, however, to find information about the exchange value of individual pieces of the material set. This can be done with records detailing the same types of materials in the same time period, though not necessarily from the particular site in question. This comparative analysis was also used during the *Modern Greece* project where records were not available from Wilmington, and instead the project compared items from similar blockade-running ports.

Determining utilitarian values of the material

set, as a whole and as individual pieces, is a larger anthropological question. In this case, gaining information is more a product of analyzing the culture of reception, while exchange value comes from the culture of production. This can also be viewed from an archaeological perspective, examining other salvage in the area if possible to see material shortages. Again, historical documents from the culture itself, rather than just from the site, would prove even more helpful for collecting these data sets. In the *Modern Greece* example, this was determined by looking at Confederate Civil War shortages as well as examples of salvage of other blockade-runners.

Given the hypothesized availability of data in a scenario where a shipwreck or site itself is not very well documented, including information about the salvage procedure, there are two conclusions that can be reached. The first is that a comparison of total exchange value v. total utilitarian value will probably prove fruitless from a lack of available data. The second is that it is possible to execute a more systematic comparison of selective salvage of individual pieces of the material set, based on relevant related historical documents and/or archaeological data that may not deal directly with the site itself. In this case, the relevant information may still be able to help explain conditions for a selective, rather than complete, salvage.

Another possibility is that this model could be used on newer ships with more representation in the historical record. A common argument against this is that it would be a waste of resources to examine sites where the historical record provides a significant amount of information to address why the salvage occurred. It is important to note, however, that especially during wartime these records can be influenced by political motivation or lack of proper documentation and as such, may not be completely accurate. In cases such as these, archaeological methodology can provide a good check to determine the accuracy of the historical record.

All of these conclusions may be adapted for use on other types of maritime sites. The main concern is that this model is specifically designed for time-dependent selective salvage, such as in the face of an impending natural disaster. For this reason, it may be necessary to significantly adapt the model for use in a situation where long-term selective salvage occurred, but the same principles could be used and modified for the change in cost-benefit analyses.

References

BARRETT, JOHN G.
1963 *The Civil War in North Carolina*. The University of North Carolina Press, Chapel Hill.

BLACKBURN, MARION
2012 A Cargo Twice Dug: Fifty Years after they were Salvaged and Placed in Wet Storage, the Contents of a Confederate Blockade Runner have Reemerged. *Archaeology* (Sept/Oct):42–43.

BOAZ, THOMAS
1996 *Guns for Cotton: England Arms the Confederacy*. Burd Street Press, Shippensburg, Pennsylvania.

BRIGHT, LESLIE
1977 *The Blockade Runner* Modern Greece *and her Cargo*. North Carolina Department of Cultural Research, Raleigh.

THE CHATTANOOGA DAILY REBEL
1862 No title. *The Chattanooga Daily Rebel* 9 August. Chattanooga, Tennessee.

DAILY NEWS
1864 The Court. *Daily News* 6 February 5538. London, England.

FAYETTEVILLE OBSERVER
1862 Firing at New Inlet – Vessel Ashore. *Fayetteville Observer* 30 June 2352. Fayetteville, North Carolina.

FONVIELLE, CHRIS E., JR.
1994 "The Last Rays of Departing Hope": The Battles of Fort Fisher, the Fall of Wilmington, North Carolina, and the End of the Confederacy. Doctoral dissertation, Department of History, University of South Carolina.

FREELAND, CHELSEA
2014 *Modern Greece*: Values of a Civil War Blockade Runner. Master's thesis, Department of History, East Carolina University, Greenville, North Carolina

GOFF, RICHARD D.
1969 *Confederate Supply*. Duke University Press, Durham, North Carolina.

HENRY, NATHAN
2014 Artifacts from *Modern Greece*. North Carolina Department of Cultural Resources, Underwater Archaeology Branch, Kure Beach, North Carolina.

KEITH, H.J.
2011 *Guns of the Cape Fear: Civil War Defenses of Wilmington, North Carolina. Vol. I: The First Nineteen Months*. Confederate Imprints, Eagle, Idaho.

LEBERGOTT, STANLEY
1960   Wage Trends, 1800–1900. In *Trends in the American Economy in the Nineteenth Century*, The Conference on Research in Income and Wealth, pp. 449–500. Princeton University Press, Princeton, New Jersey.

MARX, KARL
1887   *Capital: A Critique of Political Economy*. Progress Publishers, Moscow, USSR. Marx/Engels Internet Archive. <http://www.marxists.org/archive/marx/works/1867-c1>. Accessed 30 Sept 2013.

MCKEAN, BRENDA CHAMBERS
2011   *Blood and War at My Doorstep: North Carolina Civilians in the War Between the States*. Vol. I. Xlibris Corporation, Bloomington, Indiana.

MOHOLY-NAGY, HATTULA
2002   *The Artifacts of Tikal – Utilitarian Artifacts and Unworked Material: Tikal Report 27B*. University of Pennsylvania Museum of Archaeology and Anthropology, Philadelphia.

OFFICER, LAWRENCE H. AND SAMUEL H. WILLIAMSON
2013   "Computing 'Real Value' Over Time with a Conversion Between U.K. Pounds and U.S. Dollars, 1774 to Present." MeasuringWorth. <www.measuringworth.com/exchange>.

OFFICIAL RECORDS OF THE NAVIES
1912   *Official Records of the Union and Confederate Navies in the War of the Rebellion*. 2 Series, 22 Vol. Government Printing Office, Washington, D.C.

SURDAM, DAVID G.
2001   *Northern Naval Superiority and the Economics of the American Civil War*. University of South Carolina Press, Columbia.

TROTTER, WILLIAM R.
1989   *Ironclads and Columbiads: The Civil War in North Carolina, The Coast*. John F. Blair, Publisher, Winston-Salem, North Carolina.

WANDRUS, HARRY
1962   North Carolina Archaeological Laboratories. *Bulletin of the American Group. International Institute for Conservation of Historic and Artistic Works* 3(1):4–5.

WEBSTER, C. L. III
2010   *Entrepôt: Government Imports into the Confederate States*. Edinborough Press, Roseville, Minnesota.

WILMINGTON DAILY JOURNAL
1862   Auction Sale. *Wilmington Daily Journal* 2 July. Wilmington, North Carolina.

WISE, STEPHEN R.
1988   *Lifeline of the Confederacy: Blockade Running during the Civil War*. University of South Carolina Press, Columbia

Chelsea R. Freeland
PO Box 13522
Richmond, VA 23225
(217) 549-3075
cfreeland08@gmail.com

Results from the first excavation on the Saintes Bay's Shipwreck, Guadeloupe, FWI

Jean-Sébastien Guibert

This paper presents results from the first excavations on the Saintes Bay's wreck, Guadeloupe, French West Indies. The wreck may be linked to the loss of Anemone, *a French schooner built in 1823 in Bayonne and used as a custom ship in Guadeloupe. The July 2015 archaeological project surveyed the site. Discrete trenches were excavated to identify both shipwreck material culture and ship structure, and compare this to archival records; and facilitate archaeological interpretation of the site, with regard to accounts of its loss, design plans, construction details, etc.*

Introduction

"*Nowhere else the hurricane had been more violent than in those islands (…) It was impossible to raise the king schooner* Anémone *sunk on her anchors during the tempest. Her masts were snatched from their foot taking of all sails and rigging (…) Mr Guillotin's body has been found few days after the wreck and successively 18 men of his crew*" *(ANOM SG/GUA/CORR/68 25/3/1825).*

This extract from Governor Jacob's report was the first hint to identify the site of the Saintes Bay's wreck found in 1995 and first described in 2001. The site known as Baie des Saintes wreck was discovered by Claude Edouard in 1995. It was excavated in the 1990s by local divers, without archaeological oversight. The hypothesis that this is the wreck site of the French schooner Anémone, proposed in 2013 (Guibert 2013), is confirmed by this first excavation.

The first archaeological assessment, conducted by Michel L'Hour and Jean-Luc Massy during a DRASSM project in 2001, dated the site from before 1840 from the presence of 'Creil and Montereau' stamps on two

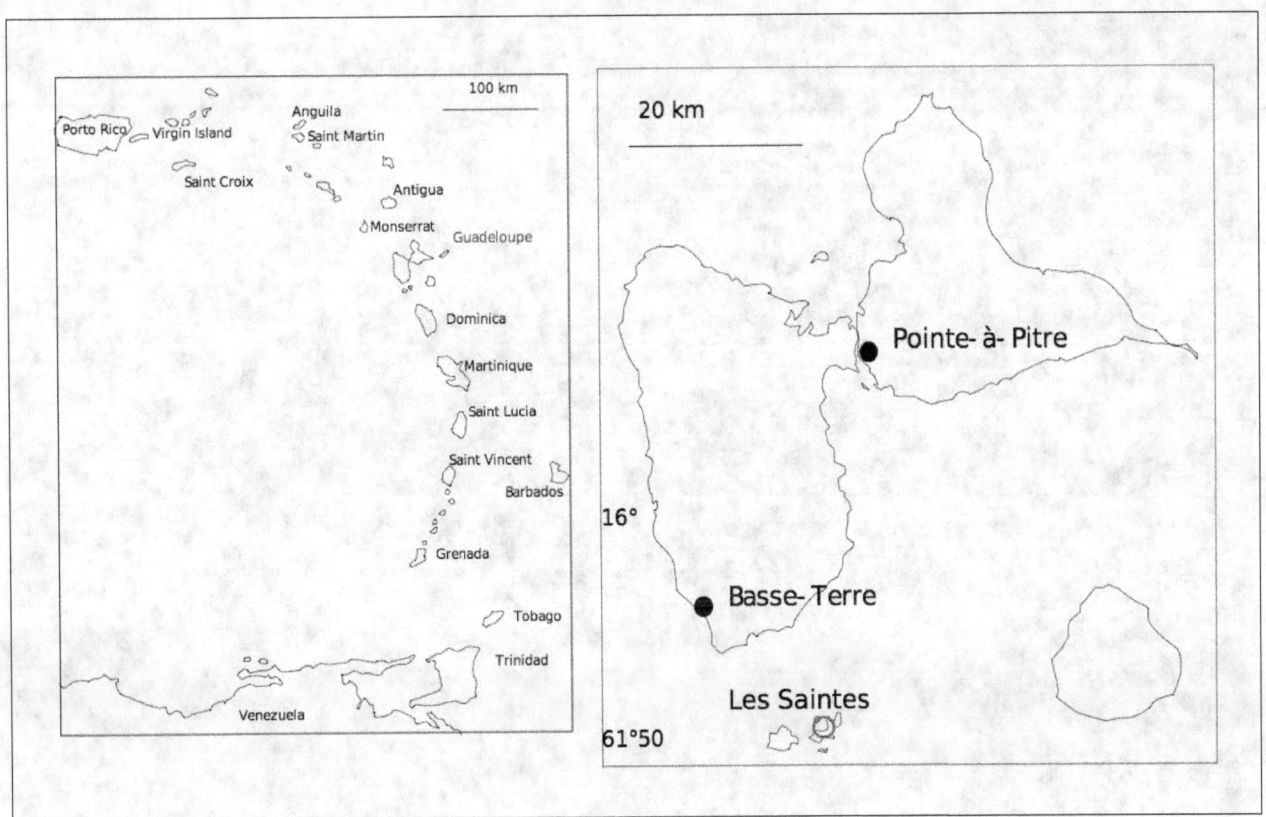

Figure 1. Site localization (Map by author, 2014).

ceramic artifacts (L'Hour and Massy 2002). In addition, copper sheathing and cast iron ballast were observed on the site. Based on the little information existing to date, the wreck may be associated with the French schooner *Anémone*. This vessel was built at Bayonne, France in 1823 and was sent to the West Indies after its involvement in the Spanish War. In Guadeloupe, the vessel was used as a tender ship, actively engaged in the struggle against the slave trade. Though the slave trade had been officially forbidden in the French colonies from 1817, the illegal trade continued until the 1830s. *Anémone* sank during the 1824 hurricane just after being sent to Saintes Bay for protection (Lacour 1855 [4]:355). All of the crew and officers were lost.

This article presents the first archaeological and historical evidence that identifies this wreck as the *Anémone*. The information was gathered in July 2015, as part of a French West Indies University research program. It lasted one week and involved nine professional and scientific divers for nearly 60 hours of diving.

Site Description and Methodology

The wreck is located in 25 m of water in the middle of the Saintes Bay by the entrance of Terre-de-Haut mooring (Figure 1). The exposed wreck site is about 30 m. long, appearing as a mound or sand tumulus orientated south north. Some metal and some elements are visible in elevation, but the actual nature of this is unclear. Copper hull sheathing is scattered around the site, and apparent pig iron is located in the south area. A cannon muzzle was visible at first dive, and the tube is identified as a carronade. A broken anchor is located 45 m. from the site, but it is unclear if it is associated with the shipwreck.

In order to locate and document accurately the remains, a base line was installed from which four trench tests were excavated. The most interesting is trench test 1, undertaken around the carronade (Figures 2-3). This trench test revealed (a) the carronade, clearly in a secondary position (not a ballast cannon); (b) faunal remains identified as salt meat underneath the carronade; and (c) hull structure (ceiling planks, frames). Trench test 4 extending to trench test 1 confirms the end of structural remains and the potential for artifact scatter. Trenches test 2 and 3 were not relevant.

In the vicinity of trench test 1 and 4, the hypothesis of a central position of below the waterline needs verification during the next campaign.

Figure 2. Divers excavating trench test 1, carronade at first plan (Photo by author, 2015).

Ordnance

One of the two presumed carronades has been studied (Figures 2-3). It is heavily concreted, but its size corresponds to the 1818 type of 12-pounders according to Boudriot's typology (Boudriot 1992: 112). Its in situ length is 128 cm; caliber 12 cm; and muzzle 20 cm. This information can be used for site identification. *Anémone* had two carronades of that type. It may indicate the central area of the hull structure, even if the ordnance was initially on deck. It is in a secondary position because a layer with faunal remains was trapped underneath (Figure 3). Its position indicates clearly it is not a ballast cannon. At least it gives a terminus post quem, and adds weight to this being a French naval wreck. The carronade has not been recovered.

Hull Structure

The analysis of hull structure near the carronade is ongoing (Figure 3). It appears to be a lightly built ship because its double frames are 24 cm wide, 1 m. apart. The frames are 11 cm wide. Locking pieces (scarfs) are 17 cm wide. One of the latter has been analyzed and is oak. Their construction alternates in the following pattern of double frame / locking piece / simple frame / locking piece / simple frame / locking piece / double frame. Those measurements have to be fully confirmed with more recording, but they match with a ship that has a lightly-built hull. A keelson is expected under the carronade but has not yet been found. However, the structural elements discovered look to be the lower part of the hull below the waterline. The hull is copper sheathed, confirming that this wreck dates from the mid or late 18th to the early 19th century. Several nails have been found in the trench test 1. They match with 19th century construction (McCarty 2005). Most nails are badly preserved. Electrolysis or poor brass alloy may explain this condition.

Material Culture

Material culture removed from trench tests are ceramics (16 elements), bottles (8 elements), faunal remains (20 elements), and metals.

Material Culture: Ceramics and Glass

The ceramic artifacts are in bad condition, excepting a Westerwald ware fragment pot found in trench test 4 from Eastern France or Western Germany. It dates from the late 18th or early 19th centuries (Figure 4). GR is for Georges Rex III from England and Hanover king from 1760-1820. This common ceramic has been found in colonial contexts; its aspect and details indicate a late fabrication (Gusset 1980, Plourde Lapointe 1996). Most of the others ceramics and glass bottles found in trench tests 1 and 2 are French and date from the same period: one is part of an ink bottle similar as the one found on France's wreck in Guadeloupe or Kejouano's wreck in

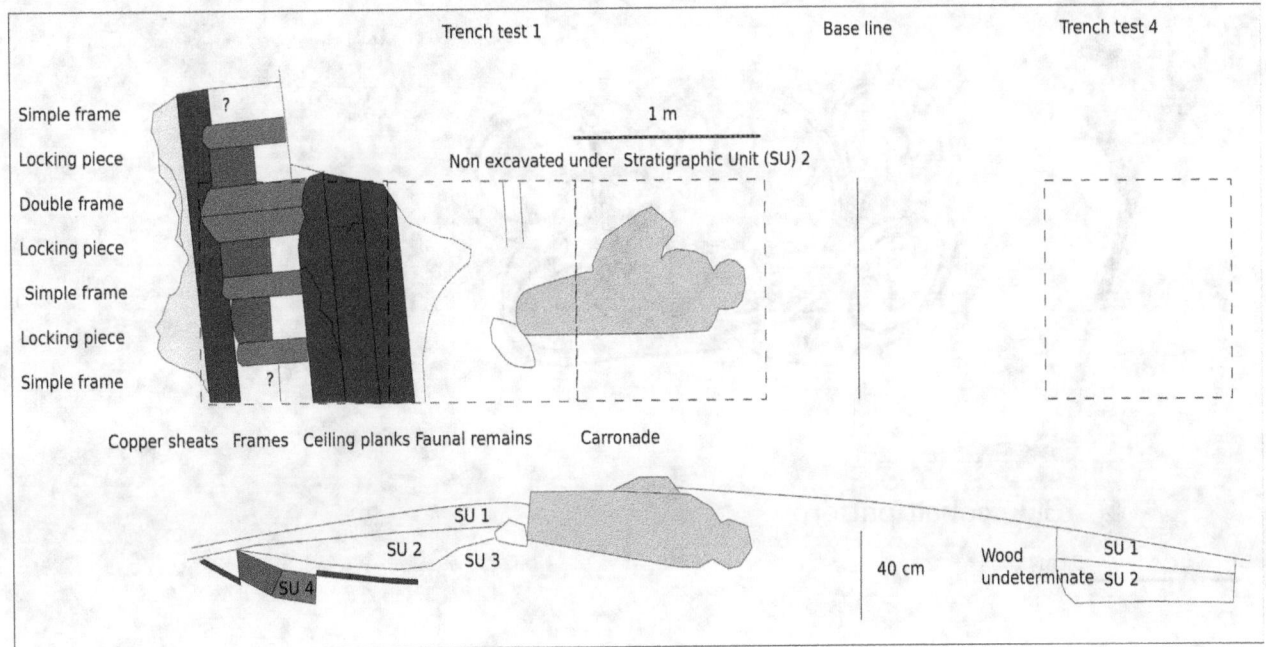

Figure 3. Drawing of trench tests 1 and 4 (Plan by author, 2015).

Britany, both are early 19th century shipwreck contexts (Guibert 2014, L'Hour Veyrat 2005). Some sherds are from Saintonge, and others from Biot.

Material Culture: Faunal Remains

Faunal remains are common in wreck contexts (Migaud 2011). This assemblage has been studied by Noémie Tomadini from the Paris Museum National d'Histoire Naturelle. Twenty elements were recovered– part of a larger group inaccessible because of their location under the carronade. Twelve are identified as vertebra and ribs of cattle (*Bos taurus*). They form a coherent stratigraphical layer trapped under the carronade (Figure 3). It is interpreted as remnants of a barrel of salted meat, because the bone was saw cut. But it is not possible to determine its origin yet.

Material Culture: Bullets

In addition to the carronade, about 135 lead bullets were found in trench test 1 in the vicinity of the ceiling planking. Their weights vary from 27-29 g; their diameters vary from 16.26 to 17.46 mm. They are linked to weapons pistols or guns used from 1786 to 1822, according to Boudriot's typology (Boudriot Berti 1992). This is another evidence for a naval identification.

Material Culture: Kersaint's Kitchen ?

Several copper alloy boxes were observed; one was recovered for detailed examination. It measures 210 mm (L) X 310 mm (H), X 144 mm. (W). Its capacity may be 9 liters. This copper box may be one of the containers of the galley in what was known as kitchen Kersaint, used on several ships since the end of 18th century and especially on schooners from the 1823 type. Some artifacts linked with everyday life on board were also recovered, including a knife handle, brush handle and hand made pipe tube.

Historical Evidence: A Ship from Bayonne

To date, all archaeological data indicate that these are the remains of a lightly-built French naval vessel lost between 1818 and 1840 with at least one gun. Research in the relevant historical archives yields only one candidate that matches the evidence: an 1823 French schooner built in Bayonne named *Anémone* that was lost in the September 1824 hurricane (Guibert 2013). *Anémone* is one of six schooners built in the 1820s after Ministry of Marine and Colony's decision to follow the 1823 plan type. *Rose* and *Anémone* were built in Bayonne, *Jacinthe* and *Jonquille* in Toulon, and *Émeraude* and *Topaze* in Cherbourg (Boudriot 1989: 26).

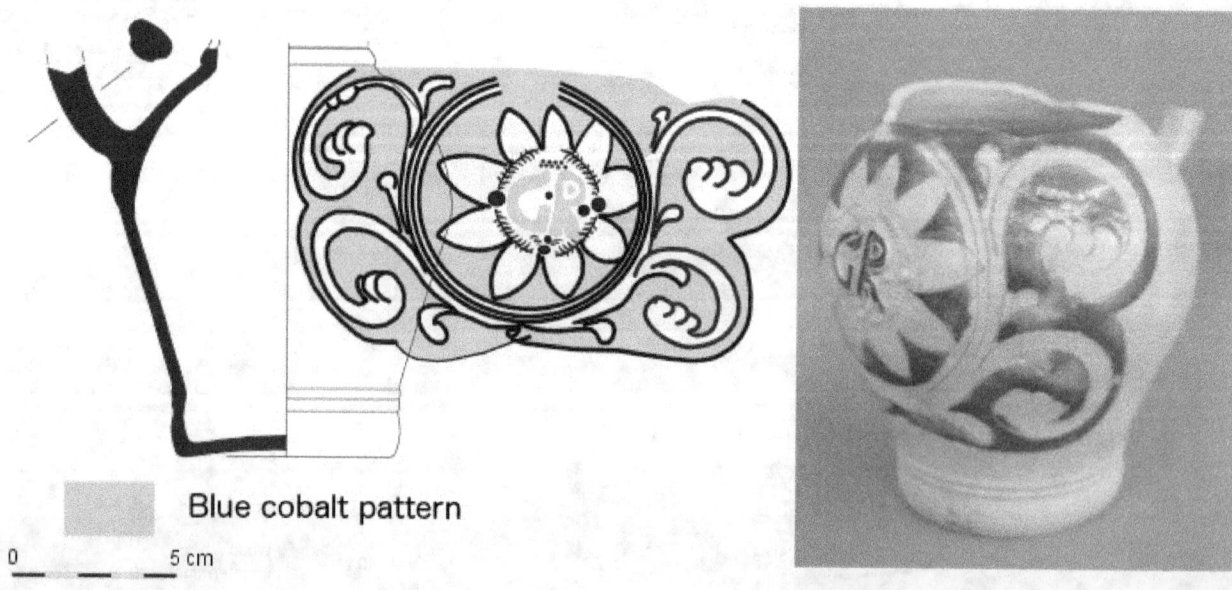

Figure 4. Westerwald ware fragment pot (1800-1820) (Drawing by Franck Bigot, Photo by author).

Archives and plans indicate the dimension of the schooners of the 1823s series: 21 m long X 5.8 m wide X 2.36 m depth-of-hold, with two carronades of the 1818 type (SHD Vincennes 8DD1 9 n°7). Several contemporary documents mention copper sheathing and pig iron ballast in the construction of these ships. In Bayonne, the schooners were built between February and July 1823. After being involved in the Spain expedition under command of Guillotin, *Anémone*, *Rose*, *Topaze* and *Émeraude* were sent in West Indies in December 1823. In spite of a demand to shorten the topmasts and equip *Anémone* with two more carronades, no change occurred to the schooner (SHD Vincennes 8DD1 5-13/11/1823).

Historical Evidence: A Custom Ship in French West Indies

The ship had just arrived in West Indies in January 1824 and was used as a customs ship, coast guarding, transport and mailing. Its mission was also to patrol for illegal slave traders in the French West Indies forbidden since 1817. For example, it took part in the May 1824 arrest in Guadeloupean waters of *Jeune Adèle*, a schooner from Bordeaux loaded with a cargo 207 slaves (ANOM SG/GUA/CORR 67 7/9/1824).

The ship under Guillotin's command was sent to Saintes Bay at the end of July 1824 for the rainy season and to prevent hurricane risk (ANOM SG/GUA/CORR/72 20/7/1824). Its mooring was considered secure from as early as the 18th century, in spite of several accidents. During the 7-8 September hurricane, the Saintes Islands were totally devastated. *Anémone* sunk at anchor in the Bay. 28 of her crew, from the captain to the Guadeloupean pilot, were lost. The location of the wreck may match the loss of the anchored ship in the bay. Considering the minimal archival information, it seems the ship sank during the tempest, and the masts that had not been reduced were snatched during the wreck. Moreover, the total loss of all the crew indicates a sudden event. One of the reports mentioned the fact that all the crewmen were fastened to the rigging and floated to the surface while decomposing (ANOM SG/GUA/CORR/68 25/3/1825).

Conclusion

The archival and archaeological evidence confirms the current identification hypothesis, that the Bay of Saintes' wreck is the French schooner *Anémone* lost in September 1824.

The site should be the focus of further excavation in 2016-2017 in order to study accurately the construction of an early 19th century schooner. To date, it is the only identified example of such a ship type and of the 1820s French series. We will also investigate the wreck's material culture (faunal and ceramic remains, etc.) in the context of a French naval ship engaged in a customs mission in the West Indies. In spite of several indications of looting, the site may have potential for good artifact preservation due to its relative water depth. A sandglass for example was removed by local divers in the 1990s (L'Hour and Veyrat 2005).

The fact that this little French schooner was policing the illegal slave trade gives this site a patrimonial element that is quite unusual and both historically and archaeologically significant.

Archival Sources

Archives Nationales d'Outre mer (Aix-en-Provence) [ANOM]: Série SG Série Géographique Guadeloupe 1815–1900. Correspondance 1815-1845, Généralités 1815–1859.

Service Historique de la Défense (Vincennes) [SHD]:Série DD Service général, Sous série 8DD Plans de bâtiments à voiles.

References

Lacour, Auguste
1855 *Histoire de la Guadeloupe*. E. Kolodziej, Paris, France.

Boudriot, Jean
1989 *La Jacinthe Goélette 1823 Monographie Étude historique*. Paris, France.

Boudriot, Jean and Berti, Hubert
1992 *Artillerie de mer France 1650-1850 Étude historique et technique*, Nice, France.

Guibert, Jean-Sébastien
2013 Mémoire de mer Océan de papiers Naufrage, risque et fait maritime à la Guadeloupe (fin XVII-mi XIXe siècles). Doctoral dissertation.

2014 A Question That Counts in French West Indies Maritime Archaeology: Linking Historical and Archaeological Sources. *2014 ACUA Proceedings*, Charles Dagneau and Karolyn Gauvin editors, p. 113-119, Advisory Council on Underwater Archaeology Publication.

Gusset, Gérard
1980 *Les grès blancs salins, rhénans et à corps sec*, Parcs Canada, Ottawa Canada.

L'Hour, Michel, and Massy, Jean-Luc (editors)
2002 *Bilan scientifique du Drassm*. Ministère de la culture, Paris, France.

L'Hour, Michel, and Veyrat, Élisabeth (editors)
2005 *La mer pour mémoire. Archéologie sous-marine des épaves atlantiques*. Somogy éditions d'art/Buhez, Paris, France.

Migaud, Philippe
2011 A first approach to links between animals and life on board sailing vessels (1500-1800), *IJNA*, 40 (2), p. 283-292.

Plourde, Guy and Lapointe, Camille
1996 *Les objets domestiques en grès fin anglais de Place-Royale*, Les publications du Québec, Québec.

Jean-Sébastien Guibert, PhD
AIHP-GÉODE EA 929 Université des
   AntillesUFR Lettres et Sciences Humaines
Campus de Schoelcher BP 7207 97275
Schoelcher Cedex, France.
00 596 (0)5 96 72 74 76
00 590 (0)6 90 65 77 31
jsebguibert2@hotmail.com
jean-sebastien.guibert@martinique.univ-ag.fr

The Maritime Archaeology of Slave Ships: Overview, Assessment and Prospectus

Jessica Irwin and Dave Conlin

In one of the most consequential historical processes in global history, over a period of approximately 300 years, more than 12 million enslaved persons were stolen from their homelands in Africa and forcibly placed in the Americas. Driven by market forces, the maritime technology utilized for this shameful trade developed rapidly, while the physical characteristics of ships designed to transport slaves changed over time due to economic, cultural and historical constraints.

This presentation will provide a brief overview of wrecks known, or thought to have been involved in the slave trade; discuss what might archaeologically define a slave ship, and then situate this discussion into the larger program of study currently being done by an international consortium of scholar with the slave wrecks project and others.

Overview

In the single most consequential historical event in human history, ships carrying human captive cargo crossed the Atlantic continuously for nearly 300 years. Over those three centuries, an estimated 12.5 million individuals were taken from their homes by force and transplanted to the Americas. Taken in context, 12.5 million people out of a global population of approximately 1 billion would equate to about 90 million people today—that's 15 Holocausts stacked on top of each other for 3 centuries. The ships that facilitated this shameful history were the single largest factor in shaping the cultural, racial and economic climate of today and of the last 400 years, and the idea that these ships have left little or no mark in the archaeological record is ludicrous. Nearly every country with access to the Atlantic participated in the slave trade, financing the building and purchase of vessels, collecting trade goods, acquiring African slaves, and distributing them across two continents in the Americas. Many of these ships may not have wrecked with slaves on board, but that does not bar them from contributing to the potential story of the slave ship.

The maritime technology utilized for this hateful trade developed rapidly and was driven by market forces, while the physical characteristics of ships designed to transport slaves changed over time due to economic, cultural and historical constraints in Europe. The material cultural that survives in the archaeological record developed and changed due to cultural and historic changes taking place in Africa rather than Europe, and these changes leave distinct markers in the archaeological record.

To this point, with few exceptions, the slave ships that have been discovered or examined archaeologically have not been investigated in a manner that allows for historic understanding or progressive knowledge to the subject. The most famous of these ships have been discovered by treasure hunters, and thus examined in a way driven by profit and not academic understanding of the global process or microeconomics. The ships that have been examined in a more acceptable archaeological manner are ships that at the time of wrecking were serving a purpose other than slaving. These ships contribute to the slave ship narrative more through historic research than through ship structure and material culture.

Only recently have ships that sank as slavers been examined archaeologically. In particular, the slave wrecks project has examined the remains of a ship off the coast of West Africa—the Portuguese slave ship *Sao Jose* (*Saint Joseph*), which sank just south of Cape Town in 1794 with the loss of 212 enslaved persons.

The nature of the economics around the slave trade and the slave ships themselves present several challenges to historic and archaeological research. One of these challenges is that a slaver could sink while working as a slaver without human cargo on board, so that researchers must look for other clues to link the ship with the active slave trade. More research of the material culture of the slave trade needs to be done to help identify ships that may otherwise be identified as merchant vessels. A study of this nature could also lead to the re-examination of unidentified shipwrecks by surveying the onboard material culture and its possible implications.

A re-examination of previously excavated vessels requires the definition of a slave ship to include any ship participating in the slave trade, regardless of country of origin or time period of participation. It also requires the definition to include ships that sank without human cargo on board, as well as ships in support of the vessels that carried enslaved humans. While the discovery of wrecks that had onboard human cargo would give by far the most insight into the structure and construction of the ship itself, ships that sank at any stage of the journey could give insight into the changing and fluid nature of the slave trade itself. When discussing previously examined wrecks in the archaeological record, it is important to distinguish the changes over time. The most logical way to do this is to differentiate between early ships; ships used at the height of the trade; and ships involved after the trade became illegal in England. Early ships transported not only slaves but also supported new and growing colonies that were not yet self-sufficient and trade routes that were not yet totally established. The height of the slave trade lasted from 1700 to 1807, when roughly 50% of the total number of Africans were taken from the continent and ship construction exploded. After 1807, ships adapted to British and American statutes that made the trade illegal, changing the overall nature of the trade and shipping, by enforcing these statutes on all slaving enterprises not just those originating in England and the United States. Although ships carrying enslaved peoples developed for speed to carry humans who died over the course of their terrible journey, as the practice became illegal to participate in more countries the ships themselves changed in a technological "arms race" that exactly paralleled those of smugglers and blockade runners.

Assessment

The potential for slave ships in the archaeological record is huge. A study done by New Castel University indicates that there are potentially 261 wrecks of slavers: 85 British wrecks, 33 Irish wrecks, 97 West African wrecks, 72 Caribbean wrecks, 17 North American wrecks, 6 South American wrecks, and some 31 mid-Atlantic wrecks. If even a small portion of these were discovered and researched by archaeologists, what is known about the structure and construction of slavers would grow exponentially (Smith, 2014).

To date the most famous slave wrecks have been those discovered by treasure hunters. These include The *Henrietta Marie*, the *Whydah*, The Manilla Wreck, and the *Fredensborg*. These wrecks have been re-examined from an archaeological perspective since their discovery, but mainly because the cultural material or historic research indicated that those wrecks were in fact slavers.

The *Queen Anne's Revenge*, *James Mathews*, *Adelaide*, and *Elmina Wreck* are all wrecks that have had extensive archaeological investigation. In the case of the *James Mathews* and the *Queen Anne's Revenge*, the vessels sank while working as something other than a slaver. However, the characteristics of the vessels (speed primarily) that made them suitable as slave ships are also what made them desirable as pirate ships. The *Adelaide* and the *Elmina Wreck* were both working as slave vessels, but slaves were not on board at the time of sinking. The findings on the *Adelaide* have yet to be published, but the *Elmina Wreck* can serve as a marker for what a slave ship could contain and how archaeological investigations can be carried out.

The *Enterprise* and the *Trouvadore* were salvaged at the time of wrecking. Neither of these vessels contained much cultural material at the time of examination, but they are examples of how the hull of a ship that worked as a slaver at any point in its life can add to the narrative of the slave trade.

A re-examination of the material culture of unidentified wrecks may also lead to further understanding of these vessels. Shackles and other articles of restraint are certainly indicative of a slaver, as are larger galleys, larger water tanks, and segregated interior spaces. Research into historic documents related to the outfitting of slaving vessels both in the United States and England show that the most common goods being sent to Africa were items that would not last in the archaeological record or may not have survived a wrecking event at all. They include foods stuffs, livestock and other organic material such as fabric. Because material going to Africa was highly localized and changed often, much like fashion today, material culture has the potential not only to reveal where ships were traveling from but also to suggest the date at which they were operating.

Fabric was an exceptionally popular slave trade item. Bale seals have enormous potential to identify slave ships. Beads have long been associated with slave ships and are small enough that they often survive among the ballast stones of a vessel long after it stopped transporting human cargo. What is missing is a comprehensive study of slave-related beads, and a method to use them as a diagnostic marker of both port of departure and destination. Taste in beads was highly regional and changed frequently, as they were utilized both as status symbols and currency. Cowries especially have led to some confusion, because these shell beads were highly sought after; they appear in the archaeological record rather frequently; and they may be mistaken for local shell. In fact, if these shell types are found on a beach, they likely washed ashore there as these particular shells are only found in specific places, none native to Africa (Lorenz and Hubert 1993, 205).

Another item that could notably change the discussion is one that would indicate that a ship sank with slaves on board. The presence of bricks from a slave stove would most likely survive in the archaeological record. While cook stoves existed on most vessels, a slave stove was constructed on deck only while slaves were on board. This feature is particularly unique to slave ships during the height of the trade. They were often placed in the middle of the vessel and served to both divide the ship into manageable sections and feed the hundreds of extra mouths now on board.

Metal items being transported also can be diagnostic. Historic documents record that many African ports preferred the import of European iron and copper in a raw state. The skill level of many smiths in Africa rivaled that of those in Europe, but the quality of the imported stock was much better than the locally available material. This resulted in vessels full of copper rods and iron bar. Manillas are often associated with the slave trade as well and have been an indicator. They rarely show up on terrestrial sites and this could be the reason. Items that are both currency and status symbols reigned supreme on the African coast (Johansson, 1967).

In addition to iron for trade is iron ballast, used extensively in slave ships like *Sao Jose*. This iron ballast speaks to the sickening physics of human transport in a ship—people take up room but don't weigh very much, so dense iron ballast blocks provided hydrodynamic stability.

Dye wood survived aboard the *Henrietta Marie*, and fabric survived on the Manilla Wreck site. Both of these wrecks lay in shallow tropical waters. This suggests that more careful excavation of other wrecks could reveal many of the materials that we often think of as unable to survive in highly aerobic environments.

Prospectus

Cargo on all three legs of a slave ship's journey held high value. Many of those items are still valuable today, which is why treasure hunters and salvors have a particular interest in finding them. Coupled with this is the incidental destruction of slave shipwreck sites that have no inherent value but are destroyed in the industrial dismemberment of history that is modern treasure hunting—particularly in less developed countries like (until recently) Mozambique. *Henrietta Marie* was not targeted; it was found during a focused search for Spanish treasure shipwrecks.

Because slavery was a global phenomenon, the international community of archaeologists needs to work together to examine these wrecks—particularly wrecks in the mid-Atlantic that may not be protected in the same way that wrecks found in the waters of flagship counties may be. There is significant potential to find well-preserved wrecks that will illuminate the construction and structure of the vessels themselves in the deeper waters managed under international jurisdiction. Open ocean wrecks are also the most likely to retain their cargoes—trade goods or enslaved humans. The development of more stringent protection of underwater cultural heritage is needed in many Latin American and African countries that were the destinations of these ships. The Slave Wrecks Project is dedicated to a global effort and a global examination of the trade in enslaved humans. The project includes archaeology, history, law and legal protection, development and capacity building for local constituencies. This shameful history is something we don't talk about. It's something that makes us uncomfortable, and it's something that we all—African, European, American—carry a piece of. We are building a coalition of scholars willing to look at the ugly and the forgotten, to give a voice to 12.5 million stolen souls, and we would welcome your help, expertise and participation.

References

JOHANSSON, SVEN-OLOF.
1967   *Nigerian Currencies: Manillas, Cowries and Others.* Skolgatan, Norrkoping: Alfa-Tryck.

LORENZ, FELIX AND ALEX HUBERT.
1993   *A Guide to World Cowries.* Wiesbaden: Verlag Christa Hemmen.

SMITH, MICHAEL.
2014   "Locating Slave Shipwrecks, Innovative approaches to digital and archival resources," (Presentation Newcastle University, School of History, Classics and Archaeology). Voyages Database. Voyages: The Trans-Atlantic Slave Trade Database. Accessed January 2014. http://www.slavevoyages.org.

Jessica Irwin
2206 BE Wheatley Drive,
Beaufort SC 29902
805-712-9466
jessicaglickman@aol.com

David L. Conlin Ph.D.
Archeologist/Chief
National Park Service
Submerged Resources Center
12795 W Alameda Pkwy.
Lakewood, CO
(303) 969-2665
(303) 378-6285 cell
(303) 969-2659 fax
daveconlin321@yahoo.com

Lake Tahoe Maritime Heritage Trail

Denise Jaffke and Tricia Dodds

Just offshore in Lake Tahoe are the remains of the Emerald Bay "Mini-fleet," ten small recreational boats once used by resort patrons. These small craft, representing a variety of vessel forms and functions, operated on Emerald Bay from 1890-1940. The Mini-fleet represents 90% of the boat styles used for leisure and work on the Lake, and the vessels are one of the largest examples of early 20th century small boats known to exist in situ. California State Parks is in the process of establishing an underwater maritime heritage trail to highlight and interpret the group.

Lake Tahoe is the third deepest lake in North America, and Emerald Bay on its southwest shore is one of the most photographed places on earth. The bay is a fjord embayment and has long been recognized for its spectacular natural beauty. At the head of the bay is the historic residence of Vikingsholm, a Scandinavian inspired "castle" listed on the National Register of Historic Places. Emerald Bay was designated California's first underwater state park in 1994 and is the resting place for many boats, launches and barges used in the lake during 19th century early settlement; during the heyday of 20th century Emerald Bay resorts; and during the 1929 construction of Vikingsholm. This is the site proposed for California's first maritime heritage trail.

Lake Tahoe, often described as the "Jewel of the Sierra," attracts more than five million visitors a year, many of whom explore the lake by boat. The first boats on Lake Tahoe were dugouts manufactured by Washoe Indians and their ancestors. Once European explorers and settlers reached the lake, they immediately took to the water using small craft, sailboats, and subsequently steamers, which supported local transportation and commerce.

Between 1860-1890, a majority of people living in the Lake Tahoe Basin were workers involved in harvesting, transporting, or milling lumber, principally for the Comstock Lode in Nevada. Most of the 19th century roads were specifically built for logging operations and not particularly suitable for the recreational visitor. At the end of the 19th century, as logging declined, the roads fell into disrepair. While the Lincoln Highway crossed the Sierra as part of the first coast-to-coast paved route in 1913, a fully accessible road did not circumnavigate Lake Tahoe until 1935 (Lindstrom 2000). Meanwhile, travelers were served by a variety of steamboats to access resorts around the lake's rim. Increased accessibility to automobiles and the inevitable improvements to the basin's roadways created competition that ultimately rendered the steamers obsolete. This created a shift in how the lake was perceived; from settlement through the 1930s, the majority of spectator's perspectives interpreted Lake Tahoe from the bow of a boat. Today, accounts of the lake are from land, looking out to the water's horizon.

Automobiles brought a tourism boom to Lake Tahoe resorts and pressured California and Nevada to construct a road around the lake. Not surprisingly, one of the last road sections to be finished was the difficult cut around Emerald Bay. For almost a decade tourists would drive south along the California side of the lake to Rubicon Point where they loaded their cars onto a barge. The barge was towed across the entrance of Emerald Bay to Camp Richardson, where tourists then off-loaded and continued on along Highway 89.

The barges were owned and operated by the lumber companies, who used them to haul cord wood part of the year and then employed them as car ferries during the summer months. Since the barges had no means of propulsion, they were either towed or pushed by steamers.

Two historic barges constructed of massive Ponderosa pine timbers are located between 10 to 40 feet of water near the southern shore of Emerald Bay. Barge I, with a remaining length of 85 feet, lies perpendicular to the shore with her northwestern hull end protruding out of the water during low water years. The hull appears to have grounded atop boulders, and wave action has since worked the hull apart. Twenty-nine of the frames, 16 hull strakes and the eastern transom remain attached to the northern hull side. The western transom and a majority of the southern hull side are disarticulated. Only one bulkhead and one bitt remain in place. There appears to have been an attempt to salvage portions of the hull, since several of the longitudinal bulkheads are neatly piled on the submerged slope just north of Barge I.

Barge II parallels the shoreline approximately 15 feet south of Barge I. Within the 106-ft.-long barge are 55 single timber frames spanning the hull. Natural deterioration has begun in the bulkheads at the southern end of the barge, and some organized salvage attempts succeeded in removing approximately 75% of her decking. However, hull integrity is almost totally intact.

Although the barges share many similarities, they appear to have been built by different shipwrights to the same general plan. Details, such as the way in which the bitts are set in the corners and the difference in scarph alignment, point to an experienced shipwright for Barge II. By contrast, Barge I may have been constructed by a carpenter (Smith 1991). Together, they represent a major transportation mode of the last quarter of the 19th and early 20th centuries. Their construction was quite practical, nothing exotic, yet the craftsmanship exhibited in the two barges of Emerald Bay reflects attention to detail and overall regard for the finished product.

During the 19th century, as the Tahoe Basin attracted more interest and more tourists, diverse resorts appeared along the shores of the lake. Growing numbers of eastern visitors joined the members of San Francisco's elite and the wealthy mining and business interests of the Comstock at the lake's best hotels. People of more modest means camped or vacationed in rustic hotels and cottages. In 1907, Russell and Margaret Graves began construction of the Emerald Bay Resort/Camp on the northwest shore of Emerald Bay. The resort boasted calm waters and offered its guests a variety of small craft for fishing and recreation. The variety of activities helped the business prosper, despite the absence of a road into and around the bay. Supplies, mail, and guests arrived by steamer, and the larger supplies arrived by barge (Marx 2002).

The Emerald Bay Resort lies in an area that is now the Boat-in Campground at Emerald Bay State Park. The resort represents one of the longest running resorts in the area, spanning 70 years of continuous operation. Compared with Tahoe's luxury hotels, the Emerald Bay Resort was a simple family resort in a unique setting on the shore of the lake's most famous bay. The resort had a hotel as well as tents, cottages, and several piers where steamers could dock (Marx 2002). It offered several forms of recreation, but the small recreational boats were undoubtedly the most popular.

Just offshore of Boat Camp are the remains of what is known as the "Mini-fleet." They were intentionally sunk as a means of disposal when they were no longer useful. The owners loaded rocks aboard and they were left to settle on the bottom. Cold water has preserved them, and it is this outstanding preservation that allows their historic significance to be recognized and enjoyed by the general public.

The Emerald Bay Resort boats represent the skill and craftsmanship available at Lake Tahoe at the time. Among them are examples of small craft powered by

Figure 1. Lapstrake motorboat, MF 5 of the Emerald Bay Mini-fleet.

outboards; a wooden fishing boat with live bait well; and boats propelled by inboard engines, such as the lapstrake motorboat (Figure 1). There is also a hard chine fishing boat–a boat originally rowed but later powered by an outboard. By contrast, there are also boats that were rowed (the live bait well fishing boats) (Figure 2); those that were paddled (the metal kayak), and a day sailor.

Probably the oldest craft in the Mini-fleet is a 27-ft. launch, indicative of turn of the century construction. Most of the Emerald Bay Resort wooden boats likely were constructed locally, but the launch could have been built in San Francisco and transported at a time when affluent families were constructing second homes at the lake. The boat probably had a second life as a work boat before it was scuttled in the bay. The hull has the

Figure 2. Wooden hard chine fishing boat with live bait well, MF 4 of the Emerald Bay Mini-fleet.

same green and white paint as a few of the other boats, indicating it was part of the Emerald Bay Resort fleet.

The submerged barges and small recreational boats of Emerald Bay Underwater State Park, speak to Lake Tahoe's transportation and recreation history. The craft that plied the waters of Lake Tahoe shed light on daily life, and the important nature of many of the Lake's resort communities. They speak to how people spent their leisure time on the water, and how important fishing was on the lake. Moreover, the boats and barges reflect changes in maritime technology. They range in construction materials and style, from wood to metal and from simple to complex. They also reflect the change in American leisure boating from sail to rowing to engine-powered, exhibiting the diversity of Lake Tahoe's maritime technology. The significance of tourism to modern-day Tahoe has a direct correlation to the historic communities that plied, fished, and visited its waters more than 100 years ago, providing a physical linkage with the past and insight into the technologies used for survival, recreation, and enterprise on Emerald Bay.

Our objective is to plan, design, and implement a historic maritime heritage trail for the existing Emerald Bay Underwater Preserve, using the submerged, historic barges and small recreational boats as links in a tour of both the onshore and underwater environments (Figure 3). Project-related tasks begin with resource monitoring fieldwork, interpretative planning, and public outreach, followed by implementation and promotion. Work will begin with archaeological monitoring of all submerged small craft and the two barges. We've started to assess the condition of the vessels, comparing what we see today

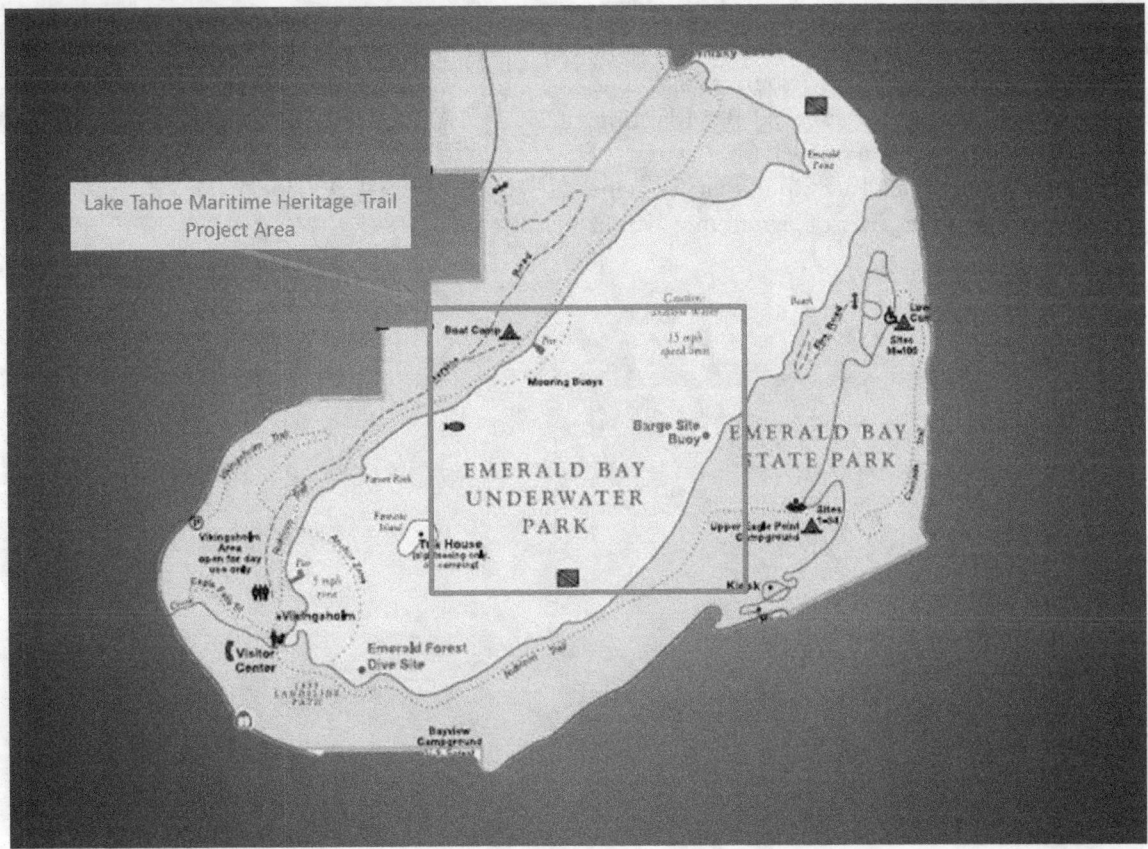

Figure 3. Emerald Bay State Park brochure map highlighting the proposed area for the Lake Tahoe Maritime Heritage Trail.

with what was initially recorded over ten years ago. We've captured video of two dories, the launch, and barges, but we need to revisit the remaining seven vessels with high-quality video equipment. We also wish to apply current photogrammetry techniques to build 3D models of each vessel, as a means to capture the current condition of the vessels before they degrade further. These records also will provide the non-diving public opportunities to view and interact with the boats.

The natural environment of the Lake Tahoe region is our greatest asset. Because of the region's unique sense of place, it draws visitors from all over the world to experience the lake's sublime beauty. About three million people visit Lake Tahoe each year, and most include Emerald Bay as part of their lake tour. This is comparable to the numbers of visitors to Grand Canyon and Yellowstone national parks. A maritime heritage trail provides a way to promote the Lake's heritage and history, while augmenting existing tourism. Emerald Bay is ideally suited to support maritime heritage attractions, since it is easily accessible and visually interesting. These key factors combine to develop an opportunity appealing to a wide audience. The narrative created through our interpretative materials will serve as a vehicle for communicating archaeological values within the broader framework of the park itself. The primary message we want to convey to the visitor is the value of preserving archaeological resources, including submerged sites, in place. The Emerald Bay Maritime Heritage Trail will serve as a model for the rest of California State Underwater Parks; one that we hope will be duplicated at other sites of significance within the park system.

References

LINDSTRÖM, SUSAN
2000   A Contextual Overview of Human Land Use and Environmental Conditions. In *The Lake Tahoe Watershed Assessment Volume 1*. Ed. By Dennis D. Murphy and Christopher M. Knopp, editors, pp. 23-130. United States Department of Agriculture Forest Service.

MARX, DEBORAH E.
2002   The Emerald Bay Resort/Camp, Emerald Bay, Lake Tahoe, California. Report prepared for California Department of Parks and Recreation.

SMITH, SHELI O.
2005   Emerald Bay Mini-Fleet DPR 523 Site Record. Prepared for California Department of Parks and Recreation, Sacramento.

1991   Emerald Bay Barges Archaeological Survey 1989-1990. Report prepared for California Department of Parks and Recreation, Sacramento.

Denise Jaffke
California State Parks
P.O. Box 266
Tahoma, CA 96142

Tricia Dodds
California State Parks
5172 Highway 78
Borrego Springs, CA 92004

The 2012 Field Season of the 1630-31 New Spain Fleet Archaeological Project in the Gulf of Mexico

Roberto Junco and Flor Trejo

This paper presents the 2012 field season of the 1630-31 New Spain Fleet Archaeological Project, as well as a succinct picture of its history. The 2012 Field season of the 1630-31 New Spain Fleet Project of the Subdirección de Arqueología Subacuática of INAH, has been a leap forward from prior work. The project started in the year 1995 and involved many people throughout the years proposing and implementing diverse search methods and surveys. The project has as one of its main objectives the location of the galleon Nuestra Señora del Juncal (NSJ). *In the case of the 2012 field season, success came from a thoroughly methodological process to propose a search area in the Gulf of Mexico where the Admiral ship of the New Spain Fleet, the* NSJ, *sank in 1631. A good survey approach implemented solid standards of work and equipment at sea. We will mention briefly the approaches previously used in the location of the* NSJ *shipwreck; our current approach; as well as the way the search was planned and how this evolved into a much more complex process that ultimately will locate the ship.*

Introduction

NSJ was an important galleon of the 17th century famous for its tragic history as the Admiral ship of the 1631 fleet that sank with its impressive cargo amidst a storm in the Gulf of Mexico. It cleared Veracruz en route to Havana (Trejo 2003: 53-61). Havana was the port from where both the fleet of New Spain and the Fleet of Tierra Firme rendezvoused to sail together to Spain (Junco 2012: 93). *NSJ* was a 650-ton ship built in Guipuzcoa, north of Spain, between 1622 and 1623. Its sides were reinforced in America. It was built to the "Ordenanzas," or 1618 nautical architecture royal decree. *NSJ* roughly measured some 34 m long X 11 m width and carried 24 cannon. It was the admiral ship of the fleet and carried two years worth of taxes for the king of Spain (Meehan 2003: 92).

The story of the 1630-1631 fleet is tragic: the ships were held for a year at port because of rumors of pirates in Cuban waters. When they were ready to depart, the

Ship	Characteristics	Cargo	Artillery
Nuestra Señora del Juncal Almiranta New Spain Fleet 1631 350 souls	650 to 700 tonnage Built in Guipúzcoa (Fuenterrabía) between 1622 and 1623. Reinforced in América De fábrica nueva (1618 ordinances) Measurements: Breadth (manga): 10.91 m Bottom floor (plan): 5.17 m Keel (quilla): 27.58 m Length (eslora): 34.65 m Draft (puntal): 5.45 m	**Silver coinage:** 1,077,840 pesos **Cochineal fine:** 17.595 tonnage **Cochineal wild:** 11.925 tonnage **Indigo:** 46.080 tonnage **Silk:** 1.185 tonnage **Brazilwood:** 18.630 tonnage **Chocolate:** 26 crates	8 demicannon: 16 lb bronze 10 third-cannons: 10 lb bronze 6 demiculverins: 10 lb bronze Total: 24 cannons

Table 1. Characteristics of the galleon: *Nuestra Señora del Juncal*.

fleet general Echazarreta died. The new general Manuel Serrano was appointed to command the Captain ship of the fleet, *Santa Teresa*. The fleet of 13 ships finally departed 14 October, late into the northern winds season. *NSJ* was the admiral ship and was commanded by Andrés de Aristizábal; onboard were 300 souls. For three days they sailed smoothly to the northeast of the Gulf of Mexico. Then the northern winds began to blow. Aristizábal decided to head back to the coast; however, excess cargo in the hold did not let them maneuver freely. After six days of sailing, the two ships of the king lost sight of the 11 merchant ships of the fleet (Trejo 2003: 55-58).

By the evening of 21 October, the crew of *NSJ* heard cannon fire from the Capitan ship Santa Teresa; the next day, *NSJ* was alone. Probably Santa Teresa sank, and the cannon fire was a signal for help. The next days the wind picked up, and *NSJ* tried to reach the coast of Campeche. However, the ship was taking on water and things became so difficult that they threw overboard cargo and cannons. Later, they even cut back the mainmast. On the evening of 31 October, the bow of the ship broke and *NSJ* sank. 39 people made it into the ship's boat (Meehan and Trejo 2008: 67-68).

Several survivor testimonies are in the Spanish archives. There is a letter of a friar of the order of San Juan de Dios, who reported the incident to his superiors. The ship's quartermaster Francisco Granillo testified to the authorities in Seville for having stolen some gold cargo, and merchant Martín de Irriberri also testified in Seville on the accident. Martin de Irriberri gave day-to-day route information, including wind, directions and clues to the nature of the storm. The friar also provided data on the route, days, number of leagues sailed, some of the maneuvers like the mainmast cutting, and the date and duration of sinking, measured in the time it takes to say a prayer. Quartermaster Granillo gave the coordinates of latitude where *NSJ* supposedly sank, and the distance to the coast of Campeche (AGI, Santo Domingo 133 No. 2 doc. 23; RAH, Colec. Jesuítas t. 114, fs. 646-647; AGI, Escribanía 1023b).

There are also important secondary testimonies by people who did not live through the event, but who provided information on what happened as they were sending expeditions to go look for the ship. Among these testimonies was one from a captain of the ship Santiago, part of the fleet. Also the General Larraspuru in Havana, who recorded news from ships that made it safely to port. Even the viceroy of New Spain gives us clues in his instructions to rescue the ship (AGI, Santo Domingo 133 No. 2 doc. 23; AGI, México 31 No. 4). A total of over 100 documents directly related to the fleet have been identified, and over 500 regarding the fleet indirectly. Flor Trejo has done exhaustive analysis on the documents.

Past Proposed Survey Areas and Fieldwork

For more than 300 years, the *NSJ* loss has remained in the memory of people trying to find its rich cargo. The first known project was in 1677 by Diego de Florencia, who asked the king's permission to look for the galleon. He searched the Campeche Bank for at least 70 days without success (Serrano 1991: 89-91). The documentation does not specify the area where he looked, but it is known that this was a common practice and such expeditions were quite frequent. There was always a contract with the king to salvage as much as possible of the lost cargos. His contract permitted him to search for 10 years. Many centuries later, the first serious proposal to search for the *NSJ* came from treasure hunter Burt Webber; in 1982 he contacted Mexican authorities to search for the ship. In 1992, he presented a proposal to search for the ship to INAH's Consejo de Arqueología, Mexico's governing body for archaeological research and in charge of approving any archaeological projects (Webber 1992). The project was denied. Parallel to this and to other proposals, the Subdirección de Arqueología Subacuática in the 1980s, led by Pilar Luna Erreguerena, stepped up to battle commercial exploitation of underwater cultural heritage (UCH). In 1986, Ofmex Inc. tried to search for *NSJ* in the Gulf of Mexico. It was a tense moment for Mexico's UCH; however, archaeology emerged victorious (Ofmex 1986). These early proposals paved the way for legislation against negotiating the UCH with treasure hunters in Mexico, and ultimately led to Mexico signing the UNESCO convention (Luna 2012: 270-273). In 1993 the project "Mexico-93" was the first to mount a long sea campaign using the Russian research ship *Keldish*. The expedition was coordinated by Joaquin Garcia Bárcena using sidescan sonar to spot potential sites and using mini submersibles to visit the targets. In 3 months, they covered 632 square kilometres (Shirshov Instituto de Oceanología de la Academia de Ciencias de Rusia 1993). Since then, several attempts have been made by treasure hunters to search for these remains, including Odyssey Marine Exploration. OME formally applied to the Mexican government in 2006 and 2012 for permits to search for this and many other shipwrecks (Odyssey Marine Exploration 2006, 2012).

All the proposals to define an area where to look for the *NSJ* share the same documentary information mentioned above. Differences stem from interpretation of historic measurements translated into modern measurements, such as what a league was in the 17th century. Thus, proposals for survey areas interpret the data and add different information to each one. For example, in 1998 Carillo and Herrera proposed a value for the league and added cartographic analysis to determine old versus new positions to understand changes in coordinates. Also, they introduced a more in-depth analysis of the content of the documents (Herrera-Carrillo 1998). Later in 1998, Cruz Apestegui also dealt with the league issue, and added a value for the magnetic declination to take into account as well as a hypothesis on the sinking of *NSJ* and the depth at which it happened, using descriptions in the documents (Apestegui 1998). Other proposals like the 2001 Rojas example add the experience of navigation in the 17th century and other sorts of historic cartographic analysis to the search (Rojas 2008: 91-102). In 2008, the Subdirección de Arqueología Subacuática of INAH had an opportunity to conduct a survey with the help of the Waitt Institute; 155 square kilometers were sonar surveyed (Luna 2009).

In 2012, historian Fernando Serrano Mangas published a book on a survey proposal, while collaborating with the 2012 campaign authors. He produced an in-depth look at the documents and on nautical expertise of the 17th century to reach his conclusions. He did this without any authorization (Serrano 2012). Although he was a good friend (now deceased), his behavior was unacceptable.

The 2012 Field Season Proposal

The authors' proposal for the 2012 season comprised several lines of inquiry and worked closely with specialists in different disciplines (Trejo and Junco 2012). For historical documents interpretation, Trejo proposed to measure the importance of the testimony according to the author and author's purpose (among other criteria) to define the credibility. For the ship reconstruction, we consulted Filipe Castro at Texas A&M University who kindly introduced us to Jose Luis Casaban. Casaban did the reconstruction of the *NSJ* (Casabán 2013). Part of our interest was to reconstruct the possible size of the remains and their characteristics, for advance details on what the shipwreck might look like.

To understand the Gulf of Mexico's oceanographic dynamics, Dr. Salas de León of the Institute of Ciencias del Mar y Limnología at UNAM University in Mexico helped produce a mathematical currents model for 31 October-10 November 1631 (Salas 2013). This model helped establish probability areas for the shipwreck. Other studies established the magnetic declination for that year. Junco reconstructed the ship's route, having studied the route from Veracruz-Habana route from the 16th century onwards (Junco 2012).

For operations planning, Jeff Morris, who had helped in the 2008 Gulf of Mexico survey, oversaw the entire technical set up together with Gordon Watts. The strategy was to tow both a digital sidescan sonar and a cesium magnetometer on one cable, the magnetometer 10 m. behind the sonar, and control them by a winch camera operated from a control room. There, the signal of the two instruments would be display along with an echo sounder for water depth. For total coverage, Jeff recommended 30-m. lane spacing. During the sea campaign, two incidents involving equipment required two days in port to wait for parts. In the end, the captain decided to sail without the equipment and followed the lanes manually.

After the remote sensing survey, Jeff Morris and Joshua Daniel undertook data analysis. 4568 side scan sonar targets were identified, and 1157 targets were identified for the magnetometer. Magnetometer targets were ranked in four categories for being shipwrecks; sidescan sonar targets were ranked into high and low priorities (Luna 2014).

Preliminary Results

From 3 May-15 June 2012 on the ship *B.O. Justo Sierra*, the SAS-INAH campaign tried to find the famed *NSJ*. In the 1700-square-km. area where we propose the shipwreck occurred, 385.50 square kilometers have been surveyed in four blocks. Now we are trying to start a new sea campaign for target verification. For the sonar we have 37 priority sonar targets and 83 priority magnetometer targets. In 2016 we hope to return to sea to resume survey work on this project.

Over the years, the New Spain Fleet of 1630-31 project has helped not only to understand the fleet itself, but has also impacted positively on the discipline of underwater archaeology in Mexico. First, it has been a flag to defend UCH in a constant fight against treasure hunters who keep seeking permits to search and exploit this and other shipwrecks. In addition, it has brought infrastructure, personnel, and education together in diverse areas. It has also encouraged other projects, such as the Inventory Project for the Location of Shipwrecks, which has located hundreds of wrecks in the Gulf of Mexico.

Acknowledgements

There have been many people involved with this project throughout the years; to all of them, thank you! And specially to those involved in the 2012 field season, Pilar Luna Erreguerena, Gordon P. Watts, Jeffrey D. Morris, Joshua A. Daniel, Susan L. Morris, Lawrence H. Tyler, Andrew J. Sherrell, Michael J. Plakos y Aubrey L. Kozak, Ricardo Borrero Londoño, Rosa María Roffiel Franco, Elva Escobar Briones, David Alberto Salas de León, Adela Monreal, Miguel Ángel Díaz Flores, Capitán Leobardo Ríos Mora and the crew of the ship *B.O. Justo Sierra*, Juanito, Match, Lalo, Belinda, Castro, Waitt Foundation (Michael Dressner and Dominique Rissolo), Filipe Castro, and José Luis Casabán among many others.

References

CASABÁN, JOSÉ LUIS
2013 Preliminary Archaeological Report. The reconstruction of Nuestra Señora del Juncal (1631). INAH, Mexico.

HERRERA, MANUEL, AND CARRILLO, LAURA
1998 Preliminary Archaeological Report. Desarrollo metodológico de la selección de áreas de búsqueda de acuerdo a la investigación archivística. INAH, Mexico

CRUZ APESTEGUI.
1998 Preliminary Archaeological Report. Propuesta INAH, Mexico.

JUNCO SÁNCHEZ, R.
2012 La ruta de Veracruz a La Habana en la época colonial. In *Arqueología marítima en México*, Vera Moya, editor, pp. 93-114. INAH, México.

LUNA ERREGUERENA, PILAR
2008 *Underwater and maritime archaeology in Latin America and the Caribbean*, Leshikar-Denton Margaret and Pilar Luna Erreguerena (eds.). Walnut Creek, California, Left Coast Press, 2008.

2013 Preliminary Archaeological Report. Proyecto de investigación Flota de la Nueva España de 1630 – 1631 e Inventario y diagnóstico de recursos culturales sumergidos en el Golfo de México. Informe 2013 INAH, México.

LUNA ERREGUERENA, PILAR, HELENA BARABA MEINEKE, FLOR TREJO RIVERA, ROBERTO JUNCO
2009 Los Arrecifes Perdidos: recent Investigations along the yucatan Coast. In *ACUA Underwater Archaeology Proceedings 2009*. Erika Laanela and Jonathan Moore, editors, SHA.

MEEHAN HERMANSON, PATRICIA
2003 Criterios y procedimientos para la elección de navíos insignia: el caso de Nuestra Señora del Juncal, capitana de la flota de la Nueva España de 1630. In *La flota de la Nueva España 1630 – 1631. Vicisitudes y naufragios*, Flor Trejo Rivera, editor, pp. 79-112 INAH, México.

MEEHAN HERMANSON, PATRICIA, AND TREJO RIVERA, FLOR
2008 Nuestra Señora del Juncal her story and her shipwreck. In *Underwater and maritime archaeology in Latin America and the Caribbean*, Margaret E. Leshikar-Denton and Pilar Luna Erreguerena, Editor, pp. 67-90. Left Coast Press, Walnut Creek, California.

ODYSSEY MARINE EXPLORATION, INC.
2006 Report. Solicitud de autorización, presentada por Odyssey Marine Exploration, Inc. ante el C. Almirante Marco Antonio Peyrot González, secretario de Marina, para realizar trabajos de exploración submarina en aguas mexicanas a fin de descubrir y rescatar tesoros. México, 10 febrero. 2006

2012 Report. Solicitud de autorización, presentada por Odyssey Marine Exploration, Inc. INAH, Mexico.

OFMEX, INC.
1986 Report. Contrato para la investigación, exploración y rescate de pecios en aguas nacionales, firmado el 30 de junio de 1986, Secretaría de Marina / Ofmex, Inc., 1986.

ROJAS, CARMEN
2008 Preliminary Archaeological Report. Flota de Nueva España, SAS, INAH.

SALAS DE LEÓN, DAVID, MONREAL GÓMEZ, M., DÍAZ FLORES, M. A., MONREAL JIMÉNEZ, R.
2012 Preliminary Archaeological Report. Estudio de corrientes y posibles trayectorias del navío Nuestra Señora del Juncal ocurridas del 16 de octubre al 2 de noviembre de 1631 en la región este de la Bahía de Campeche. Prospección de Arqueología Subacuática Nuestra Señora del Juncal. SAS INAH, México.

SERRANO MANGAS, FERNANDO
1991 *Naufragios y rescates en el tráfico indiano durante el siglo XVII*. Seglusa Editores, Lima, Perú.

2012 *Los tres credos de don Andrés de Aristizábal*. Universidad Veracruzana, México.

Shirshov Instituto de Oceanología de la Academia de Ciencias de Rusia
1993 Technical Report in the Gulf of Mexico Volume I, Report on the scientific results of oceanographic investigations provided in the expedition "Mexico-93" in Gulf of Mexico. Shirshov Instituto de Oceanología de la Academia de Ciencias de Rusia.

Trejo Rivera, Flor
2003 Adversidades en la administración de la Carrera de Indias: el caso de la flota del general Miguel de Echazarreta. In *La flota de la Nueva España 1630 – 1631. Vicisitudes y naufragios*, Flor Trejo Rivera, editor, pp. 33-78. INAH, México.

Webber, Burt, Jr.
1992 Report. Operation Arcas. The search, discovery & recovery of "Nuestra Señora del Juncal" Spanish treasure galleon sank in 1631.

Documents

Archivo General de Indias, Seville
AGI, Santo Domingo 133 No. 2 doc. 23

Archivo General de Indias, Seville
AGI, Escribanía 1023b

Archivo General de Indias, Seville
AGI, México 31 No. 4

Real Academia de la Historia
Colección Jesuitas, tomo 114, fs. 646-647

Roberto E Junco
Subdirección de Arqueologia Subacuática
Instituto Nacional de Antropología e Historia
Calle Moneda 16
Col. Centro, Ciudad de Mexico 06060
robjunco@mac.com

Flor Trejo Rivera
Subdirección de Arqueologia Subacuática
Instituto Nacional de Antropología e Historia
Calle Moneda 16
Col. Centro, Ciudad de Mexico 06060
clonopio@gmail.com

Prioritizing the Concretions from *Queen Anne's Revenge* for Conservation: A Case Study in Managing a Large Collection

Kimberly P. Kenyon

In the excavation of archaeological site 31CR314, Blackbeard's flagship Queen Anne's Revenge *(QAR), 3,140 lot numbers of concretions have been raised as of autumn 2015. With a planned full recovery, and considering that approximately 60% of the site has been excavated so far, over 5,000 lots containing concretions could eventually be recovered. A small team of conservators and the substantial amount of conservation remaining necessitates a strategy for how to proceed through the collection. Priority is based on what concretions are known to contain, taking into account urgent treatment needs and feedback from other project staff.*

Introduction

Full excavation of *QAR*, overseen by the North Carolina Underwater Archaeology Branch (UAB) within the North Carolina Department of Natural and Cultural Resources (NCR), began in 2006 and has continued, funding-dependent and with only sporadic interruptions in overall progress, beginning at the southern end of the site (Wilde-Ramsing and Ewen 2012:115). As of the Fall Field Expedition in 2015, progress has reached just forward of what is estimated to be midships. Over 10,000 lot numbers, or *QAR* numbers, have been raised to date, accounting for more than 400,000 individual artifacts and artifact fragments. Many different material types are represented, such as ceramics, glass, organics, and metals, which in turn make up a variety of artifact categories, such as galley wares, storage, navigational and medical instruments, personal arms and armament, ammunition, hand tools, trade goods, and even the ship's hull and rigging. Objects may be easily identified, such as cannon, or may necessitate further exploration using microscopy, like the traces of gold dust found in dredge spoil (Price 2016).

The most abundant *QAR* artifact material is concretion, which develops as a result of iron corrosion processes and colonization by marine life. While it may be safe to assume that each individual concretion may contain a metallic iron artifact or remnants thereof, the presence or material identification of other possible objects contained therein cannot be ascertained until x-radiography is performed. Even then, the presence of certain materials like glass, ceramics, and organics cannot always be determined in x-ray (Cronyn 1990:190). Upon recovery, artifacts are transported from the *QAR* site in Beaufort, NC to the NCR/*QAR* Conservation Laboratory (*QAR* Lab), located at East Carolina University in Greenville, NC. There they undergo documentation, treatment, research and, ultimately, preparation for transfer to the North Carolina Maritime Museum in Beaufort (NCMM), the official repository for the *QAR* collection.

A total of 3,140 *QAR* numbers bearing concretions have been recovered to date. As artifacts are located in situ, they receive a unique number, which not only corresponds to the artifacts' archaeological data but is also used to track an artifact's conservation record. A *QAR* number may consist of a single object or multiple fragments or components. As a concretion is dismantled, artifacts from the concretion receive a sub-designation of the main *QAR* number. For example for concretion QAR3111.000, copper alloy wire was assigned QAR3111.001, lead shot was assigned QAR3111.002, round cannon shot was assigned QAR3111.003, and so forth, in the order by which it was removed from concretion. The total of actual concretions recovered so far is 6,297, but for the purposes of this paper, only counts in relation to the *QAR* number are discussed, since projects are prioritized solely by that identifying number. Additionally, cannon were purposefully excluded from this study but were undertaken later by colleague Erik Farrell in a similar exercise (Farrell 2016).

Beginning in May 2013, a formalized methodological approach was developed so that there would be a categorical system by which the concretions are prioritized. Previously, informal discussions and x-ray viewings with NCMM and UAB helped determine high-priority objects for display or research purposes, namely unique artifacts or those which might yield makers' marks, essentially splitting the concretions into two categories: high or low priority. Previous priorities were also set for the purposes of deciding which concretions to x-ray based on the outer appearance of an object, which resulted in many concretions still awaiting radiography. In order to formulate an organized method of how to progress the concretions from *QAR*, it was decided to x-ray the remainder of the collection so that every concretion is not only imaged but also immediately inventoried and prioritized, allowing for a more comprehensive artifact database. Until 2013, 1,700 concretions had been x-rayed, while at present over 2,700 now have x-ray images, leaving only the largest, most cumbersome objects as unknowns. Wednesdays were designated as x-ray days, where a subset was set aside to x-ray in the morning, leaving the afternoon to inventory films and enter data into the database. While already in practice well before 2013, inventorying of films sometimes did not take place as soon as films were developed. Currently, each x-ray film is immediately inventoried, its contents counted and documented, allowing conservators to easily ascertain from the artifact records how to process any given concretion. The immediate documentation of a concretion's contents also aides in ensuring the artifact database remains as current as possible and allows for easier sharing of that information.

Methodology

Concretions are assigned a priority based on what they are known to contain, as visible in x-ray or physical examination, in order to have an easily quantifiable and searchable means for conservators to identify a potential project. Ongoing discussions between the three key parties within the *QAR* Project (QAR Lab, UAB, and NCMM) contribute to determining which types of objects should be deemed more significant, based on the needs and observations of the different participants.

From August 2013 until February 2014, the x-rays of 2,364 *QAR* numbers were studied and an assessment system was adopted from one to five, one being high priority and five being low. Values were initially assigned based on the uniqueness of an artifact, such as a pair of cufflinks or various hand tools. In reviewing all of the x-rays, it became apparent that many concretions contain certain artifacts, such as nails, lead shot and six-pound cannon shot in abundance. Other concretions hold glass beads, tools, buckles, and parts of the ship's rigging. It was decided that evaluation should additionally take into account any urgent conservation needs, such as the removal of visible glass, ceramics, or any fragile organic materials, since all *QAR* concretions are stored in a 2.5% sodium carbonate in tap water solution. Concern arose that delicate objects would continue to degrade in an alkaline environment (Cronyn 1990:134).

Project archaeologists and researchers were then consulted on suggestions for what would constitute a higher rating in terms of archaeological significance and research. Likewise, there was a need to establish what exactly NCMM considers as high-priority objects, for the purposes of public interest and the *QAR* exhibition. Input from these three main entities (fellow conservators, archaeologists, and collections managers) was taken into consideration, and values were adjusted accordingly.

The categories are roughly defined as follows. For artifacts of high consequence, a designation of Priority 1 (P1) is given. This category encompasses artifacts termed unique, diagnostic, or particularly fragile. For example, musket partials (Figure 1) and padlocks (Figure 2) were considered unique, while a chain plate assembly was deemed archaeologically diagnostic in terms of ship construction, and exposed glass or ceramic were regarded as fragile. P1 is also used as the designation for objects that NCMM has expressly stated an interest in for imminent display. With the 300th anniversary of the loss of the vessel rapidly approaching in 2018, an expanded NCMM permanent exhibit is planned. The numerical ratings have been useful in tracking that artifact list in particular.

The Priority 2 (P2) category may consist of artifacts that occur in multiples but are still noteworthy, such as survey chain, grenades, gun barrel fragments, and

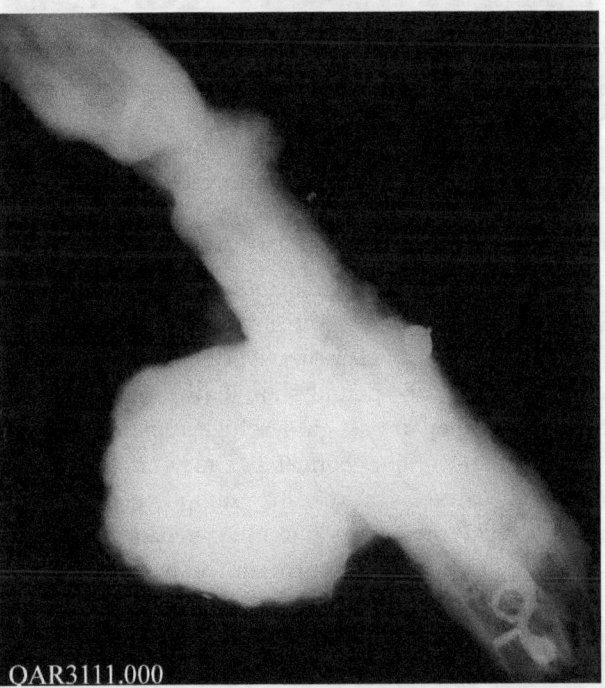

Figure 1. X-ray of QAR3111.000 concretion containing musket partial with copper alloy side plate and corroded barrel, lead shot, and cannon shot. (Photo by Wendy Welsh; Courtesy of NC Dept. of Natural and Cultural Resources, Raleigh, NC.)

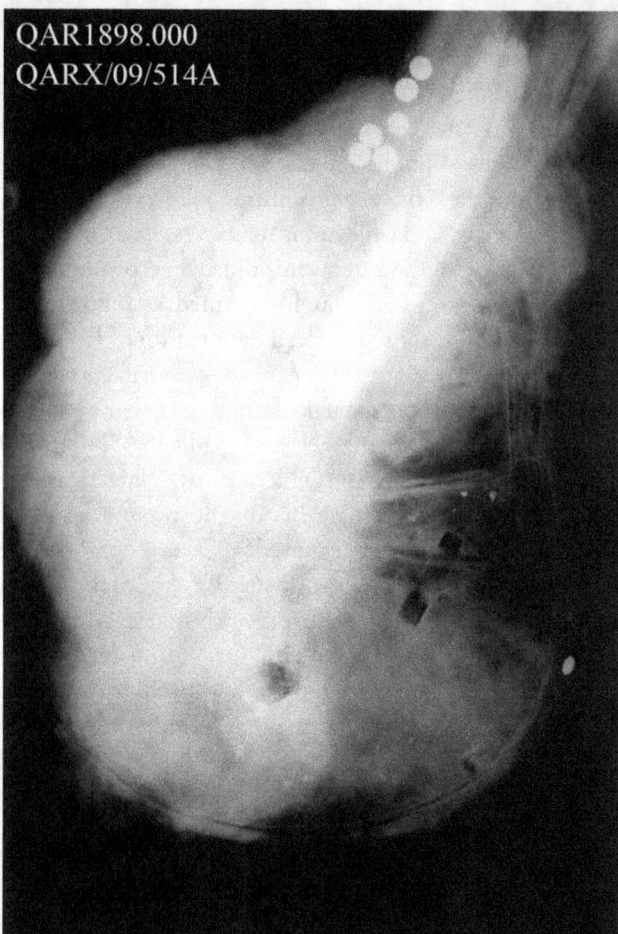

Figure 2. X-ray of QAR1898.000 concretion containing padlock, lead shot, and fastener (Photo by author; Courtesy of NC Dept. of Natural and Cultural Resources, Raleigh, NC).

smaller cannon shot. Attempts to cast the survey chain have been unsuccessful; thus more research into various epoxies is needed before an example of the chain can be safely de-concreted. While intact personal arms are generally designated P1, incomplete gun barrels have been relegated to the P2 category, due to a lack of other associated firearm elements. Very few small cannon shot, such as one-pound shot, have been conserved. Therefore, they are assigned a higher numerical value than the larger shot. Former P1s may be downgraded into this category as well; for example, grenades were assigned P1 previously, but nine grenades have now progressed through treatment and several are currently scheduled for pending transfer. Consequently, they are not presently in high demand from NCMM.

Designated as Priority 3 (P3) are the objects of moderate interest such as rigging hooks, glass beads, and unidentified objects. Four rigging hooks have already been conserved or are presently undergoing treatment, and there is hope that others will be found with associated intact rope and thimbles. Hundreds of glass bead fragments and 38 intact beads have been recovered from dredge spoil, although only seven have been successfully removed from concretion thus far. It is hoped that concretions will yield additional types and more intact examples, thanks to the protective encrustation. Also, there are always objects that elude identification upon initial study of x-rays. These unknowns are denoted as P3 in order to get a second opinion, or for an additional x-ray.

Ship's fasteners, other than nails, as well as iron rigging rings and casting sprues, are generally assigned to the Priority 4 (P4) category. The casting sprues are remnants of the cannon shot manufacturing process, which, due to extreme high temperatures necessary for casting iron, would not in all likelihood have taken place on the ship. The explanation for the sprues' presence on board remains elusive; hence, a discernible cluster may achieve a higher rating on the hope that it might provide some additional clue to their purpose, perhaps langrage or scrap metal for later reuse (Figure 3). Otherwise, several have been transferred to NCMM already and are not generally desirable for display.

The final Priority 5 (P5) category contains artifacts in abundance, such as nails, lead shot, cannon shot, and even concretions that contain no discernible objects. Lead shot is certainly the most prolific artifact type found on QAR, with over 250,000 individual examples in total. Augmenting this particular subset is not urgent (Figure 4). Though plentiful, concretions containing cast iron cannon shot provide excellent training for new graduate students and may be set aside for that purpose. Otherwise, further work on P5-designated objects will be reserved for later years, when other higher priorities have been addressed.

In cases where a single concretion contains an array of objects that would individually fall into varying categories, the concretion as a whole is granted the priority of the highest-ranking artifact. Once that particular artifact is removed, the altered concretion may be reassessed for a new priority, if remaining objects fall into a lower category.

Results

The total of numbered lots representing concretions in the *QAR* collection with an active priority rating is 2,644. This figure excludes previously prioritized concretions but following complete breakdown are now extant only in the form of concretion debitage

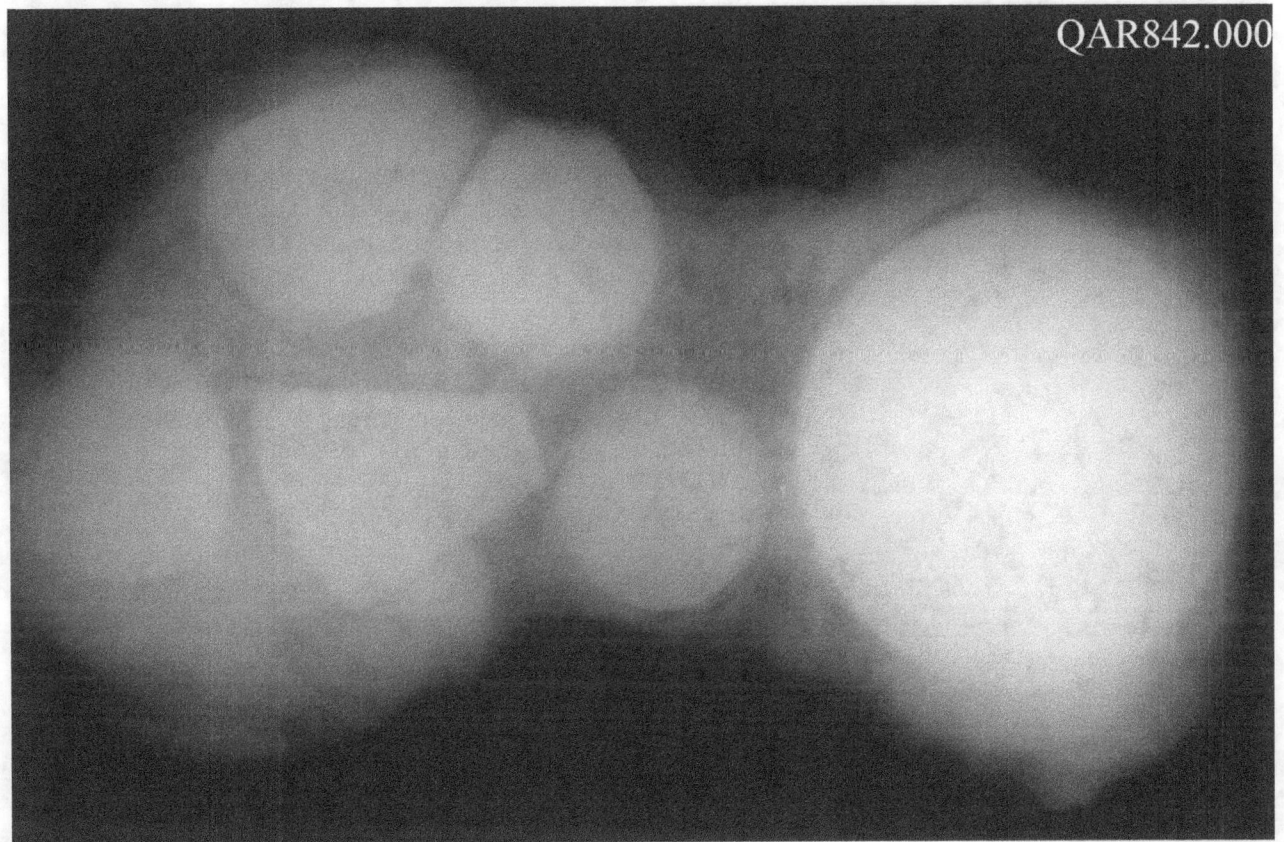

Figure 3. X-ray of QAR842.000 concretion containing cast iron casting sprues and cannon shot (Photo by Wendy Welsh; Courtesy of NC Dept. of Natural and Cultural Resources, Raleigh, NC.)

(Krop and Nordgren 2004). The counts for each of the five priority categories are as follows: (P1) 145 *QAR* numbers; (P2) 123; (P3) 172; (P4) 268; (P5) 1,936. The vast majority of concretions fall into the P5 category, due to the presence of certain artifacts of which there are many examples or because they are not considered particularly high-risk from a conservation standpoint. It is interesting as well that concretions considered as P1 objects are usually very intricate and require a more experienced eye for decision-making and more time to complete, such as a padlock. Concretions designated as P5 tend to be simpler and could be assigned to a graduate assistant as a beginning conservation project, such as cannon shot. Of course, it is most likely that the objects in high demand from NCMM's point of view will take longer not only to extract from concretion but also to treat once freed. This is true in the case of unique composites, such as a musket partial containing iron, copper alloy, and wooden elements.

To conserve more artifacts in coming years, it is hoped that staffing levels will increase, which of course is funding-dependent and not guaranteed. If current staffing is maintained in perpetuity, it is calculated that based on progress to date, *QAR* conservation will require another 50 years (Watkins-Kenney 2010). Although daunting, this time projection falls in a similar range to other excavations producing an abundance of material. One potential outcome of prioritizing the concretions may be an improved time scale for completing conservation, if certain components can be successfully managed and balanced simultaneously.

Discussion

One issue currently faced with examining x-rays is accessibility. At present, x-ray access is limited to physical inspection of the films on site at the *QAR* Lab. Digitization of the x-ray images will enhance the conservation staff's ability to consult with fellow team-members and specialists from a distance about object identification prior to deconcretion. This in turn may benefit conservators in knowing what other associated material to anticipate during de-concretion that might not otherwise be evident in x-ray, such as related organic matter or even trace residues. Digitization of the more than 3,000 x-rays currently housed at the *QAR* Lab is

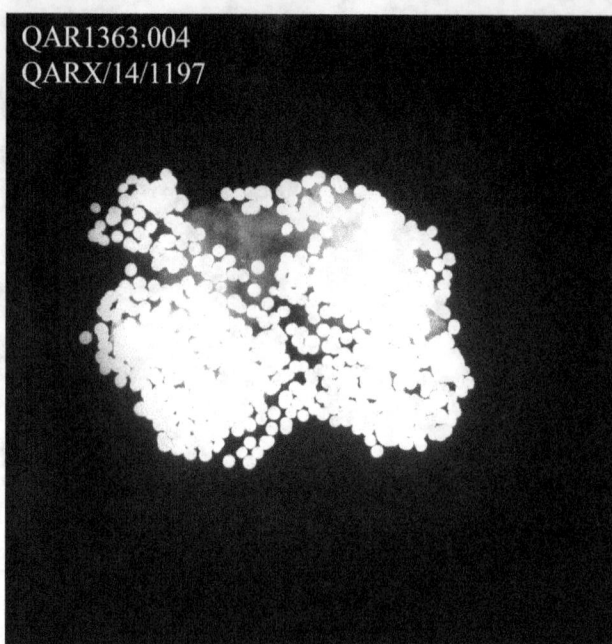

Figure 4. X-ray of QAR1363.004 concretion containing lead shot and corroded fastener (Photo by Bryan Rose; Courtesy of NC Dept. of Natural and Cultural Resources, Raleigh, NC.)

underway, not only to improve accessibility but also to ensure the longevity of those somewhat fragile primary records (Cronyn 1990:63).

As concretions are addressed and dismantled, priorities may shift and are easily adjusted. For example, if exposed glass has been removed from a concretion and there is nothing else of immediate concern in it, it may be downgraded to a lower category. Conversely, if NCMM requires a specific artifact for a special exhibit, priority can be upgraded. If project archaeologists have a specific research question in mind about a certain type of artifact, priority may just as well be reconsidered. As excavation continues, additional concretions will undoubtedly be recovered, and an established system will ensure the fluidity of incorporating new material into the lab without too much disruption in the overall concretion breakdown plan. Once a concretion is fully dismantled and all artifacts are extracted, leaving only debitage, that information is noted in the artifact's database record so that the concretion no longer appears in a query for potential projects, eliminating it from the priority system altogether. From the outset, a flexible system was deemed the most important function of any evaluation method.

As the remaining backlog of concretions and newly-recovered finds are x-rayed, annual x-ray viewing days with archaeologists and NCMM staff are scheduled at the QAR Lab in order to keep all interested parties abreast of what is identified. Feedback from those discussions is processed and considered when assessing future projects. Shifts in display needs, as well as the ever-expanding body of research ensure that priorities are evolving. Now that this system is fully integrated, it will remain easily adaptable. Since multiple entities are working together to bring such a historically prominent shipwreck into the public eye, the key to the success of QAR as a whole is communication. All efforts are made to ensure that between excavation, conservation, and exhibition, various needs are addressed and individual goals are met. Input from different points of view is strongly encouraged.

Acknowledgments

Support and feedback for the development of this project was provided by the many individuals associated with QAR: fellow conservators and staff at the QAR Lab, the underwater archaeology team at UAB, and the collections staff at NCMM. Input from outside researchers and former staff has also been most enlightening and has helped expand the priority system to accommodate a number of varied and unique research questions.

References

Cronyn, J.M.
1990 *The Elements of Archaeological Conservation.* Routledge, New York.

Farrell, Erik R.
2016 Establishing an Integrated Conservation Priority for Artillery from Site 31CR314, *Queen Anne's Revenge* (1718). *ACUA Proceedings 2016* (this volume).

Krop, David and Eric A. Nordgren
2004 Report on Examination of *QAR* Concretion Debitage. Manuscript, North Carolina Department of Natural and Cultural Resources, Raleigh, NC.

Price, Franklin H.
2016 More than Meets the Eye: A Preliminary Report on Artifacts from the Sediment of Site 31CR314, *Queen Anne's Revenge*, an Eighteenth-century Shipwreck off Beaufort Inlet, North Carolina. *Southeastern Archaeology* 35(2)=155-169.

Watkins-Kenney, Sarah C.
2010 Conservation Provision for Beaufort Inlet Shipwreck (31CR314), *Queen Anne's Revenge* Shipwreck Project: 1996-2009. Manuscript, North Carolina Department of Natural and Cultural Resources, Raleigh, NC.

Wilde-Ramsing, Mark U. and Charles R. Ewen
2012 Beyond Reasonable Doubt: A Case for *Queen Anne's Revenge. Historical Archaeology* 46(2):110-133.

Kimberly P. Kenyon
North Carolina Department of Natural
    and Cultural Resources
Queen Anne's Revenge Conservation Lab
East Carolina University
1157 VOA Site C Road
Greenville, NC 27834-2018

Legacies of an Old Design: Reconstructing *Rapid*'s Lines Using 3D Modelling Software

Ivor Mollema and Jennifer F. McKinnon

Introduction

The early 19th century American China trader *Rapid* was excavated from 1978-1982 by the Western Australia Museum (WAM) and was a formative maritime archaeological project in the Australian development of the discipline (Henderson 1978, 1979, 1981a, 1981b, 1983a, 1983b, 2007). Since then, archaeologists have continued to develop and experiment with new technologies and their applications on this shipwreck. More recently, the Shipwrecks of the Roaring Forties Project was conceived to evaluate new ways of investigating the history of Europeans in the Indian Ocean off Western Australia by revisiting and applying new technologies to several of the foundational maritime archaeology projects conducted on Australia's early shipwrecks. The wreck and legacy data of *Rapid* were chosen for the application of digital modeling software in an effort to re-evaluate the previous reconstruction efforts generated nearly 40 years ago. This paper outlines the use of Rhinoceros 3D modelling software to generate a 3-dimensional model (3D) of the China trader.

Rapid's History

Shipwright and sailing captain Nathaniel Thomas constructed *Rapid* in 1807 at a shipyard in Braintree, MA (Henderson 1981:126). The ship was registered on 23 December 1807 and owned by Andrew Ritchie of Boston at the time of registration. However, *Rapid* did not sail until August 1809 due to US President Thomas Jefferson's signing the Embargo Act only one day after *Rapid* was registered. *Rapid* was owned by Paschal Pope, William Boardman, Jonathan Amory, Ebenezer Dorr, Jonathon Dorr, and Joseph Bray when it made its first voyage to China in 1809. The success of the voyage allowed for the planning of a second voyage in 1810. Henry Dorr captained *Rapid* on both of its China voyages. American trade with China necessitated the outbound transportation of large amounts of valuable Spanish dollars, since Chinese merchants accepted little else in return for their goods. As a result, *Rapid* carried 280,000 Spanish silver dollars as its cargo. The Boston Marine Insurance Company insured the vessel and its cargo (Henderson 1981:130).

Rapid departed Boston for Canton, China on 28 September 1810 (Henderson 2007:101). It rounded the Cape of Good Hope and crossed the Indian Ocean in good time. Dorr plotted *Rapid*'s course to intersect with the North West Cape in Australia. Once there, Dorr planned to check his longitude and sail to Canton. On 7 January 1811, the 98th day of the voyage, *Rapid* struck a reef near Point Cloates. A storm struck the next day and threatened to break the ship apart. Dorr ordered the crew to abandon the ship, but before leaving, the crew burned the vessel to avoid detection and possible looting by passing ships (Henderson 1981:127).

After abandoning ship, the crew sailed for Batavia in three small boats (Henderson 2007:101). Dorr sailed in a leaky jolly boat and reached Batavia 37 days later (Henderson 2007:103). He captained *General Greene* to Philadelphia on a return voyage and arrived on 27 July 1811. Once there, Dorr arranged for the salvage vessel *Meridian* to recover the 260,000 coins left on board. It arrived in April 1812 after picking up divers in an Asian port, most probably Batavia. By this point, it is likely that illegal salvage had already occurred, as word of the silver laden shipwreck spread through Batavia. Dorr salvaged just over $90,000 of *Rapid*'s remains. Around $20,000 of silver remained in the shipwreck as deteriorating relations between the United Kingdom and the United States forced the discontinuation of the salvage mission. Dutch Java was under British control since August 1811, and war was declared by the United States on the United Kingdom in June 1812. *Meridian* risked capture by British naval vessels or privateers if it remained any longer.

Previous Work

Rapid was located again in 1978 by spearfishers Glynn Dromey, Larry Paterson, Frank Paxman, and Barry Paxman (Nash 2007:64). The shipwreck is located on a reef near Point Cloates on the central coast of Western Australia (Henderson 2007:100). Discovery and recovery of copper bolts, glass fragments, ceramic sherds, and 600 silver coins confirmed the existence of a potentially valuable shipwreck (Nash 2007:64). In accordance with the 1976 *Historic Shipwrecks Act*, the collection was turned over to WAM for treatment and conservation. Due to the monetary value of the artifacts, the finders received $30,000 as a reward (Nash 2007:65).

An initial inspection of the shipwreck site by WAM occurred in November 1978 (Nash 2007:65). It revealed a shipwreck in 6 m of water buried in sand in a channel on the edge of the reef. Extending over 36 m was a large central ballast mound. Also on site were three anchors, small cannons, and several copper artifacts amongst the ballast. Most of the silver coins and copper bolt remains were deposited in an area of the stern measuring 4 m by 6 m. The quality and quantity of valuable artifacts resulted in *Rapid's* registration as a protected historic shipwreck on 14 December 1978.

The WAM team completed three excavation seasons on *Rapid* between 1978 and 1982 (Nash 2007:65). A reference grid of 16 m by 48 m was created and 2 m sections were uncovered using an airlift. A total of over 50 tons of ballast stones was removed from the site. The third season (Jan – Feb 1982) focused on the ship's structure. Trenches uncovered the remaining hull and keel timbers and a cross section of the hull was completed (Nash 2007:72). While the stern structure was disintegrated beyond recognition, the keel and port hull structure survived in good condition (Henderson [1980s]:18). Over 70 timbers survived *in situ* attached to the keel. A total of 32 ship timbers were recovered, and profile drawings were made of them (Western Australian Museum 2015). Later, these data were used to create a lines plan based on the archaeological and historical data available (Figure 1).

Historical data focused on archival work in Boston. After archaeological data pointed to Boston as *Rapid's* homeport, registration papers revealed the official dimensions of *Rapid* upon construction and subsequent voyages to China. On 14 September 1810, *Rapid* was listed as a ship of two decks and three masts. Its length was 104 ft., beam was 28 ft. 4 in., and its depth was 14 ft. 2 in. Total displacement was stated as 366 84/95 tons (U.S. National Archives 1810:1). It was thought that the use of a fraction of 95 indicated the following equation was used historically to calculate depth at 14.1666 (Hutchins 1941:217):

$$\text{Tonnage} = \frac{(\text{length} - 3/5 \text{ beam}) \times \text{beam} \times \text{depth of hold}}{95}$$

However further research revealed it was conventional to simply set the depth at half the beam. As a result, it is impossible to establish an accurate depth for *Rapid*.

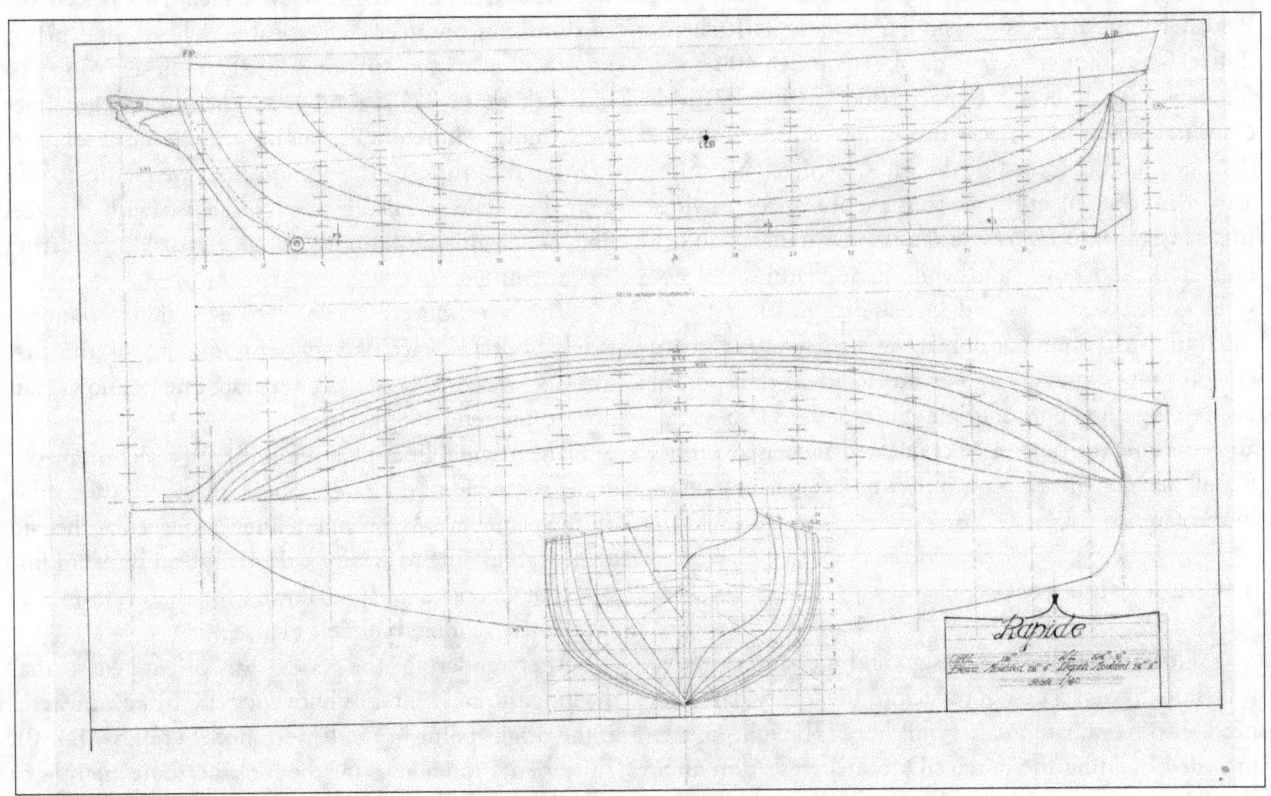

FIGURE 1. Completed 1980s lines plan. Courtesy of the Western Australia Maritime Museum.

Using the historical information above, a reconstructed lines plan was developed by WAM researchers; however, the steep angle of the stem; lack of tumblehome; and the sharp bow established on the lines plan resemble a Baltimore Clipper design more than an American China trader.

Hull design was the most important element of a Baltimore Clipper. A long and narrow hull yielded a greater length:beam ratio than other ships of similar length. Waterlines narrowed towards the bow to create a sharp bow, which cut through water easily. Draft along the keel line was twice that of the bow (Davis 1984:40). While other ships rode over waves, or pushed them aside, these design factors allowed Baltimore Clippers to cut through waves, giving them a decided advantage in speed.

Shipwrights designed Baltimore Clippers to provide stability along with increased speed. A wide deck quickly narrowed to the keel, giving the hull a bell-like, or heart shape. The center of buoyancy was thus kept high, while the center of gravity remained along a vertical center line. These two forces worked to naturally right the vessel when it heeled (Chapelle 1967:212). While this narrow hull provided clear advantages, it did not allow for large cargo capacity, limiting the Baltimore Clipper's role as a merchant vessel.

American China traders, while smaller than their British counterparts, were similar in design (Richards 2003:15). Although *Rapid* displaced under 400 tons, it likely shared several characteristics with its British cousins. While the American shipbuilding industry did keep a clear record of the lines of merchant ships, artwork and a look at British construction styles provides some insight into *Rapid*'s design. China traders had full hulls and bluff bows, and while these features did not yield great speed, they did increase cargo capacity. As the round trip often consumed more than a year, it was critical that as much cargo as possible was transported back to the ship's port of origin. Such designs also served an economic purpose, as they yielded increased profits for merchants and ship owners, who often had a stake in the cargo.

The 3D Design Process

With discrepancies in design and measurements, it was thought that a new approach to the legacy data was needed to reevaluate *Rapid*'s hull lines. The full process included building the initial 3D model recreation after the 2D lines plan which was drawn after the excavations.

From here the model will be analyzed for hydrodynamic statistics and the computed values of those from the drawn lines plan will be compared with the digital values and historical evidence. Following comparison, the 3D model will be adjusted to fit a design more suited to its function as an American China trader. Finally, the ultimate model will be used as a base for recreating the construction of *Rapid* in 3D. This paper focuses on the initial creation of a 3D model.

The program used for the 3D reconstruction was Rhinoceros 5, a computer design software based on the NURBS mathematical model. This program provides a 3D platform along with the Orca Plugin, which is designed to assist marine architects in 3D design projects of ships and other structures. In this case, its most useful feature is a hydrostatics calculator that computes dimensions, displacement, and coefficients. This tool proved useful in analyzing the 3D reconstruction of *Rapid* and allowing for adjustments to the initial model.

A number of steps were involved when converting a 2D representation to a 3D model. A base layer was created by placing the reconstructed lines plan as a background image in each viewing panel. The image was set to a 1:1 scale using the measuring tool and aligning it with key features, especially the length and breadth of the ship. The section lines on the body plan were traced in the 'Right' view panel. This placed the section lines on an even vertical and horizontal plane, but the lines were still only a 2D representation. To move them to a 3D representation, the section lines were moved horizontally along the traced keel line, stem, and sternpost. The section lines were adjusted on a smaller scale to ensure they connected with the keel line. When this was confirmed, an initial 3D rendering was attempted.

This produced two issues that required troublesooting. Part of the stem forward of the first section needed to be set as a separate line to allow a fair flow to the rendered model.

The original lines plan did not have a section placed at the stern end of the rabbit line. However, it does show on the plan view. As a result, a line was placed at the end of the rabbet line to mirror this final stern transom line as much as possible. This allowed for the creation of a completely rendered model (Figure 2).

After rendering, the model was orientated so that the longitudinal center of buoyancy (LCB) point was set at the origin point in the Rhino model (x=0, y=0, z=0). This orientation allows for the most accurate analysis of a model. The subsequent analysis yielded the following

FIGURE 2. Completed 3D model.

results: A length of 111 ft., a beam of 31 ft. 3 in., and depth of 23 ft. 2 in. Displacement was calculated at 476.05 long tons. These values differ markedly from those claimed in the historical documents.

Evaluation of 3D Model

The discrepancies between these values may reveal issues with the initial lines plan. Most notably, they call into question the accuracy of the depth used in the initial lines plan. As mentioned by Hutchins in the tonnage equation above, the lack of this measurement resulted in a hypothetical lines plan based on the notion that the depth simply equaled half the beam. While this method may provide for a historically accurate reconstruction, the convenience of simply halving the beam does not yield a model that is also scientifically accurate. As a result, some adjustments still need to be made.

This project is still underway and the model is far from complete. The lines are not fair, especially at the sheer waterline where the top of the section lines do not allow for a smooth line. This is most prevalent at the first, second, and third waterline. More work and accurate adjustments of the model will result in a fair model that can form the basis of future work in which *Rapid*'s final dimensions and shape may be revealed.

Future Work

Creating a basic 3D model paves the way for several opportunities of future research. From a basic lines model, the progression to a full 3D model of the ship's interior and structure is entirely possible. Timber measurements, feature drawings, and profile measurements all provide the archaeological data required for further digital reconstruction. Archival research also reveals comparative options of similar ship plans or contemporary artwork that would assist in reconstruction efforts. Promising datasets may be at the Peabody Essex Museum, which focuses on the China trade and the Massachusetts-built ships involved in the trade. International comparisons to similar ships could also yield significant results including the smaller East Indiamen of contemporary European nations. More work is planned for refining the 3D model and testing hypotheses related to dimensions and shape along with historical research into the design of American China traders.

Acknowledgements

This project was partially funded under and Australian Research Council Linkage Project 130100137 "Shipwrecks of the Roaring Forties: A Maritime Archaeological Reassessment of Some of Australia's Earliest Shipwrecks" Funding was provided by the grant to assist Ivor in an internship at the Western Australia Museum. Special thanks to staff at the Museum for assisting Ivor in data collection and research development. Without the pioneers of

Australia's early maritime archeology including Graeme Henderson, Jeremy Green and Myra Stanbury, work like this by later archaeologists could not continue into the digital age – so a special debt is due to those forerunners.this by later archaeologists could not continue into the digital age, so a special debt is due to those forerunners.

References

CHAPELLE, HOWARD
1967   *The Search for Speed Under Sail 1700-1855*. Bonanza Books, New York, NY.

DAVIS, CHARLES G.
1984   *American Sailing Ships: Their Plans and History*. Dover Publications, New York NY.

1993   Management Plan for the Historic Shipwreck Rapid 1807-1811. Western Australian Maritime Museum, Fremantle, Western Australia.

HENDERSON, GRAEME
1978   A Newly Discovered Shipwreck in Western Australia. *The Great Circle* 1(1):77-78.

1979   *Report on the first season's excavations of an unidentified wreck at Point Cloates, WA*, Report, Department of Maritime Archaeology, Western Australian Maritime Museum, No.14.

1980s   *Rapid Excavation Report*. Western Australian Maritime Museum.

1981a   The Identification of the Shipwreck at Point Cloates, Western Australia. *Australian Institute for Maritime Archaeology Bulletin* 5:39–41.

1981b   The American China Trader Rapid (1811): An Early Western Australian Shipwreck Site Identified. *The Great Circle* 3(2):125-132.

1983a   Update: The Identification of a China Trader. *Archaeology* 36(3):69.

1983b   The *Rapid* Excavation at Point Cloates in 1982. In W. Jeffery and J. Amess (Eds.), *Proceedings of the Second Southern Hemisphere Conference on Maritime Archaeology*:243-247, South Australian Dept. Environment and Planning and Commonwealth Dept. of Home Affairs and Environment, Adelaide.

2007   *Unfinished Voyages Western Australian Shipwrecks 1622-1850*. University of Western Australia Press, Crawley, W.A.

HUTCHINS, JOHN
1941   *The American Maritime Industries and Public Policy: 1789-1914*. Harvard University Press, Cambridge, MA.

NASH, MICHAEL (EDITOR)
2007   *Shipwreck Archaeology in Australia*. UWA Publishing, Crawley, W.A., 2007.

RICHARDS, RHYS
2003   Re-Viewing Early American China Trade 1784-1833. *Maritime Museum of San Diego*: 14-19.

WESTERN AUSTRALIAN MUSEUM
2015   RP4140-Ship's Timber. Western Australian Museum. Government of Western Australia, <http://museum.wa.gov.au/maritime-archaeology-db/artefacts/rp4140-ships-timber>.

U.S. NATIONAL ARCHIVES
1810   Boston Customhouse Register, Charlestown, 23 December 1807, ship *Rapid*, No.246.

Ivor Mollema
East Carolina University
8787 Southside Blvd., Unit 216
Jacksonville, FL 32256
ivormollema@gmail.com

Jennifer McKinnon
East Carolina University
302 E. 9th Street
Greenville, NC 27858
mckinnonje@ecu.edu

Examining Golden Age Pirates as a Distinct Culture Through Artifact Patterning

Courtney E. Page

Piracy is an illegal act that does not survive well in the archaeological record, making it difficult to study pirates as a distinct culture. There is, however, potential to use artifact patterning to illuminate behavioral differences between pirates and other sailors during the Golden Age (ca. 1680-1730). Artifact frequencies of two early-18th-century British pirate wrecks, Queen Anne's Revenge *and* Whydah *were compared to frequencies aboard the Royal Navy's HMS* Invincible *and slaver* Henrietta Marie. *There is not currently enough data to predict a pattern for identifying pirates archaeologically, but there are several avenues of further study for describing this sub-culture.*

Introduction

Pirates are a frequently encountered cultural group with a very defined image, but the stereotype of a pirate may not be as accurate as we are led to believe. Some historians suggest that pirates were members of a gentleman's society, where things were democratic and equal, and while by nature they clearly participated in violent and illegal acts, their day-to-day behavior did not differ greatly from other sailors, and their appearance and possessions may not have differed significantly either. At the same time, however, most of the primary sources on pirate behavior, from which these conclusions are made, are biased accounts by those who were captured by pirates or who were trying to save themselves from the noose. So what are the prospects for studying pirate behavior archaeologically?

This research suggests the possibility of using artifact patterning to study pirate behavior. Made popular by Stanley South, pattern recognition in historical archaeology can be used to illuminate specialized behaviors on sites based on the frequencies of specific functional groups of artifacts recovered from those sites. South's Carolina Artifact Pattern suggests frequencies of artifacts one would expect to find on an 18th century British colonial domestic site. Any deviations from these artifact frequencies at a site of unknown function would indicate a differing function or behavior (South 1977:90-93, 110-112).

This method assumes two things: (1) that the site represents a subset of a larger system that imposes a degree of uniformity on the behavior of the members of the subset, and (2) that as part of the larger system, members of the subset will have the same sets of beliefs, attitudes, and artifacts regardless of where they are geographically (South 1977:86-88). As pirates fit into the greater system of British maritime culture and global economy, they should exhibit uniformity in behavior that would result in regularities in the archaeological record. Similarly, because of shared behaviors and attitudes, any deviations from the frequencies of artifacts found on pirate vessels would indicate a differing function.

This artifact patterning was applied to English pirates in the Atlantic in the early 18th century. Only two positively identified English pirate wrecks with accessible inventories were available for this study: *Queen Anne's Revenge* and *Whydah*. Obviously, these two wrecks cannot represent the full range of pirate behavior. Similarly, very few comparative non-pirate examples have been fully documented. This research, therefore, is intended to erect a framework for this type of study of pirate behavior through categorizing the artifact assemblages of *Queen Anne's Revenge* and *Whydah*, and the comparative sites HMS *Invincible* and the slaver *Henrietta Marie*.

History

Queen Anne's Revenge

After its first voyage as a French privateer in 1710, *La Concorde* operated as a French slave ship for most of four years (Wilde-Ramsing 2009:109-111). In November 1717, *La Concorde* was captured by the pirate Blackbeard and his crew as it headed to Martinique to deliver slaves. Blackbeard released the French crew on the island of Bequia, increased the armament of his new prize, and renamed it *Queen Anne's Revenge* (Lusardi 2006:196). After plundering the Caribbean and blockading Charleston, SC, the large pirate fleet sailed to the poor coast of North Carolina, where *Queen Anne's Revenge* ran aground on a sandbar at Topsail Inlet, in present-day Beaufort (Lusardi 2006:197).

The wreck of *Queen Anne's Revenge* was discovered in 1996 by the maritime salvage company Intersal. The North Carolina Underwater Archaeology Branch formed a partnership with Intersal, beginning site surveying in 1997 and recovery in 2006 (Wilde-Ramsing 2006:164-166). Excavation and conservation of the site and its artifacts continue today. The identification of the wreck was considered tentative until 2012, when the preponderance of evidence overwhelmingly pointed toward the wreck being that of *Queen Anne's Revenge* (Wilde-Ramsing and Ewen 2012). As of the Fall 2013 excavations, approximately 60% of the site (6,625 square-feet) had been excavated, and 244,000 artifacts were recovered applicable to this research.

Whydah

Whydah was a London-built slaver operating between England, Africa, and Jamaica. The vessel was captured by the pirate Samuel Bellamy in the northern Bahamas in February of 1717 en route home to London. Keeping about a dozen members of the *Whydah* crew, Bellamy set the rest free in one of his other ships and sailed north with his fleet along the coast of North America, heading for present-day Maine. In late April 1717 off Cape Cod, MA, the vessel was caught in a heavy northeaster, smashing the vessel into a shoal and capsizing it. Only two men survived the wreck, and they stayed in the area for a few days, salvaging what washed ashore before being arrested for piracy. The wreck was also salvaged immediately by locals and the Massachusetts government (Hamilton 2006:131-132).

Barry Clifford's search for the wreck of *Whydah* began in 1978, and the first artifacts were discovered in 1984. The identity of the wreck was confirmed in 1985 with the discovery of the ship's bell, bearing the words "The Whydah Galley 1716." Full excavation began in 1988 and continued intermittently as funding allowed (Hamilton 2006:134-135). Approximately 7,500 square-feet were excavated, with the recovery of just under 106,700 artifacts used in this research (Hamilton 1992:108-136).

HMS *Invincible*

HMS *Invincible* was a French naval vessel, built in 1741 and captured by British Admiral Lord Anson in 1747. *Invincible* was considered an unlucky ship, almost exploding in 1752 and losing its mast and rudder in a hurricane in 1757. In 1758 as the vessel left Portsmouth for Louisburg, Nova Scotia, the anchor became stuck, and strong winds and waves caused the ship to run aground on Horse Sand Tail. It could not be freed, and salvage of the ship's guns and much of its stores occurred over subsequent weeks (Bingeman 2010:15-19).

The wreck was discovered in May 1979 by a fisherman in the Solent Straight in England. Full-scale excavation began in 1981 under the direction of Commander John Bingeman, and the same year the ship was positively identified as *Invincible* with the discovery of a tally stick bearing the name (Bingeman 2010:22-24). Excavation continued intermittently through 1991, with approximately 29,000 square feet excavated and just over 10,000 artifacts recovered that apply to this research (Bingeman 2010:44, 46; Hampshire & Wight Trust for Maritime Archaeology 2011).

Henrietta Marie

The *Henrietta Marie* first appears in the documentary record in 1697, on its first voyage from London to Africa. After arriving in Barbados, it returned to London in 1698. The Barbados shipping records state that *Henrietta Marie* was a foreign-built, London-registered vessel. It arrived in Jamaica in May of 1700 with a second shipment of slaves. On the return to England the ship ran aground on New Ground Reef in the Dry Tortugas, off the coast of Florida (Moore and Malcom 2008:21-27).

The wreck of *Henrietta Marie* was discovered by the salvage company Treasure Salvors Inc. in 1972, while searching for the Spanish treasure ship *Nuestra Señora de Atocha*. Permitted recovery began in the summer of 1973, and continued intermittently under various subcontractors through September of 1991. Excavation yielded approximately 14,000 artifacts used in this research (Moore and Malcom 2008:21-23).

Methodology

To effectively compare the activities performed on these ships, each assemblage was divided into groups based on the functional attributes of the artifacts that reflect behavior. Arms and Armament are those things related to weaponry, including ammunition, artillery, and personal arms. This group reflects the fighting function of the ship and its crew. Cargo items are storage containers, treasure, and commodities carried on the ship either to be traded or used by the crew, representing its commercial or plundering function. The Kitchen Group includes artifacts involved in food preparation and consumption. The volume of these objects found on a ship may represent its purpose as a short-term transportation vessel or a living space for extended periods.

Personal Effects are those things that would have been privately owned and used, excluding small arms. These artifacts may suggest the type of entertainment or status enjoyed by the crew or the types of personal belongings they possessed and how they may vary by the type of crew. The Tools and Instruments Group covers a wide variety of materials associated with the functioning of the ship and repair activities that occurred onboard. The proportions of these groups of artifacts may suggest the extent to which the crew had to keep their tools and ship functional. Each of these groups were further divided into several artifact classes for more detailed inter-assemblage comparison.

Artifacts related to the architecture and basic functioning of the ship, such as wood planks, sail cloth, and rigging, were excluded from this study because these things are necessary to all ships. The artifacts in each assemblage were categorized into the appropriate groups and a percentage that each group represents of the whole assemblage was calculated, as well as a frequency for classes of artifacts within each group.

Important Considerations

Each shipwreck represents a unique assemblage of artifacts resulting from many uncontrollable variables, beginning before the wrecking event and continuing through the recovery and documentation of the wreck as an archaeological site. The small sample size and large range of dates is an unavoidable problem due to the limited availability of work conducted and published on 18th-century wrecks. Ethnicity has been limited to British crews, but the dates during which these ships operated and the locations to which they sailed cannot be strictly controlled.

Several factors affecting the sites will alter the artifact types and frequencies on each shipwreck. A violent wrecking will favor the preservation of more durable artifacts, as the light ones float away or are not protected from degradation. A grounding, on the other hand, both allows time for immediate salvage, and traps smaller objects inside the vessel as the water rises around it, enhancing their preservation. Scavenging wrecks for valuable items by locals, divers, and salvaging companies in the 200-plus years since deposition also skews the artifact frequencies (Page 2014:100-101).

The aquatic environment, including water temperature, depth, and currents, will cause some artifacts, such as clothing, wooden objects, or light gold pieces to be more prevalent in conditions that favor their preservation. Hurricanes, natural seabed movements, and dredging displace artifacts. Finally, excavation techniques will dictate what artifacts are kept and the quality of the record keeping, which will significantly influence a wreck's inventory (Page 2014:101-102). All of these variables affect each wreck to varying degrees, making underwater archaeological sites unique units with the archaeological record and presenting difficulties in normalizing several sets of data. This is a problem that can only be remedied by a larger data set in the future.

Results

At this time, there is not a clear pattern differentiating pirate archaeological assemblages as unique when compared to the assemblages of ships of other functions. While the pirate vessels are more like each other than the other two vessel types, differences among the assemblages occur in small frequencies (Figure 1). There is a noticeable difference between the pirate vessels and the merchant vessel, as the pirates vessels are predominated by Arms and Armament artifacts while the merchant vessel is dominated by Cargo artifacts with very few Arms artifacts. However, it is more difficult to distinguish between the pirate vessels and the naval vessel.

A logarithmic transformation of the frequencies of each group was also performed to more clearly define the differences between the groups of artifacts, because the pirate assemblages are over 90% lead shot, and the *Henrietta Marie* over 90% glass beads. Logarithmic transformations of data sets can be used in archaeology when data that are skewed, contain outliers, or differ by orders of magnitude, result in graphic representations absent of finer details (Baxter 1994:38-41). Visually, this logarithmic transformation reinforces the fact that the pirate assemblages are more similar to each other than to the other assemblages, and provides finer detail of the differences, although minute, between the pirate and naval assemblages (Figure 2).

While an overall "pirate pattern" cannot be illuminated without more data, a look at the artifacts within the Arms and Armament, Cargo, and Tools and Instruments artifact groups points to some avenues for further research into pirate behavior.

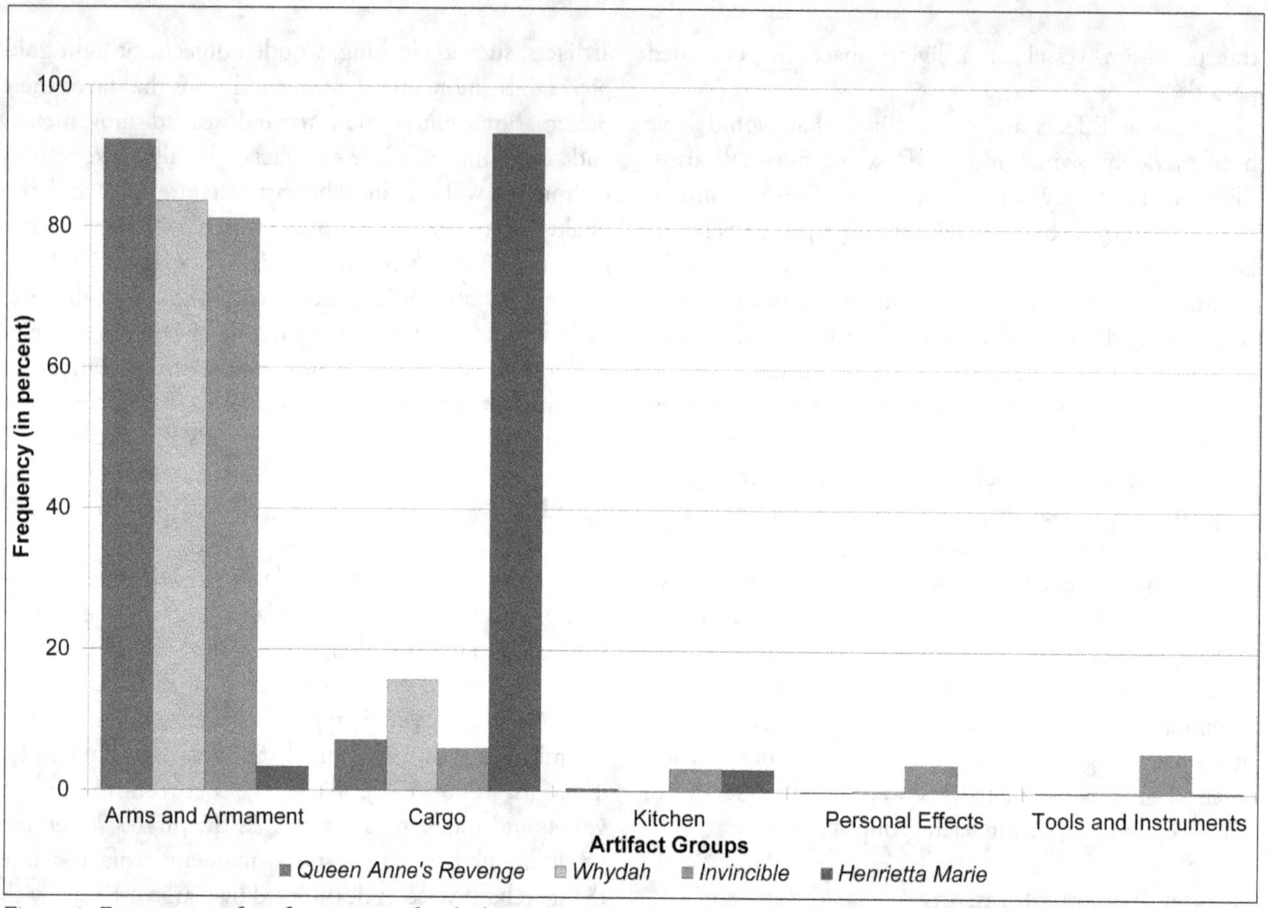

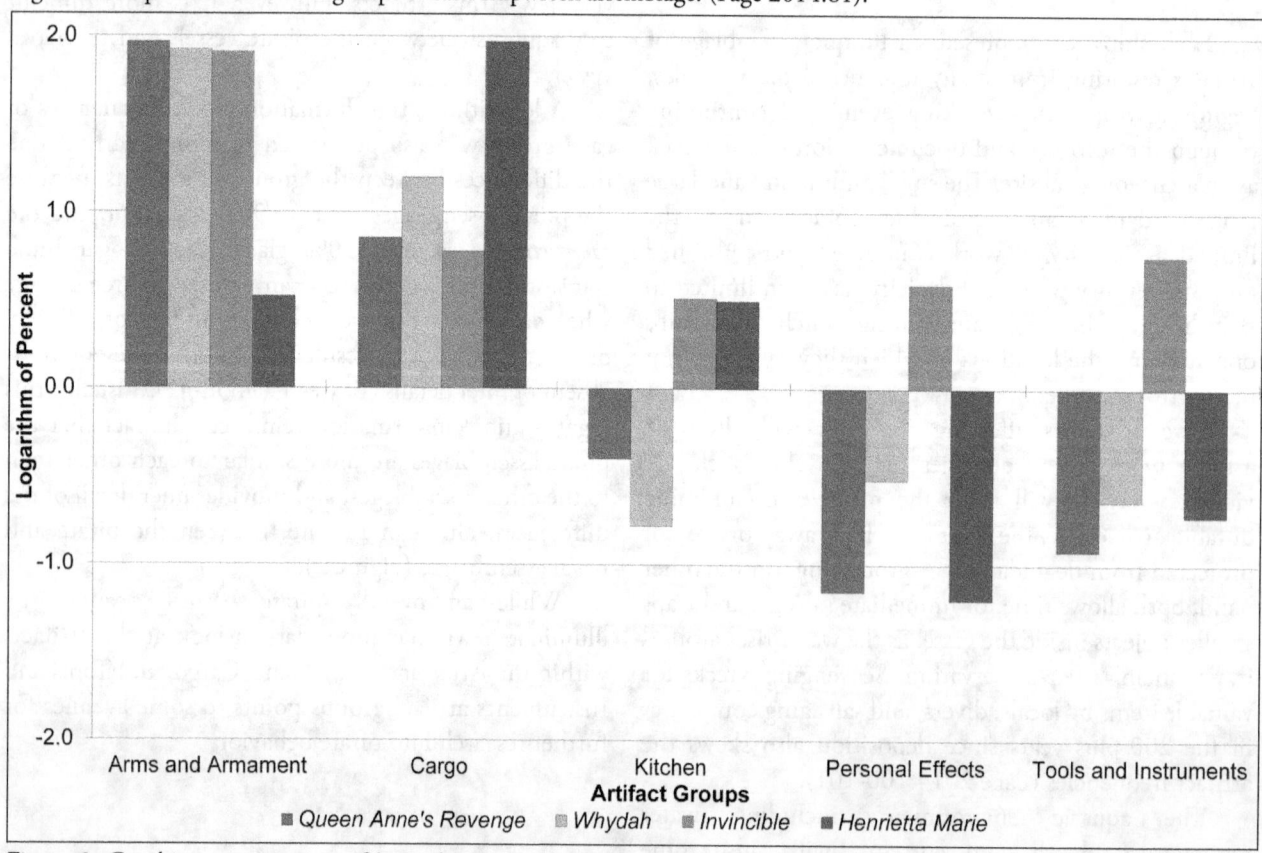

Figure 1. Frequencies of artifact groups of each shipwreck assemblage. (Page 2014:81).

Figure 2. Graphic representation of logarithmic transformation of the percent frequency for each artifact group of all four assemblages (Page 2014:84)

Arms and Armament Group

There is little differentiation among the assemblages in the classes of the Arms and Armament group, which is strongly affected by the fact that over 99% of both the *Queen Anne's Revenge* and *Whydah* Arms and Armament artifacts are lead shot. While artillery represents very little of all assemblages, the cannon may be an artifact with clues to pirate behavior. For their size, the pirate vessels seemed to have a greater quantity of cannon. *Whydah* was a 300-ton vessel carrying 18 guns, which Bellamy increased to as many as 30 guns. Similarly, *Queen Anne's Revenge* was between 200 and 300 tons, carrying between 16 and 18 cannon, which Blackbeard increased to 40 guns. By comparison, a contemporary vessel used by the Royal Navy in 1702 during the War of Spanish Succession carried 40 guns, but it was over twice *Whydah*'s size at 662 tons (Winfield 1997:31-33).

Cannon size may also provide a clue. While no cannon were recovered from *Invincible* in the present day, historical records state that the ship carried guns as small as 9-pounders and as large as 32-pounders. Cannon recovered from both pirate wrecks are much smaller; *Whydah* cannon range from 3- to 6-pounders, and *Queen Anne's Revenge* cannon range from 0.5- to 6 pounders. This, however, could also be due to rapidly changing technology.

Different countries of origin for the cannon on these wrecks may be another clue of pirate behavior. Guns of at least two nationalities (English and Swedish) have been recovered from *Queen Anne's Revenge* and *Whydah* (Page 2014:89). Pirate crews would have been acquiring cannon to heavily arm their own ships from the vessels they captured, and there was no discrimination in the nationality of captured vessels. Naval vessels, on the other hand, would have most likely had uniform collections of guns onboard and obtained more from their home port.

Several cannon recovered from both the *Whydah* and *Queen Anne's Revenge* were still loaded, some with miscellaneous materials like nails, glass, or bags of lead shot. While cannon being kept at the ready for action may not be a characteristic of pirate behavior, as it was common for warships to keep their guns loaded when away from home (Bingeman 2010:114), what they were loaded with might point to a differentiation in behavior.

Cargo Group

The classes within the Cargo group help differentiate the pirate and naval assemblages, as *Invincible* cargo is composed almost entirely of Container/Storage artifacts, while the Cargo group of both *Whydah* and *Queen Anne's Revenge* is mostly Treasure artifacts of gold and silver (Figure 3). This difference likely relates to the militaristic rather than commercial function of *Invincible*. The high frequency of *Henrietta Marie* treasure is almost entirely glass beads used in the slave trade.

There is a large disparity in the weight of the Treasure found on the two pirate wrecks; the total weight of the 14,000 pieces of gold dust from *Queen Anne's Revenge* is only about 24 grams, while it would take only 40 of the over 8300 coins recovered from *Whydah* to equal 24 grams. When compared to the volumes of the ships there is much less Treasure recovered from *Queen Anne's Revenge*, likely a factor of the wrecking process, as there was time and accessibility for salvage of valuable materials by the pirates and locals. The completed excavation of *Queen Anne's Revenge* in the future could also result in a different picture. Further analysis involving weights, including the precious metals and also glass beads and other treasure, might shed additional light on assemblage differentiation through the Treasure class.

Tools and Instruments Group

The Tools and Instruments group makes up less than 6% of all assemblages, but the frequencies of classes within this small group show an interesting trend. The Fabric Working and Miscellaneous classes represent the highest frequency of artifacts of the pirate assemblages, while these two classes represent low frequencies of the merchant and naval assemblages (Figure 4). Over 80% of those Miscellaneous artifacts found on the pirate ships are lead fishing weights. Both *Invincible* and *Henrietta Marie* assemblages are dominated by Ship Maintenance artifacts, while this class represents the minority of the *Queen Anne's Revenge* and *Whydah* Tools and Instruments group.

The fixing of clothing and acquisition of their own food might have been a behavior that both naval officers and merchantmen performed while docked. Therefore, they would only needed a small quantity of associated materials onboard, whereas the pirate crews would need these tools while at sea, as sailing into a port was not an option. Ship maintenance while at sea, on the other hand, may not have been of high priority to the pirates, as they were constantly taking new ships, while the naval and merchant crews would need to keep their ships in good functioning shape at all times.

As more data become available, these things should

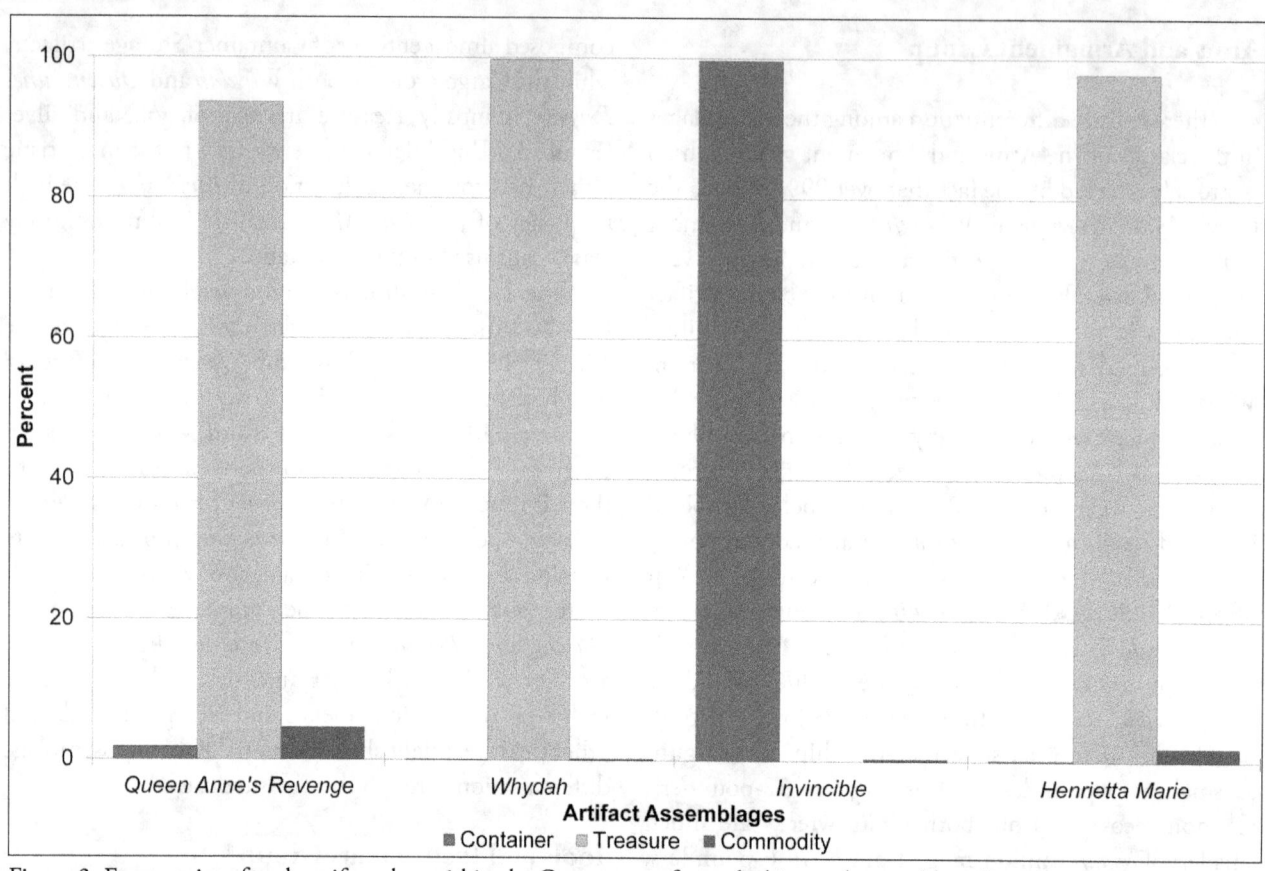

Figure 3. Frequencies of each artifact class within the Cargo group for each shipwreck assemblage (Page 2014:91).

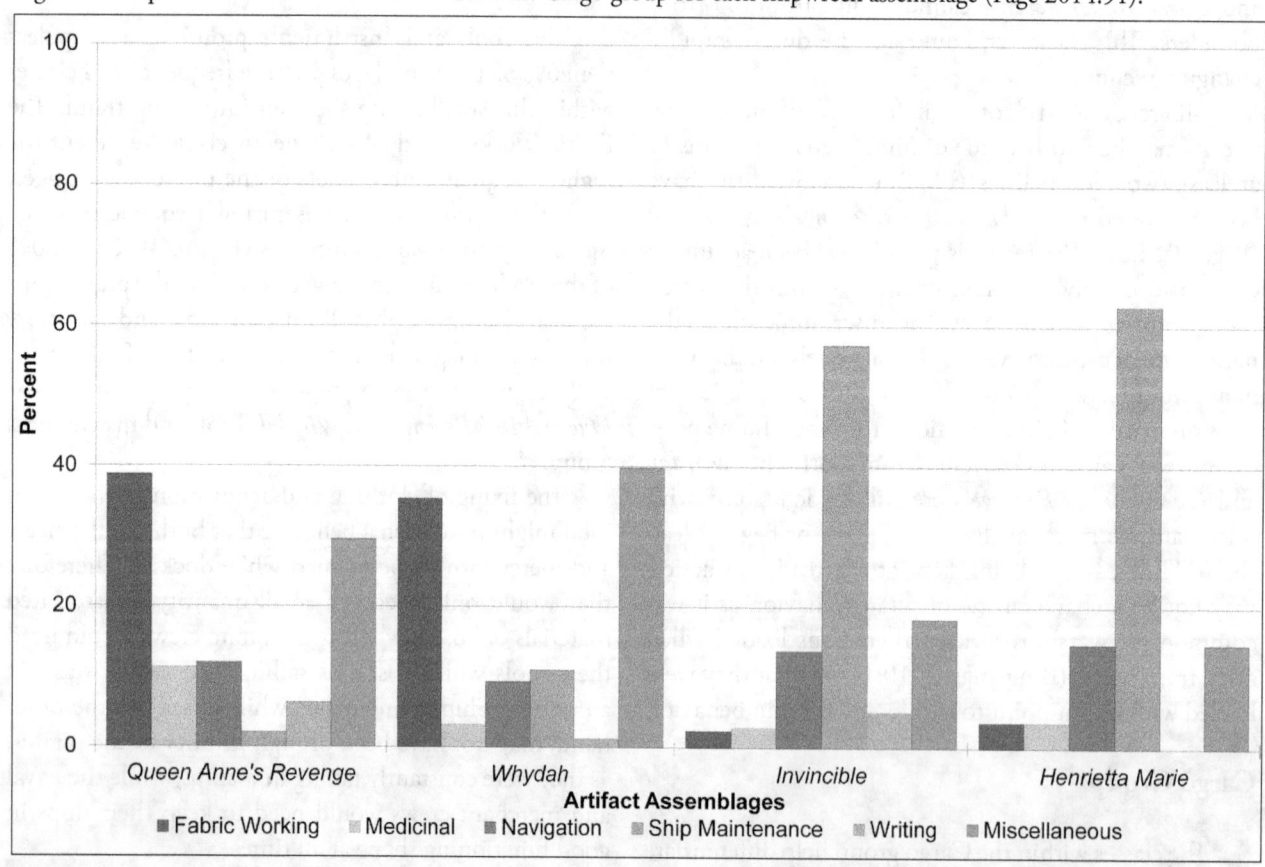

Figure 4. Frequencies of each class within the Tools and Instruments group for each shipwreck assemblage (Page 2014:98).

be investigated further, and the model presented should be reassessed. While a clear pattern of pirate behavior does not currently exist, this research demonstrates the potential for the use of artifact patterning in maritime archaeology.

Acknowledgements

I would like to acknowledge my thesis committee, under whom I conducted this research, and past and present staff of the Queen Anne's Revenge Conservation Lab who provided support during data analysis. An additional thanks to Dr. Charles Ewen and Dr. Russell Skowronek for the opportunity to publish this research in a book.

References

BAXTER, M. J.
1994   *Exploratory Multivariate Analysis in Archaeology.* Edinburgh University Press, Edinburgh, UK.

BINGEMAN, JOHN
2010   *The First HMS* Invincible *(1747-58): Her Excavations (1980-1991).* Oxbow Books, Oxford, UK.

HAMILTON, CHRISTOPHER E.
1992   Final Report of Archaeological Data Recovery: Text; The *Whydah* Shipwreck Site WLF-HA-1 1982-1992. Report to US Army Corps of Engineers Planning Division, Waltham, and The Massachusetts Historical Commission State Historic Preservation Office, Boston, from Maritime Explorations, Inc. and The *Whydah* Partners, L.P., South Chatham.

2006   The Pirate Ship *Whydah*. In *X Marks the Spot: The Archaeology of Piracy*, Russell K. Skowronek and Charles R. Ewen, editors, pp. 131-159. University Press of Florida, Gainesville, FL.

HAMPSHIRE & WIGHT TRUST FOR MARITIME ARCHAEOLOGY
2011   HMS *Invincible* (1758) – Interactive Site-viewer. Hampshire & Wight Trust for Maritime Archaeology, Southampton, UK, <http://www.hwtma.org.uk:8008/mapguide/invincible/main.php>. Accessed 9 Dec. 2011.

LUSARDI, WAYNE R.
2006   The Beaufort Inlet Shipwreck Artifact Assemblage. *In X Marks the Spot: The Archaeology of Piracy*, Russell K. Skowronek and Charles R. Ewen, editors, pp. 196-218. University Press of Florida, Gainesville, FL.

MOORE, DAVID D. AND COREY MALCOM
2008   Seventeenth-Century Vehicle of the Middle Passage: Archaeological and Historical Investigations on the *Henrietta Marie* Shipwreck Site. *International Journal of Historical Archaeology* 12:20-38.

PAGE, COURTNEY
2014   *Going on the Account: Examining Golden Age Pirates as a Distinct Culture Through Artifact Patterning.* Master's thesis, Department of Anthropology, East Carolina University, Greenville NC.

SOUTH, STANLEY
1977   *Method and Theory in Historical Archaeology.* Academic Press, New York.

WILDE-RAMSING, MARK U.
2006   The Pirate Ship *Queen Anne's Revenge*. In *X Marks the Spot: The Archaeology of Piracy*, Russell K. Skowronek and Charles R. Ewen, editors, pp. 160-195. University Press of Florida, Gainesville, FL

2009   Steady as she goes… A Test of the Gibb's Model Using the *Queen Anne's Revenge* Shipwreck Site. Doctoral dissertation, Program in Coastal Resource Management, East Carolina University, Greenville NC.

WILDE-RAMSING, MARK U. AND CHARLES R. EWEN
2012   Beyond a Reasonable Doubt: A Case for *Queen Anne's Revenge*. Historical Archaeology 46(2):110-133.

WINFIELD, RIF
1997   *The 50-Gun Ship.* Caxton Publishing, London.

Courtney Page
1157 VOA Site C Road
Greenville NC 27834
Work: 252-744-6721
courtney.page@ncdcr.gov

A Maritime Context for Richmond, Virginia and Environs: Assessment and Recommendations for Future Study

Bruce G. Terrell

The Fall Line at Virginia's James River has drawn people throughout human history to take advantage of the river's resources for sustenance, transportation and industry, and it figures in Richmond's placement and growth over time. Often portrayed as one of North America's most historic waterways, the intersection of tidewater and the uplands at Richmond has a "maritime" identity that is not often recognized. Natural and human forces have eroded much of the river's historic cultural landscape, but there may still be potential for archaeological discovery.

Context of Richmond as a Port

Few modern citizens of Richmond, Virginia are likely aware of their city's historic links to the Atlantic Ocean. The city's historic economy was, in fact, based on its geographic siting as a connection between the ocean and a fertile upland river valley. Richmond's founding at the falls of the James River created opportunities for commerce between upland plantations and major American and European ports. The lure of lucrative trade was great enough that merchants overcame obstacles to navigation and adapted technologies from shallow draft sailing vessels and steamboats to upland canals to overcome currents, twisting channels and rocky falls [Figure 1].

Historic documentation of early navigation on the upper James is sparse. William Byrd II established Shockoe plantation at the falls early in the 18th century, but left no mention of the condition of the river for ships. He stimulated settlement and trade by having the town of Richmond platted in 1733. Just downstream from the new town was a ferry landing established by Robert Rocketts in 1730 called Rocketts' Landing. Located at the head of navigation, Rocketts became the entrepot for trade between tidewater and piedmont (Sayre 2004).

In 1748 a tobacco inspection warehouse, or "rolling house," was established at Shockoes (Hening 1819:VI, 142). Tobacco, the earliest upland export, was generally

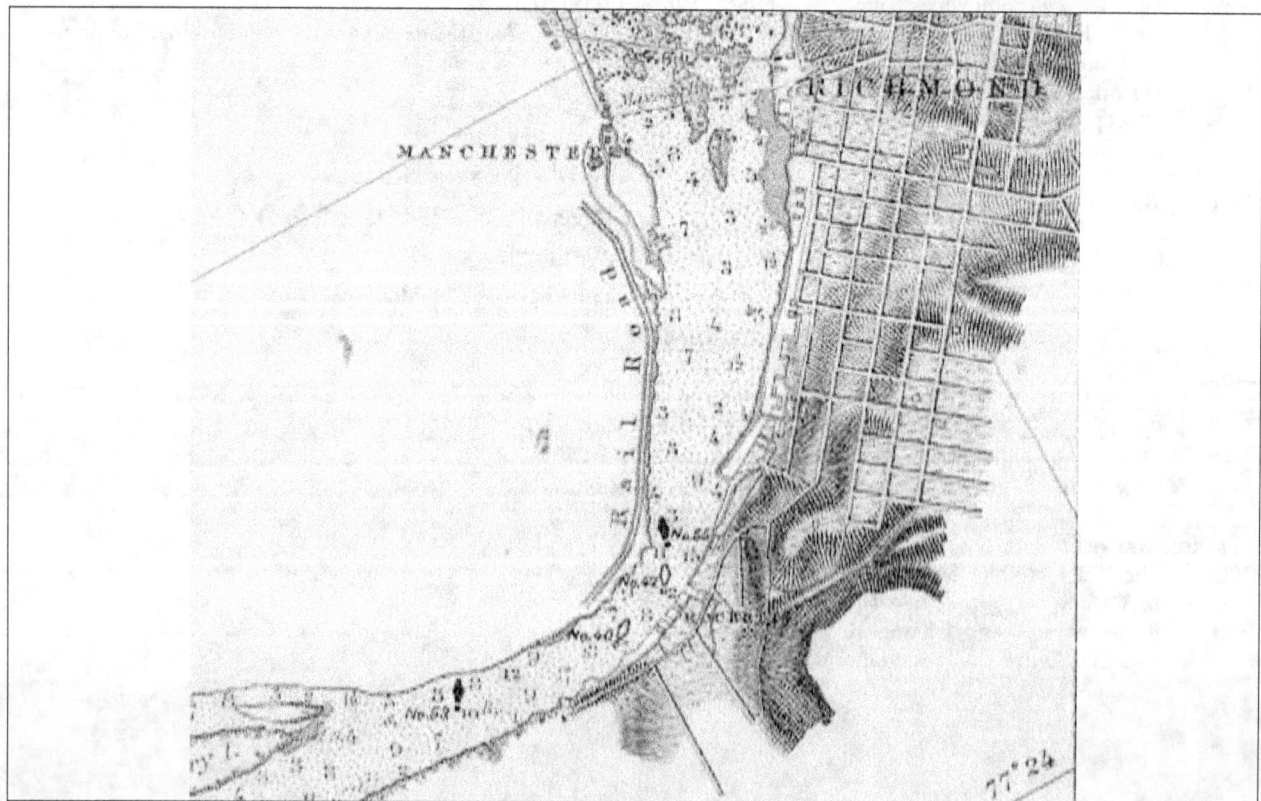

Figure 1. Richmond at James River, 1855. Publisher: NOAA.

conveyed by shallow upland watercraft or rolled to market in standardized hogsheads of about a ton. As Richmond's economy grew, so did the settlement at Rocketts. Wharves, warehouses, housing, and taverns were built for the merchants, sailors, factors, slaves, and others involved in the port's commerce (Tyler-McGraw 1994:44, Tatham 1800:210).

Although the exports were plentiful, merchants faced geographic problems shipping the cargo to England. The shallowness of the river restricted the size of ship that could carry a shipment. Thomas Jefferson reported in 1781 that the river was navigable by a 40-gun ship up to Harrison's bar, which was about 15 feet deep (at about Berkeley Plantation). From there he wrote, "Vessels of 250 tons [burden] may go to Warwick; those of 125 go to Rocket's, a mile below Richmond…." (Jefferson 1781) Port towns and warehouses were established downstream at Warwick and Bermuda Hundred in 1740 (Hening 1819:VI, 142, *Virginia Gazette* 18 January 1740).

Several approaches to shipping were practiced at Rocketts and the south bank of the James at Rocky Ridge (later Manchester). William Tatham wrote that prior to the Revolutionary War, large European vessels waited 10-15 miles below town where the water was deeper. From Richmond, merchant-owned flatboats, or scows carried up to 40 hogsheads downriver, maneuvered by enslaved black crewmen. Tatham noted that the crews were "…very dexterous in their profession as fresh water sailors; and many of them made excellent skippers, and good river pilots" (Tatham 1800:210, 211).

Tatham wrote that prior to the Revolution, larger sloops and schooners occasionally came to Richmond, but anchored in mid-channel while cargoes were carried to them on scow lighters. Many schooner owners also owned large ocean-going ships docked in Norfolk. The Richmond boats transferred the hogsheads to the ships, which would sail to foreign ports when a full load was accumulated (Snediker 1992:12–13).

In May 1771, the "Great Freshet" caused massive damage along the banks of the James River. Boats and warehouses were swept away, the entire harvest of tobacco was ruined and English goods destined for upland plantations were washed away at the wharf. Silt built up at the already shallow sand bars and further impeded navigation to Richmond (Tyler-McGraw 1994:54, Tatham 1800:93, Ward 1977:130, *Virginia Gazette* 11 July 1771).

The Revolution also upset trade patterns. Many Virginia merchants found trade in the West Indies. Small fast schooners slipped through the British blockade carrying upland goods to the Caribbean, trading them with European agents. Vessels from the Indies also reached Richmond, as in April 1777 when the schooner *Molly* entered Rocketts carrying a load of arms (Ward 1977:127). Richmond suffered a blow from a British raid led by Benedict Arnold in January 1781. British troops destroyed public property as well as tobacco, warehouses, navy stores and the ropewalk at Rocketts where rope and sailcloth were made. Arnold returned later in April and attacked shipyards and surprised the remnants of the Virginia State Navy squadron at Osborne's Landing below Richmond, destroying nine ships and capturing ten merchant vessels loaded with full cargoes (Goldenberg 1981:195, Ward 1977:136 – 137).

Virginia gradually shifted away from a tobacco economy in the late 18th century in favor of wheat, which led to Richmond's rise as a flour manufacturer. The James River Valley was the leading exporter of wheat after 1750. In 1793, Jefferson was informed that most Virginia planters had turned to wheat over tobacco (John Clarke to Thomas Jefferson, 15 July 1793, Jefferson 1976:349-350). Richmond's Haxall and Gallego flourmills were the largest in the United States, and Richmond was second behind Baltimore in national flour export. By 1837, Richmond's flour export commanded both the Brazilian and Australian markets. The Virginia-milled flour was known for maintaining its quality on long sea voyages. The returning ships carried Brazilian coffee, making Richmond the largest coffee market in the country by 1860 (Tyler-McGraw 1994:123, Duke 1983:89).

In 1789, Richmond led Norfolk in the value of exports by virtue of the upland goods that were shipped. While Norfolk clearly had the superior port, Richmond had the prized location. Richmond merchants, however, did not often deal directly with foreign entities as its cargo continued to be sent in multiple small vessels to Norfolk for European shipment in larger hulls. Goods transferred to larger ships at Warwick and Bermuda Hundred usually went to larger U.S. coastal ports of Boston and New York (Losse 1944:161 – 178, Duke 1983:24-25). After the War of 1812, the state legislature sought to revive the city's flagging trade by approving funds to clear the river between Rocketts and Shockoe Creek. The sand bars between Rocketts and Warwick were dredged and deepened as well (Christian 1912:93).

The ubiquitous vessels at Rocketts' wharf during the first half of the 19th century would have been small two-masted schooners and occasional single-masted sloops. Both were rigged with triangular "fore and aft" sails, which were more maneuverable than square sails on the narrow Virginia rivers. The deep draft Virginia and Baltimore schooners of the era were not able to ascend the upper James. Other less refined schooners were used on the shallower waters. These "Chesapeake Bay" type schooners were small and full-bodied with shallow keels. Chesapeake schooners had droppable centerboards, housed in trunks along the keel. Deployed, a schooner could maintain speed and maneuverability in the deeper Chesapeake Bay and coastal waters, but the centerboard could be retracted for negotiating shallow, narrow rivers. Sometimes called "clump" schooners, these boats were used in both freight and passenger trades. They were ubiquitous on most 19th century Virginia rivers and were used in many trades including fishing, oyster harvest and bulk cargo transport (Blanton 1994:31, Snediker 1992:58-60).

A rich bituminous coal field ten miles west of Richmond on both sides of the James provided another source of commerce. Coal from the Henrico County side was shipped down the canal to Richmond, where it fed Richmond's iron manufacturing industry. Coal from the south-side Midlothian mines was transported down to Manchester to waiting schooners by a gravitational railway whose coal cars used the natural incline of the topography to roll down tracks to the wharves. During the last half of the 19th century, the bituminous trade shifted to Warwick and, ultimately, Newport News (Wilkes 1988, Duke 1983:90).

In June 1815, steam navigation came to Richmond. The Philadelphia-built steamer *Eagle* conducted a promotional voyage from Norfolk to Richmond. It returned to Norfolk in 19 hours. A Richmond newspaper reported that it carried a party of ladies and gentlemen downriver at 4 miles an hour and returned at 2 miles an hour. It was noted, "She turns, runs backward as well as forward with wonderful ease. All those who saw the splendid stranger hailed her with enthusiasm" (Christian 1912:91). The *Eagle* ran regularly scheduled trips between Richmond and Philadelphia. Soon, another steamer, *Powhatan*, ran between Richmond and Norfolk. The shallow draft, side-wheel steamers brought growth and regularity to the fall line commerce. However, the steamers did not immediately boost Richmond's economy. They were expensive to operate and fuel took up valuable space, while sailing craft were still a slow but reliable way to move bulk cargoes. Steamers mainly carried passengers and compact merchandise for Richmond's stores (*Enquirer* 8 July 1815, Bauer 1988:108).

Several steam lines eventually began to service the Chesapeake Bay tributaries. The Maryland & Virginia Steam Boat Company built *Pocahontas* in 1829 for commerce between Richmond, Norfolk and Baltimore. The steamer was considered "in all respects a boat of the first class and...combines the most improved arrangements...on the score of elegance as comfort." By 1840, that company was replaced by the Baltimore Steam Packet Company, known by all as The Old Bay Line. The steamers of the Old Bay Line ran until 1962, when at last they were rendered obsolete by trains and trucks. By the 1880s, at least eight other lines provided regular service between U.S. coastal and inland towns and the steamboat landing at lower Rockets (Blanton 1994:32, Brown 1961:16-17, Chataigne 1881).

Richmond also maintained various watercraft around the harbor, including scows to pound pilings and perform yard duties, and a city tugboat to assist vessels to the docks. The *Thomas Cunningham Sr.* was a small steam tug that operated as a tugboat as well as a fireboat between 1897 and 1977. *Cunningham* was noted in 1912 for bringing in the largest ship to ever enter Richmond's harbor, the three-masted wooden barkentine *Mabel Myers* from Buenos Ayres with a consignment of guano for the Richmond Guano Company (*Times Dispatch* 11 March 2013). Throughout Richmond's merchant shipping history, the main vessels that entered the harbor were shallow draft coastal schooners. Small sailing oyster and fishing boats brought their catch to market at Rocketts and Shockoes. Somewhat larger vessels that entered included two-masted brigs and brigantines with a mix of square and fore and aft sails. By the decade prior to the Civil War, vessels of 1,000 tons capacity and a draft of 11 ½ feet entered Richmond's harbor (Callahan 1952:10, Wood 2010:71).

Another craft used in the river commerce was similar to Tatham's tobacco scows. Diarist George R. Wood wrote of working on a "tobacco ark" in about 1861. He recounted meeting incoming cargo vessels at shallow downstream bars where part of the load was transferred to the ark to lighten the sail vessel. They were then towed by tug or poled to Rocketts. Arks were also towed downstream by the schooners, where they were re-loaded after passing the bar. Wood described them as having a "sharp head and square stern so as to put the stern to the wharf to load with flour or tobacco and also to roll them on board of ships" [Figure 2]. They were open boats and were propelled either with poles, or were towed by steamers (Wood 2010:70-72).

Between the colonial period and the Civil War,

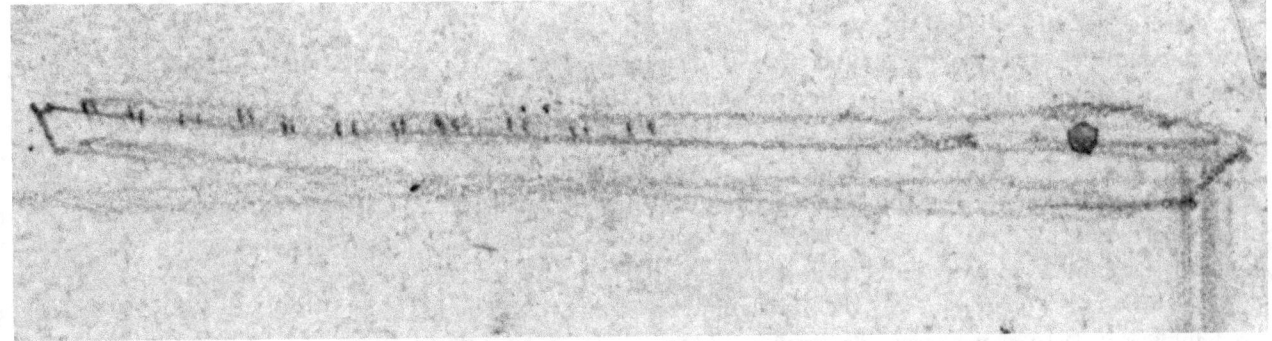

Figure 2. Possible tobacco ark (A. Waud). Publisher: Library of Congress.

Richmond became acknowledged as the "Great slave Market for the South." It was a hub for slave collectors, traders and buyers. Richmond's real rise came in the antebellum era creating a large market that sold enslaved laborers to plantations in the Cotton South. Although many enslaved people were marched in gangs or *coffles*, sources show that they were also sent south in ships from Chesapeake ports. For example, Solomon Northrop reported being transported from Richmond to New Orleans in the brig *Orleans* in 1841. This author has found no statistics regarding ship-borne transport from Richmond, but it is hoped that ongoing research will reveal the maritime aspect of Richmond's abhorrent commerce in human life (*Virginia Memory*, Northrop 2012:36).

The Civil War halted Richmond's growth. A victim of its own economic and manufacturing success, the city was made the capitol of the Confederate states in May 1861. The James was effectively cut off from international and coastal trade by the Union forces's control of Hampton Roads. Steamers, schooners and arks continued to move along the upper James as far down as City Point, bringing supplies and ammunition to Confederate troops and carrying hay and wood back up to Richmond from the plantations. Steamers also carried exchanged prisoners between Richmond and Howlett's near Varina. Dodging U.S. Navy expeditionary ships, the open arks were used to transport goods from Petersburg to the Commissary Department in Richmond. All river commerce came to an end when the Union forces occupied City Point in May 1862. Steamers and schooners were, then, scuttled to create several Southern defensive lines of obstruction below Richmond (Wood 2010:85-95).

After the Confederate abandonment of Norfolk in May 1862, Richmond's harbor converted from commerce to warship construction and became the South's largest naval shipyard. The Rocketts Navy Yard commanded the warehouses, sheds and landings and was connected to iron foundries by railroad lines. On the south side, the William A. Graves Confederate Shipyard accessed the Richmond and Danville Railroad and was the site of wooden ship construction. With access to rail transportation and Richmond's iron manufacturing, the shipyards turned out four ironclads (CSS *Richmond, Virginia II, Fredericksburg, Texas*) and converted existing steamers to naval standards. The wooden New York-built side-wheel passenger steamer *Yorktown* was converted to the Confederate Navy school ship CSS *Patrick Henry*. Several armed wooden gunboats and smaller spar-torpedo boats were also built there (Coski 1996).

Confederate Secretary of the Navy Stephen Mallory referred to the vessels that constituted the James River Naval Squadron as his "chained bulldogs," because their strength was restrained by the Union forces and the Confederate government's fear of their possible loss. Famed Confederate naval commerce raider Admiral Raphael Semmes of the CSS *Alabama* returned in Richmond in 1865 to find himself assigned command of a squadron that he was soon ordered to scuttle when Petersburg and Richmond fell in early April 1865. After blowing up the ironclads at Drewry's Bluff, the remaining sailors steamed upriver in the squadron's wooden gun and torpedo boats and put ashore at the Richmond and Danville Railroad Bridge at Manchester. They set fire to the gunboats and pushed them off to float downstream (Coski 1996, Semmes 1869:813).

The interruption and devastation to wartime Richmond destroyed her commerce, and the city was a long time in recovering. Scuttled ships downstream restricted navigation to Richmond for several years after the war. Commerce was able to resume after 1870, following removal of the obstructions. As commerce revived, factories and rail facilities were built along the riverbanks. Cargo and passenger steamboat traffic resumed. The Richmond channel was deepened to 17 feet in 1883, which allowed larger vessels to dock. Richmond saw renewed economic growth during this period until 1890, when it began to decline, due in part to a lack of ability to dredge deep enough to accommodate new deep-draft steamboats. Railroad rates for passengers and shipping also became cheaper, and steamships could not compete. The city was unable to maintain the needed upkeep of Rocketts' wharf. The brief career of the Trigg Shipbuilding Company on Chapel Island by the Tidewater Connection Locks between 1899 and 1903 produced several steel warships but had little effect on commerce. The last significant dredging was in 1916, which ensured a depth of 22 feet. (Callahan 1952:18–29,53,57)

The port showed growth again between 1920-1950 due in part to the export of tobacco to Turkey, and an influx of bulk goods and sugar used primarily in the tobacco industry. By the early 20th century, only a few individual companies such as Richmond Cedar Works and Richmond Guano maintained small fleets that serviced their own docks and warehouses. Most shipping commerce declined after the 1950s due to competition from Hampton Roads and other forms of transportation (Callahan 1952:19-54, Times Dispatch 27 Sep 1914, Blanton 1994:36-37).

Assessment for Potential Cultural Resources

The historically documented number of ship losses in the environs of Richmond is small. If the radius is expanded to include the downstream areas of Henrico, the number increases. Wrecks within an expanded zone include the Virginia State Navy and merchant ships destroyed in Benedict Arnold's raid. That zone would also include the scuttled ironclads of the James River Squadron, as well as the steamers and schooners used to create Union and Confederate lines of river obstructions. Some of these vessels have been identified but continue to be threatened by channel widening.

Known historic losses in the immediate Richmond area include the six James River Squadron gunboats that were cast off as the sailors abandoned the city in 1865:

3 April 1865, CSS *Hampton*, screw steam gunboat
3 April 1865, CSS *Nansemond*, screw steam gunboat
3 April 1865, CSS *Patrick Henry*, side wheel steamer
3 April 1865, CSS *Shrapnel*, steamer
3 April 1865, CSS *Beaufort*, screw steam gunboat
3 April 1865, CSS *Raleigh*, screw steam gunboat

Donald Shomette's index of historic shipwrecks within the Chesapeake Bay region includes six vessels between 1840 and 1961 for Richmond:

28 Aug 1840, *James Gibbon*, side-wheel steamer, boiler explosion
8 Aug 1873, *Bonita*, screw steamer, fire
5 Mar 1920, *Lillie*, gas screw, fire
8 Apr 1922, *Ada*, schooner, abandoned
22 Dec 1959, *Joyce Ann*, gas screw, burned
5 Jul 1961, *Raven*, oil screw, burned

An additional wreck found through newspaper research was the gas yacht *Mascot*, which burned at the Richmond Cedar Works dock on 21 August 1910 (Shomette, *Times Dispatch*).

Historic shipwrecks potentially hold information on past events, watercraft construction techniques, material culture and human behavior. Remains and artifacts can contain cultural information on places of origin as well as the people who operated them. In addition to known ship losses are possibilities for small, unrecorded workboats used in day-to-day tasks from pounding pilings to performing dock maintenance and repair on ships in port. These nameless vessels were often abandoned where they sank. The deposition of such vessels on the riverbed is exemplified in the numerous bateaux and canal boats found in the James River Canal turning basin during construction in the 1980s, as well as small craft found in the Richmond ship lock when it was drained for maintenance in the 1980s.

A potential historical resource associated with port activities may be extant remains of wharves and docks. Remains of early phases of Rocket's and Manchester's wharf structures may be submerged along the wharves in the water. As an example, the excavation of Keith's wharf and Battery Cove in Alexandria, Virginia in 1989 revealed structures from an 18th century colonial wharf (Engineering-Science 1993). Many ports have a record of their history buried where the shore meets the water. In the past, it was not uncommon to create new land by depositing rubble into cribwork created from derelict vessels to expand useable wharf space. This is seen as recently as December 2015 in Alexandria, where remains of an 18th century ship were excavated from an old wharf area where it was apparently used to bring the wharf closer to the deep river channel. Any physical remains of Rocketts' wharf are likely encased in concrete dating to the 1930s and '40s (Richards 2013, Callahan 1952:60).

Another potential for historical ship remains may be the presence of abandonment areas farther downstream from Rocketts. Derelict ship abandonment was a common use pattern in the past. A modern example on the James River is the collection of abandoned barges and tugs assembled at Farrar's Island/Trent's Reach. It is possible that in the pre-steam area, owners may have deposited their vessels closer to Rocketts than these 20th century abandonments (Richards 2013).

Types of events likely to have a negative effect on the preservation of submerged cultural remains at Richmond's waterfront include erosion or destruction by floods, contemporary salvage and dredging. As the upper James was industrialized after the Civil War, sunken vessels that obstructed commerce were likely removed. It is probable that the multiple dredgings that occurred between 1870-1916 would have impacted earlier sunken vessels.

A series of dikes, or wing dams can be seen today along the river banks, created to control the velocity of water flow and sediment deposition in the channel. They appear as far back as the late 19th century on Coast Survey charts. The author's inspection of one next to the Ancarrow's Landing boat launch in the last ten years showed the presence of fragmented wooden ship timbers mixed with rock and gravel. It is the author's assumption that this may be where the cast-off, burning James River Squadron gunboats sank. Photographic images from 1865 show Union boats in the apparent salvage of one or more vessels in that spot [Figure 3]. The dikes may have included dredge spoil that incorporated historic wooden ship parts. The photograph also shows the remains of the CSS *Patrick Henry* near the Richmond Gas Works at the north bank. An 1897 image also shows a steam boiler on shore near the same spot.

Events that may promote the preservation of submerged historic cultural remains include silting that helps to preserve organic materials such as wooden ship remains and wharf structure. Low salt content also restricts many marine organisms that feed on organic wooden ship structure. Also, the decline and neglect of port activities that occurred in the mid-20th century may have reduced exposure of submerged cultural resources to physical threats. A new threat to existing remains is development at Rocketts Landing, which could impact what remains of Richmond's connection to its maritime past.

This brief context and assessment suggests that the port of Rocketts was influential in Richmond's economic development and growth during much of its history. As a heavily industrialized river, much maritime

Figure 3. Rocketts looking South, 1865 (Brady). Publisher: Library of Congress.

activity has come and gone on the banks and riverbed. However, it was a heavily used and constricted area and seems to have had several phases of dredging as well as shoreward change. Material remains may exist in the riverbank and underwater, but it would require diligent survey and cultural resource mitigation by responsible agencies. It is recommended that further documentary research be conducted to attain a fuller understanding of the later port development at Rocketts and also to locate primary sources on early 19th century activities. Remote-sensing studies with side scan sonar and magnetometer is recommended for research-targeted areas to identify submerged historic resources.

References

Bauer, K. Jack
1988 *A Maritime History of the United States: The Role of America's Seas and Waterways*. Columbia, University of South Carolina Press.

Blanton, Dennis B. and Samuel G. Margolin
1994 An Assessment of Virginia's Underwater Cultural Resources. Williamsburg, William and Mary Center for Archaeological Research.

Brown, Alexander Crosby
1961 *Steam Packets on the Chesapeake: A History of the Old Bay Line Since 1840*. Centreville, Tidewater Publishers.

Figure 4. Rocketts 1897, Boiler. Publisher: Virginia Commonwealth University Library.

CALLAHAN, MYRTLE ELIZABETH
1952 History of Richmond As Port City. Thesis submitted to University of Richmond for a degree of Master of Arts in Economics.

CHATAIGNE, J.H.
1881 *Chataigne's Directory of Richmond, VA*. Richmond, Baughman Bros.

CHRISTIAN, W. ASBURY
1912 *Richmond: Her Past and Present*. Richmond, L.H. Jenkins.

COSKI, JOHN M.
1996 *Capital Navy: The Men, Ships and Operations of the James River Squadron*. Campbell, Savas Publishing Company.

DUKE, MAURICE AND DANIEL P. JORDAN
1983 A Richmond Reader: 1733-1983. Chapel Hill, The University of North Carolina Press.

n.d. Encyclopedia Virginia, Eyre Crowe's Images of the Slave Trade .http://www.encyclopediavirginia.org/Slave_Trade_Eyre_Crowe_s_Images_of_the_slave_Trade

ENGINEERING-SCIENCE, INC.
1993 Maritime Archaeology at Keith's Wharf and Battery Cove (44AX119): Ford's Landing Alexandria, Virginia. Washington, D.C., Engineering-Science, Inc.

GOLDENBERG, JOSEPH A. AND MARION WEST STOER
1981 *The Virginia State Navy in Chesapeake Bay in the American Revolution*. Centreville, Tidewater Publishers.

HENING, WILLIAM WALLER
1819 *Hening's Statutes at Large*. 13 vols. Richmond, Franklin Press.

JEFFERSON, THOMAS
1791 *Notes on the State of Virginia*. Chapel Hill, University of North Carolina Press, 1955.

1977 *Thomas Jefferson's Farm Book*. Ed. Edwin Morris Betts. Charlottesville, University Press of Virginia.

LOSSE, WINIFRED J.
1944 The Foreign Trade of Virginia, 1789-1809, in *The William and Mary Quarterly*, Vol. 1, No. 2 (Apr., 1944).

NORTHROP, SOLOMON
2012 *12 Years a Slave*. London, Penguin Classics.

RICHARDS, NATHAN
2013 *The Archaeology of Watercraft Abandonment*. Nathan Richards, ed. New York, Springer.

SAYRE, DAVID M. AND AHMET BULBULKAYA
2004 Rocketts Landing, Richmond, Virginia, USA, Brownfield Redevelopment Under Voluntary Remediation. IAEG2006 Paper number 678.

SEMMES, RAPHAEL
1869 *Memoirs of Service Afloat During the War Between the States*. Baltimore, Kelly, Piet & Co.

SNEDIKER, QUENTIN, AND ANN JENSEN
1992 *Chesapeake Bay Schooners*. Centreville, Tidewater Publishers.

TATHAM, WILLIAM
1800 *An Historical and Practical Essay on the Culture and Commerce of Tobacco*. London, Vernor and Hood.

TYLER-MCGRAW, MARIE
1994 *At the Falls: Richmond, Virginia, and Its People*. Chapel Hill, The University of North Carolina Press.

VIRGINIA MEMORY WEBSITE
n.d. http://www.virginiamemory.com/online-exhibitions/exhibits/show/to-be-sold

WARD, HARRY M. AND HAROLD E. GREER, JR.
1977 Richmond During the Revolution: 1775-83. Charlottesville, University Press of Virginia.

WILKES, GERALD P.
1988 Mining History of the Richmond Coalfield of Virginia. Charlottesville, Department of Mines, Minerals and Energy, Commonwealth of Virginia.

WOOD, GEORGE RANDOLPH
2010 *A Young Virginia Boatman Navigates the Civil War: The Journals of George Randolph Wood*. Charlottesville, University of Virginia Press.

Bruce G. Terrell
1305 East-West Highway, 11th Floor
Silver Spring, MD 20910
Work Phone 301-713-7255
Home Phone 703-807-0235
Cell Phone 703-919-1101
bruce.terrell@noaa.gov

An Initial Site Assessment of Submerged Naval Aircraft off the Coast of Pensacola, Florida

Hunter W. Whitehead and Nicole Mauro

Known as the U.S. Navy's 'Cradle of Aviation,' Naval Air Station Pensacola has been a fundamental aviation training ground since the beginning of the 20th century. During World War II, inexperienced pilots were quickly processed through an accelerated flight-training program that resulted in the loss of numerous aircraft. This paper presents the initial steps undertaken to recognize site formation processes of previously undocumented submerged aircraft in the Gulf of Mexico. Through the use of photogrammetry, site assessments will allow local archaeologists to establish baseline data for these aircraft for future monitoring and management.

Introduction

"Ever since ships first voyaged on the sea, there have been shipwrecks, and these in turn have always attracted the attentions of potential salvors ..." (Muckelroy 1978:10). At the turn of the 20th century with the advent of aviation, submerged aircraft sites have likewise drawn similar attention. Conversely, within the field of archaeology, submerged aircraft have only recently become of interest. This is partly due to legislation requiring cultural resources to be 50 years or older to be eligible for the National Register of Historic Places. Terrestrial military aircraft sites have largely disappeared due to salvage efforts of government-sanctioned salvors and souvenir collectors. As others have pointed out, "in the future, the best available examples of aircraft will be found underwater" (Fix 2014: 1007). UNESCO's Manual for activities directed at Underwater Cultural Heritage considers in situ preservation as the first option to manage a site's integrity (Maarleveld, Et al. 2013: 20). In order to determine the long-term variability of in situ monitoring, this study will help to elucidate field methods and establish photogrammetric techniques for the use of site monitoring.

The primary focus of this study is the initial site assessment of submerged U.S. naval aircraft, hereafter referred to as naval aircraft, off the coast of Pensacola, FL. Pensacola has been a training ground for naval pilots since 1911, which has resulted in various aircraft lost in the Gulf of Mexico. With notable assistance from Dr. Bill Howe, a local sport diver in the community, University of West Florida (UWF) archaeologists have located four submerged naval aircraft sites. Dr. Howe has been SCUBA diving in the area since 1982 and has extensive knowledge of local underwater cultural resources. His observations noted in this paper have been taken into consideration and have helped considerably due to a lack of previous scientific investigations. Through preliminary archival research and initial site visits, the Grumman-manufactured F6F Hellcat and F8F Bearcat were chosen for examination. Although only four aircraft have been investigated initially, several additional sites are in the research area, ranging from TBF Avengers to F4U Corsairs.

Several recent studies indicate increased archaeological interest in submerged aircraft (Jung 2001; Ford 2006, MacLeod 2006, Bell 2015). A recent examination of four WWII aircraft sites in Saipan demonstrated examples of in situ documentation (Bell, 2015). Archaeologists involved in this study proposed, "One of the best ways to broaden our theoretical knowledge of these sites is by researching and understanding their site formation" (Bell 2015:49). Current research has sought to add to theoretical knowledge of submerged aircraft through understanding of the site formation processes of submerged naval aircraft in the Gulf of Mexico through site assessments.

History Of Naval Air Station Pensacola (1911-1945)

The U.S. Navy became interested in aircraft as early as 1898. Samuel P. Langley's flying machine and the Wright Brothers public demonstrations a few years later brought about new technology that caught the eye of the military. To look into it, Captain Washington I. Chambers was appointed head of naval aviation matters, and he assembled a team of engineers. By 1911, the U.S. government had allocated funds for flight training, and ideas of flying overseas were forming. Chambers called for expansion in research and in the fleet itself. On 7 October 1913, naval directors recommended establishment of a ground and flight training center at Pensacola, FL (Grossnick 1991-1995: 1).

The U.S. Navy allocated $1,297,700 to implement the program (Grossnick 1991-1995: 12), and a few months later, officers, gear, and aircraft hangars were transferred from Annapolis, MD to Pensacola, FL. The flight school at Pensacola continued to develop over the next several years. Only 30 years after the Navy incorporated aviation, WWII brought one of the first tests of its usefulness. Naval Air Station (NAS) Pensacola played its role in the war by providing primary air training during this time. In 1943, the base was officially established as the Naval Air Training Command, where all Naval Aviation training was to be coordinated and directed (Grossnick 1991-1995: 134). A number of aircraft types were utilized for training at NAS Pensacola throughout its history, including the F6F Hellcat and the F8F Bearcat.

The F6F Hellcat

The U.S. Navy considers the Grumman F6F Hellcat (Figure 1), which evolved from the F4F Wildcat, the most important fighter of WWII (Mondey 2002: 142). With an innovative low-wing layout, the landing gear retracted into the center of the wing section instead of the fuselage. Ammunition capacity and armor also were increased. The Hellcat had a span of 42 ft. 10 in. (13.06m), an overall length of 33 ft. 7 in. (10.24m) and a max speed of 380 mph. Based on similarities in design, the transition from flying the F4F to the F6F was smooth; with quick and efficient production, squadrons were equipped with the new model within a year of the order date. This was a manufacturing record.

The aircraft first saw action in Norway in December 1943 and remained in first-line service with the U.S. Navy for the remainder of the war. In air-to-air combat, the Hellcat was credited with 4,947 destroyed enemy aircraft (Mondey 2002: 144). With increased aerodynamics and increased armament and armor, the final version of the Hellcat, the F6F-5, saw extensive action over Sumatra and participated in attacks on Sumatra's oil refineries. It remained in service after VJ-Day and was modified for use as target drones.

The F8F Bearcat

The F8F Bearcat (Figure 2) is smaller and 20%

Figure 1. An F6F Hellcat located at the National Naval Aviation Museum in Pensacola, Florida (photo by author).

Figure 2. An F8F Bearcat located at the National Naval Aviation Museum in Pensacola, Florida (photo by author).

lighter than the Hellcat, with a 30% greater climb rate. The Bearcat's main purpose was as an interceptor fighter, which required excellent maneuverability, good low level performance and a high rate of climb (Mondey 2002: 147). An order was placed in October 1944 but the Bearcat never saw battle. Squadrons were still learning how to operate the aircraft, when VJ-Day put an end to WWII. The aircraft were modified post-war to serve in a drone capacity. The Bearcat had a span of 35 ft. 10 in. (10.92m), an overall length of 28 ft. 3 in. (8.61m), and a max speed of 421 mph. It was capable of operating on aircraft carriers of all sizes (Mondey 2002: 148). Understanding the history of the F8F Bearcat and F6F Hellcat was key to implementing a site-specific research design.

Methodology

Investigators organized three phases of research: archival work, archaeological site assessments, and post-processing of images for use in creating photogrammetric models. Preliminary archival research at the U.S. Navy Yard within the office of Naval History and Heritage Command (NHHC) produced aircraft history cards, accident reports, and other documents that would assist in aircraft identification. Fieldwork in 2015 included four aircraft sites, which UWF archaeologists dived on to identify the aircraft type, site extent, and site integrity. Divers attempted to locate identification plates containing bureau numbers unique to each aircraft. Investigators also utilized video and still photographs taken with a GoPro Hero 4 Black to document the aircraft's current condition and facilitate future studies. Archaeologists took basic hull, wing and tail measurements for the F8F Bearcats to determine what is currently exposed.

The authors intend to create site maps and monitor degradation over time through the use of photogrammetry. Since no earlier scientific documentation has been conducted on submerged aircraft in Pensacola, this will set a precedent for future site monitoring. For the initial steps of this research, investigators took photographs with a GoPro Hero 4 Black in burst mode to capture as many angles of the aircraft as possible. UWF archaeologists edited the resulting images with Photoshop to reduce the fisheye effect and to adjust color balance. Processed images were uploaded into Agisoft's Photoscan for 3D-site models.

Results

The NHHC database indicates seven F6F-5 Hellcat aircraft crashed in Pensacola. Investigators were able to locate aircraft history cards and accident reports on microfilm, which contained accidents from 1949-1952. Two of the records indicated GPS locations, though only referencing degrees and minutes. Aircraft records revealed lost aircraft with bureau numbers 77979, 78130, 78773, 94433, 94279, 78620, and 80226.

Researchers selected two contrasting Hellcat wreck sites for assessment. The first site, F6F Hellcat 1, is 86 ft. (26m) deep. Heavy marine growth cover the remains, and the aluminum skin that would have covered the internal elements is degraded. The mid and aft sections are absent, and the minimal surrounding debris field lacked any recognizable components. According to Dr. Howe, the tail portion was present before Hurricane Ivan in 2004. The aircraft's propeller was also missing, possibly the result of natural processes or site looting. In addition, the gauges in the cockpit were absent, perhaps the result of sport diver salvage. Since a majority of the aircraft's structure lies beneath the sediment, divers could assess only visible remains. A bureau number plate that would have determined the aircraft's history was present, although the portion containing the serial numbers was missing, reducing the chances of identifying the aircraft. Surveying the immediate vicinity revealed several cinder blocks, probably from fishermen altering the site to attract fish.

The second Hellcat site, F6F Hellcat 2, lies 76 ft. (23m) deep. In comparison to F6F Hellcat 1, the marine growth and missing aluminum skin are similar, but the tail portion is missing. The key difference between the two wrecks is that F6F Hellcat 2 lies upside down with extended landing gear. It is possible that this feature has provided a large portion of the wreck with an anaerobic environment and additionally one that has kept the aircraft's components out of the hands of looters.

In addition to the Hellcats, UWF archaeologists surveyed two F8F Bearcat sites. The Bearcats generally exhibit better preservation than the Hellcats. The first Bearcat examined, F8F Bearcat 1, lies 96 ft. (29m) deep. Like the Hellcats, this aircraft is covered in marine growth and lacks its aluminum skin. Though the tail is present, the sand covers a large portion, revealing a broken rudder barely protruding from the sea floor. The starboard wing is above the sediment, yet missing a substantial portion. While the port wing is covered by sediment and possibly intact, it needs further investigation to determine its preservation. The remains of the starboard wing measured 10 ft. 5 in. (3.2m) in length. The length of the remains from fuselage to rudder is 21 ft. 9 in. (6.64m), indicating approximately 75% of the length of the original structure is intact. The engine and one blade of the propeller lay 19 ft. 10 in. (6.05m) away from the port side of the aircraft, which is mostly buried. Almost all of the cockpit gauge components were missing, again suggesting looters. To test photogrammetric field methods, the authors chose F8F Bearcat 1 as the best-preserved example, with its fuselage mostly intact and engine with propeller near by. UWF archaeologists collected 1,563 photos.

The second Bearcat site has been designated F8F Bearcat 2. It lies 107 ft. (32m) deep, in a depression that appears to be the result of natural scouring. Like the other sites assessed, marine growth, aluminum skin degradation and missing gauges are evident. The tail

Figure 3. The first attempt of a photogrammetric model of a submerged F8F Bearcat in Pensacola, Florida (Agisoft Photoscan).

portion was present; like F8F Bearcat 1, sediment covers a larger portion with the top of the rudder incomplete. The length from the foremost intact portion of the aircraft to the rudder is 22 ft. 3 in. (6.80m), indicating approximately 75% of the original length of the aircraft is present. The wings currently extend beneath the seabed, although before Hurricane Ivan, Dr. Howe observed them undamaged and above sediment. The engine and propeller are absent, although divers discovered several possible engine components. The canvas canopy cover was a unique feature.

In the early stages of this study, the authors were unable to create photogrammetric models due to the abundance of marine organisms on the site. To overcome this problem, several solutions were considered including feeding the fish away from the site throughout the dive. Eventually, with enough photographs allowing more overlap, Agisoft Photoscan created the first recognizable 3d model (Figure 3). The model, though still not an accurate representation of the site, displayed anomalous fish "globules" above a bluish green aircraft. With further experimentation and editing, a higher quality model was achieved (Figure 4). Researchers then supplemented the model with measurements taken from the field to create a scale model. To test the accuracy of the model, additional measurements will be taken in the field to ground truth model-created dimensions.

Conclusion

The archival research and site assessments of submerged naval aircraft in Pensacola have created a baseline for future monitoring and site formation studies. Non-intrusive methods of recording the sites have resulted in basic measurements and photographs that can be referenced for ongoing degradation. Photographic data will "allow meaningful comparisons to be made in the future to ascertain if any significant changes to a particular site have occurred" (Richards, Carpenter 2015: 119). Tools such as photogrammetric models will assist in recording spatial data in conjunction with traditional methods. Future monitoring will rely on archival research, regular site assessments, and previously documented analysis. With continued assistance of the local community, additional historic submerged aircraft may be located and incorporated in this study. A larger sample will provide broader comparisons for greater understanding of the site formation of submerged aircraft in the Gulf of Mexico and off the Pensacola coast. Aircraft history cards and accident reports should supplement site assessments in identifying aircraft by supplying bureau numbers or providing further contextual information. With aircraft accident accounts, specific site formation processes may become discernible.

Although outside the scope of this initial assessment, environmental conditions may provide an understanding of biological degradation rates. Investigators will assess salinity, temperature, dissolved oxygen content, and a host of other water quality samples at each site. The study may require the installation of sediment pins in order to understand accumulation or scouring processes. Together with side scan sonar imagery, these data sets may provide a look at broad changes in these sites through time. The analysis of natural conditions will facilitate a more complete understanding of how to efficiently manage in situ preservation.

The reliance of this study on consistent site assessment surveys is paramount. "Any archaeologically informed interventions and stabilization regimes should include multi-year and incremental monitoring

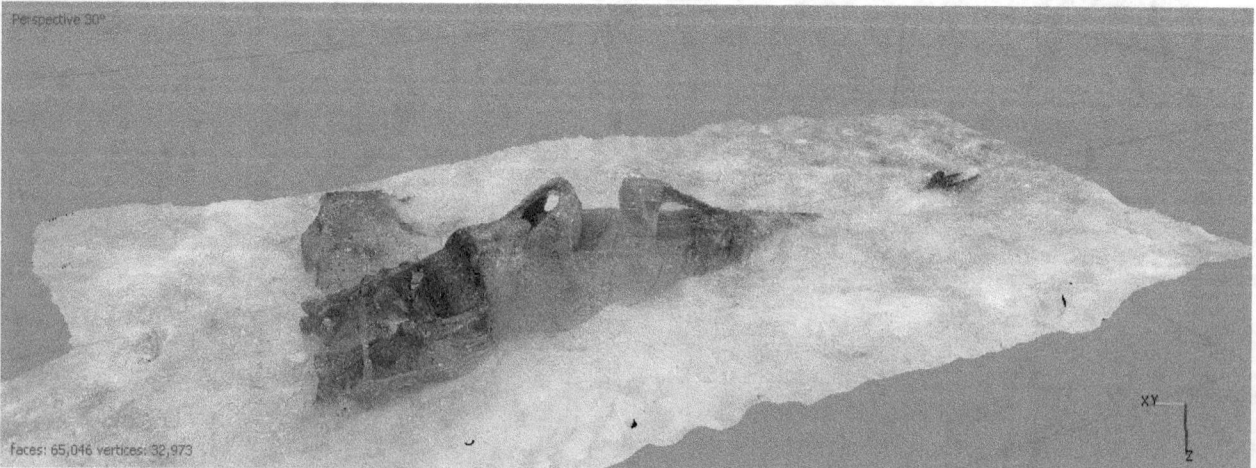

Figure 4. Higher quality photogrammetric model of a submerged F8F Bearcat in Pensacola, Florida (Agisoft Photoscan).

programs" (Shefi 2015: 378). Once the research potential of these underwater cultural resources is realized, natural and social risks of the site's integrity must be determined. With the apparent looting of these sites, site monitoring and the active engagement of the community hopefully will serve as a deterrent. The U.S. Navy holds an interest in the preservation of naval archaeological resources and seeks to "monitor U.S. Navy underwater wrecks sites; ... discourage looting of naval artifacts; ... and encourage nonintrusive surveys of wreck sites" (Dudley 1998: 109). With multi-agency cooperation, these goals may be realized and the submerged aircraft sites might be eligible for the National Register of Historic Places.

Acknowledgements

This research is supported by The University of West Florida Division of Anthropology and Archaeology. We would like to show our gratitude to those at the UWF who have offered insight and advice throughout this effort. The authors wish to thank Dr. Bill Howe for his remarkable assistance. We also thank Blair Atcheson and George Schwarz at the Naval Heritage and History Command. We are grateful to Dr. Gregory Cook, Joe Grinnan, and Charles Bendig for offering comments on rough drafts of this paper. Finally, we thank Kotaro Yamafune for his assistance with 3d photogrammetric methods.

References

Bell, Samantha
2015   In the Drink: Sunken Aircraft of the Battle of Saipan. In *Underwater Archaeology of a Pacific Battlefield: The WWII Battle of Saipan*, Jennifer F. Mckinnon, Toni L. Carrell, editors, pp. 49-62. Springer, New York, New York.

Dudley, William S.
1998   American Naval Archaeology: Past and Prologue. In *Maritime Archaeology: A reader of Substantive and Theoretical Contributions*, Lawrence E. Babits, Hans Van Tilburg, editors, pp. 105-109. Plenum Press, New York, New York.

Ford, Julie
2006   *WWII Aviation Archaeology in Victoria, Australia*. Flinders University Maritime Archaeology Monograph Series, Number 1. Shannon Research Press, Adelaide, South Australia.

Grossnick, R. A.
1997   *United States naval aviation: 1910-1995*. Naval Historical Center, Dep. of the Navy. Washington D.C.

Jung, Silvano Vittorio
2001   *Wings Beneath The Sea: The Aviation Archaeology of Catalina Flying Boats in Darwin Harbour, Northern Territory*. Masters Thesis, Faculty of Law, Business and Arts. Northern Territory University, Darwin, Northern Territory.

Maarleveld, Thijs, Ulrike Guérin, and Barbara Egger
2013   *Manual for Activities directed at Underwater Cultural Heritage: Guidelines to the Annex of the UNESCO 2001 Convention*. United Nations Educational, Scientific and Cultural Organization, Paris, France.

MacLeod, Ian D.
2006   In-situ corrosion studies on wrecked aircraft of the Imperial Japanese Navy in Chuuk Lagoon, federated states of Micronesia. *The International Journal of Nautical Archaeology*, 35(1), 128-136.

Mondey, David
2002   *The Hamlyn Concise Guide to American Aircraft of World War II*. Chancellor Press, London, United Kingdom.

Muckelroy, Keith
1978   *Maritime Archaeology*. Cambridge University Press, London, Great Britain.

Naval Heritage and History Command Archives
1949-1952   Aircraft History Cards and Accident Reports of listed Bureau Numbers: 77979, 78130, 78773, 94433, 94279, 78620, and 80226. Microfilm. Washington D.C.

Richards, Vicki, and Jonathan Carpenter
2015   On-Site Conservation Surveys. In *Underwater Archaeology of a Pacific Battlefield: The WWII Battle of Saipan*, Jennifer F. Mckinnon, Toni L. Carrell, editors, pp. 97-116. Springer, New York, New York.

Shefi, Debra, and Peter Veth
2015   A Critical Analysis and Philosophical Review of 'Rapid Reburial': the *Clarence* Project. *The International Journal of Nautical Archaeology* (2015) 44(2), 371–381.

Hunter W. Whitehead
The Division of Anthropology and Archaeology
University of West Florida
9560 Sunnehanna Blvd. Apt E202
Pensacola, FL 32514
hww5@students.uwf.edu

Nicole Mauro
The Division of Anthropology and Archaeology
University of West Florida
711 Underwood Ave. Apt 102D
Pensacola, FL 32504
nom1@students.uwf.edu

Shallow Water Hydrographic Surveys in Support of Archaeological Site Preservation: *Queen Anne's Revenge* Wreck Site, North Carolina

Mark U. Wilde-Ramsing, David J. Bernstein, and Christopher W. Freeman

In 2006, the NC Department of Cultural Resources/Underwater Archaeology Branch and the US Army Corps of Engineers undertook an experimental project by placing a mound of dredge spoil sediments on the updrift side of the Queen Anne's Revenge shipwreck site. The experiment was designed to promote site preservation and decrease exposure of subaqueous cultural artifacts. A series of high-resolution multi-beam sonar surveys was conducted to quantify and monitor the morphology of the sediment mound and its interaction with the wreck site. After each survey, a spatio-temporal assessment was performed using modern GIS techniques. Over the course of five years, the sediment mound dispersed gradually over the wreck site, reducing the erosional trend at the site and protecting the remaining artifacts. Hydrographic surveys carried out for the experimental sediment mound project helped to understand the effectiveness of this preservation technique for shipwreck artifacts lying in an energetic coastal environment.

Introduction

North Carolina shipwreck 31CR314 lies in an energetic, shallow marine environment where natural impacts are often extreme (Figure 1). Discovered in 1996, these shipwreck remains are of the pirate Blackbeard's flagship *Queen Anne's Revenge (QAR)* and thus have been determined to be an archaeologically significant, internationally recognized cultural heritage site (Wilde-Ramsing and Lusardi 1999; Plakos 2004; Wilde-Ramsing and Ewen 2012). The vessel reportedly ran aground on the ebb-tidal delta while attempting to enter Beaufort Inlet in 1718. The vessel quickly settled into the unconsolidated shoal sands and for much of

Figure 1. Map showing the location of the *Queen Anne's Revenge* shipwreck relative to the ebb-tidal delta of Beaufort Inlet, North Carolina.

the past three centuries lay buried (Wells and McNinch 2001). Natural re-configuration of Beaufort Inlet, channel stabilization, and a more resistant substrate at the site left the wreck site exposed over the last several decades, threatening the integrity of the artifacts and archaeological information. In 2006, an experimental project was initiated by State managers and archaeologists to preserve the wreck site until major recovery efforts could be completed. This project took advantage of a US Army Corps of Engineers' (USACE) offer of well-sorted quartz sand from a nearby dredging project to create a mound of sediments on the updrift side of the wreck site (Wilde-Ramsing and Rodrigues 2009).

In order to study the dispersal characteristics of the sediment mound, a series of high-resolution multi-beam sonar surveys was conducted over five years. After each survey, a spatio-temporal assessment of the sediment mound morphology and its interaction with the site was performed using GIS techniques. Volume changes over time were quantified relative to the entire experiment site and the wreck site itself, to better understand the sediment transport and mound dispersion around the wreck site.

The Experiment

Purpose

The experiment was designed to examine the effectiveness of an indirect sand disposal method on the short-term protection and long-term preservation of the *QAR* site (Figure 2). It was thought that the sediment mound would reduce the wave energy created during large storm events and decrease scour and erosional trends by re-nourishing the wreck site with a local sediment source. Furthermore, the submerged sand deposit was not expected to hamper full-scale recovery operations nor introduce modern contaminants to the existing archaeological record.

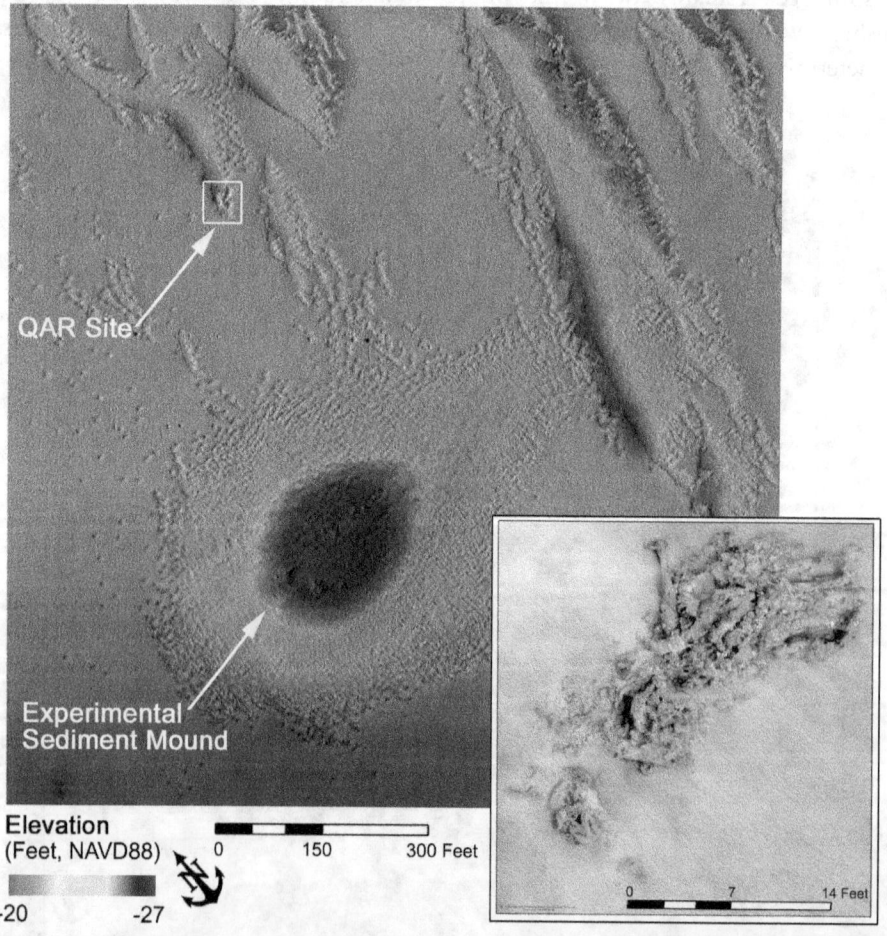

Figure 2. Bathymetric map (March 2006) showing the experimental sediment mound in relation to the *QAR* site and general seabed morphology. Inset in the lower right is a photo mosaic of the main wreck pile (courtesy of the National Geographic Magazine).

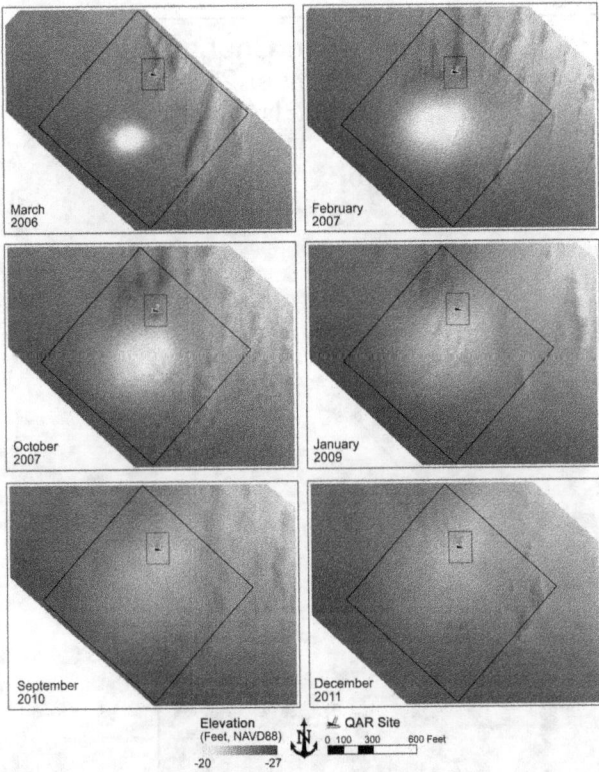

Figure 3. Map series illustrating seafloor elevation derived from each multibeam sonar survey throughout the experiment. Overlaid on each map is the experiment-wide area and the smaller area referred to as the *QAR* site in which geo-spatial and volumetric analysis were performed.

Creation of the Sand Berm

The USACE performed maintenance dredging of the Bulkhead Channel, near Beaufort, North Carolina, less than two miles from the shipwreck. Dredge material was removed by the hopper dredge *Currituck* and transported to a dump site located 400 ft. seaward of the shipwreck site. The dredging and disposal work began in February 2006 and continued through March 2006, during which 40,925 cubic yards of material were deposited. This activity created a sediment mound, or submerged sand dune approximately 600 ft. long (east-west), 200 ft. wide and 6 to 12 ft. high over the surrounding seabed (Wilde-Ramsing and Rodrigues 2009).

Methodology

In the years prior to the 2006 mound placement, an assortment of research activities was conducted in the vicinity of the wreck site. This research ranged from diver observations of relative seafloor elevation, hydrographic surveys in support of inlet management, in-situ current measurements, sub-bottom profiling, sediment analysis, and a variety of hydrographic surveys for equipment calibration and acceptance. The hydrographic surveys ranged from side scan, single-beam, swath interferometric, and multi-beam sonar surveys. These datasets provided a cursory understanding of sediment transport and seafloor morphology around the *QAR* site and aided in the experimental design of the mound placement and size. Impressed by the resolution and repeatability in the multi-beam sonar surveys, the NC Underwater Archaeology Branch contracted for additional multi-beam surveys to further support the experiment.

Six high-resolution, ellipsoidally-referenced multi-beam sonar surveys were acquired with Kongsberg EM3002 and EM3002-D systems integrated with an Applanix POS MV inertial navigation system and AML Oceanographic sounds speed instrumentation. The surveys began in March 2006 and spanned through December 2011.

Upon acquisition of each bathymetric survey, CARIS HIPS-SIPS was used to process, clean, and export the sonar data into XYZ datasets ready for GIS. Each bathymetric dataset was converted from an XYZ vector file into a 5-foot resolution raster surface in ArcGIS. Once each bathymetric surface was created, GIS layers such as contour plots, slope, and curvature surfaces were generated to make general assessments of the seafloor and document seabed features.

To assess the morphology of the sediment mound and changes at the wreck site over time, geo-spatial and volumetric analyses were performed using the Raster Math Toolset and Image Analysis extension in ArcGIS. Raster-based arithmetic functions were applied to each successive bathymetric survey in order to calculate seabed elevation change and to monitor morphological evolution spatially across the monitoring area. Volume change was calculated within two areas; a larger experiment-wide area and a smaller area referred to as the *QAR* site. This approach was selected in an effort to assess the overall dispersal of the sediment mound and capture any burial or scour that occurred directly at the wreck site.

Results

The March 2006 survey revealed the recently-placed sediment mound and a more complex seabed feature with a shore-oblique, ripple-scour depression to the

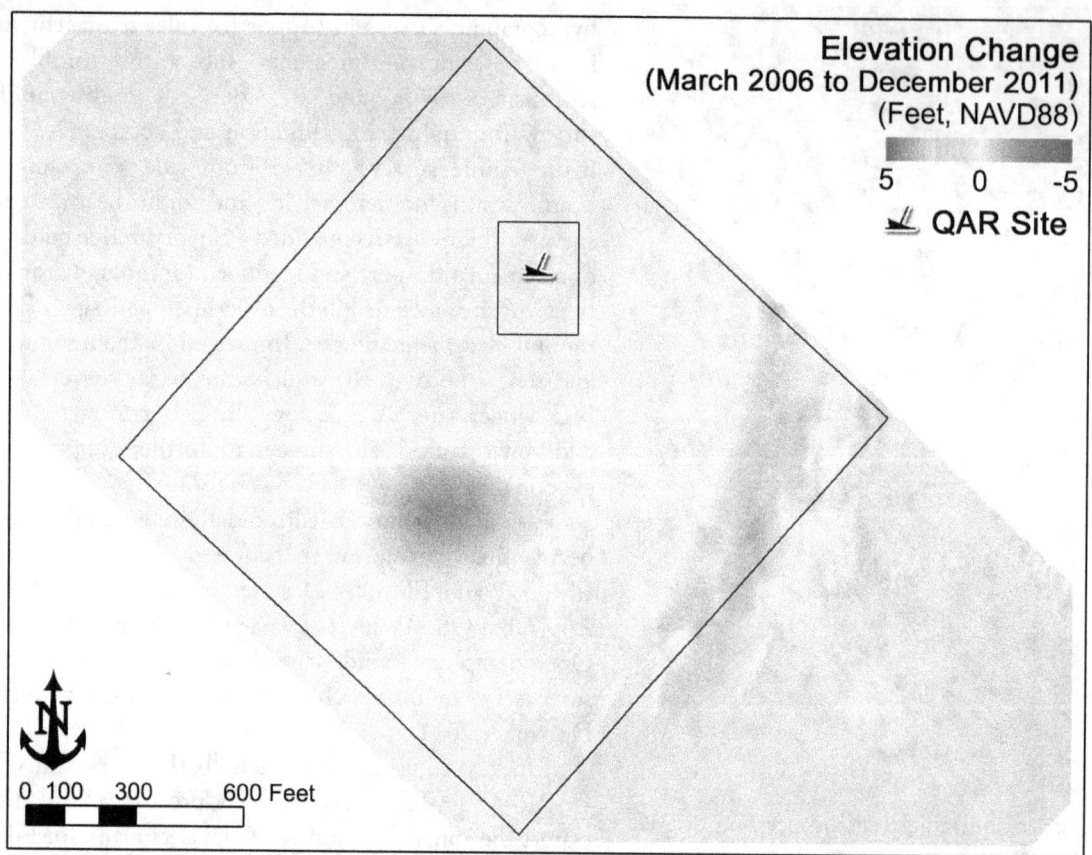

Figure 4. Map showing change in seafloor elevation from the start of the experiment to the end (March 2006 to December 2011). Red indicates loss in elevation and green indicates gain in elevation.

north and east of the mound (Figure 3). From March 2006 to February 2007, the mound began deflating and spreading toward the north. As of February 2007, the wreck site was still erosional and showed scour north of the exposed artifact pile. The October 2007 survey revealed a larger dispersal of the sediment mound to the north with the leading edge progressing approximately 250 ft. since the placement occurred. The wreck site area began to show volumetric gains and less evidence of scour, indicating the beginning of sediment accretion at the site. Between October 2007 and January 2009, the sediment mound and majority of the experimental area showed a more significant loss in volume (-7785 cubic yd.) while the wreck site itself had its most significant accretion (+1033 cubic yd.). About 4 years after placement, in September 2010, the remains of the mound had now spread out substantially in area and appeared to migrate over the wreck site and further to the north. While the volumetric assessment still showed a small amount of accretion (77 cubic yd.) at the wreck site, scour behind the site was now apparent again. With much less sediment available in what was left of the mound, the December 2011 survey showed small material gains at the wreck site and illustrated that the material had now fully encroached the wreck site area and began migrating past it to the north. Cumulatively, the *QAR* site had a net accretion of 1376 cubic yards since the placement of the sediment mound in March 2006.

Discussion

The analysis of six multi-beam sonar surveys from March 2006 to December 2011 shows that the experimental sediment mound had spread out and moved in the general direction of the *QAR* site (Figure 4). This mobilization and northerly transport of sediment increased sand volumes relative to the exposed artifacts at the *QAR* site and acted to protect them from the erosive physical and biochemical action of waves and seawater. The slow migration of sediment associated with the indirect sand disposal method still allowed for on-going archaeological excavations that were conducted after implementation (Wilde-Ramsing and Rodrigues 2009).

The use of high-resolution multi-beam sonar surveys proved instrumental in gaining an understanding of the spatial dispersion and volumetric life-cycle of the sediment mound. Raster-based analysis has allowed marine hydrographers to understand sediment transport processes and the interaction of an anthropogenic sediment source to determine the feasibility of this method to preserve the site through the final excavation phases. Results of this interdisciplinary study have provided the marine archeological community with a viable method to support the protection and longer-term preservation of historically significant cultural resources within energetic nearshore environments.

Acknowledgements

We would like recognize our many colleagues who played a role in this study, particularly: Dan Sumners, Geodynamics; Tony Rodriquez, UNC-CH Institute of Marine Sciences and Department of Marine Sciences; Phil Payonk, US Army Corps of Engineers – Wilmington District; and Chris Southerly, NC Underwater Archaeology Branch.

References

Plakos, Michael J.
2004   *Queen Anne's Revenge* Shipwreck Site. Nomination to the National Register of Historic Places, National Trust for Historic Preservation. Washington DC.

Wells, John T. and Jesse E. McNinch
2001   Reconstructing shoal and channel configuration in Beaufort Inlet: 300 years of change at the site of *Queen Anne's Revenge. Southeastern Geology*, 40.1, 11-18.

Wilde-Ramsing, Mark U. and Charles R. Ewen
2012   Beyond Reasonable Doubt: A case for *Queen Anne's Revenge, Historical Archaeology*, Volume 46, Number 2.

Wilde-Ramsing, Mark U. and Wayne R. Lusardi
1999   Management Plan for North Carolina shipwreck 0003BUI: *Queen Anne's Revenge*, North Carolina Department of Cultural Resources, Raleigh, NC.

Wilde-Ramsing, Mark U. and Antonio B. Rodriguez
2009   Final Report – Using the *Queen Anne's Revenge* Shipwreck Site as a Testing Ground for a New Method of Artifact Protection and Preservation in Shallow-Marine Environments. North Carolina Sea Grant Project Number: R/MG-0620, Raleigh, NC.

Mark U. Wilde-Ramsing
NC Underwater Archaeology Branch (Retired)
3934 Edgewood Road
Wilmington, North Carolina 28403

David J. Bernstein
Geodynamics
310 A Greenfield Drive
Newport, North Carolina 28570

Christopher W. Freeman
Geodynamics
310 A Greenfield Drive
Newport, North Carolina 28570

The Archaeological Investigation of the Storm Wreck, a Wartime Refugee Vessel Lost at St. Augustine, Florida at the End of the Revolutionary War: Overview of the 2010-2015 Excavation Seasons

Carolane Veilleux and Chuck Meide

The Storm Wreck was discovered in 2009 by the Lighthouse Archaeological Maritime Program (LAMP) near St. Augustine's historical inlet. Excavations were conducted 2010-2015 in conjunction with LAMP's field summer school. A wide range of artifacts, including personal items, household items, tools, ship fittings and rigging, cookware, tableware, artillery, and firearms, were recovered for conservation at the St. Augustine Lighthouse & Maritime Museum. The wreck has been identified as one of 16 British ships lost on 31 December 1782, part of the last fleet evacuating British troops and Loyalist refugees from Charleston, SC, at the end of the Revolutionary War.

Introduction

The colonial shipwreck site known as the Storm Wreck (8SJ5459) was discovered by LAMP archaeologists in 2009 and has been the subject of an intensive archaeological excavation every summer from 2010-2015 (Turner and Kennedy 2010; Meide 2013a, 2015a, 2015b; Meide et al. 2011:104-190; Meide et al. 2014:143-322). The shipwreck is located within 1.6 km of shore near the relict St. Augustine Inlet, an

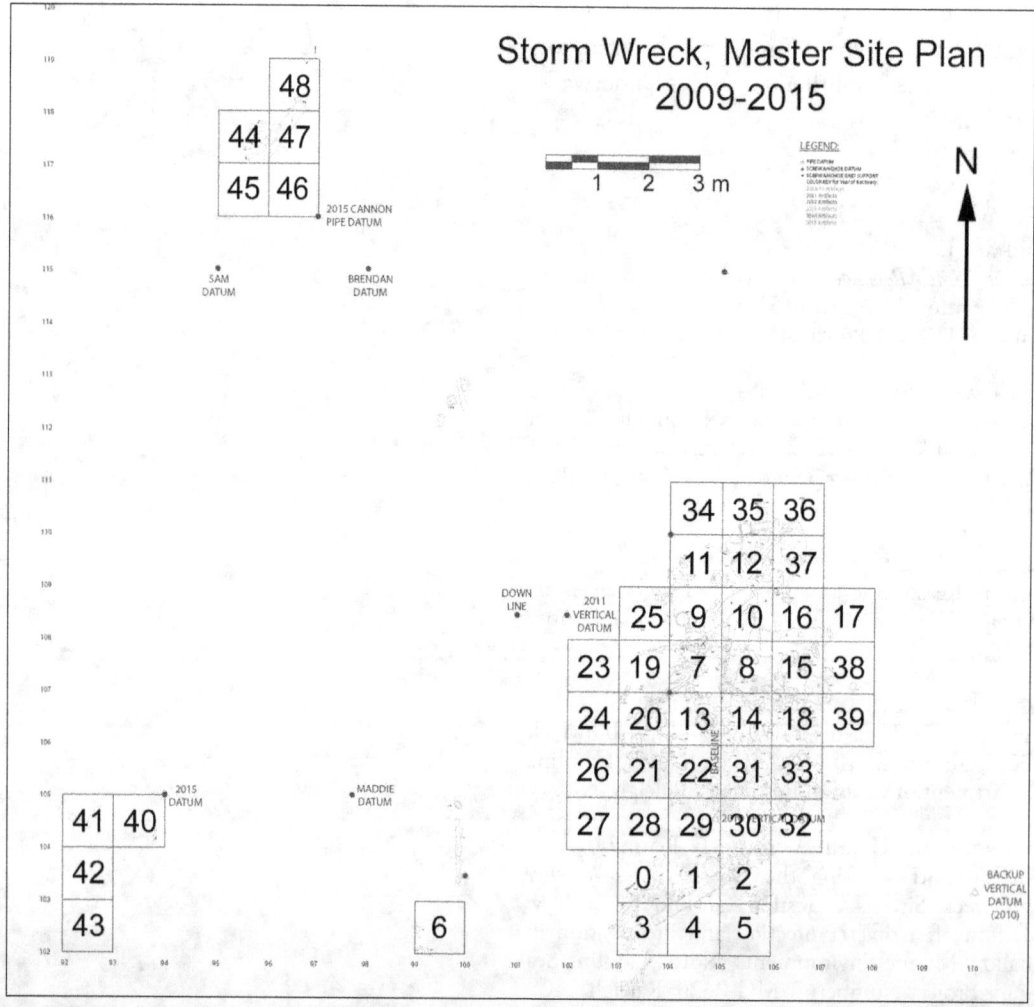

FIGURE 1. The Storm Wreck master site plan, 2009-2015. The main excavation area at right was excavated between 2009 and 2014, and the two outlying areas to the left and upper left were excavated in 2015 (by Chuck Meide and Olivia McDaniel, digitized by Tim Jackson, 2015).

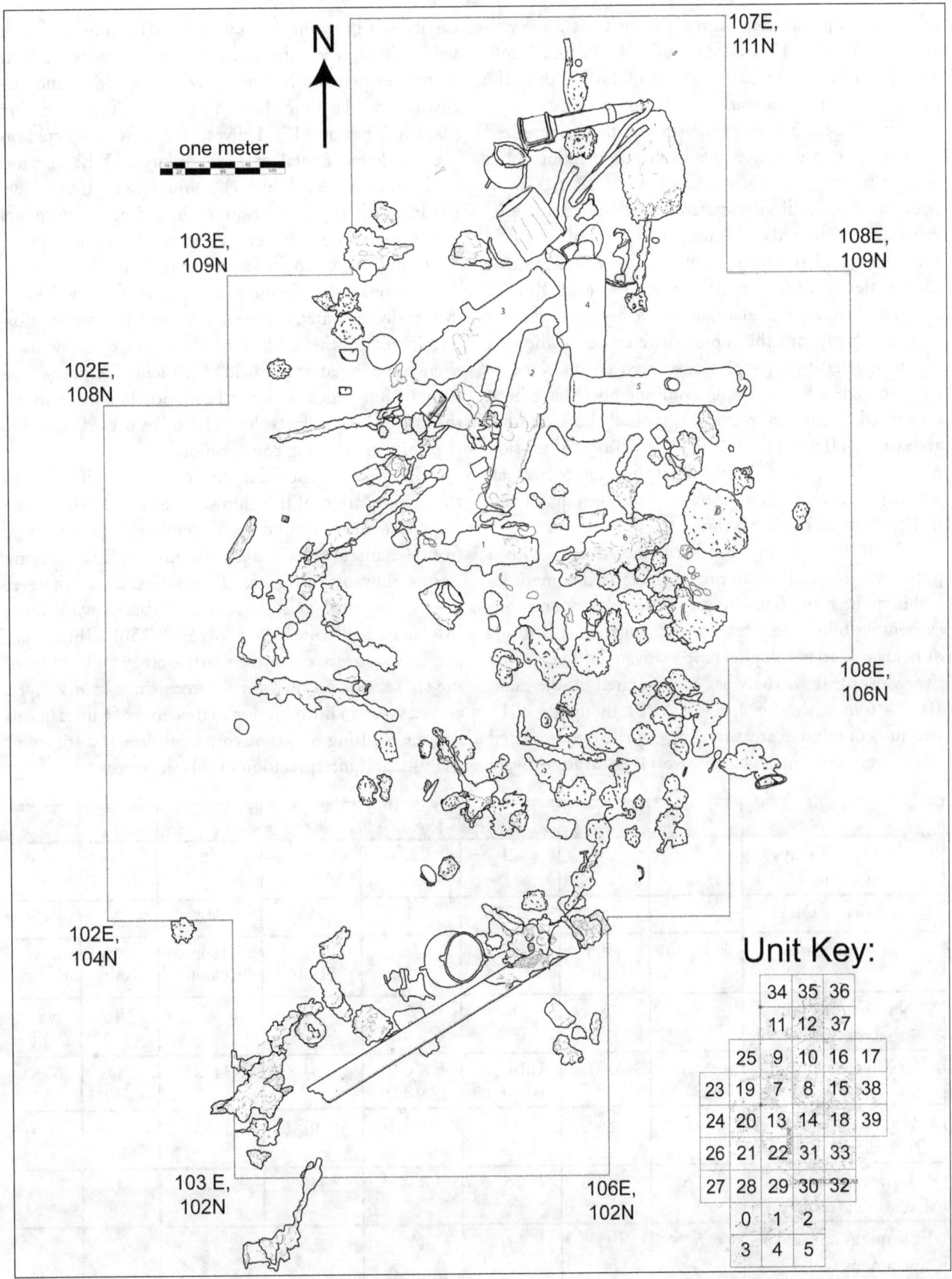

FIGURE 2. The Storm Wreck main excavation area site plan, 2009-2014 (by Chuck Meide and Olivia McDaniel, digitized by Tim Jackson, 2015).

infamous ship trap that claimed as many as 24 vessels annually in the 1780s (Schoepf 1788:226-229,248; Meide 2015a:356-357). It is about 4.8 km south of the present inlet and in about 7.6 to 9.1 m of water.

The physical nature of the site can be characterized as a very dense scatter of buried concretions and other artifacts covering an area of about 10 m X 6 m, with more sporadically scattered and buried material expanding outwards (Figures 1-2). Metal detector surveys beyond the main excavation area indicate that the less dense scatter covers an area of at least 30 m X 26 m, and a few isolated artifacts have been found as far away as 45 m from the approximate center of the site. No articulated hull remains have been encountered to date, though a few individual hull members have been unearthed. Shipwreck material is typically buried under at least 30-60 cm of sand, though periods of erosion periodically expose artifacts. When first discovered, all wreckage was buried, and there were no signs that divers had ever visited the site before.

Conditions on this wreck can be adverse, with a propensity for sudden storms characterized sometimes by heavy surge and frequently by extremely poor or nonexistent visibility. Despite these challenges, in six seasons of fieldwork archaeologists have excavated 48 m² of the site. Most of this activity has concentrated on the main 10 m X 6 m excavation area (Figure 2), though in 2015 two noncontiguous areas totaling 9 m² were excavated to the west and northwest (Figure 1). Excavations were carried out in conjunction with LAMP's annual 4-week field school, with the research vessel *Roper*, a 36 ft. ex-trawler generously loaned by David Howe and the Institute of Maritime History, serving as the main diving platform. To date, 1,371 dives have been completed on the wreck for a total of 1,094 hours and 12 minutes of bottom time (Table 1). Ninety-two divers have participated in the excavation, including 55 students and dozens of volunteers. A total of 481 numbered field specimens have been collected, many of which are concretions containing multiple artifacts which are eventually separated and treated in the lab. Conservation has increased the artifact count, and at this writing there are 653 cataloged field specimens. Including lead Rupert shot which have not been individually counted, thousands of artifacts have been recovered and are currently undergoing conservation.

The archaeological data collected to date have led to the identification of this shipwreck as one of 16 refugee ships lost on or around 31 December 1782, on route from Charleston, SC to St. Augustine, FL, carrying troops, Loyalist civilians, their slaves, and whatever possessions they could manage to bring with them (McNamara 2014; Meide 2015a,2015b). This paper presents an overview of the methodology and results of the six seasons on the Storm Wreck since its discovery, and serves as an introduction to the series of papers in this volume focusing on various aspects of the investigation, analysis, and interpretation of this shipwreck.

	2009	2010	2011	2012	2013	2014	2015	Total
Number of Days Diving	3	30	21	22	29	16	15	136
Number of Dives	6	181	237	226	253	244	224	1371
Bottom Time	3h 20min	150h 37min	222h 27min	138h 11min	221h 31min	180h 59min	177h 7min	1094h 12min
Number of Units Excavated	N/A	6	10	5	12	6	9	48
Excavated Units	N/A	U0-U5	U8-U10, U12-U18	U7, U10, U19-U21	U22-U33	U34-U39	U40-U48	N/A
Highest Elevation Recorded (in cmbd)	N/A	24	15	45	20.5	25	9	N/A
Lowest Elevation Excavated (in cmbd)	N/A	108	85	144	150	137	137	N/A
Number of Field Specimens Collected	5	94	96	111	92	41	47	486

TABLE 1. Summary of 2009-2015 Field Seasons (from LAMP 2015)

General Methodology

Horizontal and Vertical Control

A grid system established on site in June 2010 was expanded over the years to provide horizontal control for excavation. A polypropylene baseline, marked at one meter intervals, was stretched across the length of the initial 10 X 10 m site area, running from south to north along the 105E line. The baseline was placed so that its center point lined up with the original magnetic anomaly STM001 at 105E, 105N. The baseline was secured with screw anchors and, in 2011, it was extended an additional 5 m to the north.

Excavation grids were fashioned of PVC piping in 1 m X 1 m or 1 m X 2 m sizes, and marked at 10 cm intervals with black electrical tape discernable by touch for divers in low visibility. The PVC grid units were initially suspended from ten meter long polypropylene gridlines, which were aligned east-west and secured by screw anchors. The line diameter and alignment was purposely chosen to aid divers orienting themselves in low or zero visibility: all gridlines were 2.54 cm line running east-west, while the baseline and additional travel lines holding the units in place were 0.64 cm running north-south. As the excavation expanded in subsequent years, gridlines were omitted and new grids were pinned to the seafloor using long fiberglass rods. Most grids were recovered at the end of each field season, though several have been left in place, firmly secured by sinking 3.05 m lengths of pipe down into the sand and lashing them to grid corners, allowing an accurate reestablishment of the grid system in the future. These grids tend to remain buried once excavation in the area has ceased.

Over six years, a total of 48 meter square units have been designated and excavated, Units 0 through 48 (U6 was designated in 2006 but never excavated). The units are also referred to by the Cartesian coordinates of their southwest corner (i.e., U13 is also 104E, 106N) but the simple numbering system was easier for working divers.

A vertical datum was set in place at the start of the 2010 field season by driving a 4.57 m long steel pipe into the seafloor using the hydraulic probing system. It provided a secure anchor for the datum in an otherwise dynamic underwater landscape. A wire tie loop, point designated zero, was fixed to the upper portion of the pipe, so that a level line could be extended from there and vertical measurements taken below that point could be expressed as cmbd (cm below datum). Four additional vertical datums were established at various locations throughout the excavation areas, all being marked at the same level for vertical control across the site. In 2013, a secondary datum was established on each pipe datum, 30 cm higher than the primary datum, which allowed for accurate vertical measurements when the visibility was zero on the seafloor but somewhat better higher in the water column.

Excavation and Recording

Two handheld 10.2 cm diameter induction dredges were used for excavation. The dredges were normally operated simultaneously by two teams to excavate two units at a time. They were powered by individual water pumps mounted on the research vessel above which was kept stationary on a three-point mooring. The exhaust end of each dredge hose was left on the seafloor downcurrent from the site (to the north or northwest), and all dredge spoil was filtered through an attached mesh bag. After the discovery of tiny lead pellets in the dredge spoil early in the first season, doubled mesh bags were used to ensure the complete recovery of even the smallest of artifacts. This resulted in a sizable amount of dredge spoil, mainly in the form of shell hash, which was sorted by laboratory volunteers during and after the close of fieldwork.

Divers excavated in arbitrary levels. Before the start of excavation, elevation measurements (in cmbd) were recorded, usually in all four corners and the center of the unit. After an excavation dive, divers recorded closing

FIGURE 3. The 4-pounder long gun, designated Cannon 2 or Field Specimen 11S-153.14, was raised from the Storm Wreck site on 28 June 2011 using the lifting davit on the research vessel *Roper* (Courtesy of LAMP, 2011).

elevations, and the volume excavated was treated as a single provenience. The site is characterized by deep deposits of sand that constantly shift, typically with no discernable sediment stratigraphy. Sometimes clay deposits have been observed around some clusters of artifacts, and in some rare cases discernable sediment strata have been observed, most typically a dark layer of more organic sediment which seems to represent mud deposits brought by outgoing tides from estuarine rivers which have filled voids left by scouring events (including previous archaeological excavation). Excavated areas left untouched for more than a day or two would fill as sand in surrounding areas slumped into the unit; backfilling is rarely required. A more thorough discussion of site formation processes on this and other St. Augustine shipwrecks is presented by Burke (this volume).

There was usually no need for pre-disturbance drawings before excavation, as all cultural material was buried. The exception was in 2011, when an eroded portion of the site revealed buried cannons and other artifacts. When erosion or excavation revealed concretions or other artifacts, detailed 1:5 scaled drawings were made of each unit on mylar sheets when visibility allowed. All underwater drawings were re-drafted onto large sheets of mylar at the same 1:5 scale after the field season closed. These were scanned and then digitized (vectorized) using Adobe Illustrator for the final site plan.

Artifact Recovery

Once recorded, artifacts were brought to the surface in sturdy plastic baskets lined with window screen, preventing the loss of tiny objects. A lightweight winch capable of lifting 136.3 kg is mounted on *Roper*, though in most cases divers used a lift bag to do so. In the case of the heaviest objects, such as the cannons raised in 2011, a heavy-duty davit capable of lifting up to 1,590 kg was employed (Figure 3).

In some cases the decision was made to return an artifact to its original location underwater after documentation. This was done with a large nail cask, a plank, and concretions determined by x-ray to offer little diagnostic value (for example, redundant clusters of nails). The proximity of LAMP's headquarters to the site makes repatriation relatively simple.

A binomial Field Specimen number was assigned to each individual object or group of like objects. The prefix or project code refers to the year and site, and the subsequent catalog number represents the consecutive number of specimens recovered from the site. The number is provided a decimal number extension for any object removed from the original specimen. Thus, Field Specimen 13S-310.1 is a concretion recovered from Storm Wreck in 2013, and was the 153rd field specimen to be recovered from the site since its discovery, while 13S-310.2 was a spoon and 13S-310.3 a key from that concretion.

Fieldwork Summary 2009-2015

2009 Discovery

The Storm Wreck was discovered in August 2009 when target testing magnetic anomalies identified during LAMP's 2009 remote sensing survey in June of 2009 (Turner and Kennedy 2009:11-13). The Storm Wreck survey area produced one 20 gamma magnetic anomaly, designated Target STM001. Its exact location was refined using a handheld magnetometer on 17 August, and it was tested using a hydraulic probe on 24 August. On this day, the diver used a 3.05 m long probe to jet beneath the sand, encountering material on the second probe test. Using the probe to clear sand in what would the following year be designated U1-U2 and U5, a wooden plank, several concretions, two ballast stones, and a large, concreted cauldron were encountered in zero visibility conditions. Five field specimens were recovered for analysis. As the discovery had been made on the last week of the field season, the site was marked with a submerged buoy and other than a brief clean-up dive it was not visited again until summer 2010.

2010 Season

The 2010 season began with a pre-disturbance sidescan sonar survey of the site, the first use of sonar to image the site in a regular monitoring effort that continues to this day (Burke, this volume). Diving began immediately afterwards, starting with a handheld magnetometer survey. Divers surveyed a 10 m² area centered on the original anomaly STM001, recording the magnetic field in gammas every meter along 11 transect lines. The 121 readings were plotted using Surfer software to generate a magnetic contour map of the immediate site environs (Meide 2013a:Figure 3).

A total of 181 dives was completed over 30 days between June and August, and six units (U0-U5) were excavated (Table 1). The 2 X 3 m excavation area revealed the 2.7 m long plank and large cauldron encountered previously, and a dense scatter of concretions.

Ninety-four field specimens were recovered, including the cauldron (the largest found), three smaller cauldrons, the plank and a timber, and numerous concretions and small finds including a brass buckle, wine glass base, and vast numbers of tiny lead shot (Meide et al. 2011; Meide 2013a; McNamara 2013). Post-season x-ray analysis revealed many interesting objects within concretions, including clothing irons, ship fittings, tools, a coin (deconcreted in 2014 and found to be a gold guinea dated 1774), navigational dividers, and a small boxlock pistol (Hanks 2013; Cox 2013). Amazingly, an intact green pea was found embedded within the concreted contents of the smallest cauldron (Carter, this volume).

On 17 December, LAMP archaeologists conducted an off-season site visit for monitoring. To their surprise, divers found five cannons and the ship's bell, recently exposed by shifting sands. Given its rarity and vulnerable exposure, the bell was documented and recovered. It was almost completely intact, missing only part of its wooden headstock and its clapper. These two missing components would be located the following year. The bell was cleaned in January but bore no inscription or indication of the year or ship's name (Jasper 2013:51-53; Meide et al. 2014:201-208; Andes, this volume).

2011 Season

Diving in 2011 was limited to three days in May, most of June, and three days in August. Over these 23 days, 247 dives were conducted, ten new units (U8-U10, U12-U18) were excavated, and 96 field specimens were recovered (Meide et al. 2014:147-160). Most of the June field school was dedicated to fully exposing and recording the recently discovered cannons in order to select two for recovery (Turner and Meide 2013; Meide, this volume). Excavation revealed a sixth gun, totaling four traditional cannons and two carronades. One of each type was raised, and the carronade was dated 1780, which remains the *terminus post quem* for the wrecksite (Figures 2-3). Dozens of concretions and finds such as iron and copper cookware, pewter spoons and plates, clothing irons, buttons, bricks, casks of nails, cannonballs, and a shoe buckle were also unearthed.

Another significant find was a heavy, lead deck pump. It displayed cut marks indicating that it was forcibly removed from the ship to jettison overboard in hopes of saving the grounded vessel, providing some of the first clues as to the circumstances of the wrecking event itself (Meide 2015b:375-376; Andes, this volume).

2012 Season

2012 saw unusually rough weather in June, preventing most work that month, and inundating the site with sand overburden. Two hundred twenty-six dives were completed over 22 days mostly in July and August. Five new units (U7, U11, U19-21) were excavated, expanding outwards from the previous year's excavation area, along with two partially excavated the year before (U8, U15). One hundred eleven field specimens were collected (Meide et al. 2014:147-160). Excavation also took place in the 2010 units to rebury a number of concretions from that season. Despite the heavy sand accretion in June, some areas underwent erosion in July, exposing several concretions, including the first musket found on site.

2012 yielded more artifacts similar to those found previously, including spoons, cauldrons, pins, shot, buttons, shoe buckles, clothing irons, tools, and coins (including a gold guinea dated 1776) (Brendel, this volume; McCarron, this volume). This was also the first year that British military artifacts were discovered (McNamara, this volume), including regimental buttons and three Brown Bess muskets. Subsequent x-rays showed two of them were loaded and half-cocked, ready for use (Meide et al. 2014:182-192; Cox, this volume). A button from the 71st Regiment of Foot from U19 dredge spoil provided the first conclusive evidence that the Storm Wreck was a member of the Charleston evacuation fleet.

2013 Season

In 2013 excavation continued to expand southward, connecting the 2011-2012 excavation area with the 2010 area. Twelve new units (U22-U33) were excavated and two previous units (U18, U21) were completed. The season included 29 days of diving from June to August, during which 253 dives were conducted with the recovery of 92 field specimens.

Visibility in 2013 was unusually good, allowing for the first extensive underwater video footage and the first *in situ* artifact photographs. In addition to familiar items such as spoons, cannonballs, clothing irons, and buttons, a multitude of unique objects were recovered, including a sector rule, brass keg tap, furniture drawer pull, a door lock wrapped up with its key in cloth, a false watch face, an assortment of lead weights, a livestock tether, and a well-preserved British sea service pistol (Burkett, this volume; Brendel, this volume; McCarron,

FIGURE 4. Detail of the right trunnion of the carronade, showing "9 P" or the caliber of the gun (9-pounder) over the date of manufacture, "1780." The opposite trunnion displayed the serial number of the gun identified in the Carron Company records (Courtesy of LAMP, 2011).

this volume; Thomson, this volume; Cox, this volume).

2014 Season

In 2014 the Lighthouse secured grant support from Florida's Bureau of Historic Preservation, which funded two additional conservators and significant laboratory expenses for two years. Nevertheless, the backlog of artifacts in storage resulted in less field excavation. Only 16 days in June were spent diving on the Storm Wreck, with 244 dives completed and six new units (U34-U39) excavated along with four previously excavated units (U16-U17, U33, U37). Only 41 field specimens were recovered. More metal detecting began, to better understand the buried extent of the site while minimizing artifact recovery. Five survey areas typically measuring 10 X 12 m to the north, south, east, and west of the main excavation area were completed. Divers followed a series of transect lines spaced two meters apart, sweeping the metal detector back and forth to cover both sides of the transect, marking noticeable hits on a pre-drawn mylar map. A total area of 560 m² was surveyed in this manner. Sporadic hits were noted throughout the surveyed areas, more concentrated close to the main excavation area and becoming less frequent further away towards the north, east, and south. This was not the case towards the west, where sporadic metal detector hits remained relatively consistent as far as 13 m from the main excavation area. One location about 13 m northwest of the primary excavation area featured several strong readings in a concentrated area. This anomaly led to the test excavation and a cannon discovery the following year.

2015 Excavation Season

As with the year before, excavation was less aggressive in the 2015 season. Only 15 days of diving were executed during the June field school, for a total of 224 dives. Nine new units were excavated, and 47 specimens recovered (of these, 35 were sediment samples). For the first time, excavation took place well outside the primary excavation area, in an attempt to better understand the buried extent of the site to the west. Two distinct areas outside the main excavation were targeted to groundtruth results of the 2014 metal detector survey (Figure 1). A cluster of four units (U40-U43) eight meters to the west produced only a few scattered concretions. However, the more promising anomaly around ten meters to the northwest resulted in an exciting find, a seventh cannon with its carriage partially intact (Meide, this volume:Figure 4). Five units were excavated here (U44-U48), exposing not only the gun but also a deadeye in its iron strop and several other concretions which appear to be tools or fittings.

A new activity in 2015 was the systematic collection of sediment samples. In previous seasons sediment samples were collected only sporadically, when sand was trapped within the confines of an excavated cauldron. In 2015 samples were taken in each excavated unit at the beginning of each arbitrary level, and at the bottom of the final level. This resulted in 35 samples collected from nine units. Thirty-six gallons (136.27 L) of sediment, including the 2015 samples and the few collected in previous seasons, were analyzed by Jacob Shidner (this volume) of University of Arkansas. He identified six invertebrate specimens, including ant and beetle remains, along with a cut, cooked fish vertebra from within cauldron 13S-308.1.

The 2015 excavation season was the final major field operation planned for the foreseeable future. Investigations will continue in the laboratory, and artifact conservation will continue for years. Public archaeology is ongoing, as the site has been interpreted for St. Augustine Lighthouse & Maritime Museum visitors since the inception of fieldwork (McDaniel et al., this volume). A major new exhibit titled "Wrecked!" is scheduled to open by early May 2016 (Swann and

Vessel Name	Date	Nationality	Vessel Type	Location
Unnamed 1782 sloop	Oct 1782		Sloop	On St. Augustine Bar
Rattlesnake	31 Dec 1782	English	Ship (galley?)	On St. Augustine Bar
Sixteen unnamed Loyalist refugee vessels from Charleston	31 Dec 1782	English		On St. Augustine Bar
Mary	19 Apr 1783	English	Ship	On St. Augustine bar
Tony	Oct 1783	English	Vessel	On St. Augustine Bar
Flounder	1783	English?	Ship	Driven ashore (Anastasia?)
Unnamed English vessel	1784	English		St. Augustine Bar
Unnamed St. Augustine pilot boat	1784	English		On St. Augustine Bar
James	7 Nov 1787	American?		On St Augustine Bar
Hope	2 Jun 1789	American?		On St. Augustine Bar
Santa Maria	1790	Spanish?		On St. Augustine Bar
Nuestra Señora del Carmen	22 Nov 1792	Spanish?		On St. Augustine bar.
Phoebus	1802	American	Schooner	On St Augustine Bar
Santa Maria	13 Jan 1803	Spanish?		On St. Augustine Bar
Friendship	14 Apr 1803	American?	Sloop	On St. Augustine Bar
Diligencia	2 Jun 1803	Spanish?	Schooner	On St. Augustine Bar
Betsy	20 Sep 1803	American?		N of St. Augustine Bar
Amiable Antoinette	26 Dec 1816		Ship	Near St Augustine
Due Bell	Jun 1816		Schooner	Near St Augustine
Water Witch	Jun 1816		Schooner	Near St Augustine
Huron	Jun 1816		Snow	Near St Augustine
Frolic	Dec 1816	American		Anastasia Island
Several unnamed 1816 Vessels	1816			St. Augustine

TABLE 2. Ships known to have been lost near the Storm Wreck, 1778-1820 (from LAMP 2011)

McDaniel, this volume).

Discussion and Conclusion

Identifying the Storm Wreck

The first datable artifacts found on the shipwreck were tiny lead pellets concentrated throughout the 2010 excavation area (Meide et al. 2011:127-131). Known as Rupert shot after their alleged inventor, they were first publicized in 1665, but then used throughout the colonial period. The date range for the ship was further narrowed as more recovered artifacts were dated to the 18th century, with some—such as the base of a drinking glass dated to ca. 1780-1805—suggesting origins in the late 18th century. Hopes that the ship's bell would provide a date or ship's name were quelled once it was cleared of concretion. There have been three dated objects recovered from the wreck, however. The *terminus post quem* of 1780 was provided by the recovered carronade (Meide, this volume). In addition, two gold guinea coins from the reign of George III were dated 1774 and 1776.

The various absolute and relative dates suggested the Storm Wreck was lost sometime in the final two decades of the 18th century, or perhaps early in the 19th. With this in mind, researchers compiled a list of potential shipwreck candidates lost between 1780 and 1820 (Table 2). By the end of the 2011 season, the primary working hypothesis was that this wreck represented one of 16 Loyalist refugee ships lost on the bar in December 1782 (Schoepf 1788:228; Meide 2013a:17,24-25). These were all from the last fleet employed by British authorities to evacuate Charleston of troops, Loyalist civilians, and enslaved Africans (Meide 2015b; Trivelpiece and Meide, this volume). The regularity of 18th-century British material culture, with a high frequency of domestic items expected of refugees fleeing their homes, convinced researchers of this scenario.

In 2012 the first military button was identified, a Royal Provincial regimental button (McNamara, this volume:Figures 1-2). Having come from an unspecified Loyalist regiment, it was considered strong circumstantial evidence that Storm ship carried Loyalists. Shortly thereafter, a 71st Regiment button (McNamara, this volume:Figure 2) provided the first definitive evidence linking this shipwreck with the Charleston evacuation fleet (Meide 2015a,2015b; Trivelpiece and Meide, this volume). Since then, buttons from three additional British Army regiments known to have been aboard the same fleet have been identified in the assemblage (McNamara, this volume:Figure 2).

These buttons, together with the archaeological data as currently understood, have convinced researchers that the Storm Wreck was indeed one of these military transports evacuating troops and civilians which was lost on or around 31 December 1782 on the St. Augustine bar (McNamara 2014). This prompted several research trips to the British National Archives and other repositories which have resulted in a rich historical context and fuller understanding of this shipwreck (Meide 2013b; Trivelpiece, this volume). As is often the case, however, archaeology has raised as many questions as were answered. None of the aforementioned regiments on the fleet were destined for St. Augustine, and they arrived safely in New York, Jamaica, and other destinations. Why these buttons, which are clearly associated with the evacuation fleet but not with a vessel bound for Florida, ended up on a transport wrecked off St. Augustine remains a mystery (Meide 2015b:181).

Interpreting the Storm Wreck as a Refugee Vessel

As a vessel carrying Loyalist refugees to Florida in 1782, the Storm Wreck promises considerable insight into an underappreciated but dynamic period of Florida's history, that of the Loyalist influx at the end of the American Revolution (Meide 2015b). But this site can also provide a much broader perspective into the archaeology of the refugee. It is believed that the Storm Wreck represents the only wartime refugee shipwreck from any time period to be archaeologically investigated. As such, and with its well-preserved assemblage of material culture coupled with a rich documentary context, it has the potential to enable a better understanding of the behavior of wartime refugees diachronically and cross-culturally.

The quantity, diversity, and preservation of material culture from this shipwreck allow for a meaningful study of refugee behavior. These artifacts give us an extraordinary glimpse of what British colonists used in their everyday lives in a situation that was anything but ordinary. The range of artifacts provides insight into the assortment of people caught up in forced exodus. Specialized tools suggest craftsmen such as shoemakers and shipwrights were present alongside soldiers, merchants, and farmers. Personal objects reflecting various levels of social status—from a spoon inscribed with an "X" by its probably illiterate owner, to the gold coins, decorative shoe buckle, and boxlock pistol undoubtedly belonging to a gentleman—suggest a spectrum of colonial society was aboard, from enslaved laborers to landed gentry. Ongoing study of these artifacts demonstrates what items were chosen during a crisis as absolutely essential, not only for survival but also to keep life as normal as possible when faced with a dangerous and uncertain future. These refugees brought cookware, tableware, and fireplace hardware to feed the family, kettles and porcelain teawares to maintain the stability and comfort of daily teatime, and the hardware, furnishings, and tools with which to rebuild new homes and new lives. The papers that follow this one provide more detailed discussions of these topics and bring into focus the stories of these desperate Loyalists seeking safe haven in St. Augustine.

Acknowledgements

While the excavation of Storm Wreck has been self-funded by LAMP and the St. Augustine Lighthouse & Maritime Museum, the original survey, the exhibit, and much of the conservation were funded with grants from the Bureau of Historic Preservation, Division of Historical Resources, Florida Department of State with the Florida Historical Commission. Dave Howe and the Institute of Maritime History generously provided the research vessel *Roper*. This project's great success ultimately lies with the team of LAMP/Lighthouse staff, students, and volunteers who have given their time, talent, and passion to this shipwreck. Thanks to them all.

References

Cox, Starr
2013 Personal Items Recovered from the Storm Wreck, a Late 18th Century Shipwreck off the Coast of St. Augustine, Florida. In *ACUA Underwater Archaeology Proceedings 2012*, Brian Jordan and Troy Nowak, editors, pp. 44-49. Advisory Council on Underwater Archaeology, Baltimore, Maryland.

Hanks, Matthew
2013 The Storm Wreck Concretions: A Look Beneath the Surface. In *ACUA Underwater Archaeology Proceedings 2012*, Brian Jordan and Troy Nowak, editors, pp. 32-37. Advisory Council on Underwater Archaeology, Baltimore, Maryland.

Jasper, Michael
2013 Ship's Fittings and Equipment Recovered from the Storm Wreck, a Late 18th Century Shipwreck off the Coast of St. Augustine. In *ACUA Underwater Archaeology Proceedings 2012*, Brian Jordan and Troy Nowak, editors, pp. 51-59. Advisory Council on Underwater Archaeology, Baltimore, Maryland.

Lighthouse Archaeological Maritime Program (LAMP)
2011 *LAMP Shipwreck Database, First Coast Shipwrecks 1520-1995*. Lighthouse Archaeological Program, St. Augustine, Florida.

McNamara, Brian
2013 Cooking with Fire: What Cookware and Tableware Can Tell Us About an Unidentified 18th Century Shipwreck. In *ACUA Underwater Archaeology Proceedings 2012*, Brian Jordan and Troy J. Nowak, editors, pp. 38-43. Advisory Council on Underwater Archaeology, Baltimore, Maryland.

2014 Out of Exile: Identifying the Storm Wreck, a Colonial Shipwreck off St. Augustine, Florida; Finding Context through Artifactual and Archival Research. Master's Thesis, Department of Archaeology, Flinders University, Adelaide, Australia.

Meide, Chuck
2013a Investigation of the Storm Wreck, a Late 18th Century Shipwreck Off the Coast of St. Augustine, Florida: Results of the First Two Excavation Seasons, 2010-2011. In *ACUA Underwater Archaeology Proceedings 2012*, Brian Jordan and Troy Nowak, editors, pp. 17-25. Advisory Council on Underwater Archaeology, Baltimore, Maryland.

2013b Archival Research on the Storm Wreck: Using Documentary Evidence to Corroborate the Archaeological Record. Paper presented at the 65th annual meeting of the Florida Anthropological Society, May 10-12, 2013, St. Augustine, Florida.

2015a "Cast Away off the Bar": The Archaeological Investigation of British Period Shipwrecks in *St. Augustine. Florida Historical Quarterly* 93(3):355-387.

2015b An Archaeological Perspective on East Florida's Loyalist Influx: The Excavation of a Loyalist Refugee Vessel Lost at St. Augustine on 31 December 1782. *FCH Annals* 22:172-186.

Meide, Chuck, P. Brendan Burke, Olivia McDaniel, Samuel P. Turner, Eden Andes, Hunter Brendel, Starr Cox and Brian McNamara
2014 *First Coast Maritime Archaeology Project 2011-2012: Report on Archaeological Investigations*.

MEIDE, CHUCK, SAMUEL P. TURNER, P. BRENDAN BURKE AND STARR COX
2011   *First Coast Maritime Archaeology Project 2010: Report on Archaeological Investigations.* Lighthouse Archaeological Maritime Program, St. Augustine Lighthouse & Maritime Museum, St. Augustine, Florida.

TURNER, SAM AND CHUCK MEIDE
2013   Artillery of the Storm Wreck. In *ACUA Underwater Archaeology Proceedings 2012,* Brian Jordan and Troy Nowak, editors, pp. 26-31. Advisory Council on Underwater Archaeology, Baltimore, Maryland.

Carolane Veilleux
University of Montreal
5616 Jules-Auclair,
Montréal, Qc, Canada
H1G 1S4

Chuck Meide
Lighthouse Archaeological Maritime Program (LAMP)
81 Lighthouse Avenue
St Augustine, FL 32080
cmeide@staugustinelighthouse.org

Archival Research and the Historical Background of the 1782 Evacuation of Charleston and the Loss of the Storm Wreck

Molly L. Trivelpiece and Chuck Meide

During the American Revolution, thousands of Loyalists displaced by war sought refuge in East Florida. As the war drew to a close, British authorities organized massive evacuations of major ports. On 18 December 1782, more than 120 ships loaded with troops and refugees left Charleston, SC. Of the ships destined for East Florida's capital, St. Augustine, 16 were wrecked trying to cross its notorious sandbar. One of these, known as the Storm Wreck, has undergone archaeological investigations from 2009-2015. This paper overviews the archival research and the historical context of the Loyalist Influx, the evacuation of Charleston, and the shipwreck event.

Introduction

The Lighthouse Archaeological Maritime Program (LAMP), the research arm of the St. Augustine Lighthouse & Maritime Museum, has been excavating the Storm Wreck since its discovery in 2009 (Meide 2015a, 2015b). Serving as a military transport and member of the last fleet to evacuate British troops, Loyalist civilians, and enslaved Africans from Charleston, South Carolina

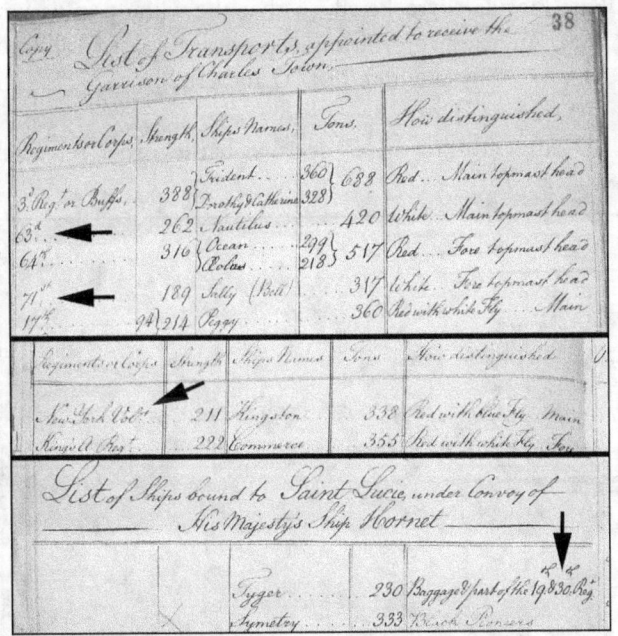

Figure 1. Excerpts from "List of transports appointed to receive the Garrison of Charles Town" dated 19 November 1782. Compiled a month before the fleet departed, the document lists all of the ships, their tonnages, and what Army regiments, cargo, or numbers of refugees and slaves were assigned to each vessel. The black arrows point to regiments whose uniform buttons have been found on the Storm Wreck (McNamara, this volume:Figure 2). Ships had not yet been assigned for the East Florida fleet when this document was produced so the Storm Wreck is not included (BNA 1782:CO5/108,ff.38-40, courtesy of the British National Archives).

(Meide 2015b:376-378), it wrecked on the infamous St. Augustine sandbar in 1782. It promises insight into an unappreciated and mostly forgotten chapter in Revolutionary War history.

The association of the shipwreck with the evacuation of Loyalists from the southern colonies meant that there was a rich documentary record to supplement and better understand the archaeological data. Waging a war that spanned the globe, the British were experts in military logistics and recordkeeping (Syrett 1970). But, in large part because the victors write the history books, the paper trail was cold. Few American scholars have focused their research on the Loyalist experience (with notable exceptions including Siebert 1929; Wright 1971; Williams 1976; Troxler 1981; Lambert 2010; Smith 2011).

LAMP researchers therefore conducted a series of archival research trips to depositories in the United Kingdom (Meide 2013; McNamara 2014:27-30). The first of these was a five-day visit to the British National Archives (BNA) by Chuck Meide in January 2013. Around 900 pages of relevant documents were photographed at that time. These were primarily official correspondences pertaining to the military operations, evacuations, and Florida's Loyalist influx; they also included logbooks and muster rolls from naval escorts HMS *Belisarius* and the armed galley *Viper*. Other documents were related to the 71st Regiment, at that time the only specific British Army unit represented in the artifact assemblage (subsequently buttons from the 3rd American, 30th, and 63rd regiments have been recovered, in addition to unspecified provincial units; see McNamara, this volume). Among the most significant finds was a document titled "List of transports appointed to receive the Garrison of Charles Town" dated 19 November 1782 (BNA 1782:CO5/108,ff.38-41). This list, compiled before the evacuation, detailed the transports slated to evacuate the city (Figure 1). It survived among the papers of the Commander-in-Chief of the British Army in New York, General Sir Guy Carleton. Also discovered was the "abstract," or summary, of the ships that actually did sail with the fleet (BNA 1783:CO5/108,f.76). This latter document, dated 3 January 1783 (after the fleet sailed) gave the number and aggregate tonnage, but not the names or individual tonnages of the ships sailing to St. Augustine and other destinations (Figure 2).

A second research trip was undertaken by Lillian Azevedo, who spent five days in the BNA and also the National Maritime Museum in January 2014. She discovered additional information on the evacuation fleet, including its sailing instructions, along with the log of HMS *Belisarius'* lieutenant. Additional research was carried out by Loren Clark, who spent four days in the National Archives of Scotland in Edinburgh, also in January 2014, and found Carron Company records related to the Storm Wreck carronade. In September 2014 Clark also spent three days in the BNA, research that was coordinated by Brian McNamara (2014:29) for his master's thesis. This resulted in the acquisition of all of the remaining escort vessels' logs from the Charleston evacuation fleet. McNamara has conducted a study of these logs, resulting in a sophisticated understanding of the fleet's movement and the weather patterns between Charleston and St. Augustine. He has also studied the 1782-1783 online editions of Lloyd's *Register of Shipping*, successfully identifying most of the privately-owned transport vessels that sailed in the Charleston evacuation fleet (McNamara 2014:43-53,61-64).

The remainder of this paper is a historical overview of Florida's Loyalist Influx, the evacuation of Charleston, and the wrecking event that resulted in the loss of the Storm Wreck informed by the research carried out in British archives.

The Loyalist Influx of East Florida, 1775-1782

As early as 1775, Loyalist refugees displaced by the American Revolution in Virginia sought haven in East Florida (Smith 2011:262). This followed a November 1775 proclamation issued by East Florida's Governor Patrick Tonyn offering asylum and land grants to loyal subjects displaced by the insurgence. Tonyn's declaration was distributed throughout the southern colonies, and rebel governments passed laws encouraging Loyalists to flee to St. Augustine (Williams 1976:465). As the war progressed, the numbers of Loyalist refugees arriving in East Florida skyrocketed, so that the white population of St. Augustine grew from its pre-war figure of 1,000 to over 4,500 by late June 1782 (Lambert 2010:187; Smith 2011:262,271).

After Yorktown, as decisive battles were replaced

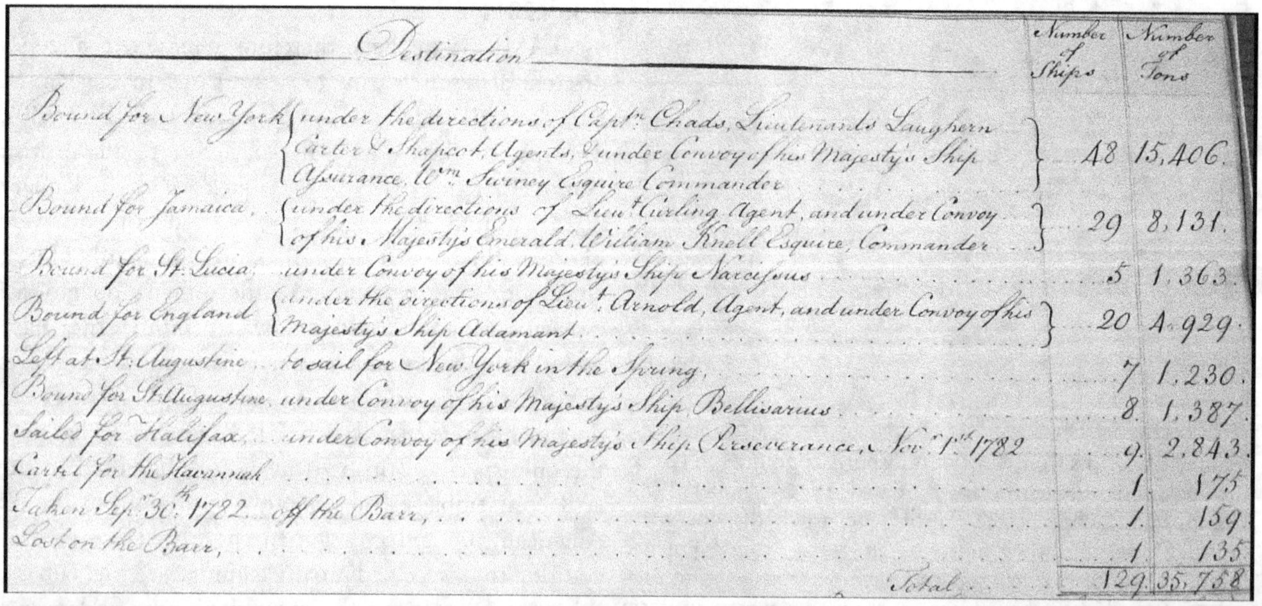

Destination		Number of Ships	Number of Tons
Bound for New York	under the directions of Capt.n Chads, Lieutenants Laughern Carter & Shapcot, Agents, & under Convoy of his Majesty's Ship Assurance, Wm. Swiney Esquire Commander	48	15,406.
Bound for Jamaica,	under the directions of Lieut. Curling Agent, and under Convoy of his Majesty's Emerald, William Knell Esquire, Commander	29	8,131.
Bound for St. Lucia,	under Convoy of his Majesty's Ship Narcissus	5	1,363.
Bound for England	under the directions of Lieut. Arnold, Agent, and under Convoy of his Majesty's Ship Adamant	20	4,929.
Left at St. Augustine	to sail for New York in the Spring	7	1,230.
Bound for St. Augustine,	under Convoy of his Majesty's Ship Bellisarius	8.	1,387.
Sailed for Halifax,	under Convoy of his Majesty's Ship Perseverance, Nov. 1st 1782	9.	2,843.
Cartel for the Havannah		1	175
Taken Sep. 30th 1782	off the Barr,	1.	159
Lost on the Barr,		1	135
	Total	129	35,758

Figure 2. Detail from "Abstract of the distribution of Transports, Army & Navy Victuallers, and Oat Vessels, appointed to receive the Garrison at Charles Town, Stores, Inhabitants, etc., etc." Dated 3 January 1783, some 16 days after the fleet set sail, this is a summary of the preceding pages, now missing, which would have listed details for all of the ships in the evacuation fleet grouped by destination, similar to the document in Figure 1. The fleet bound for St. Augustine (and also St. Johns) included eight ships registering a total of 1,387 tons (BNA 1783:CO5/108,f.76, courtesy of the British National Archives).

by hinterland skirmishes, treaty negotiations took precedence for the remainder of the war. Panicked Loyalists spread rumors that Britain was planning to abandon her colonies to the rebels. By March 1782 public notice was given in Savannah that an agent was available to meet "Refugees who are desirous of going to East Florida to settle there, agreeable to the encouragement contained in Governor Tonyn's proclamation" (Lambert 2010:178). Throughout the summer and fall of that year, the anxieties of southern Loyalists and the energies of British officials were dominated by the problems of evacuation.

The lack of available shipping necessitated separate evacuations for each major port. Savannah, seen as vulnerable to rebel attack, was first. On 11 July 1782, some 11,014 tons of shipping, representing all available military transports on the continent, were assembled to remove civilians, slaves, troops, and supplies from the city. Almost a fifth of the fleet, seven ships totaling 1,880 tons, were bound for St. Augustine with 485 white refugees, 748 slaves, provisions, and trade goods intended for Indians. The fleet lacked the capacity for these masses, so even after Lieutenant Governor John Graham chartered five additional ships, many evacuees had to make their way to St. Augustine on "canoes, boats, and such small craft" (BNA 1782:CO5/106,ff.166-169; Siebert 1929[1]:107; Syrett 1970:236-237). Siebert estimated that some 5,148 souls—1,042 Loyalists, 1,956 slaves, 500 militiamen, 350 Indians, and 1,300 regular troops—arrived in St. Augustine by 18 July, doubling the white population of East Florida and increasing the black population by one fourth or more (Siebert 1929[1]:105-106,109).

This opened the floodgates, heralding a demographic explosion in St. Augustine, which beforehand had been the smallest colonial capital in British North America. East Florida was the closest safe haven for southern Loyalists. Many from the Carolinas and Georgia, especially planters, preferred Florida to the Canadian colonies due to its geographical similarity, which made it more suitable for the slave-based economy under which they had flourished (Smith 2011:279; Troxler 1981:21). It was also a relatively easy move, and many refugees likely saw East Florida as a potential opportunity to re-take possession of their lost properties should the war take a turn in their favor or if the fledgling republic collapsed, as many anticipated (Lambert 2010:186; Smith 2011:279; Wright 1971:377).

The Evacuation of Charleston, Fall 1782

Charleston was the next major port to be evacuated (Barnwell 1910). It was a much greater organizational challenge, believed to require three times as much shipping as was used in Savannah (BNA 1782:CO5/106,ff.166-169). By mid-August more than 4,200 Loyalists had registered for evacuation, including around 2,500 women and children and 7,200 slaves (Lambert 2010:182). Because of the sheer volume of humanity and requisite supplies, Charleston had to be evacuated in stages. Enough ships were gathered for the first evacuation fleet by the end of September, though it would not depart until the second week of October. Of those departing for East Florida was its new military commander, Lt. Colonel Archibald McArthur, along with a number of provincial regiments, and many Loyalist families, including some "substantial" merchants and planters. Rations sent to East Florida for these refugees were sufficient for 1,000 whites and 2,000 slaves (Siebert 1929[2]:114,124,133-136; Lambert 2010:182).

A British officer in Charleston reported a particularly vivid eyewitness account of the tribulations of the beleaguered refugees:

To provide in some measure for these poor wretches, the commanders of the garrisons (though contrary to their orders) protracted the evacuations as long as they possibly could without offending the Ministry. Transports were procured, and several hundreds with their personal property went to St. Augustine, in Florida, the Governor of which granted each family a tract of land upon which they sat down and began the world anew.... There were old grey-headed men and women, husbands and wives with large families of little children, women with infants at their breasts, poor widows whose husbands had lost their lives in the service of their King and country, with half a dozen half-starved bantlings taggling at their skirts, taking leave of their friends. Here you saw people who had lived all their days in affluence (though not in luxury) leaving their real estates, their houses, stores, ships, and improvements, and hurrying on board the transports with what little household goods they had been able to save. In every street were to be seen men, women, and children wringing their hands, lamenting the situation of those who were about leaving the country, and the more dreadful situation of such who were either unable to leave or were determined, rather than run the risk of starving in distant lands, to throw themselves upon, and trust to, the mercy of their persecutors, their inveterate enemies, the rebels of

America (Jones 1879[2]:235-236).

The next fleet to depart, comprised of nine ships, left for Halifax with troops, munitions, and about 500 refugees on 1 November (BNA 1783:CO5/108,f.76; Lambert 2010:183). Charleston's final evacuation fleet was assembled and laded by the middle of December. A total of 111 transports set sail from Charleston, the last crossing the bar on 18 December 1782 (BNA 1782:CO5/108,ff.38-41; BNA 1783:CO5/108,f.76; Lambert 2010:183). This considerable fleet had been separated into five squadrons, each bound for a different destination: 48 ships to New York with troops and supplies, 20 ships to England with officers, colonial officials, and some (probably wealthier) refugees, 5 ships bound for St. Lucia with 200 Black Pioneers (comprised of free blacks judged too "obnoxious" to stay behind without facing retribution), 29 ships to Jamaica with, 1,260 refugees (591 men, 291 women, and 378 children), and 2,613 slaves (a total of 3873 souls), and eight ships totaling 1,387 tons to St. Augustine with refugees and their possessions. Governor Tonyn estimated that the St. Augustine convoy included 1,000 Loyalists and 1,500 slaves on board the convoy (BNA 1782:PRO30/55/57/6476:5).

The names and individual tonnages of the ships departing for East Florida remain unknown, along with numbers of refugees, slaves, troops, and the nature and amount of cargo. The previously mentioned document "List of Transports" (BNA 1782:CO5/108,ff.38-41) dated 19 November 1782, a month before the fleet departed, makes no mention of a Florida-bound fleet. The "Abstract of the distribution of Transports" (BNA 1783:CO5/108,f.76) dated 3 January 1783, a fortnight after the fleet departed, does note the number and total tonnage of the Florida-bound ships escorted by HMS *Belisarius*, but the preceding pages of this abstract or summary, which would have listed these ships and their tonnages individually, appear to be missing from the BNA. As the Storm Wreck's artifact assemblage indicates it carried at least some troops in addition to civilian refugees, researchers believe that it was a hired military transport (as opposed to a civilian merchantman leaving Charleston under its own authority). As such, it definitely would have been listed by name in these missing pages.

There were actually many more ships evacuating Charleston for East Florida with the fleet. The St. Augustine squadron was escorted by the sixth-rate 24-gun frigate HMS *Belisarius* and a number of smaller armed galleys, including *Viper* and *Rattlesnake*. There was almost certainly an additional, unknown number of vessels owned and operated by civilians (i.e., not hired transports) taking advantage of the convoy's protection leaving Charleston. Two examples from the documentary record support this hypothesis. *Belisarius'* captain's log noted 120 sail in the convoy headed south (the combined St. Augustine, Jamaica, and St. Lucia flotillas, with their naval escorts), suggesting that as many as 72 vessels in addition to those on "List of Transports" were sailing with the convoy (BNA 1782-1783:ADM52/2161 Book 3, 19 December 1782). The other evidence indicating more ships were bound for St. Augustine than the eight hired transports comes from two accounts of the wrecking, each independently noting that 16 ships from Charleston's final evacuation fleet wrecked at St. Augustine. This was double the number of Florida-bound ships arranged by the evacuation planners (Johnston 1901:210; Schoepf 1911:227-228).

The Convoy to Florida

McNamara's analysis of the logs from eight naval escorts accompanying the combined south-bound squadrons, has reconstructed the events that took place between 14 December 1782, four days before the entire fleet departed Charleston, to 1 January 1783, believed to be the day after the wrecking event (McNamara 2014:48-53). As was usual practice, all three fleets—Florida, Jamaica, and St. Lucia—sailed together in one convoy as long as their courses lay together. Within 48 hours of departure, various escort vessels began to report problems common enough for naval vessels on convoy duty: a galley fell out of the position; a schooner had to be taken under tow; and a strange sail, likely a rebel privateer, was spotted and temporarily pursued. On 20 December, *Belisarius* took the galley *Viper* under tow back to its station; the 32-gun frigate HMS *Emerald* saw another possible privateer and gave brief chase; and HMS *Magicienne* (another 32-gun frigate) took the schooner *Polly* with an unshipped rudder under tow. The following day, the weather began to worsen, and another potential privateer was pursued, this time by the 44-gun HMS *Endymion* (McNamara 2014:48).

On 23 December, in rainy weather, *Belisarius* sighted St. Simons Island, Georgia, and *Endymion* gave chase to another strange sail. At 11 am that morning the convoy arrived off the St. Johns River bar (present-day Jacksonville, 55 km or 34 mi. north of the St. Augustine Inlet). In the afternoon, the Jamaica and St. Lucia squadrons parted company with the Florida fleet and sailed on to the Caribbean. *Belisarius*, the only frigate remaining, lingered off the St. Johns for seven days (McNamara 2014:51-52).

The St. Johns River, which offered safer access than the St. Augustine Inlet, was an important destination during the Loyalist Influx. A new and rapidly growing settlement had sprung up near St. Johns Bluff on river, known as St. John's Town or simply St. John's (Siebert 1929[1]:117-188; Williams 1976:474; Lambert 1987:187). By this time the nascent town saw over 300 hastily-built frame houses, several stores and taverns and even a freemason's lodge. After arriving, most refugees gathered at either St. John's or St. Augustine, until arrangements were made to secure property and agricultural tools (BNA 1782:PRO30/55/57/6476:5; Williams 1976:474).

It was not uncommon for incoming fleets to linger at the mouth of the St. Johns for a week or longer before continuing on to St. Augustine, despite the potentially dangerous exposed position between the Atlantic and the sandbar. That is what happened to refugee Elizabeth Johnston (1901:210) who was delayed a week there "waiting for a convoy round" before her ship's captain decided to risk the last leg of the voyage to St. Augustine without an escort. According to *Belisarius'* master's log, upon their arrival (23 December) the transports bound for St. Johns were ordered across the bar, but those bound for St. Augustine, likely concerned about their exposed position (in terms of both weather and privateers), stood on for their final destination "without leave contrary to their instructions" (BNA 1782-1783:ADM52/2161 Book 4, 24 December 1782). On Christmas Day *Belisarius* busied itself laying buoys on the St. Johns Bar, and signaling for pilots for what remained of the convoy. Still at anchor two days later, a privateer attacked a vessel in the convoy, the brig *James*, but was driven off when a boatload of *Belisarius'* crew came to its aid (BNA 1782-1783:ADM52/2161 Book 3, 27 December 1782). That same day, the schooner *Sally*, perhaps spooked by the privateer attack, "Weigh'd down for St. Augustine contrary to orders," (BNA 1782-1783:ADM52/2161 Book 4, 27 December 1782).

After several days of seeking pilots for the waiting vessels, *Belisarius* finally did so on 31 December. That afternoon, *Belisarius's* officers appeared frustrated as they frequently ordered vessels to cross the St. Johns bar, while the captains of these vessels repeatedly refuse to do so even with pilots aboard. Sometime after 5 pm, *Belasarius* and the ships that had long been waiting to depart for St. Augustine finally did so. They arrived off the St. Augustine bar at 8 am the following morning, New Year's Day. The pilot boat *Kathy* arrived on 2

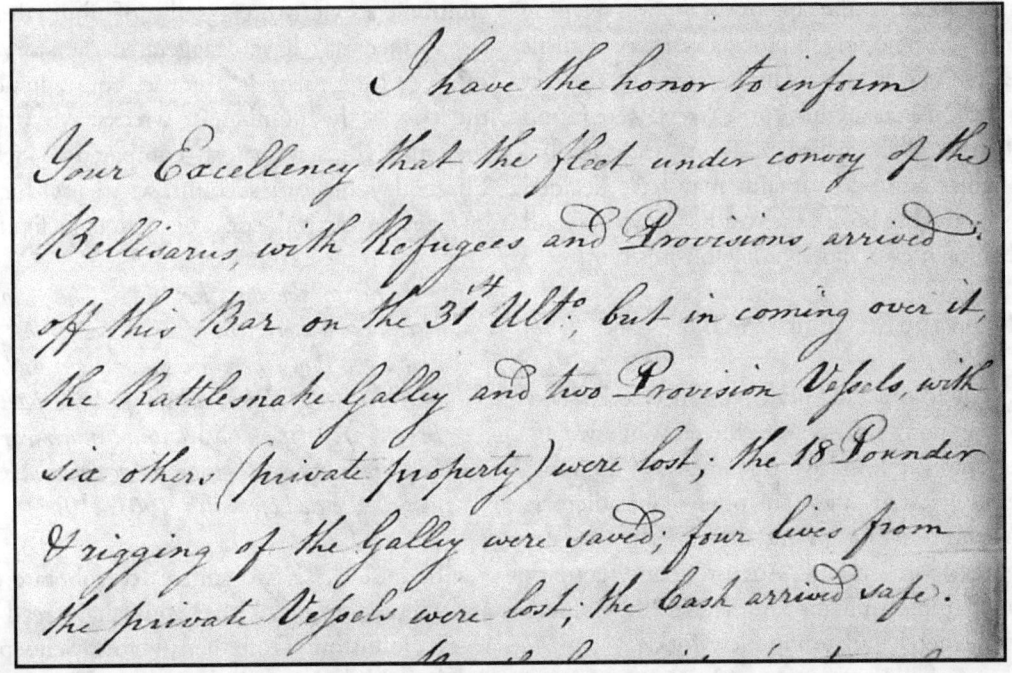

Figure 3. Detail from a letter from Lt. Colonel Archibald McArthur, commander of East Florida to General Sir Guy Carleton, Commander-in-Chief of the North American British forces. It was written on 9 January 1783, and reports the loss of the armed galley Rattlesnake along with two provision vessels and six privately-owned transports at St. Augustine on or around 31 December 1782 (BNA 1783:PRO30/55/60/6728:1, courtesy of the British National Archives).

January and itself was driven ashore trying to cross the bar.

Analyzing the logs of all the frigates spread across the region, McNamara speculated that Florida was affected by an offshore weather system known as a nor'easter between 31 December 1782 and 3 January 1783 (McNamara 2014:63). Johnston (1901:210) seemed to corroborate this hypothesis as she wrote on 3 January that the weather was "constantly wet or cloudy" without "a fair day" since her arrival several days earlier (Johnston 1901:210). While nor'easters may not seem alarmingly windy on land, they can have a great effect on the St. Augustine inlet, where incoming swells are intensified in the narrow channel and the sandbar is prone to shifting (McNamara 2014:63). These conditions would be even more dangerous for transports that were likely too large to comfortably navigate the inlet and unfamiliar with its idiosyncrasies. It is little wonder that some captains refused to comply with *Belisarius's* orders to cross the St. Johns bar.

Why would captains risk their vessels navigating the inlet in these conditions? It is clear that the *Belisarius* officers, who undoubtedly like any self-respecting Royal Navy frigate crew loathed convoy duties, were deliberately pressuring ships to cross the bar so they could complete their mission. But a greater pressure may have come from the fear of privateers. It is clear from the various frigates' logs that the convoy's wake was teeming with rebel privateers hoping to pluck an easy prize. This anxiety over privateer attacks is underscored by the fact that two of the muskets on the Storm Wreck were found loaded and in the half cocked position, ready to fire. Even in rough conditions, captains may have decided to risk crossing the bar before the weather worsened and trapped them in an even more vulnerable position.

Shipwrecks on the St. Augustine Bar

Exactly when did the multiple shipwrecks take place, and how many wrecks were there? While we are fortunate to have at least five documentary accounts of this wrecking event, they are often contradictory. Only one account gives a specific date for the tragedy: a letter (Figure 3) written in St. Augustine on 9 January 1783 by East Florida's military commander, Lt. Colonel McArthur to General Carleton in New York.

"I have the honor to inform Your Excellency that the fleet under convoy of the Bellisarius, with Refugees and Provisions, arrived off this Bar on the 31st Ult° but in coming over it, the Rattlesnake Galley and two Provision Vessels, with six others (private property) were lost; the Eighteen pounder and Rigging of the Galley were saved, four lives from the private vessels were lost, the Cash arrived safe (BNA 1783:PRO30/55/60/6728:1)."

This letter is the source of the 31 December date that researchers have assumed corresponds to the Storm Wreck's loss (note the title of Meide 2015b). However, *Belisarius* logs indicate it actually arrived off St. Augustine the following morning, so McArthur may have mistakenly provided the wrong date. There is also no way to know whether all of the ships were lost in one day, or if some or even all may have been lost before the arrival of *Belisarius* (which would explain why no such losses are recorded in its logbooks). The German military surgeon Johann Schoepf (1911:227-228), who visited the city about a year after the wreckings, wrote that "After the surrender of Charleston in 1782, within two days no less than 16 vessels, bearing refugiés and their effects, went to pieces here and many persons lost their lives." It was not immediately clear if Schoepf meant the wrecking occurred two days after Charleston's surrender, or if he meant the wrecks occurred over a two-day period, but the latter seems likelier. Schoepf's statement that there was great loss of life directly contradicts McArthur's tally of four dead, though the former may have exaggerated the story to make a more exciting memoir. Another contradiction between the two is the number of wrecks. McArthur reports that nine ships were lost, compared to Schoepf's 16. Elizabeth Johnston's account, written within three days of *Belisarius'* arrival, confirms Schoepf's figure:

"Out of the last fleet from Charleston there have been sixteen sail of small vessels lost on and about the Bar. There are six or eight high on the beach. One of these had the greatest part of Dr. Baron's property on board, and I much fear he will be a great sufferer. 'Tis amazing how such a place was ever settled (Johnston 1901:210)."

Because these two sources corroborate each other, and there is no way either could have read the other's work (Johnston wrote hers before Schoepf did, but didn't publish hers until decades after his), it seems likely that 16 was the actual number of wrecks, and that was remembered by the local community. Why would McArthur's number differ? Probably he only felt the need to report the loss of military-owned and hired transports to his superiors, and omitted mention of the loss of additional civilian ships. There is also some question as to whether Johnston meant there were six or eight wrecks on the beach in addition to those lost on the bar, though it seems likely she refers to 16 wrecks in total. It is also significant that Johnston specifies that the 16 shipwrecks were from the last fleet to evacuate Charleston, which is the same fleet escorted by *Belisarius* referenced by McArthur. Her letter provides a *terminus ante quem* of 3 January 1783 for the shipwreck event.

A fourth account of the wrecking was found in a Philadelphia newspaper, *The Freeman's Journal*, dated 12 March 1783, only about two and a half months after the wreckings. It states that "Ten sail of vessels and twelve lives were lost in a hard gale of wind proceeding over Augustine bar last December. They were part of the Charlestown fleet." This article has discrepancies in both the number of wrecks and the lives lost, which may simply represent errors of the type not uncommon in journalism of both the 18th and 21st centuries.

One final reference to shipwrecks from the *Belisarius* convoy has recently caused researchers to reevaluate their interpretation that the wrecking event took place on 31 December. In a letter (Figure 4) from Governor Tonyn to General Carleton dated 23 December 1782, Tonyn writes:

"A thousand Loyalists and about fifteen hundred negroes are supposed to have arrived under the convoy of the Belisarius, the exact number I cannot as yet ascertain, General Leslie's information on that head will no doubt be particular. They are disembarked with the loss of some small craft owing to their rashness in venturing over the bar without sufficient guides." (BNA 1782:PRO30/55/57/6476:5-6).

It is clear that Tonyn is referring to vessels from *Belisarius'* convoy lost while crossing a bar. It is also clear that Tonyn has not yet made contact with *Belisarius*, but has heard reports of its arrival, perhaps through the shipwreck survivors. His letter is dated 23 December, the same day *Belisarius* arrived at the St. Johns, and the day some ships in the convoy disregarded orders and continued sailing for St. Augustine. The earliest these ships could have left was noon, and they may have departed along with the Caribbean squadrons which left at 2 pm. If a group of these ships were impatient enough to ignore orders in order to get to St. Augustine, they probably would have sailed as rapidly as possible, to reduce the risk of capture by privateers. A small group of ships could sail faster than large convoys, which were notoriously slow. It is plausible, then, that a group of ships could sail the 55 km (34 mi.) to St. Augustine

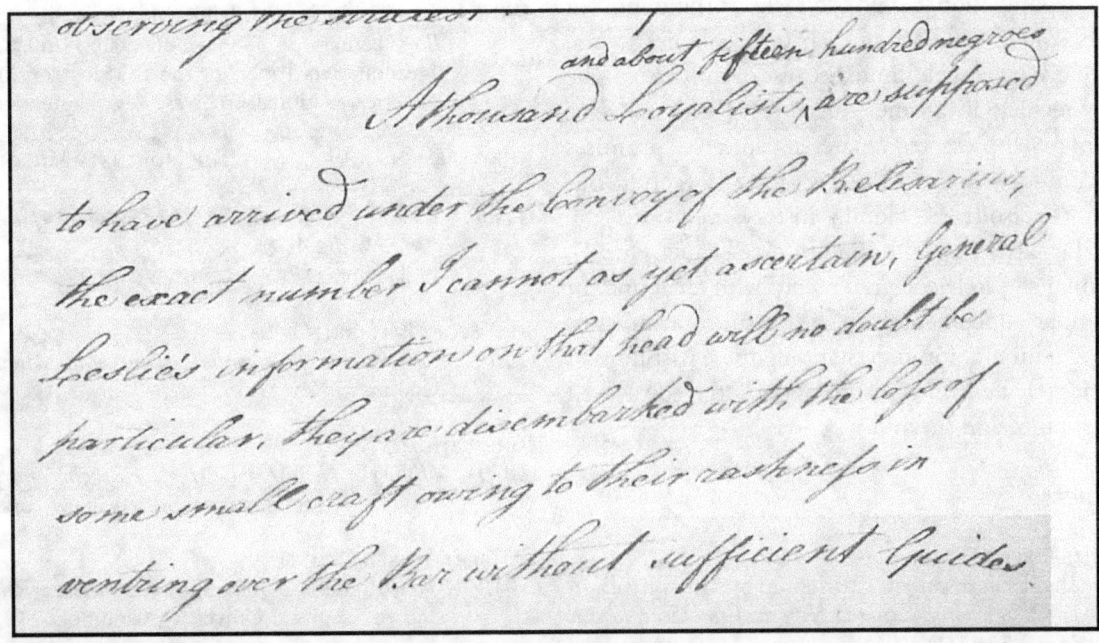

Figure 4. Excerpt from a letter written by East Florida's Governor Patrick Tonyn, to General Carleton in New York. It was written the same day that the convoy under command of HMS *Belisarius* arrived off the St. Johns River, and it reports that some of its ships wrecked due to their "rashness in venturing over the bar without sufficient guides" (BNA 1782:PRO30/55/57/6476:5-6, courtesy of the British National Archives).

and wreck while crossing the bar, with the survivors reporting the arrival of *Belisarius* at St. Johns, in time for the Governor to write a hasty letter noting both the wrecks and the arrival of the convoy, which he had not yet confirmed. The news of the convoy's arrival got to Tonyn very quickly (within 13 hours), and this scenario might explain how that was possible. Tonyn's description of the "rashness" of captains willing to cross the bar without pilots would also describe impatient captains willing to disobey orders to stay with the convoy. Bold action could get them to their destination in a matter of hours, or it could cost them their ships.

This hypothesis is a relatively new one and has not yet been reported elsewhere. The fact that none of *Belisarius'* logs reported any convoy members wrecking can be seen as supporting the interpretation that these renegade transports were lost on 23 December. Had any of the 16 shipwrecks happened under the frigate's watchful eye, then surely they would have been recorded, as was the loss of the pilot boat *Kathy*. It seems plausible that some wrecks occurred on the 23rd, and others, up to 16 in all, may have taken place at any point from then until the arrival of *Belisarius* at 8 am on 1 January.

Conclusion

The American Revolution was a dynamic period in St. Augustine's history, when in just a few short years the city's population would skyrocket. Thousands of Loyalists sought refuge from war-torn colonies to the north, many arriving destitute because of shipwreck. The Storm Wreck, as a wartime refugee vessel with a diverse range of well-preserved material culture, promises to give unique insights into this largely forgotten but important episode of Florida history, and into the lives of Loyalists during a time of extraordinary crisis. Combining the archaeological record with an abundant and complex documentary record results in an even more powerful tool for understanding these past human experiences that encompass suffering and tragedy as well as perseverance and survival.

References

BARNWELL, JOSEPH W.
1910   The Evacuation of Charleston by the British in 1782. *The South Carolina Historical and Genealogical Magazine* 11(1):1-26.

BRITISH NATIONAL ARCHIVES (BNA)
1782   General Sir Guy Carleton to the Earl of Shelbourne, 15 August 1782. CO5/106, ff. 166-169, Colonial Office Papers, National Archives, Kew, United Kingdom.

1782   List of Transports appointed to receive the Garrison of Charles Town, 19 November 1782. CO5/108, ff. 37-42, Colonial Office Papers, National Archives, Kew, United Kingdom.

1782   Governor Patrick Tonyn to Carleton, 23 December 1782. PRO30/55/57/6476:1-8, Headquarters Papers of the British Army in North America, National Archives, Kew, United Kingdom.

1782-1783   Logg Book on Board His Majesty Ship Belisarius, Richard Graves Esq. Commanding from August 30 1782 to Oct 18 1783. ADM52/2161, Book 3, Admiralty Records, Masters' Logs, National Archives, Kew, United Kingdom.

1782-1783   Log & Journal on Board His Majestys Ship Belisarius, Richard Graves Esq. Commanding by Wm James Master from September 1 1782 to Oct 18 1783. ADM52/2161, Book 4, Admiralty Records, Masters' Logs, National Archives, Kew, United Kingdom.

1783   Abstract of the distribution of Transports, Army & Navy Victuallers, and Oat Vessels appointed to receive the Garrison of Charles Town, Stores, Inhabitants, &c, &c., 3 January 1783. CO5/108, ff. 76-77, Colonial Office Papers, National Archives, Kew, United Kingdom.

1783   Lt. Colonel Archibald McArthur to Carleton, 9 January 1783. PRO30/55/60/6728:1-8, Headquarters Papers of the British Army in North America, National Archives, Kew, United Kingdom.

THE FREEMAN'S JOURNAL: OR THE NORTH AMERICAN INTELLIGENCER
1783   New York, March 5. *The Freeman's Journal: Or The North American Intelligencer* 99:12 March. Philadelphia, PA.

JOHNSTON, ELIZABETH LICHTENSTEIN
1901   *Recollections of a Georgia Loyalist*. M. F. Mansfield & Company, New York.

JONES, THOMAS
1879   *History of New York During the Revolutionary War*. 2 vols. New York Historical Society, New York.

LAMBERT, ROBERT STANSBURY
2010   *South Carolina Loyalists in the American Revolution*. 2nd ed. Clemson University, Columbia, SC

McNamara, Brian
2014 Out of Exile: Identifying the Storm Wreck, a Colonial Shipwreck off St. Augustine, Florida; Finding Context through Artifactual and Archival Research. Master's Thesis, Department of Archaeology, Flinders University, Adelaide, Australia.

2013 Archival Research on the Storm Wreck: Using Documentary Evidence to Corroborate the Archaeological Record. Paper presented at the 65th annual meeting of the Florida Anthropological Society, May 10-12, 2013, St. Augustine, Florida.

2015 An Archaeological Perspective on East Florida's Loyalist Influx: The Excavation of a Loyalist Refugee Vessel Lost at St. Augustine on 31 December 1782. *FCH Annals: Journal of the Florida Conference of Historians* 22:172-186.

2015 "Cast Away off the Bar": The Archaeological Investigation of British Period Shipwrecks in St. Augustine. *Florida Historical Quarterly* 93(3):355-387.

Schoepf, Johann David
1911 [1788] *Travels in the Confederation (1783-1784)*. William J. Campbell, Philadelphia.

Siebert, Wilbur Henry
1929 *Loyalists in East Florida, 1774 to 1785: The Most Important Documents Pertaining Therto Edited with an Accompanying Narrative*. 2 vols. The Florida State Historical Society, De Land, Florida.

Smith, Roger, Clark
2011 The Fourteenth Colony: Florida and the American Revolution in the South. Doctoral dissertation, University of Florida, Gainesville, Florida.

Syrett, David
1970 *Shipping and the American War 1775-83: A Study of British Transport Organization*. University of London Historical Studies. University of London, Athlone Press, London.

Troxler, Carole Watterson
1981 Loyalist Refugees and the British Evacuation of East Florida, 1783-1785. *Florida Historical Quarterly* 60(1):1-28.

Williams, Linda K.
1976 East Florida as a Loyalist Haven. *Florida Historical Quarterly* 54(4):465-478.

Wright, James Leitch
1971 Lord Dunmore's Loyalist Asylum in the Floridas. *Florida Historical Quarterly* 49(4):370-379.

Molly Trivelpiece
2310 Leighton Ct.
Richmond, Va 23238
(804) 212-7805
mtrivelpiece@aol.com

Chuck Meide
81 Lighthouse Avenue
St. Augustine, Florida 32080
(904) 829-074
cmeide@staugustinelighthouse.org

Bang Bang! Cannons, Carronades, and the Gun Carriage from the Storm Wreck

Chuck Meide

In December 2010, four cannons and two carronades were discovered on the Storm Wreck, apparently jettisoned in an attempt to re-float the grounded ship. One 4-pounder cannon and one 9-pounder carronade were raised in 2011 and have been conserved. The carronade, whose serial number was identified in Carron Company records, was dated 1780 and is believed to be the second-oldest surviving example. In 2015, excavations revealed another cannon, 12 meters away from the main cannon pile. It was still attached to the partially preserved remains of its carriage. This paper presents an overview of these seven guns and the carriage.

Introduction

The Storm Wreck, identified as a transport carrying civilian refugees and British soldiers during the December 1782 evacuation of Charleston, subsequently lost off St. Augustine, Florida, has undergone six seasons of excavation by the Lighthouse Archaeological Maritime Program (LAMP) (Meide et al. 2011; Meide et al. 2014; Meide 2015a, 2015b). On 17 December 2010, during a routine monitoring dive after the close of the initial excavation season, four cannons and a carronade, along with the ship's bell, were unexpectedly encountered at the shipwreck site (Meide et al. 2011:144-150; Turner and Meide 2013). Previously buried just four meters north of the 2010 excavation area, they had been partially exposed by shifting sands sometime after 9 September. After this discovery, the primary objective of the 2011 season was to fully expose and record all of the artillery in order to choose two representative specimens to raise for conservation, analysis, and display (Meide et al. 2014:160-179). During that excavation, an additional carronade was revealed, making a total of six guns: four 4-pounder cannons (one of which might be a 3-pounder) and two 9-pounder carronades. These were assigned numbers 1-6 to facilitate field recording and easy reference. Cannons 1 and 6, a long gun and a carronade, were recovered on 28 June 2011 (Veilleux and Meide, this volume: Figure 1) and, after almost four

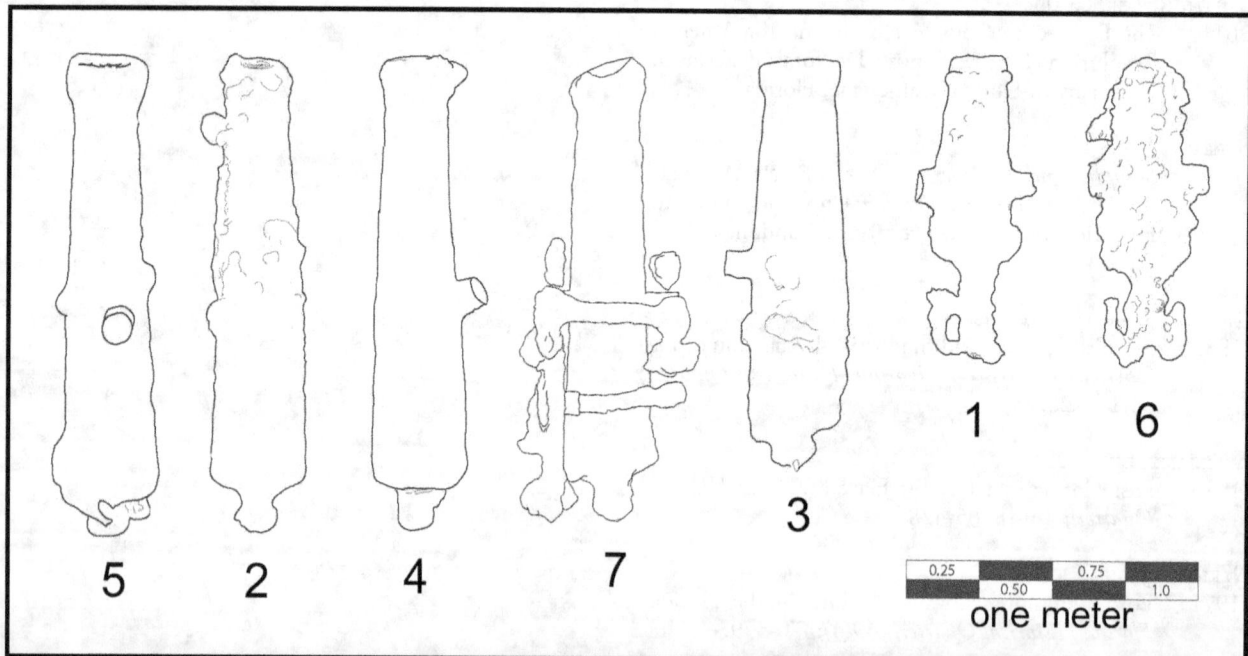

Figure 1. The 9-pounder carronade, designated Cannon 6 or 11S-154.1, recovered from Storm Wreck on 28 June 2011. Photographs were taken after initial de-concretion; this carronade has since undergone four years of electrolysis and as of March 2016 is in the final stage of treatment (Photographs courtesy of LAMP, 2011. Illustration by Brian McNamara and Tim Jackson, courtesy of LAMP, 2012).

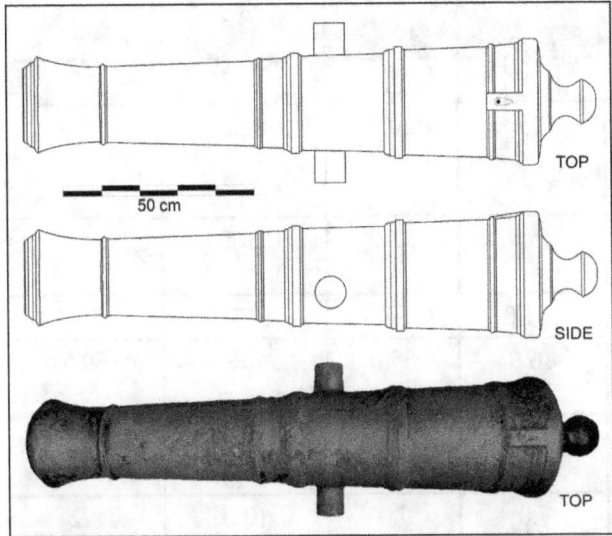

Figure 2. Cannon 2 (11S-153.14), the 4-pounder long gun recovered from Storm Wreck on 28 June 2011. Photograph was taken after initial deconcretion; this cannon has since undergone almost four years of electrolysis and as of February 2016 has been fully conserved. (Photograph courtesy of LAMP, 2011. Illustration by Brian McNamara and Tim Jackson, courtesy of LAMP, 2012).

years of electrolysis in sodium carbonate solution, they have been successfully conserved and are currently on display at the St. Augustine Lighthouse & Maritime Museum.

During 2015, the final season of major excavation at the site, a seventh piece of ordnance was discovered. Cannon 7 is another long gun, like the others believed to be a 4-pounder. It is unique in that it was found isolated from main portion of the site and from the other guns, and it featured the remnants of its carriage still attached.

Cannons 1-6 were found in a pile near the center of the site or where the scattered wreckage is most concentrated (Veilleaux and Meide, this volume: Figure 2). The distribution and orientation of these guns appears consistent with a spill or dump pattern, leading researchers to believe that the cannons were jettisoned by the crew after the ship ran aground, to lighten the vessel in an attempt to save it. This hypothesis was strengthened when evidence was uncovered that other heavy ship fittings were indeed jettisoned in this manner (Meide 2015b:180; also see discussion of the deck pump in Andes, this volume). No evidence for gun carriages has been uncovered in association with these cannons, though it is believed that these guns were originally mounted for use. These guns were discarded at the same time, perhaps after removing them from their carriages, and it remains a mystery why Cannon 7 was jettisoned separately while still in its carriage (or perhaps accidentally lost during grounding).

The Storm Wreck guns comprise a typical armament for a small to medium-sized merchant vessel of the late 18th century. Before the discovery of Cannon 7, it was noted that the known battery from the wreck was almost identical to that reported on board the 190-ton vessel *Sally*, which like the Storm Wreck was a member of the Charleston evacuation fleet. *Sally* was armed with four 3-pounder cannons and two 9-pounder carronades (Lloyd's 1782: entry S623). Ships chartered by the British government during the war, including the 122 transports used for the evacuation of Charleston, were required by the Navy Board to have a minimum number of guns and amount of ammunition on board: "at least six Carriage Guns of six pounders, or less bore as the Board shall think proper according to the size of the ship" (Syrett 1970:115). This mandate was modified on 29 November 1779 "to permit the owners of the transports to fit them with carronades instead of common guns, taking care they are not less than 12 pounders" (Syrett 1970:115). The seven guns found thus far reflect the requirement for at least six cannon or carronades, and the fact that their calibers are lower than the standard might suggest that the Storm Wreck was a relatively small vessel. The discovery of Cannon 7 makes the battery as we now know it odd-numbered. This may indicate there is another cannon on the site yet to be discovered, or that the odd cannon out served as a bow or stern chaser.

Table 1 presents measurements taken of various attributes of each gun, recorded *in situ*. Because these measurements were from concreted specimens, they are only relatively representative of the original dimensions of the guns. Table 2 shows the actual dimensions of the two guns that were recovered and de-concreted. Comparison of the two tables shows that measuring a concreted gun can easily exaggerate attribute size by between 10 and 35%, and sometimes significantly more. Overall length measurements were only minimally larger, though, by only 3.9% and 7.2% in the case of the two de-concreted guns. The weights of the concreted guns were estimated mathematically with a customized spreadsheet formula, which greatly exaggerated weight. In part this was done deliberately, as the weights of the concreted guns were being calculated for lifting purposes, and it was necessary to overestimate for safety reasons. But this process did significantly exaggerate the weight of each gun, by 36.6% for Cannon 2 and 89.4% in the case of Cannon 6.

Attribute	Cannon 1	Cannon 2	Cannon 3	Cannon 4	Cannon 5	Cannon 6	Cannon 7
Type of Gun	Carronade	Cannon	Cannon	Cannon	Cannon	Carronade	Cannon
Cascabel to Breech Reinforce	20.0	20.0	22.0	25	20.0	26.0	18.0
Cascabel to Trunnion	63.0	81.0	78.0	73.0	72.0	n/a	89.0
Overall Length	105.0	165.5	142.0	161.0	166.0	105.0	153.8
Trunnion to Muzzle Length	48.0	75.0	70.0	86.0	85.0	n/a	69.5
Muzzle Diameter	31.0	25.0	22.0	21.0	25.0	27.0	29.5
Bore Diameter	9.0	5.5	n/a	7.0	7.0	10.0	8.2
Bore Depth	n/a	18.0	n/a	9.0	n/a	n/a	n/a
Diameter Behind Muzzle Flare	27.0	22.0	8.0	22.0	20.0	n/a	25.3
Diameter in Front of Breech Reinforce	30.0	29.0	40.0	36.0	34.0	32.0	n/a
Diameter of Tube at Trunnions	44.0	27.0	54.0	34.0	30.0	n/a	n/a
Diameter of Cascabel	27.0	13.0	20.0	9.0	12.0	n/a	14.1
Length of Trunnions	Left: 8.0 Right: 8.0	Left: n/a Right: 11.5	Left: 9.0 Right: n/a	Left: 10.0 Right: n/a	Left: 9.0 Right: n/a	n/a	n/a
Estimated Weight (Exaggerated for lifting calculations)	900 lbs	1283.7 lbs	1449.9 lbs	1402.7 lbs	1515.3 lbs	833.2 lbs	n/a

TABLE 1. Measurements of the Concreted Storm Wreck Cannons Taken in Situ (in cm)

Long Guns

Five long guns or traditional cannons have been found on the Storm Wreck (Figure 3). The long guns all appear mostly similar in form to each other and are typical representatives of 18th-century cannons. All feature trunnions and the usual rounded knob-like button at the cascabel. Their dimensions are included in Tables 1-2. Four of the guns, Cannons 2, 4, 5, and 7, are similar in length and diameter, and likely all 4-pounders. The other long gun, Cannon 3, is shorter, by approximately 7.9 in. (20.0 cm), but also more robust than the others,

Attribute	Cannon 2 (11S-153.14)		Cannon 6 (11S-154.1)	
Type of Gun	Cannon		Carronade	
	cm	inches	cm	inches
Cascabel to Breech Reinforce	14.7 cm	5.79	31.5	12.40
Cascabel to Trunnion	73.6	28.98	53.5	21.06
Overall Length	154.4	60.79	101.0	39.96
Trunnion to Muzzle Length	80.1	31.54	40.5	15.94
Muzzle Diameter	24.0	9.45	15.0	5.91
Bore Diameter	8.41	3.31	10.5	4.13
Bore Depth	21.0	8.27	7.5	2.95
Diameter Behind Muzzle Flare	18.8	7.40	20.6	8.11
Diameter in Front of Breech Reinforce	29.0	11.42	24.7	9.72
Diameter of Tube at Trunnions	25.6	10.08	22.0	8.66
Diameter of Cascabel	11.2	4.41	10.3	4.06
Length of Trunnions	Left: 8.8	Left: 3.46	Left: 8.2	Left: 3.23
	Right: 8.6	Right: 3.39	Right: 8.6	Right: 3.39
Weight	426.4 kg	940 lbs	199.6 kg	440 lbs

TABLE 2. Measurements of the Recovered and De-concreted Storm Wreck Cannons

displaying a notably wider diameter along its length. Its shorter length may indicate that it is a smaller caliber gun, perhaps a 3-pounder. Its concreted length, 4.66 ft. or 1.42 m, is slightly longer than the length of 4 ½ ft. (1.52 m) mandated by Thomas Walton in 1780 for a 3-pounder (Caruana 1997:219). If Cannon 3 is a 3-pounder, it could be that another similarly-sized gun is yet to be found on the site, or it may simply indicate the ship had slightly mismatched armament. Alternatively, Cannon 3 could represent another 4-pounder, as its dimensions still fall within the range of that caliber. It should be noted that while many 4-pound (1.81 kg) and

9-pound (4.08 kg) cannonballs have been found on the site, no 3-pound (1.36 kg) shot has been encountered.

Cannon 5 displays an anomalous feature: a breeching ring or loop at its cascabel. The presence of a breeching ring on a long gun is unexpected on a shipwreck dated to 1782 and raises an interesting implication. While breeching rings were already standard on carronades at this time, their first use on long guns is attributed to Thomas Blomefield, who was appointed as Britain's Inspector of Artillery in 1780 and started to experiment with a new style of cannon in 1786, the Blomefield pattern (Lavery 1989:22-27; Caruana 1997:257-271). The addition of a loop to the breech was intended to facilitate firing at an angle to the side of the ship (Lavery 1989:24). Previously, the breech rope had been spliced over the cascabel, so that the length of rope on either side was fixed. This meant that when the cannon was fired at an angle to the ship one side of the breeching rope took the full brunt of the recoil, a dangerously enormous strain. When the rope could be passed through a ring in the breech, it was free to run and both ends of the rope could restrain the recoil at any angle. By 1787, the advantage of the breeching loop was recognized by the Royal Navy, as reported by Blomefield himself in a letter dated 10 January of that year: "the Board of Ordnance wish to have loops on all sea service guns, and have wrote to the founders to cast them accordingly" (Lavery 1989:24). What makes Cannon 5 so interesting is that while it has a breeching loop, it pre-dates the Blomefield pattern gun by at least four years. This suggests that Blomefield was probably not the earliest to use this innovation on a long gun. It is speculated that perhaps the Carron Company, which had been using breeching rings in their carronades since at least 1779, was the first to incorporate this feature on a long gun (Turner and Meide 2013:31). It should be noted, however, that cascabel dolphins serving the same purpose as 18th-century breeching loops were known on 16th and 17th-century cannons, evidenced by guns from *Trinidad Valencera* (1588), *Atocha* and *Santa Margarita* (1622), and *Vasa* (1628) (Padfield 1973; Mathewson 1986:74; Martin 1997:5; Shaughnessy 2004:38-39).

Cannon 2, afterwards designated Field Specimen 11S-153.14, was the long gun chosen for recovery (Figure 2). When first deconcreted, no markings were visible on its surface, which is typical of a cannon meant for the civilian market. After electrolysis, however, faint markings were observed at the breech end of the gun. The number "9" and the number "3" can be discerned, along with another mark that could represent either

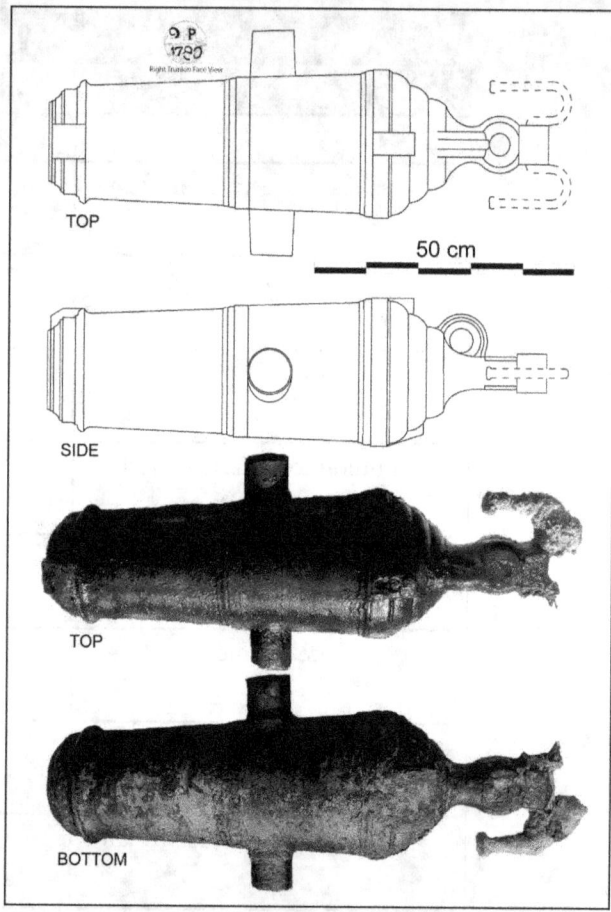

Figure 3. Comparative view of the five cannons and two carronades on the Storm Wreck on the site plan. Guns are shown to scale and arranged by length. Numbers refer to the gun designation (i.e., Cannon 5 is at far left) (Illustration by Chuck Meide and Tim Jackson, courtesy of LAMP, 2015).

a "1" or a "4" between them, on the first reinforce towards the right of centerline. If these indeed are three numbers, it is most likely they represent the weight of the gun in hundredweights, quarters, and pounds. If this is the case it should have weighed 1,039 lbs. (471.28 kg), which suggest that this cannon, weighed with a hydraulic hanging scale at 940 lbs. (426.4 kg), has lost about 9.5% of its original weight. This scope of weight loss is plausible; Australian conservators working on six 4-pounder cannons from the HMB *Endeavor* grounding site and two 18-pounder carronades from HMS *Sirius* have reported weight loss ranging between 4.75% and 26.88% (Pearson 1972:Table 4; MacLeod 1996:113)

The diameter of the cannon's bore upon initial deconcretion was recorded as only 2.95 in. (7.49 cm), slightly too small too small to accept a four pound cannonball, according to a gunnery table published in 1780 by Thomas Walton which indicated a required bore diameter of 3.21 in. (8.15 cm) (Caruana 1997:218-219). This had been a standard size since at least 1725, when John Armstrong's 4-pounder design mandated the identical bore diameter (Caruana 1997:66), and it conforms closely to his predecessor Albert Borgard's required bore measuring $^{21}/_{20}$ of the shot's diameter, or 3.20 in. (8.13 cm) for a 4-pdr (Collins 2014). The discrepancy between the bore measurement and the historical standard was reconciled after further airscribing of the muzzle, which still displayed remnants of concretion. After this final cleaning, the bore was definitively measured at 3.31 in. (8.41 cm). This confirms the cannon is indeed a 4-pounder, with its bore exceeding the required diameter by only 0.1 in. (0.25 cm).

Carronades

First developed by the Carron Company in Falkirk, Scotland, carronades were shorter and lighter than traditional cannons and featured a large bore—and thus fired a heavy shot—relative to their weight (Lavery 1987:104-109, 1989; McConnell 1988:103-111; Tucker 1989:120-130; Caruana 1997:161-214; Watters 1998; Turner and Meide 2013:28-30). Their radical design represented the most important innovation in naval artillery of the late 18th century. Carronades were significantly lighter than traditional cannons of the same firepower, which meant that they were cheaper to manufacture and required fewer men to operate in battle. They could be used to significantly increase the firepower of a ship (by four- or five-fold) while maintaining or even reducing the overall weight of its armament, thus improving both sailing qualities and its fighting prowess. Their savings in weight, space, and manpower made them especially popular on smaller vessels, and they were adopted early by merchant ship owners.

Carronades did have a few disadvantages, due primarily to their light weight and diminutive size. Their recoil was violent and sometimes resulted in carriage damage or dismounting, and their short barrels presented a fire hazard to the outer hull and rigging. Their greatest drawback was their limited range, which could result in a devastating situation when facing a maneuverable foe armed with long guns. But despite these problems, the carronade grew steadily in popularity after its introduction to the market in December 1778. A more detailed treatment of the characteristics of carronades and the history of their development can be found in Turner and Meide 2013 and Meide et al. 2014:168-172.

Two carronades were found on the Storm Wreck, Cannons 1 and 6, and the latter was recovered and conserved. They appear to be a matched set, identical in form and size. They can be seen in Figures 1 and 3 and their dimensions are presented in Tables 1-2. Both were equipped with a pair of handles on the cascabel (neither of which survived intact), a feature referred to by ordnance specialist Ruth Rhynas Brown (2011:1) as a "double handlebar tiller." These short handles projected back and then curved forward. They were wrought-iron and attached to a collar screwed onto the threaded end of the button. No other archaeological examples of this particular handle arrangement are known, though a few specimens exist in museum collections (Blackmore 1976:145) along with at least one historical drawing (Turner and Meide 2013:Figure 4).

Cannon 6 (Field Specimen 11S-154.1) was chosen for recovery since its handlebar tiller was intact, though one handle had deteriorated and fell away once deconcreted. The other handle survived electrolysis, and in other respects the carronade like the cannon has survived in an excellent state of preservation. It is a cast-iron, trunnioned, 9-pounder carronade with its barrel divided in two by a broad band with ogee curves just in front of the trunnions (Brown 2011:1). The button is pierced for an elevating screw and has a ribbed breeching loop. The breech of the gun has the typical three convex curved ribs. There is a raised rectangular patch with oval indent at the touch-hole and a flat plate or quoin patch below on the underside. The muzzle is very short, with no muzzle cup or nozzle, and displays a strong flare and a raised sight. A number of markings cast into the surface of the gun have been observed on the two trunnions. On the right trunnion appears "9 P" over "1780" which represents the caliber and date of manufacture (Veilleaux and Meide, this volume:Figure 4). On the left trunnion is the serial number "34478." The Carron Company always inscribed this number on the trunnion face, until around ca. 1782-1783 when the trunnions were eliminated from the carronade design. At that point it was placed on the quoin patch on the bottom of the gun (Watters 1998:184; Caruana 1997:185). Serial numbers were assigned to guns as they were cast, irrespective of their model or type (Watters 1998:184).

Archival research carried out in the Scottish National Archives by LAMP researcher Loren Clark in January 2014 resulted in the discovery of the Company's Invoice Book dated 1778-1781. Volume 2, which includes all products inventoried in 1780, includes the Storm

Wreck carronade (Carron Company Invoice Books 1778-1781[2]:229). Carronade no. 34478 is described as one of "17 Carronades 9 pounders 6 diameters with Snugs at the Mediun [sic] Weight of 3..3..26 Each." The 17 carronades of this lot are listed with serial numbers (often non-consecutive) ranging between 34448 and 34483. The "6 diameters" refers to the length of the bore or the gun itself expressed in calibers (bore diameters). The "snugs" which are mentioned have not been identified and remain somewhat of a mystery, though they could possibly refer to the handlebar tiller. Other carronades in the inventoried shipment are described as having either "Joints & Screws" or "Joints & Cheeks," as opposed to snugs. As the term "joint" is associated with the loop mounting which became ubiquitous on carronades (Watters 1998:173), it is possible that snugs refer to trunnions.

The averaged or median weight of the guns in this lot of 9-pdr carronades is expressed in the standard British manner, comprised of hundredweights (112 lbs.), quarters (28 lbs.) and pounds. Thus "3..3..26" refers to hundredweights, quarters, and pounds for a total of 446 lbs. (202.30 kg), which is only six pounds heavier than the weight of the carronade (440 lbs. or 199.58 kg) as measured with a hydraulic hanging scale. The weight of the entire lot was 3 tons, 7 hundredweights, 2 quarterweights, and 22 lbs., which total 7,582 lbs. (3,439.14 kg). The value assigned for this lot of 17 carronades is 34 pounds, 13 shillings, and 10 pence. This listed price per ton is 10 pounds, 3 shillings, though the total listed value for the lot actually represents a price of 10 pounds, 5 shillings per ton, suggesting that the company clerks rounded up their calculations to Carron's favor. At the listed price of 10 pounds, 3 shillings per ton, the Storm Wreck carronades should have cost around 2 pounds, 5 pence apiece.

According to the Invoice Book (1778-1781[2]:229), this lot of 17 carronades was included with a total shipment of "99 Guns & Carronades" transported to London on the company ship *Carron* under command of "Robert Paterson & consigned to Mr. Robert Sinclair per Bill of Loading." When or to whom carronade number 34478 was sold after its arrival in the Carron warehouse in London remains unknown.

Archaeologists had also expected to find the word "CARRON" on the Storm carronade trunnion in conjunction with the serial number (Brown 2011:1; Watters 1998:184), but no legible trace of this inscription was visible. Another visible marking is the casting seam, running along its sides over the entire length of the gun,

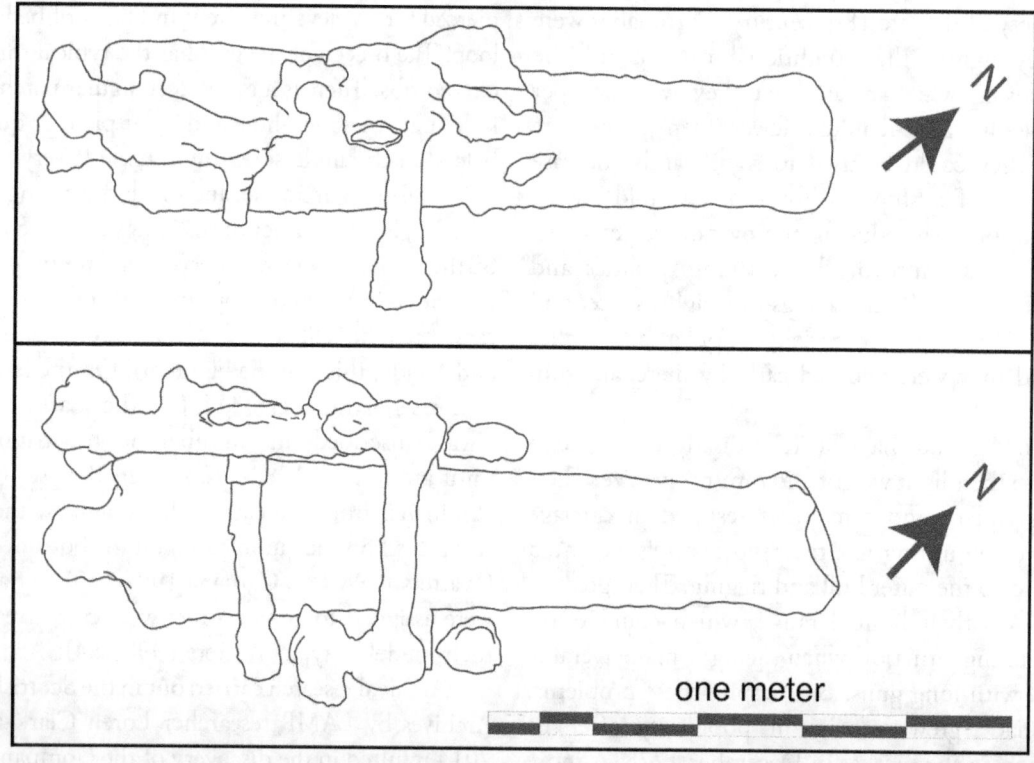

Figure 4. Two plan views of Cannon 7 with its attached gun carriage. Top: View of Cannon 7 as it originally appeared in situ. Bottom: View of Cannon 7 after it shifted and rolled as a consequence of excavation. (Illustration by Chuck Meide and Tim Jackson, courtesy of LAMP, 2015).

bisecting the trunnions.

No broad arrow mark appears on this carronade, indicating it was not marked as British government property. This is not surprising, because 9-pounder carronades were marketed exclusively to the private sector and were never adopted by the Royal Navy.

The diameter of the bore, measured after electrolytic cleaning, at 4.13 in. (10.49 cm) is almost the exact size required for a 9-pounder carronade. Carron Company engineers reduced the windage of the carronade by using a bore sized $^{35}/_{34}$ of the shot diameter, which for a 9-pounder shot of 4 in. (10.16 cm) results in a bore diameter of 4.12 in. (10.46 cm) (Collins 2014).

The recovered carronade, cast sometime in the seven months before 31 July 1780, was believed to be the oldest carronade to have survived anywhere in the world, until LAMP researchers were contacted in 2014 by Wopke Roukema and Roy Håvard Løseth from Flekkefjord, Norway (23 April 2014, 8 May 2014, elec. comm.). These two are affiliated with a local naval historical society which had just cast two working replicas of a 12-pdr carronade dated 1779. Like the Storm Wreck carronade, this example featured its caliber (12-pdr) and date on the right trunnion, along with the serial number (30077) on the left trunnion. The Flekkefjord carronade was made for the Royal Navy, evidenced by the British Broad Arrow on its upper surface. It was probably captured from a British ship or salvaged from a wreck, before ending up in a local Napoleonic War-era fort in southern Norway.

Other examples of early, trunnioned carronades have been encountered on shipwreck sites, most notably from two Royal Navy vessels lost in Australia, the *Sirius* lost in 1790 and the *Pandora* wrecked the following year (Carpenter 1986; Stanbury 1994:74-77; Andy Viduka 21 November 2011, elec. comm.; Ruth Rhynas Brown 21 November 2011, elec. comm.). Both wrecks produced very early 18-pdr carronades that were recovered for conservation and analysis; two were raised from *Sirius*, and one was recovered from *Pandora* while a second was left *in situ* attached to a sacrificial anode (Andy Viduka, 12 February 2016, elec. comm.). Other than their greater size, these examples appear similar in form to those from the Storm Wreck, though they did not feature a threaded hole in the button and therefore were not intended for use with an elevation screw. One of the *Sirius* carronades, SI 58, also bears a Carron serial number. Like the Storm and Flekkefjord carronades, this serial number on the left trunnion was depicted with its first two digits positioned over the remaining three. Its number, 37953, was also found in the Carron Company Invoice Book. It was one of 57 carronades inventoried on 13 August 1781 (1778-1781[2]:378). It is believed that five years later, in 1786, *Sirius* was renamed and outfitted with its carronades before departing for Australia in May 1787 (Lyon 1993:230; Stanbury 1994:1)

A few other early trunnioned carronades still exist, including one at Dover Castle and another at Bamburgh Castle, both in England (Carpenter 1986:44; Lavery 1989:18; Stanbury 1994:75).

Gun Carriage

Cannon 7 was discovered on 19 June 2015; upon initial inspection, divers observed a mass of concretion with two transverse linear extensions attached to the gun. It soon was realized that this concretion was actually the remains of a gun carriage, with the linear components apparently representing the two axles (historically known as axletrees). After recording it *in situ*, excavation continued around the cannon to document as much of the carriage as possible. This had an unintended consequence: enough sand was removed from one side of the gun that it shifted, rotating about 40° downwards and towards the northwest. This was not a catastrophic collapse and was not even noticed until a subsequent dive. In fact, the repositioning of the cannon was fortuitous, as it resulted in the gun and carriage reoriented on a level plane, so researchers looking down on it could now see the gun carriage as if from directly below. This new perspective greatly aided the interpretation and understanding of the structural remains of the carriage, especially given the poor visibility. Figure 4 shows both the original and repositioned views of the gun in its carriage.

The remaining wood components, while apparently well-preserved, are obscured by a layer of concretion, so that no timber is visible. Much of the right side or cheek of the carriage has survived, measuring 3.02 ft. (92 cm) in overall length with a surviving height as great as 11.82 in. (30 cm) at the forward axletree. Less of the left side remains, spanning only 2.03 ft. (62 cm). The extant overall width of the carriage, measured along the forward axletree and including the width of both cheeks, is around 2.03 ft. (62 cm). The cheeks are about 3.54 in. or 9 cm thick. Considering that this measurement has been exaggerated by concretion, this is almost exactly the correct size for a 4-pounder. Carriage cheeks were designed to be the same thickness as the bore of the gun they supported (Manucy 1962:49; Caruana 1997:359), and Cannon 2 had a bore diameter of 3.31 in. (8.41 cm).

The capsquares are visible, still locked to the trunnions. The forward axletree, which is situated just aft of and below the trunnions, measures 2.56 in. (6.5 cm) in diameter. The trucks or wheels of the carriage are no longer extant. What was initially believed to be the aft axletree is now understood to be a robust transverse bolt, known as the bed-bolt, which held the two cheeks together and is located 12.40 in. (31.5 cm) behind the forward axletree. It measures 1.97 in. (5 cm) in diameter and has a collar or wider portion (2.95 in. or 7.5 cm in diameter) where it meets the right cheek. The aft axletree, which would have been positioned under the base ring or forward portion of the cascabel, has not survived.

Conclusion

The Storm Wreck was likely a relatively small merchantman in service to the British crown as a military transport. Its armament was typical for a vessel of this class, though there are certainly some atypical aspects of its archaeological assemblage. While the 4-pounder cannon recovered and conserved does appear to be a standard and even rather generic piece made for the civilian market, some of the other long guns stand out as more than ordinary. Cannon 3, which is shorter and robust, presents something of a mystery. Was this a 4-pounder of a different design, or was it a 3-pounder? If the latter, was there an asymmetrical battery, or could there be another matching piece? A similar question can be posed given the odd number of long guns encountered to date; was an extra cannon used as a bow or stern chaser, or is there yet another undiscovered cannon on the site somewhere? The most intriguing question regarding the cannons pertains to the apparent breeching loop on Cannon 5. If this is indeed a ring cast onto the cascabel, then it pre-dates the Blomefield pattern by at least four years. While there are no current plans to raise and conserve another cannon from the wreck, an argument could be made to recover this gun, given its potential to rewrite what we know of British artillery history. Further study may also be warranted on the carriage attached to Cannon 7, as it may represent one of the few examples of a civilian gun carriage in the archaeological record. Why this cannon was deposited separately and still in its carriage, compared to the other guns jettisoned without carriages, remains an unanswered question.

The carronades are also of interest and worthy of further study. Their discovery provided the first reliable means of narrowing the date range for the shipwreck. The recovered carronade, the first object found with an inscribed year, provided what remains the *terminus post quem* for the shipwreck. The significance of this piece, one of the earliest known carronades to have survived anywhere, cannot be overstated. Further study of this carronade and the Carron Company records will continue to lend insight into this unique weapon and the ship that carried it.

Acknowledgements

The successful raising of the cannons was a group effort but one that relied particularly on the exceptional talents and experience of Brendan Burke. St. Johns County, Leonardi's Nursery, and Xynides Boatyard provided heavy machinery to move the cannons. Ruth Rhynas Brown undertook a long-distance analysis of the carronade which proved very helpful. Dave Howe and the Institute of Maritime History provided the research vessel *Roper* and acquired the lifting davit to raise these cannons. My sincere thanks to the superlative team of LAMP/Lighthouse staff, students, and volunteers who have given their time, talent, and passion to this shipwreck.

References

Blackmore, Howard L.
1976   *The Armouries of the Tower of London* Volume I: Ordnance. H. M. Stationery Office, London.

Brown, Ruth Rhynas
2011   1780- 9-pdr Carronade. Report No. 153 Manuscript, Lighthouse Archaeological Maritime Program, St. Augustine Lighthouse & Maritime Museum, St. Augustine, FL.

Carpenter, Jon
1986   *Conservation of a Carronade from the Wrecksite of HMS Sirius (1790), Norfolk Island* Report to the Australian Bicentennial Authority. Department of Materials Conservation, Western Australian Maritime Museum, Fremantle, Australia.

Carron Company Invoice Books
1778-1781   2 vols., GD 58/4/19/14-15, Invoice Books 1762-1813, Accounting Records, Records of the Carron Company, National Archives of Scotland, Edinburgh.

Caruana, Adrian B.
1997   *The History of English Sea Ordnance, 1523-1875: Volume II, The Age of the System*. Jean Boudriot Publications, Rotherfield, England.

Collins, A. R.
2014   British Cannonball Sizes. Miscellany: Miscellaneous Technical Articles <http://arc.id.au/Cannonballs.html>. Accessed 13 February 2014.

Lavery, Brian
1987   *The Arming and Fitting of English Ships of War, 1600-1815*. Naval Institute Press, Annapolis, MD.

1989   Carronades and Blomefield Guns, Developments in Naval Ordnance, 1778-1805. In *British Naval Armaments*, Conference Proceedings 1, R. D. Smith, editor, pp. 15-27. Royal Armouries, London.

Lloyd's
1782   *Lloyd's Register of Shipping*. The Gregg Press Limited, London.

Lyon, David
1993   *The Sailing Navy List: All the Ships of the Royal Navy Built, Purchased and Captured, 1688-1860*. Conway Maritime Press, London.

MacLeod, Ian Donald
1996   In Situ Conservation of Cannon and Anchors on Shipwreck Sites. In *Preprints of the Contributions to the Copenhagen Congress, 26-30 August 1996, Archaeological Conservation and Its Consequences*, Ashok Ro and Perry Smith, editors, pp. 111-115. The International Institute for Conservation of Historic and Artistic Works, London. Manucy, Albert C.

1949   *Artillery through the Ages*. U.S. Government Printing Office, Washington, D.C.

Martin, Colin J.M
1997   Ships as Integrated Artefacts: theArchaeological Potential. In *Artefacts from Wrecks: Dated Assemblages from the Late Middle Ages to the Industrial Revolution*, Oxbow Monograph 84, Mark Redknap, editor, pp. 1-13. Oxbow Books, Oxford.

Mathewson, R. Duncan
1986   *Treasure of the Atocha*. Pisces Books, New York.

McConnell, David
1988   *British Smooth-Bore Artillery: A Technological Study to Support Identification, Acquisition, Restoration, Reproduction, and Interpretation of Artillery at National Historic Parks in Canada*. Parks Canada, Ottawa, Ontario.

Meide, Chuck
2015a   "Cast Away off the Bar": The Archaeological Investigation of British Period Shipwrecks in St. Augustine. *Florida Historical Quarterly* 93(3):355-387.

2015b   An Archaeological Perspective on East Florida's Loyalist Influx: The Excavation of a Loyalist Refugee Vessel Lost at St. Augustine on 31 December 1782. *FCH Annals* 22:172-186.

Meide, Chuck, P. Brendan Burke, Olivia McDaniel, Samuel P. Turner, Eden Andes, Hunter Brendel, Starr Cox and Brian McNamara
2014   First Coast Maritime Archaeology Project 2011-2012: Report on Archaeological Investigations. Lighthouse Archaeological Maritime Program, St. Augustine Lighthouse & Maritime Museum, St. Augustine, FL.

Meide, Chuck, Samuel P. Turner, P. Brendan Burke and Starr Cox
2011   First Coast Maritime Archaeology Project 2010: Report on Archaeological Investigations. Lighthouse Archaeological Maritime Program, St. Augustine Lighthouse & Maritime Museum, St. Augustine, FL.

PADFIELD, PETER
1973   *Guns at Sea*. H. Evelyn, London.

PEARSON, COLIN
1972   *Restoration of Cannon and Other Relics from HMB Endeavour*. Australian Defence Scientific Service, Defence Standards Laboratories, Maribyrnong, Victoria, Australia.

SHAUGHNESSY, CAROL
2004   *Diving into Glory: The Mel Fisher Maritime Museum*. The Mel Fisher Maritime Heritage Society, Key West, FL.

STANBURY, MYRA
1994   *HMS Sirius 1790: An Illustrated Catalogue of Artefacts Recovered from the Wreck Site at Norfolk Island*. Special Publication No. 7. Australian Institute for Maritime Archaeology, Adelaide, South Australia.

SYRETT, DAVID
1970   *Shipping and the American War 1775-83: A Study of British Transport Organization*. University of London Historical Studies. University of London, Athlone Press, London.

TUCKER, SPENCER
1989   *Arming the Fleet: U.S. Navy Ordnance in the Muzzle-loading Era*. Naval Institute Press, Annapolis, MD.

TURNER, SAMUEL P. AND CHUCK MEIDE
2013   Artillery of the Storm Wreck. In *ACUA Underwater Archaeology Proceedings 2012*. Brian Jordan and Troy Nowak, editors, pp. 26-31. Advisory Council on Underwater Archaeology, Baltimore, MD.

WATTERS, BRIAN
1998   *Where Iron Runs Like Water! A New History of Carron Iron Works 1759-1982*. John Donald Publishers Ltd., Edinburgh, Scotland.

Chuck Meide
Lighthouse Archaeological Maritime Program (LAMP)
81 Lighthouse Avenue
St. Augustine, FL 32080
904-829-0745
cmeide@staugustinelighthouse.org

Pew Pew! Small Arms from the Storm Wreck, a Loyalist Evacuation Ship from the End of the American Revolutionary War

Starr Cox

On or around 31 December 1782, several ships from a larger fleet evacuating Charleston, South Carolina wrecked while attempting to enter the St. Augustine Inlet. One of these ships, the Storm Wreck, has been the focus of six seasons of excavation for the Lighthouse Archaeological Maritime Program (LAMP), the research arm of the St. Augustine Lighthouse & Maritime Museum. The firearms recovered from this site include both muskets and pistols. This paper will discuss these small arms recovered from the site, conservation challenges, and what these firearms mean for the interpretation of the site.

Introduction

The Storm Wreck was discovered by the Lighthouse Archaeological Maritime Program (LAMP) in August 2009, during a remote sensing survey conducted as part of the state-funded First Coast Maritime Archaeology Project (Meide et al. 2010:184-186). Systematic excavations began the following summer and continued every summer through 2015, in conjunction with LAMP's annual field school. Many artifacts, some still encased in concretions, were collected and are undergoing conservation at the St. Augustine Lighthouse & Maritime Museum.

Artifacts recovered include ship fittings and equipment, arms and munitions, cookware and tableware, personal items, and military items. This paper focuses on the small arms recovered. No edged weaponry has been encountered on the site to date, though the remains of a dirk scabbard were recovered in 2010 (Meide et al. 2011:158-160; Cox 2013:48). In addition, the remains of a couple of knives have been recovered (Cox 2013:47-48; McNamara 2013a:41-42), though these are believed more likely to represent eating or utilitarian tools, and will not be discussed here. The firearms recovered from the shipwreck include three Brown Bess muskets, a Queen Anne's style boxlock pistol, a British sea service pistol, and the remains of a wooden handle from an additional small pistol. They are believed to represent both military and civilian pieces. All of the items presented here are still undergoing conservation either at the St. Augustine Lighthouse & Maritime Museum or at the Florida Division of Historical Resources. The information provided below is based on scrutiny of x-ray images and physical examination whenever possible.

2010

In 2010 a concretion was recovered from Unit 3 (Veilleux and Meide, this volume: Figure 1) containing a small flintlock pistol (Field Specimen 10S-44.1). X-rays revealed this pistol to be a Queen Anne style boxlock pistol measuring 8.4 in. in length. All of the operational elements of the pistol can been seen in their proper places, including the frizzen, wooden grip, barrel, and trigger guard, although not all of the elements are in good condition (Figure 1). The cock or hammer is hung in the middle of the frame and the pistol, which is sightless, is intended for close range firing (James Levy 2010, elec. comm.). A boxlock is distinguished by having its trigger plate, lock plate, and breach of the barrel all as one piece, but the hammer can be either inline or side-cock (Burgoyne 2002:9).

Unlike most flintlock small arms of the time, this weapon was not loaded from the muzzle. Instead the barrel was unscrewed with a barrel key or wrench, the threaded stub was filled with powder, and the ball was put in place before reattaching the barrel. When fired, the ball, which was slightly oversized for the bore, was compressed down to bore size, which eliminated windage and resulted in a more powerful and truer shot (James Levy 2010, elec. comm.). This pistol was designed for close action as personal defense and was not military issue (Burgoyne 2002:13).

Conservation continues to reveal more information. The barrel and lock are brass, while the trigger guard, trigger, hammer, and frizzen are all iron. The handle is slab-sided and made of wood with metal inlay. The pistol has not been fully deconcreted due to the need to cast the iron components, which are mostly voids left inside the concretion. While uncovering the brass components, three marks were found upon the barrel. The two shown here (Figure 1) are one of the two Birmingham private proofs and the gun manufacturer's mark. The third mark

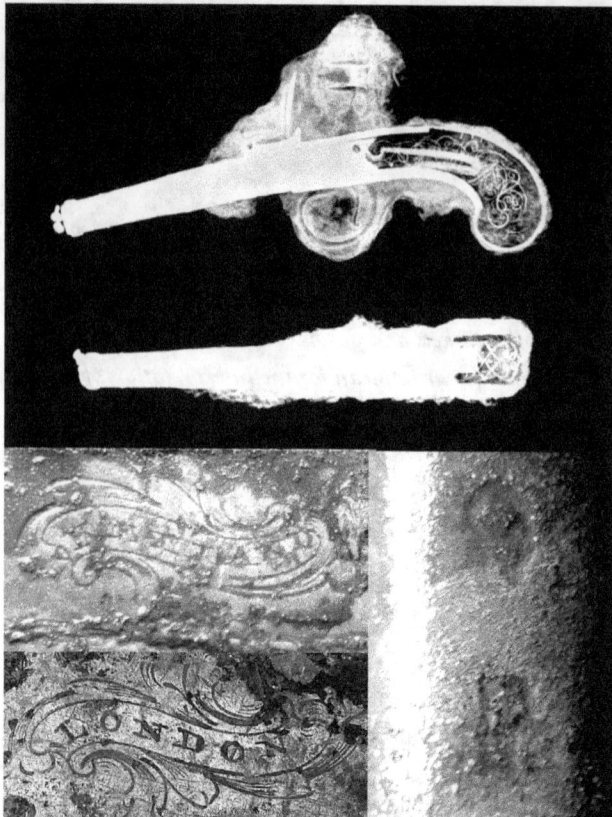

Figure 1. Top: x-ray of Queen Anne style boxlock pistol. Bottom left: Ketland and London inscriptions. Bottom right: one Birmingham proof with a crown and P and a maker's mark with the letters TK (St. Augustine Lighthouse & Maritime Museum).

(not shown) is the second Birmingham private proof. Along the sides of the box portion of the gun are the words "Ketland" and "London" (Figure 1). Ketland refers to the manufacturer, and at first glance London would refer to its location of manufacture. However, the proofs, as well as known history of the Ketland business, indicate this gun was manufactured in Birmingham (Puleo 2011:15-16). Thomas Ketland Sr. was most likely the maker of this gun, because the maker's mark in Figure 1 includes a TK. The upper portion of that mark is unclear.

This style of pistol originated in the mid-17th century and was typified by a side lock action with the grip ending in a ball-shaped pommel (Burgoyne 2002:13). Throughout the 18th century, the style evolved from a firearm reserved for the wealthy to a common sidearm used more broadly, as more manufacturers produced them. This pistol has a slab-sided grip and no buttcap. These two attributes alone, as argued by Burgoyne (2002:54), indicate a move away from the artistic zenith of the Georgian-era towards a firearm favoring functionality over elegance. However, it is clear that some amount of decoration exists on the pistol grip as the x-ray image displays what appears to be flourished inlay work (Meide et al. 2014:191-192).

2011

The partial remains of a handle from a second small pistol, only 1.97 in. in length, were found within concretion during cleaning of the 4-pounder cannon recovered in 2011. Designated Field Specimen 11S-153.3, it is a wooden fragment similar in shape to the handle of the boxlock pistol inside concretion 10S-44.1. The shape of this pistol grip is typical of the small boxlock family of pocket pistols. No metallic portions of this pistol survive, although the handle was carved and drilled to accommodate a metal butt cap. The ventral surface has a carved channel 0.35 in.wide to accommodate a trigger guard tang. There is no evidence of any further decoration or embellishments. The fore end of this piece is roughly fractured, indicating that the handle might have broken off and separated from its lock and barrel before or during the wrecking event. Boxlock pistols were commonly sold in matched pairs, but this piece is not a mate to the pistol within 10S-44.1. Its profile is rounded, terminating in a bulbous butt-end 1.34 in. wide. The pistol grip in 10S-44.1 is slab-sided (Meide et al. 2014:191 – 192).

2012

The remains of three nearly intact muskets and an additional short musket fragment were recovered during the 2012 season (McNamara 2013b). All are identified as Brown Bess muskets, the standard British military arm for most of the 18th century (Goldstein and Mowbray 2010). They are undergoing conservation at the Florida Division of Historical Resources state laboratory in Tallahassee, FL. The Brown Bess was used by the British Army for well over a century, from 1722 to 1838, with many incremental design changes, including the Long Land Pattern, Short Land Pattern, India Pattern, New Land Pattern, and Sea Service Pattern. It was the most common firearm of the American colonial period. The Brown Bess was a muzzle-loading, smoothbore, .75 caliber musket. Land Pattern muskets and their derivative versions were used by both sides during the Revolution (Meide et al. 2014:182).

During the Revolutionary War, all infantrymen were armed with a flintlock musket, which fired a lead ball, and was furnished with a detachable socket bayonet.

This turned the musket into a formidable pole arm (Frey 1981:100). An accurate date of manufacture can be obtained by carefully observing several design features on each gun. It is generally acknowledged that the original Land Pattern musket evolved over a period of about 20 years, incorporating elements from contemporary Dutch muskets, Board of Ordnance procured British muskets, and privately purchased Colonel's muskets (Goldstein 2000:41). British Ordnance adopted the land pattern family of muskets in 1720, and with modifications and improvements the basic design was produced into the middle 1800s (Goldstein and Mowbray 2010:18,152).

As improvements and modifications were made to the manufacture of these muskets, a change in the pattern was adopted, resulting in a new model or pattern. These patterns were the approved design of the time, and were to be replicated exactly as specified. The original Long Land Pattern was the longest version, with a 46-in. barrel, but later versions were shorter once it was realized that shortened barrels were easier to handle without reducing accuracy. Land Pattern muskets can be dated fairly accurately by matching the nuances in their design and construction with these example 'patterns' (Meide et al. 2014:183).

Field Specimens 12S-197.1, 12S-206.1, 12S-223.1, and 12S-236.1 were recovered during the 2012 field season, and brought to the Flagler Hospital for CT scanning. The resultant imagery revealed the concreted metal components of Brown Bess muskets from the period of the American Revolution. Examination revealed a fairly accurate and telling identification of musket patterns with date ranges supporting the working hypothesis that the Storm Wreck was a Loyalist ship that lost in December 1782 (Meide et al. 2014:183).

Musket 12S-197.1 was discovered outside the main excavation area, to the southwest, from an undesignated unit at 99E, 103N (Veilleux and Meide, this volume:Figure 1). No further excavations were conducted in that area. It measures 51.65 in. cm in length. A brass trigger guard and the general shape of a musket lock were observed with the naked eye prior to CT scanning. This musket is the most intact specimen, though it is missing a large portion of its butt (Meide et al. 2014:183). It has been identified as a British 1769 Short-Land Pattern musket.

At the onset of the Revolution, this model was the newest and most modern musket available to the British infantry (Goldstein and Mowbray 2010:92). These muskets were a shortened variant of the Land Pattern, with a 42 in. barrel rather than the older 46-in. length.

This particular variant of the Land Pattern musket was produced between 1768 and 1777, numbering less than 68,000 (Goldstein and Mowbray 2010:93). Two thousand four hundred of these muskets were issued to the 71st Regiment of Foot during the British campaign in North America (Bailey 2009:170). Out of this issue, seven muskets survive today in collections with regimental markings of the 71st (Goldstein and Mowbray 2010:94). Regimental markings are typically observed on the musket's barrel or on the brass wrist plate (Meide et al. 2014: 183). The barrel on this musket is too poorly preserved to reveal any markings, but the corrosion product around the barrel revealed a proof mark consisting of a crown and crossed scepters. The brass wrist escutcheon survives in excellent condition, but upon deconcretion it was found to bear no inscription or identifying marks.

The visible profile of the extant brass furniture within this concretion matches that of English manufactured Land Pattern muskets from the Tower of London, and not of the Irish arms produced by Dublin Castle (Goldstein and Mowbray 2010:78). The flat style of side-plate and the absence of a "Pratt pipe" ramrod pipe (Figure 2) seen in later models helped in dating this piece, along with the corroded remnants of a steel ram rod. All of these characteristics are typical of muskets manufactured between 1768 and 1777 (Meide et al. 2014:185).

The musket lock is possibly a Pattern 1755 lock. CT scanning imagery revealed remains of the cock assembly: a slotted cock-screw, flat comb, and goose neck (Figure 3). This pattern of lock was stockpiled and used by the Tower of London armorers as the main component for Short Land pattern muskets until phased out by the later 1777 pattern lock. This further supports the identification of a 1769 Land Pattern musket (Meide et al. 2014:185).

The most startling discovery revealed by the CT scan was the fact that this musket is still loaded, and in the "half cock" position (Figure 3). There were three types of standard musket service cartridge: ball, buck and ball, and buck shot (Bailey 2009:247). This musket has been loaded with a cartridge of buck and ball, which was developed to inflict greater damage by a unit's volley of fire. Buck and ball consisted of the standard load of a .69 caliber musket ball accompanied by three or four .32 caliber buckshot acquired from the Royal Artillery (Meide et al. 2014:185).

The next intact musket encountered, 12S-223.1, was over 12 feet away in Unit 7 (Veilleux and Meide, this volume:Figure 1). Additional excavation revealed that this musket extended into Unit 20. The musket concretion measures 49.21 in. in length, and displays a distinct curvature due to the warping of the wooden musket stock. Musket 12S-223.1 is intact for the entire length of its barrel, but is missing most of its butt (Meide et al. 2014:185-186). After x-ray analysis, this specimen was identified as a 1777 Short Land Pattern British musket, produced between 1777 and 1782. By the end of the Revolution, it is estimated that half of the 350,000 muskets procured by the British were of this pattern (Goldstein and Mowbray 2010:113).

Very little of the iron components remains on this musket. However, two key diagnostic pieces on the gun did survive. The most noticeable of these is the brass "Pratt pipe" (Figure 2) designed by John Pratt and adopted by the Board of Ordnance in 1777. This pipe features a wide mouth and taper that facilitated a speedier return of the ramrod to quicken the loading process between shots (Goldstein and Mowbray 2010:62). This replaced the second ramrod pipe, immediately behind the forward "trumpet mouthed pipe" in Pattern 1777 muskets and all subsequent patterns. This musket also has the remains of a steel ramrod housed within its four brass ramrod pipes. Later variants of the Land Pattern family reduced the number of ramrod pipes from four to three as the overall musket lengths shortened over time (Meide et al. 2014:187).

The second diagnostic feature is the remnant of the

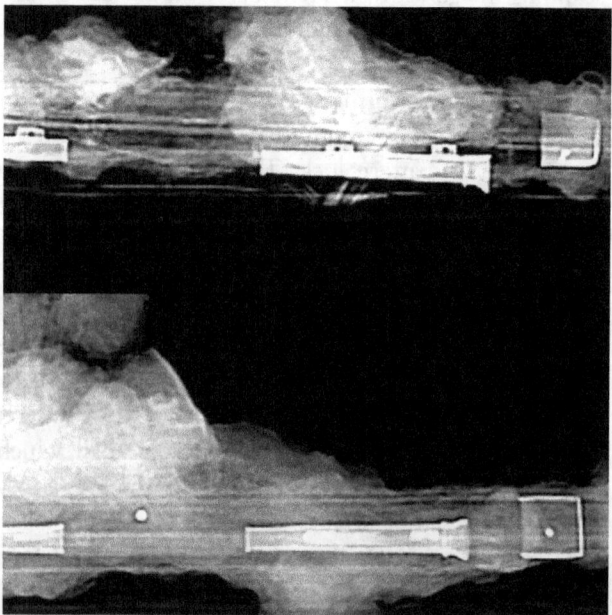

Figure 2. Top: x-ray of 12S-197.1 showing the standard pipe. Bottom: x-ray of 12S-223.1 showing the pratt pipe (St. Augustine Lighthouse & Maritime Museum).

new variant of shortened sear spring, introduced with the 1777 Short Land Muskets. This spring is normally easy to spot because the two screws were located behind the cock on the tail of the lockplate, but the lock has not survived within the concretion. We can see the spring itself, however, with its two mounting holes located exactly where they should be behind the shadow of the now nonexistent cock (Meide et al. 2014:187-198).

The last of the three mostly intact muskets, 12S-236.1, was also found in Unit 7 (Veilleux and Meide, this volume:Figure 1), roughly parallel with and within a yard of Musket 12S-223.1. It extended into Unit 19 for most of its length. The distal end of the musket is curved, again due to warping of the wooden stock. It is less complete than the other two specimens, as it is missing most of the butt and also its forward most end or nose (Meide et al. 2014:189).

Diagnostic features revealed by x-ray identified this gun as a 1756 Long Land Pattern. Produced from 1756-1790, this was the pattern musket carried by British forces at the onset of the American Revolution. This pattern musket was originally fitted with a 46-in. barrel, though the length of this example cannot be confirmed since it is missing the fore-end, which includes the brass nose cap and "trumpet pipe" or first ramrod pipe. The measured distance between rammer pipes suggests a long land pattern with the 46-in. barrel as opposed to a Short Land musket with a 42-in. barrel. This was the first musket in the Land Pattern series to be fitted with the trumpet pipe (Meide et al. 2014:198 – 191).

Another feature revealed in the x-ray imagery identifying the pattern of this musket is the contoured edges of the Long Land pattern side plate. When scanned from above the side plate exhibits a rounded profile, which is inletted to accommodate the heads of the side screws used for mounting the lock. This piece was replaced in all later patterns with a flatter side plate that was simpler to produce. Another visible feature is the shadowed remains of a pattern 1755 lock. This was the first musket in the Land Pattern lineage to be fitted with this lock, also used in the later Short Land patterns (Meide et al. 2014:191). As this musket is being conserved at the Florida Division of Historical Resources state laboratory, marks have been uncovered on some of the brass furniture. The underside of the side plate contains a broad arrow, and two of the ramrod pipes have roman numerals scratched into them. The aft pipe contains two scratches that could represent the roman numeral II, and the forward pipe contains one scratch in addition to the roman numeral VII. The difference in

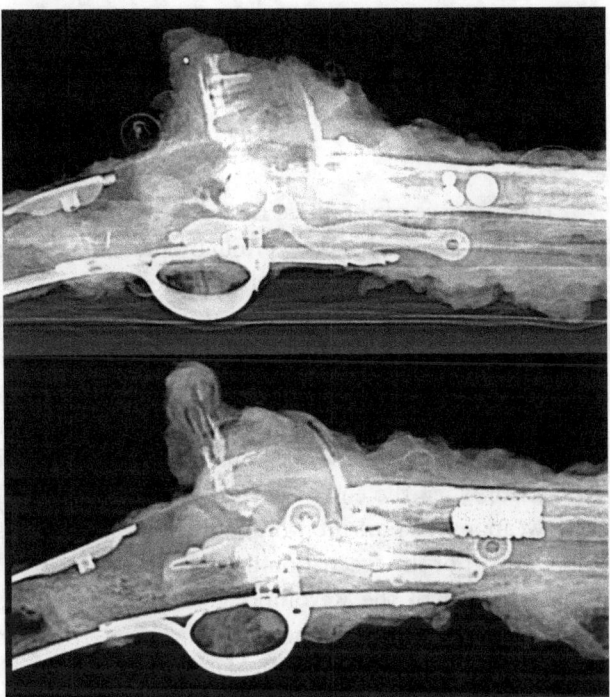

Figure 3. Top: x-ray of 12S-197.1 showing the load of buck and ball. Bottom: x-ray of 12S-236.1 showing a load of Rupert shot (St. Augustine Lighthouse & Maritime Museum).

numbers could indicate a possible repair, since most brass furniture was made and marked with matching numbers or marks so they could be kept together as matching sets for final assembly, and also marked with the order of assembly (Amy Borgens 2016, elec. comm.).

This musket was recovered loaded with its lock in the half-cock position, ready for firing at a moment's notice (Figure 3). The load is not military issued ammunition of .32 caliber buck-shot, but rather a load of Rupert shot or birdshot, tiny lead pellets which are omnipresent across the Storm Wreck. The Loyalists evacuated Charleston under the perpetual threat of predation by American privateers (Trivelpiece and Meide, this volume). This danger is reflected in the weaponry "locked and loaded," ready for rapid use if the need for self-defense did arise. Muskets loaded with these pellets, like a modern shotgun, would probably have been quite effective against a boarding party (Meide et al. 2014:191).

The final musket find, 12S-206.1, consists of only a short surviving segment. This concretion, found within Unit 7 (Veilleux and Meide, this volume:Figure 1), was only a few inches away from Musket 12S-223.1. It is 10.24 in. long, 1.77 in. wide, and has a visible channel or groove along its length. When x-rayed by Monahan's Chiropractic, it was revealed to be the fore-end of a musket stock with brass furniture still intact, matching that of an English Pattern 1756 Long Land musket or possibly a later model of the Land Pattern musket family (Meide et al. 2014:191).

The two brass components within this concretion are a sheet brass nose cap and a trumpet-mouthed ramrod pipe. The trumpet mouthed ramrod pipe was not featured on British muskets until the pattern 1756 Long Land Musket was approved for issue, and is present in every subsequent model of Land Pattern muskets manufactured from that date on. The wooden portion of stock is grooved to accommodate a ramrod; partial remains of a steel ramrod are visible from the mouth of the ramrod pipe to the face of the nose cap (Meide et al. 2014:191). The British began issuing steel ramrods with the 1756 pattern muskets and by 1779 almost all muskets issued of both the Long and Short land patterns in North America were using steel rammers rather than wood (Bailey 2009:34).

While this fragment could represent a fourth musket, it is also possible that it is the missing front-portion of Musket 12S-236.1. The fragment does include the correct furniture for this pattern musket. However, the trumpet pipe from the field specimen lacks marks like those found on the ramrod pipes removed from 12S-236.1, and the break pattern in both pieces of wood do not align.

2013

Found in the East wall of Unit 33 (Veilleux and Meide, this volume:Figure 1), Concretion 13S-353.1 was CT scanned at Flagler Hospital, and found to contain an excellent example of a British Sea Service flintlock pistol numbered 13S-353.2 (Figure 4). Unlike the more ornate Land Service pattern of handguns, the Sea Service variants were of a minimalist design that simplified production and maintenance of weapons destined to serve a shorter life in the saltwater environs of a ship at sea. This particular example was readily identifiable in CT imaging by the overly simplified yet heavily reinforced "skull crusher" style butt cap, flat side plate, and the use of a single brass trumpet pipe to hold a wooden ramrod. This pistol was missing its lock and the barrel corroded away, but otherwise it was in near perfect condition. As conservation progresses, markings have been found on the brass furniture removed thus far. The trigger guard has a crown engraved in the inner curvature, and three scratches and an X on the inner side of the tang. The side plate has a broad arrow and four scratches located on the interior surface (Figure 4). The butt cap has not been removed yet.

There were two variants of the Sea Service Pattern pistols in circulation during the American Revolution, the difference being the barrel lengths. This example is of the "long" variant with a 12-in. 56 caliber tapered round barrel, no sights, secured by two wire pins. The rammer is wood with a tapered brass cap, to avoid rusting in service. A shorter variant with a 9-in. barrel was coming into circulation during the 1780s, but was not as common (Bailey 2009:89-92). Sea Service Pistols were stocked to the muzzle, and the brass furniture consisted of one nearly cylindrical collared rammer pipe, with no tailpipe or trigger plate. The side plate sat flush with the wood stock and had an upward curving tail (Bailey 2009:89-92)

At sea it was often necessary to arm the crew of a ship to capture an enemy vessel or repel boarders. Sea Service pistols were typically stowed in the powder room or shot locker of a ship and kept under lock and key, under the guard of a Marine sentry. Only when the officers of the ship deemed it necessary for the conduct of the vessel, did they issue the order for pistols, muskets, cutlasses, boarding pikes and axes to be distributed among the crew. These weapons only went to specific men within the cannon crews who were to act as boarders, and then quickly re-collected when no longer needed to lessen the danger of mutiny (Gilkerson 1991:5). These were not items that a common sailor would have been allowed to carry on his person.

Discussion

The presence of the three Brown Bess muskets and the sea service pistol indicate a military presence aboard this ship. The fact that two of the muskets were loaded and ready to fire indicates the ship was under some sort of duress. The two smaller pistols were not military issue, but personal belongings. These could have either belonged to civilians or to military officers, who would sometimes purchase these weapons themselves as a last defense for when the enemy got too close. Together, all these weapons support the working hypothesis that this ship was part of the evacuation fleet leaving Charleston, SC at the end of the Revolution. While none of the muskets contained regimental markings, buttons recovered and discussed in McNamara (this volume) support a military presence. However, this ship was not a military vessel. The presence of two non-military carronades discussed by Meide, this volume, indicate that it was chartered for the evacuation. Because of this, the small pistol, which could be either officer owned or civilian owned, still fits the hypothesis.

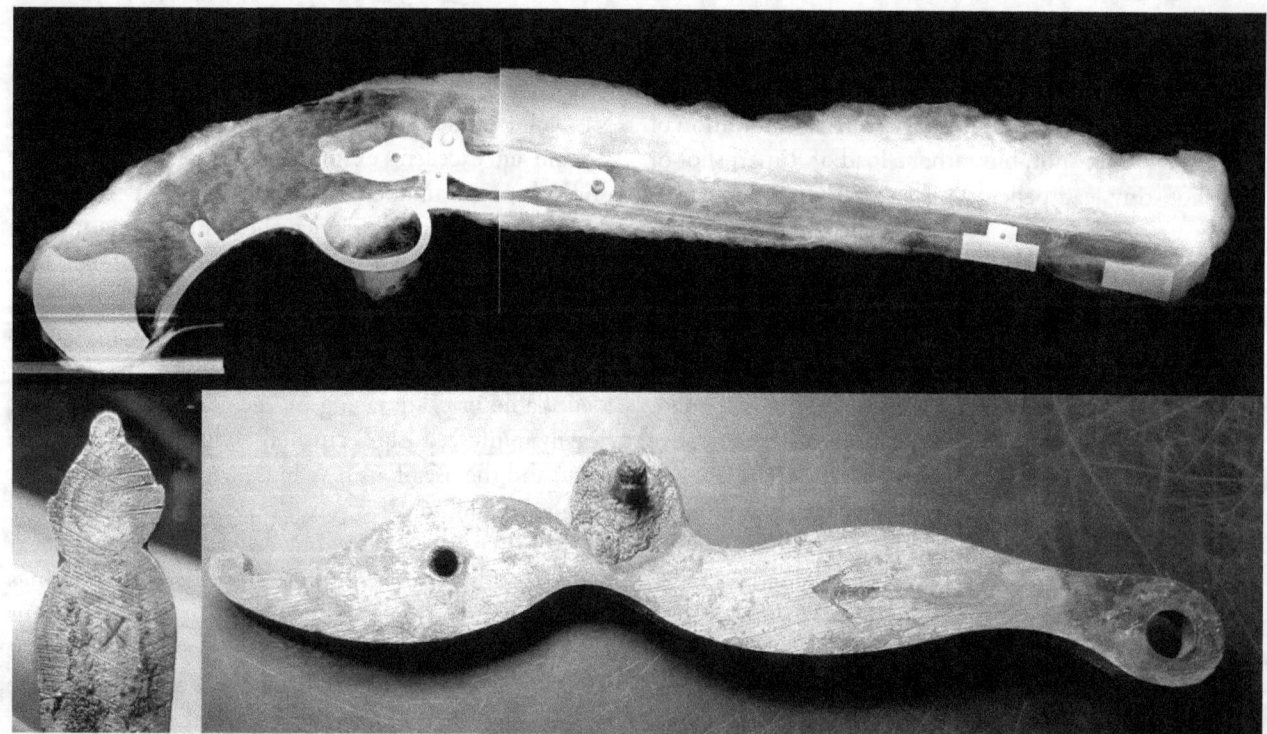

Figure 4. Top: x-ray showing sea service pistol 13S 353.2. Bottom left: 3 scratches and an X on the trigger guard tang. Bottom right: 4 scratches and a broad arrow on the side plate (St. Augustine Lighthouse & Maritime Museum).

References

Bailey, De Witt
2009   *Small Arms of the British Forces in America 1664-1815*. Andrew Mowbray Inc. Publishers, Woonsocket, Rhode Island.

Burgoyne, John W.
2002   *The Queen Anne Pistol 1660 – 1780: A History of the English Turn-off Pistol*. Museum Restoration Service, Bloomfield, Ontario, Canada.

Cox, Starr
2013   Personal Items Recovered from the Storm Wreck, a Late 18th Century Shipwreck off the Coast of St. Augustine, Florida. In *ACUA Underwater Archaeology Proceedings 2012*, Brian Jordan and Troy Nowak, editors, pp. 44-49. Advisory Council on Underwater Archaeology, Baltimore, Maryland.

Frey, Sylvia R.
1981   *The British Soldier in America*. University of Texas Press, Austin, Texas.

Gibbs, N. H.
1965   Armed Forces and the Art of War. In *The New Cambridge Modern History, Vol. 9, War and Peace in an Age of Upheaval 1793-1830*, C. W. Crawley, editor, pp. 60-76. University of Cambridge, Cambridge.

Gilkerson, William
1991   *Boarders Away with Steel – Edged Weapons and Polearms*. Andrew Mowbray, Inc., Lincoln, Rhode Island

Goldstein, Erik
2000   *The Socket Bayonet in the British Army 1687 – 1783*. Andrew Mowbray Publishers, Lincoln, Rhode Island.

Goldstein, Erik, Stuart Mowbray
2010   *The Brown Bess: An Identification Guide and Illustrated study of Britain's Most Famous Musket*. Andrew Mowbray Inc. Publishers, Woonsocket, Rhode Island.

McNamara, Brian
2013a   Cooking with Fire: What Cookware and Tableware Can Tell Us About an Unidentified Eighteenth Century Shipwreck. In *ACUA Underwater Archaeology Proceedings 2012*, Brian Jordan and Troy Nowak, editors, pp. 38 – 43. Advisory Council on Underwater Archaeology, Baltimore, Maryland.

2013b   Small Arms from the Storm Wreck, a Revolutionary War Period Shipwreck off St. Augustine, Florida. Paper presented at the 65th annual meeting of the Florida Anthropological Society, May 10-12, 2013, St. Augustine, Florida.

Meide, Chuck, Samuel P. Turner, and P. Brendan Burke
2010   First Coast Maritime Archaeology Project 2007-2009: Report on Archaeological and Historical Investigations and Other Project Activities. Report to Florida Division of Historical Resources, Tallahassee, from Lighthouse Archaeological Maritime Program, St. Augustine Lighthouse & Museum, St. Augustine, FL.

Meide, Chuck, P. Brendan Burke, Olivia McDaniel, Samuel P. Turner, Eden Andes, Hunter Brendel, Starr Cox, and Brian McNamara
2014   First Coast Maritime Archaeology Project 2011-2012: Report on Archaeological Investigations. Report to Florida Division of Historical Resources, Tallahassee, from Lighthouse Archaeological Maritime Program, St. Augustine Lighthouse & Museum, St. Augustine, FL.

Neumann, George C.
1998   *Battle Weapons of the American Revolution*. Scurlock Publishing Co., Inc., Texarkana, Texas.

Peterson, Harold L.
1956   *Arms and Armor in Colonial America 1526 – 1783*. Bramhall House, New York, New York.

Puleo, Joseph V.
2011   Ketland Guns in America: A Fresh Look at the Family of English Industrialist Who Dominated the Early American Firearms Trade. *Man at Arms* 33(6):14 – 23, 46.

Starr Cox
St Augustine Lighthouse & Maritime Museum
81 Lighthouse Avenue
St Augustine, FL 32080
904-829-0745
scox@staugustinelighthouse.org

Rigging and Equipment from the Storm Wreck: a late 18th Loyalist Refugee Ship

Eden Andes

The Storm Wreck is a late 18th century sailing vessel that ran aground on the coast of St Augustine. FL in an attempt to relocate British loyalists after the Revolutionary War. Among the artifacts recovered were vital pieces of ships' equipment and rigging elements. Several of these artifacts, in particular the rigging, show that those aboard were unable to save the ship.

Introduction

In 2009, a wreck found by the Lighthouse Archaeological Maritime Program brought to light a forgotten portion of our country's past: Florida, as a British colony, was still loyal to the King after the Revolutionary War. Loyalists fleeing our newly independent nation boarded ships in Charleston, SC, headed for Saint Augustine, FL. On 31 December 1782, several of these refugee vessels wrecked at the treacherous inlet. Historical documents reveal that although no lives (or money) were lost, many people lost their worldly possessions. Artifacts from this wreck, named the Storm Wreck, reveal the everyday goods these people brought with them to start over in a new territory. While many of these artifacts are still in concretion awaiting conservation, many more have been deconcreted and provide an interesting story about the 1782 events.

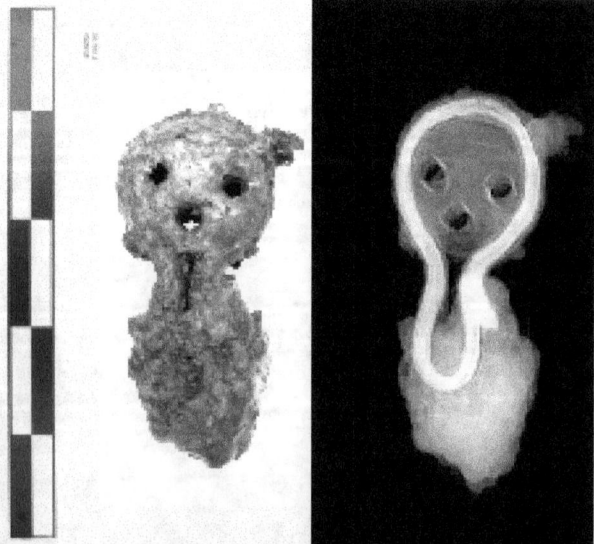

Figure 1. Left: photo of concretion 15S-450.1 showing distinctive shade of the dead-eye as found on the Storm Wreck. Right: x-ray reveals the attached iron strop (St. Augustine Lighthouse and Maritime Museum).

Hanks and Hooks

Hanks are crucial in rigging and are still in use today on modern sailing vessels. Used to attach sails to stays, hanks were made of wood or line until more durable iron gained popularity in the later half of the 18th century (Marquardt 1992:204-205). Iron hanks, like the one found in concretion 10S-044, were slow to catch on because they tended to wear down stays much faster than wood or line hanks (Meide et al. 2010:170-171). Their presence on the Storm Wreck is noteworthy because this ship predates wire rigging by several decades (Stone 1993:69). Iron hanks were employed more commonly after wire rigging replaced line rigging.

The hank's signature omega shape is owed to its function: the stay would pass through the larger eye, allowing the hank to move along it freely without jamming, despite tension from the sail. A smaller bolt-rope would attach to the eyelets on either end of the omega, securing the sail without it chafing against the hank or the stay (Meide et al. 2010:170-171). A sail would employ several dozen hanks, when bent onto a stay. Since so few hanks were identified on the Storm Wreck, it is possible that those found were spares and that the ones in use floated away with the sail after the mast was cut down and jettisoned in an attempt to save the ship.

Reverse-eye hooks were found throughout the Storm Wreck's artifact assemblage, particularly in concretions 13S-336 and 10S-041. Their numbers could account for their probable use aboard the ship: to secure cannons and their carriages fast to the gunwales with block-and-tackle; to secure the breeching lines to soften the guns' recoil, and as an integral part of the running rigging when trimming sails (Boudriot 1986; Desmond 1997).

Deadeyes and Strop

Named for their spooky "human" faces, deadeyes are used in standing rigging to adjust tension on a ship's

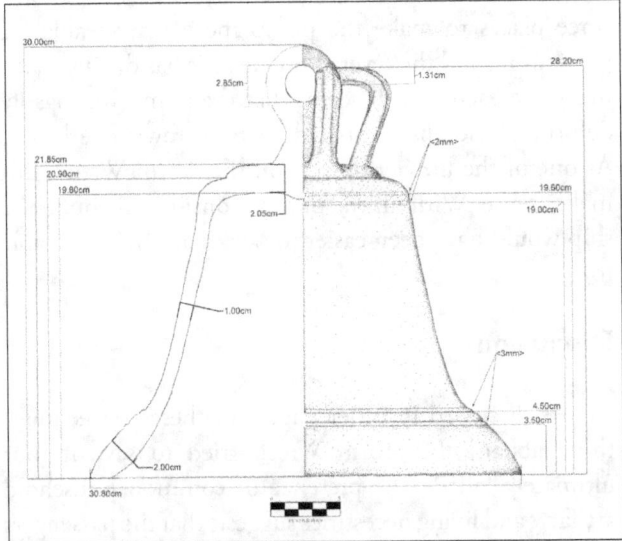

Figure 2. An illustration of 10S-64.4, the ship's bell. Note the molding wires at the soundbow and at the head and shoulder of the bell. A cross section at right illustrates its thickness relative to its height.

spars. Generally found in pairs, one deadeye attaches to a turnbuckle attached to the hull while the other attaches to the line securing the spar via a shroud. The pair is threaded together through their eyes with a lanyard, allowing for easy adjustment when needed. Each deadeye is scored around its outer edge, dividing them into two groups. Depending on the deadeye's function, the scoring could be rounded to accept the rope of the shroud or square if attached to an iron strap (Corder 2007:49-50).

The Storm Wreck's deadeye still has its iron strap attached; it is therefore assumed that the scoring around its outer edge is square and that it was attached to the hull via a turnbuckle. Going through such effort to jettison a light and hard to reach element of rigging would be superfluous, strenuous, and time-consuming considering the chaotic circumstances and other more relevant and weighty objects to be tossed overboard.

Ships Bell

In 2010 archaeologists recovered an intact bronze bell and attached headstock (10S 64.4). X-ray images revealed much of the headstock's hardware as well as a pewter spoon concreted to the bell. However, x-rays did not pick up a pewter "RP" military button also found in the bell's concretion (Meide et al. 2010:133-144). Much to the chagrin of the archaeologists and conservators, the bell had no maker's mark or decoration of any kind, making it virtually impossible to use for dating or identifying the wreck. Its lack of décor or ship's name suggests that it was a merchant ship and its owners were attempting to save money (Meide et al. 2011-2012:201-208). However, the headstock of the bell is one of few found in the archaeological record, making it unique within the Storm Wreck's assemblage. Iron hardware found within the headstock includes several large fasteners running vertically on either side of the bell's crown, and two very large iron fasteners running horizontally from either end of the headstock as the fulcrum on which the bell swung. Two very large bolts are visible on the outer ends of the headstock, although none of the hardware survived conservation. The only decorations found on the bell were the molding wires around the top of the soundbow and on the head and shoulder.

Lead Deck Pump

A very large and heavy cylindrical artifact was recovered during the 2011 season (Meide et al. 2014: 208). Researchers originally thought it to be a pissdale; the precursor to the ship's head. However, comparisons of contemporary pissdales proved the Storm Wreck's artifact to be too large and intricate. The earliest pissdales were rather rudimentary and not much more than sheetmetal shaped and soldered into a funnel (Daniel 2009). Piping recovered from a previous season was another pump component; it was too thin to allow the passage of solid waste. Further research into another 18th century wreck, the *San Jose*, led researchers to believe that

Figure 3. Shows 10S-64.4 in its entirety, with its headstock. Complete bell headstocks are rare occurrences in the archaeological record, making the Storm Wreck's headstock unique.

they had found the ship's deck pump, which pumped sea water onto the deck for various purposes (Oertling 1996:35-38; Skowronek 1984a:78, 83). Several more examples of contemporary deck pumps served to back this claim (Meide et al. 2011-2012:209).

Something very interesting struck the researchers almost immediately about the pump: it appears to have been purposely bent in several places, and portions of the intake piping were severed from its body. The intake piping still attached to the reservoir was bent in three places to make the pump more manageable for jettisoning, and the severed intake pipe has distinct hack marks on each end. It seems that the pump was hastily deformed and dismembered to be thrown overboard. As one of the heavier objects on the Storm Wreck, this makes sense. Without the pump's considerable bulk, the ship would have been easier to save (had they been able to).

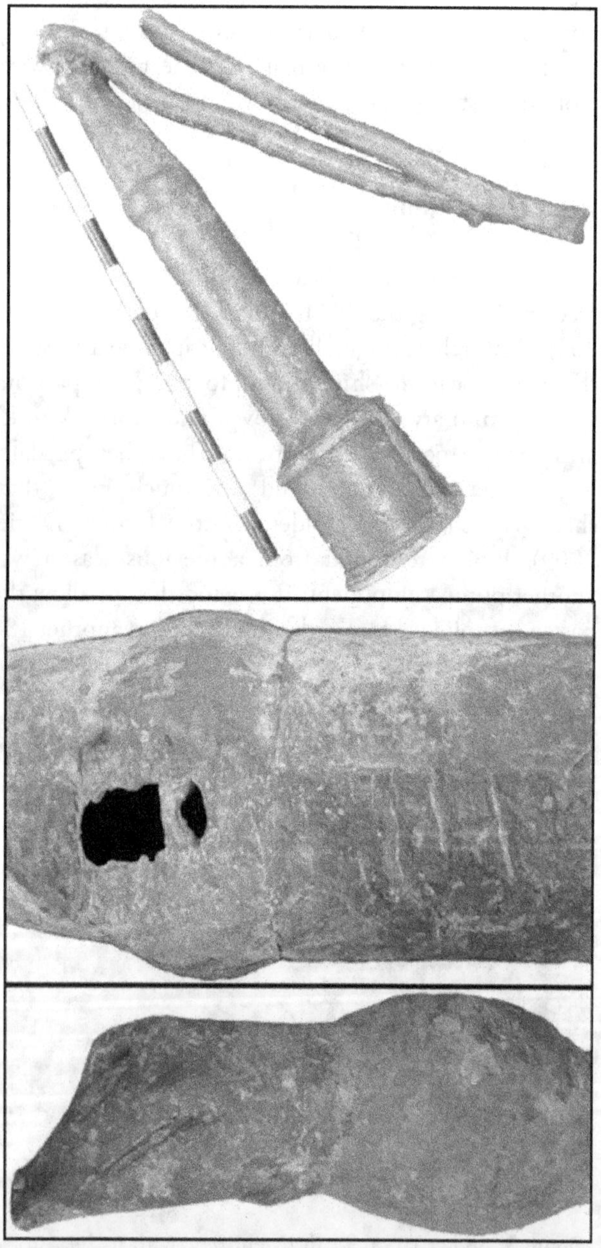

Discussion

As discussed in other papers in these proceedings, those aboard the Storm Wreck tried to save it, but ultimately failed. The presence of common household artifacts and living necessities suggests that the passengers were looking forward to starting anew, while preserving what normalcy they could. The absence of valuables and specie suggests that salvage efforts after the wreck were successful. However, the ship itself could not be saved, as shown by various rigging and equipment artifacts found within the assemblage.

References

BOUDRIOT, JEAN
1986 *The Seventy-four Gun Ship: a Practical Treatise on the Art of Naval Architecture*. Naval Institute Press, Annapolis, Md.

CORDER, CATHERINE LEIGH INBODY
2007 *La Belle: Rigging in the Days of the Spritsail Topmast; A Reconstruction of the Seventeenth-Century Ship's Rig*. Texas A & M University College Station

DESMOND, CHARLES
1997 *Wooden Ship-Building*. Vestal Press.

MARQUARDT, KARL HEINZ
1992 *Eighteenth-Century Rigs & Rigging*. Conway Maritime Press, London.

MEIDE, CHUCK, SAMUEL P. TURNER, AND P. BRENDAN BURKE
2010 First Coast Maritime Archaeology Project 2007-2009: Report on Archaeological and Historical Investigations and Other Project Activities. Report To Florida Division of Historical Resources, Tallahassee, from Lighthouse Archaeological Maritime Program, St. Augustine Lighthouse & Maritime Museum, St. Augustine, Florida.

Figure 4. Top shows Storm Wreck's deck pump after conservation. Middle and bottom are details of the modifications found, apparent hack marks from an axe.

Meide, Chuck, Samuel P. Turner, P. Brendan Burke, and Starr Cox
2011 First Coast Maritime Archaeology Project 2010: Report on Archaeological and Historical Investigations and Other Project Activities. Report To Florida Division of Historical Resources, Tallahassee, from Lighthouse Archaeological Maritime Program, St. Augustine Lighthouse & Maritime Museum, St. Augustine, Florida.

Meide, Chuck, P. Brendan Burke, Olivia McDaniel, Samuel P. Turner, Eden Andes, Hunter Brendel, Starr Cox, and Brian McNamara
2014 First Coast Maritime Archaeology Project 2011-2012: Report on Archaeological and Historical Investigations and Other Project Activities. Report To Florida Division of Historical Resources, Tallahassee, from Lighthouse Archaeological Maritime Program, St. Augustine Lighthouse & Maritime Museum, St. Augustine, Florida.

Oertling, Thomas J.
1996 *Ships' Bilge Pumps: A History of Their Development, 1500-1900*. 1st ed. Studies in Nautical Archaeology No. 2. Texas A&M University Press, College Station.

Skowronek, Russell K.
1984 *Trade Patterns of Eighteenth Century Frontier New Spain: the 1733 Flota and St. Augustine*. Master's Thesis, Department of Anthropology, Florida State University, Tallahassee. Volumes in Historical Archaeology No. 1. South Carolina Institute of Archaeology and Anthropology, Columbia.

Stone, David Leigh
1993 *The Wreck Diver's Guide to Sailing Ship Artifacts of the 19th Century*. Underwater Archaeological Society of British Columbia, Vancouver, British Columbia.

Eden Andes
2775 CR 214
St Augustine, FL 32084
edenjandes@gmail.com

Navigational Instruments Found on the Storm Wreck

Mary H. Burkett

Between 2009 and 2015, excavations of the Storm Wreck (8SJ5459), an 18th-century British shipwreck off the coast of St. Augustine, FL, by the Lighthouse Archaeological Maritime Program (LAMP) have revealed a variety of navigational instruments. The primary navigational instruments found were a pair of dividers, octant elements, and a sector rule. This paper presents a historical analysis of each instrument, examines the context of these artifacts in relation to the Storm Wreck, and offers insight into the methods used for determining a ship's position in the late 18th century.

Introduction

In 2009, LAMP completed a remote sensing survey as part of the First Coast Maritime Archaeology Project, during which the Storm Wreck was discovered. This 18th-century shipwreck (designated 8SJ5459) encompasses a wide array of artifacts including several navigational instruments, and components of such instruments (Meide et al. 2010:184-186). Excavations between the 2010 and 2013 summer field schools revealed a pair of navigational dividers, an adjustor knob, an octant eyepiece, and a sector rule. These items are currently undergoing conservation at the St. Augustine Lighthouse & Maritime Museum. This paper examines navigation methods and navigational instruments of the 18th century, focusing on those instruments found on the Storm Wreck.

Navigation in the 18th Century

For hundreds of years, mariners around the world struggled with one thing in particular: longitude. Although acquiring a ship's latitude had become fairly routine by the 18th century, this was not the case with longitude. To determine longitude the exact time at the ship's location and at the Prime Meridian is needed. With rolling seas and changes in temperature and humidity, the commonplace pendulum clock was unreliable. Without a method for determining longitude, even the greatest navigators ended up lost at sea, and in many cases did not survive (Sobel 1995:5-6).

As a result, in the early 1700s mariners and astronomers began searching for a solution. Some governments even offered monetary prizes in exchange for a working method. For example, the British Longitude Act of 1714 granted the inventor of a solution an amount equal to several million dollars in today's currency. This incentive eventually led to John Harrison's 1773 invention of the marine chronometer, and also inspired the development of the octant and sextant, navigational instruments more reliable and efficient than their predecessors (Sobel 1995:7-10).

Octant Piece (Pinnula)

In 2012, LAMP archaeologists found a copper alloy peep sight, or sighting pinnula, (12S-266.1) from an octant in the Unit 19 dredge spoil (See 2015 Site Plan, Veilleux and Meide, this volume:Figure 1). An important navigational instrument of the 18th century, the octant measured the altitude of celestial bodies at varying degrees to determine latitude. Unlike earlier instruments, the octant utilized two reflecting mirrors (Meide et al. 2014:218). These features made it possible to obtain latitude from small, point-like stars, not solely the much larger sun. This reduced measurement error and therefore greatly improved accuracy of the device (Denny 2012:68).

To use the instrument, the observer established a line of sight to the horizon through the sighting pinnula. Then, by using the index mirror and swinging index arm, the reflection of a particular celestial body was lined up with the horizon and the observer recorded altitude measurements from the graduated arc on the instrument's side. Several colored glass panels located between the index and horizon mirrors adjusted the amount of light reaching the eye, allowing for measurements with both the sun and the stars (Meide et al. 2014:218). Developed independently in 1731 by English mathematician John Hadley and American glazier Thomas Godfrey, the octant remained in use until the 20th century. By 1780, the accuracy of the octant, and later the sextant, rendered the use of earlier devices unnecessary (Meide et al. 2014:218; Denny 2012:68).

Figure 1 shows complete measurements of artifact 12S-266.1. The pinnula is 3.6 cm (1.44 in.) in length and 2.1 cm (0.84 in.) in width at its widest point. The peephole at the center of the object is 0.2 cm (0.08 in.) across, and the circular depression around the peephole is 0.6 cm (0.24 in.) across. The slight bend at the narrow end of the object would allow this piece to fit into the instrument. The pinnula has recently completed

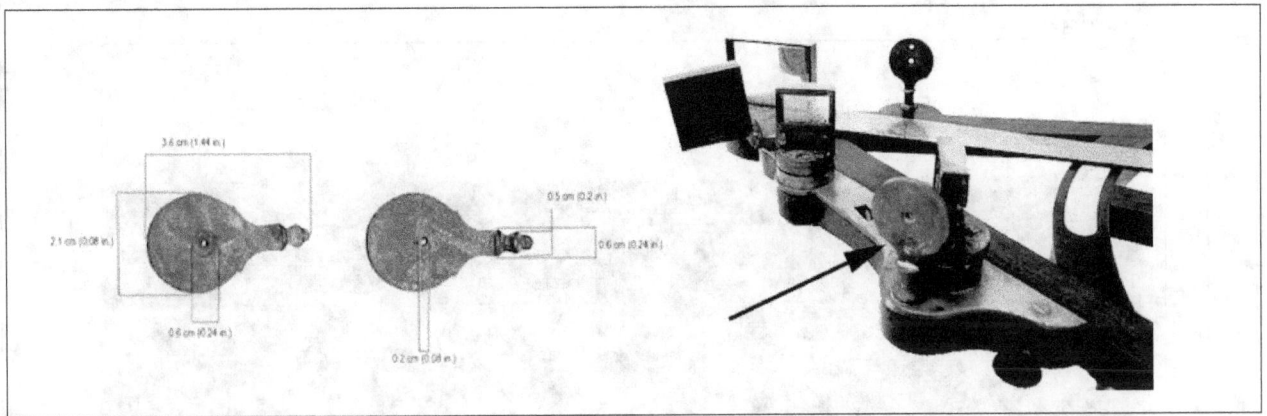

Figure 1. Left: Artifact 12S 266.1. Copper alloy sighting pinnula from an 18th century octant with complete measurements, front and back. Photographs taken before conservation. Right: Octant from the Land And Sea Collection; arrow points to sighting pinnula. (Jacobs 2013) (Copyright 2016 by Land And Sea Collection).

electrolysis at the St. Augustine Lighthouse & Maritime Museum. Other examples of sighting pinnulas and octants in the archaeological record include an octant pinnula from the French Auguste (1761), and octant fragments from the Mardi Gras Wreck (1815). An octant made by Jesse Ramsden circa 1795 (Figure 1) has a sighting pinnula that is almost identical to artifact 12S-266.1 (Meide et al. 2014:218; Jacobs 2013).

Developed shortly after the octant, the sextant had many similarities. The only significant functional difference between the octant and the sextant is the sweep of the arc. The octant has a 45 degree arc with a 90 degree measurement capacity, whereas the sextant has a larger arc of 60 degrees with a 120 degree measurement capacity. Also, the materials (metal, wood, and ivory) used to make octants and sextants were the same. Having only found the sighting pinnula (12S-266.1), identification of the instrument was difficult (Meide et al. 2014:218). However, sextants typically use sighting telescopes or sighting tubes, so the presence of a pinnula almost always signifies an octant (Ford et al. 2008:152). It is reasonable to assume that the pinnula found on Storm belonged to an octant, and not a sextant.

Adjustor knob

An adjustor knob (11S-144.2) removed from concretion 11S-144.1 may be associated with the octant pinnula (12S-266.1) (Figure 2). Two of the knob's features suggest that this artifact came from a scientific instrument, and possibly from an octant (Meide et al. 2014:218). First, the narrow end of the knob is threaded, like a screw. Scientific instruments almost always employ knobs for tuning and adjusting. For example, adjustor screws found on octants and sextants are threaded to allow the instrument to be zeroed, or

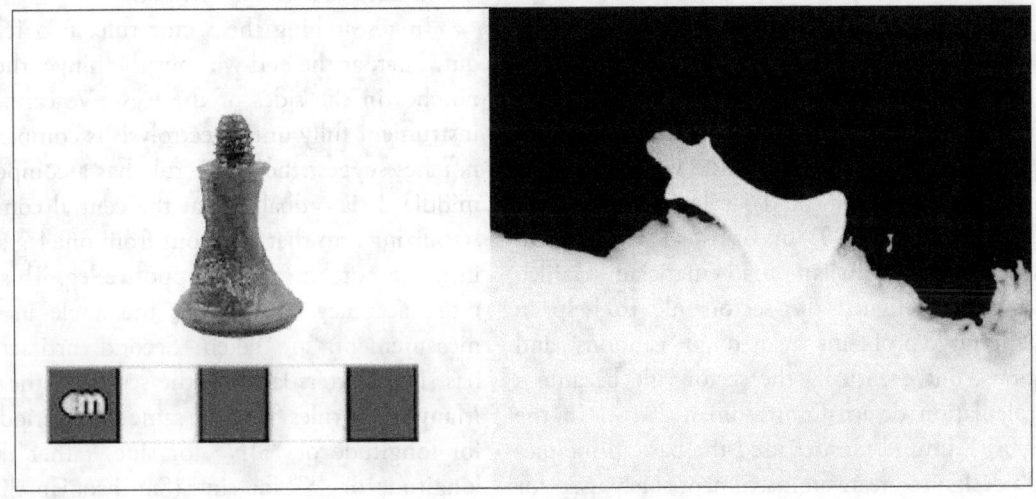

Figure 2. Artifact 11S 144.2. Copper alloy adjustor knob with x-ray.

2016 Underwater Archaeology Proceedings

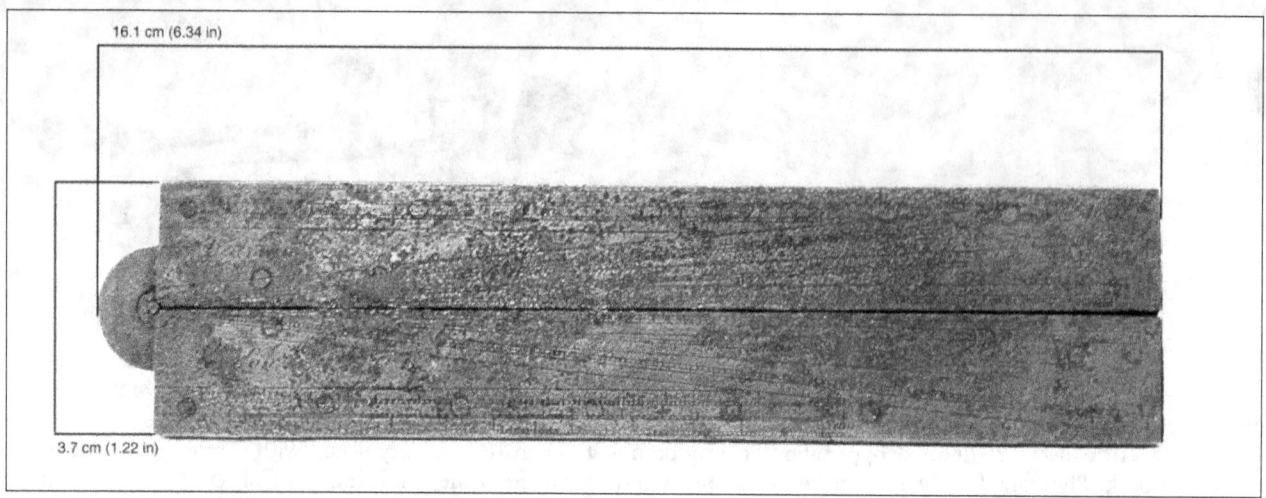

Figure 3. Artifact 13S 341.1. Brass sector rule with measurements.

allow the index arm to be locked in place on the scale (Ford et al. 2008:152). Second, the outer edge of the wider end of the object is knurled. Knurling is common on tuning and adjusting knobs, because it makes turning and gripping easier.

Made of copper alloy, the knob measures 2.58 cm (1.03 in.) in length and 1.73 cm (0.69 in.) in diameter at its wider end. The threaded end of the knob is 0.31 cm (0.12 in.) in diameter. This artifact is currently in a sodium carbonate solution at the St. Augustine Lighthouse & Maritime Museum and will begin electrolysis soon. While we believe this knob came from a scientific instrument based on its features, research to date does not show adjustor knobs of this shape or size on octants and sextants (Meide et al. 2014:218). Therefore, although it is a possibility, we cannot be certain that artifact 11S-144.2 came from the same octant as the sighting pinnula (12S-266.1).

Sector Rule

In 2013, LAMP archaeologists recovered a brass sector rule (13S-341.1) from the northeast quadrant of Unit 31 (Figure 3). The sector rule was a common navigational instrument and calculation device developed in the late 1500's by British mathematician Thomas Hood and Italian mathematician Galileo Galilei. Galileo designed the sector rule to help in solving military problems related to cannons and fortifications, but eventually the sector rule became a simple calculation device (Smithsonian 2016). In the early 1600s, Edmund Gunter used the basic principles of Hood's design to create an instrument solely used for calculation. He noticed that a device capable of quick and simple calculations was much needed, especially among seamen. His book *De Sectore & Radio* (1623), allowed widespread understanding and application of the principles of an instrument that would be in common use for over 250 years (Waters 1958: 416-417; Hopp 2009: 7).

The sector rule follows the principle that corresponding sides of similar triangles are proportional. The two sides, or legs, of the instrument move about a central joint, and measurements are taken using dividers from scales inscribed on the legs. The scales included on sectors vary, but most include scales for measuring inches, decimals, chords, sine, tangent and longitude. Sector rules differ in length, although six in. rules are most common. They were typically made of boxwood, ivory, or brass (Hopp 2009: 7). Artifact 13S-341.1 is 16.1 cm (6.34 in.) long, 3.7 cm (1.22 in.) wide and is currently undergoing electrolysis at the St. Augustine Lighthouse & Maritime Museum.

In researching the sector rule, two features stood out. First, at the end without the hinge, there are small notches in the sides of the legs. We cannot open the instrument fully until electrolysis is completed, but the notches suggest the sector rule has a component in the middle. It is probable that the central component is a stabilizing arm that pulls out from one leg and then fits into the notches on the opposite leg. This arm allows more accuracy, as it holds the angle in place while measurements are taken. Second, artifact 13S-341.1 has single letters labeling the scales on the instrument. Many sector rules from the same time period say "LON" for longitude or "SIN" for sine, rather than "L" for longitude or "S" for sine (Smithsonian 2016). While an "L" and "S" are discernable on this sector, other markings are still obscured by a dark patina. When treatment is completed, we hope to learn more about the scales and markings on the instrument. Examples of similar sector rules can be found in the Smithsonian's National Museum of American History collections. The sector rule in the Smithsonian collection manufactured by Williams Harris has several similarities to artifact 13S-341.1, including a stabilizing arm (Smithsonian 2016).

Dividers

In 2010, LAMP recovered a concretion (10S-041.1) containing hooks, hanks, nails, and a set of navigational dividers (10S-041.2) (Figure 4). Dividers were an important navigational instrument used to take measurements and plot points on nautical charts (Meide et al. 2011:162-163). Like the sector rule, dividers are composed of two legs that open from a hinge at the top of the tool. Unlike the sector rule, they have sharp points, typically iron, at the ends of each leg (West 2005:69). The pair of dividers found on the Storm Wreck did not survive conservation fully intact and no longer have sharp iron tips.

Dividers were not only essential for navigation and piloting, but also for sector rule calculation. Without them, the sector rule would be useless. Navigators used dividers to take distance measurements from the sector rule, and then transferred those measurements to the scales on the instrument (Smithsonian 2016). With more than one purpose, this small but efficient tool remains in use today.

Most dividers were made of brass or iron. Typically, iron dividers were used in carpentry for taking and transferring measurements, and brass dividers were used at sea for navigation (West 2005:68). Made of brass, the dividers from the Storm Wreck are currently in a sodium carbonate solution until electrolysis begins. They measure 7.2 cm (2.83 in.) in length and 1.3 cm (0.51 in.) in width at the end farthest from the hinge. The diameter of the hinge is 1.4 cm (0.55 in.), and the width of the hinge is 1.0 cm (0.39 in.). Navigational dividers are commonly found on shipwreck sites. Some examples include: 1798 *Colossus* (1 pair), 1653 *Lastdrager* (80 pairs-brass), and 1707 *Association* (3 pairs) (West 2005:70).

Conclusion

The navigational instruments found on the Storm Wreck can show us that even on a ship evacuating Loyalists at the end of a war, wayfinding instruments were essential and in common use. There will always be unanswered questions. Did the adjustor knob we found come from the same octant as the sighting pinnula? Did someone on the ship use the navigational dividers to take measurements from the sector rule? The possible connections among these tools are fascinating, and although some answers are lost to the sea, there is at least one question to contemplate. What can these artifacts tell us about the Storm Wreck? Our theory is that the ship hit the sandbar off the coast of St. Augustine, and when it started taking on water the crew unsuccessfully tried to lighten the load to save the ship. Had they succeeded in saving the ship, it would be very unlikely to find a sector rule, dividers and possibly an octant on the site. With a

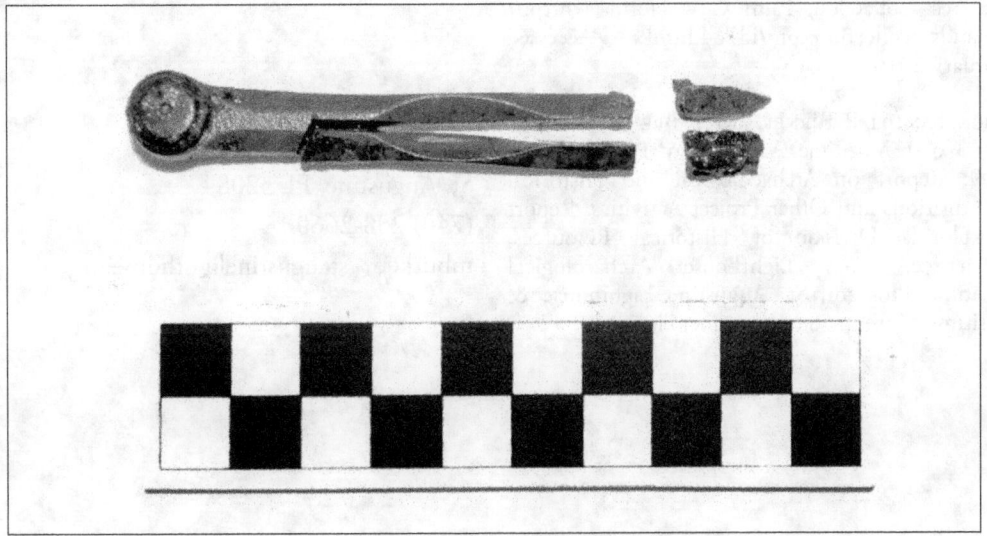

Figure 4. Artifact 10S 041.2. A pair of brass navigational dividers.

watertight ship they would have needed these important instruments, and they would not have ended up on the ocean floor.

Acknowledgements

I would like to thank all of the archaeologists at the Lighthouse Archaeological Maritime Program - Chuck Meide, Brendan Burke, Starr Cox, Sam Turner, Andrew Thomson, and Olivia McDaniel - for their support and guidance. I would also like to thank the entire staff at the St. Augustine Lighthouse & Maritime Museum.

References

DENNY, MARK
2012   *The Science of Navigation: From Dead Reckoning to GPS*. The Johns Hopkins University Press, Baltimore, Maryland.

FORD, BEN, AMY BORGENS, WILLIAM BRYANT, DAWN MARSHALL, PETER HITCHCOCK, CESAR ARIAS, AND DONNY HAMILTON
2008   Archaeological Excavation of the Mardi Gras Shipwreck (16GM01), Gulf of Mexico Continental Slope. OCS Report MMS 2008-037. Prepared by Texas A&M University. U.S.Department of the Interior, Minerals Mangement Service, Gulf of Mexico OCS Region, New Orleans, Louisiana.

HOPP, PETER M.
2009   *Joint Slide Rules: Sectors, 2-Foot 2-Fold, and Similar Slide Rules*. Hexagon Press.

JACOBS, JOEL HARRY
2013   Early Period English Backsight Octant, Jesse Ramsden Anchor Imprint Ca. 1795. The Land And Sea Collection, Palm City, Florida <http://landandseacollection.com/id764.html> Accessed February 2016.

MEIDE, CHUCK, SAMUEL P. TURNER, AND P. BRENDAN BURKE
2010   First Coast Maritime Archaeology Project 2007-2009: Report on Archaeological and Historical Investigations and Other Project Activities. Report To Florida Division of Historical Resources, Tallahassee, from Lighthouse Archaeological Maritime Program, St. Augustine Lighthouse & Maritime Museum, St. Augustine, Florida.

MEIDE, CHUCK, SAMUEL P. TURNER, P. BRENDAN BURKE, AND STARR COX
2011   First Coast Maritime Archaeology Project 2010: Report on Archaeological Investigations. Report To Florida Division of Historical Resources, Tallahassee, from Lighthouse Archaeological Maritime Program, St. Augustine Lighthouse & Maritime Museum, St. Augustine, Florida.

MEIDE, CHUCK, P. BRENDAN BURKE, OLIVIA MCDANIEL, SAMUEL P. TURNER, EDEN ANDES, HUNTER BRENDEL, STARR COX, AND BRIAN MCNAMARA
2014   First Coast Maritime Archaeology Project 2011-2012: Report on Archaeological Investigations. Report To Florida Division of Historical Resources, Tallahassee, from Lighthouse Archaeological Maritime Program, St. Augustine Lighthouse & Maritime Museum, St. Augustine, Florida.

SMITHSONIAN INSTITUTION
    Sectors. The National Museum of American History Collections, Smithsonian Institution <http://americanhistory.si.edu/collections/object-groups/sectors?ogmt_page=sectors-introduction>. Accessed 21 February 2016.

SOBEL, DAVA
1995   *Longitude: The True Story of a Lone Genius Who Solved the Greatest Scientific Problem of His Time*. Bloomsbury Publishing Place, New York, New York.

WATERS, D.W.
1958   *The Art of Navigation in England in Elizabethan and Early Stuart Times*. Yale University Press, New Haven, Connecticut.

WEST, MICHAEL
2005   An Intact Chest from the 1686 French Shipwreck La Belle, Matagorda Bay, Texas: Artifacts from the La Salle Colonization Expedition to the Spanish Sea. Master's thesis, Department of Anthropology, Texas A&M University, College Station, Texas.

Mary H. Burkett
2775 County Road 214
St. Augustine, FL 32084
(740) 258-2660
mburkett@staugustinelighthouse.org

Household Artifacts from the Storm Wreck

Christopher McCarron

When Loyalist families evacuated Charleston, SC in December 1782, they carried with them all they could bring from their homes. Various domestic artifacts have been recovered from the Storm Wreck including tableware, cookware, and household hardware, among others. The domestic artifacts presented here provide an idea of what British colonial subjects from a variety of social backgrounds used in their everyday lives, and what items were deemed critical for survival and for attempting to cultivate a sense of normalcy when these Loyalists were forced to flee their homes and start new lives in an unfamiliar colony.

Introduction

In December 1782, the final Loyalist evacuation of Charleston, SC set sail for places in Canada, Florida, and the Caribbean, where those loyal to the British Crown were still welcome. As these Loyalists prepared to leave, they were told to grab what they could at a moment's notice and leave town with no promise of return. These items were picked specifically to help rebuild a community away from home. An eyewitness description from a British officer in Charleston describes the hardships of the Loyalists escaping Charleston:

> "To provide in some measure for these poor wretches the commanders of the garrisons (though contrary to their orders) protracted the evacuations as long as they could without offending the Ministry. Transports were procured, and several hundreds with their personal property went to St. Augustine, in Florida, the Governor of which granted each family a tract of land upon which they sat down and began the world anew. ... There were old grey-headed men and women, husbands and wives with large families of little children, women with infants at their breasts, poor widows whose husbands had lost their lives in service of their King and country, with half a dozen half-starved bantlings taggling at their skirts, taking leave of their friends. Here you saw people who had lived all their days in affluence (though not in luxury) leaving their real estates, their houses, stores, ships, and improvements, and hurrying on board the transports with what little household goods they had been able to save. In every street were to be seen the situation of those who were about leaving the country, and the more dreadful situation of such who were either unable to leave or were determined, rather than run the risk of starving in distant lands, to throw themselves upon, and trust to, the mercy of their persecutors, their inveterate enemies, the rebels of America (Jones 1879: 1-5)."

Of the hundreds of ships that left Charleston in the final evacuation, 16 arrived in St. Augustine on December 31, 1782. In their attempt to enter the inlet, all 16 were lost upon the bar (Meide et al. 2014: 314-316). One of these 16 ships was discovered in 2009 by archaeologists with the Lighthouse Archaeological Maritime Program (LAMP), the research arm of the St. Augustine Lighthouse & Maritime Museum. Over the course of excavations on this site, now designated the Storm Wreck (8SJ5459), archaeologists recovered a number of domestic items. These help provide an idea of what these particular British Loyalists were using in their everyday lives, and what they believed was necessary to begin a new life upon their arrival in St. Augustine.

Of the domestic items found on the Storm Wreck, few are as practical and important as those involved in cooking and eating. The kitchen hearth has been described as the heart of a county home; ideally, the same would be true for the evacuees' potential new homes in Saint Augustine, FL. Occasionally, a colonial family might display their prized kitchenware silver or fine china, but survival in developing colonies typically meant relying on an array of functional items made from more practical materials such as wood, horn, pewter, brass, copper, iron, tin, leather, and clay. During the 1600s, rough pottery, wooden implements, iron pieces, and pewter pieces were found most frequently in the kitchen. By the 1700s, homes expanded and so did their domestic wares. Wrought and cast iron increased the variety of andirons, fire backs, kettles, pots, tools, lighting devices, and eating utensils. Brass and copper were largely imported from Europe, and their uses in the colonial home also expanded over the years by contributing slender candlesticks, teakettles, warming pans, tobacco boxes, and furniture brasses (Neumann

1984:155). These metals were also used to protect homes and valuables as locks both large and small. Some containers were made of glass of varying strength and styles, both practical and decorative.

Pewter Spoons

A large portion of the domestic artifacts from the Storm Wreck are pieces of flatware. Fourteen flatware specimens were recovered from the site between the 2010-2015 field seasons, 13 of which are spoons, and one of which is a broken handle, possibly representing a spoon or other piece of flatware. All the spoons and the handle are pewter. Standard pewter was a mix of approximately 95% tin, 3 to 4% lead, 1% copper, with slight traces of bismuth, arsenic, and zinc; for centuries it was a common alloy for use in tablewares (McNamara 2013:38).

10S-064.1 was a spoon from a concretion on the ship's bell that remained concreted until removed in late 2011. Until that point, this spoon was visible only in x-ray images. Its handle was attached to the bowl by a drop rather than a rat tail, and its handle has been truncated and most of it is missing. It is unknown if this was done deliberately or if it was broken during natural site formation (Meide et al. 2014:251). The shortening of spoon handles is a historically and archaeologically documented practice among sailors intended to make the implements easier to fit in pockets (Broadwater 1996[1]:133; Smith 2008:88-90). The missing handle makes dating this spoon difficult, and stylistic identification all but impossible. Its bowl is elongated, measuring 8.4 by 4.2 cm (3.3 by 1.7 in.), and its surviving length, whose extant handle is bent, is around 15.0 cm or 5.9 in. This artifact has undergone electrolysis and is fully conserved.

Spoon 11S-104.1 was the first intact, unconcreted spoon discovered on the wreck. It came from the southeast quadrant of Unit 12 under a brick that was lodged under the cascabel of Cannon 4. Its overall length is 19.0 cm (7.5 in.), and its bowl measures 7.6 cm by 4.0 cm (3.0 by 1.6 in.). The pattern and shape of its handle is typical of the fiddle-back design, which was gaining popularity in the late 18th and early 19th centuries

Figure 1. Spoon 14S-420.2 recovered from Storm Wreck. This spoon features the most common spoon design found on the Storm Wreck, showing the rat tail handle attachment on the back of the spoon (top), and the dog nose design at the end of the handle. Image courtesy of LAMP.

(McNamara 2013:38; Cox 2013:44). The attachment between the bowl and handle is in the shell-back style, with the shell portion cast to resemble an acanthus leaf or similar floral design. This is also a common pattern on neoclassical spoons, showing a strong French design influence (Sheridan 2009:3). While there are no maker's marks on the spoon, there is a crude "X" etched into the back of the handle; this was a common sign of ownership among illiterate sailors (Brendel, this volume).

Spoon 11S-115.1 was also unconcreted and recovered by hand in 2011 from the northwest quadrant of Unit 14. It is a dog-nose spoon, also known as the wavy-end style, so-called because of the shape at the end of its handle. The dog-nose pattern is older than the fiddle-back design and was popular from 1690 into the 1800s (McNamara 2013:39). It bears a rat-tail ridge along the bottom of its bowl, which is a distinctive characteristic of this pattern. Its bowl measures 6.3 cm by 4.2 cm (2.5 by 1.7 in.). Its overall length is difficult to define due to a notable bend in its handle, but it appears to measure 17.6 cm (6.9 cm) long. It is not known if the spoon was purposely bent by its owner or if the bending was a result of site formation processes (Meide et al. 2014: 115). There also appears to be a series of asterisk-like marks scratched into the underside of the finial, possibly denoting ownership (Brendel, this volume).

Spoon 11S-122.2 was embedded in a concretion found in the southeast quadrant of Unit 14. Made of pewter, its bowl measures 6.8 cm × 4.1 cm (2.68 by 1.61 in.) and its handle has been broken off. Spoon 11S-122.2 has a rat-tail attachment under the bowl, but its handle pattern cannot be ascertained from its preserved length (Meide et al. 2014:254).

Specimen 12S-202.1 is a simple pewter handle with no decorations. It may belong to a spoon or other piece of flatware. Spoon 12S-203.1 measures 18.5 cm (7.28 in.) in length with a bowl of 6.3 cm by 4.5 cm (2.48 by 1.77 in.). It is also made of pewter and has a dog-nose handle with a rat-tail bowl attachment—the most common style found on the Storm Wreck (Meide et al 2014: 254).

Another pewter spoon, 12S-239.4, is a dog-nose spoon with a rat-tail much like that of 11S-115.1 and12S-203.1. It measures 17 cm (6.69 in.) in length and its bowl is 6.5 cm by 4.0 cm (2.56 by 1.57 in.). Any decorations or markings that might be present on this spoon are obscured by concretion. Spoon 12S-241.1, like several other specimens, is missing part of its handle. This spoon's preserved length is 14.2 cm (5.59 in.), and its bowl measures 8.3 cm (3.27 in.) long and 4.5 cm (1.77 in) wide (Meide et al. 2014:255-256).

Spoon 13S-338.4 is an intact specimen with the usual rat-tail and dog-nose combination. Spoon 13S-355.1 also is complete with a handle that is exceptionally straight compared to most of the other spoons in the catalog. It has a dog-nose decoration at the end. 13S-386.1 has a truncated handle, elongated bowl, and no decorations.

Spoon 14S-420.2 (Figure 1) is in slightly better condition overall compared to the other spoons. It has a dog-nose and rat-tail combination with a carved double anchor decoration on the handle as well as another possible, but partially obscured, decoration in the bowl. This spoon also has cast decorations, but they are not easily visible. 14S-425.1 is in fairly good condition and has a dog-nose handle design. Spoon 15S-440.1 has an elongated bowl and no decorations. Typically, other spoons found on the Storm Wreck of this design are truncated, while this example is intact.

Despite the prevalence of the dog-nose, rat tail design, those spoons that feature this design are of different dimensions, and the remaining specimens feature different designs all together. In addition to the individual marks present on some of the spoons, this suggests that the spoons were all individually acquired by their owners and were therefore personal possessions of sailors or passengers on board (McNamara 2013:39; Brendel, this volume).

Pewter Plates

Two pewter plates were recovered from the Storm Wreck (Figure 2). The first plate, 11S-134.1, measures 30 cm (11.81 in.) in diameter with a bowl depth of 2.5 cm (0.98 in.) and a brim width of 2.5 cm (0.98 in.). Chargers were often used as serving platters for meals that were then divided onto smaller plates called trenchers for individual consumption (Neumann 1984:277). The second plate, 11S-153.1, is a trencher measuring 25 cm (9.84 in.) in diameter with a bowl depth of 1 cm (0.39 in.). The plate's design has a smooth-faced, wide-brim with a single reed on the underside of the rim. This design was popular in the 18th and 19th centuries (Neumann 1984:276; McNamara 2013:41).

Brass Candlestick

A candlestick designated 11S-126.1 was recovered in 2011. It is made of brass or a similar copper alloy, and measures 17.3 cm (6.81 in.) in preserved length. Its base

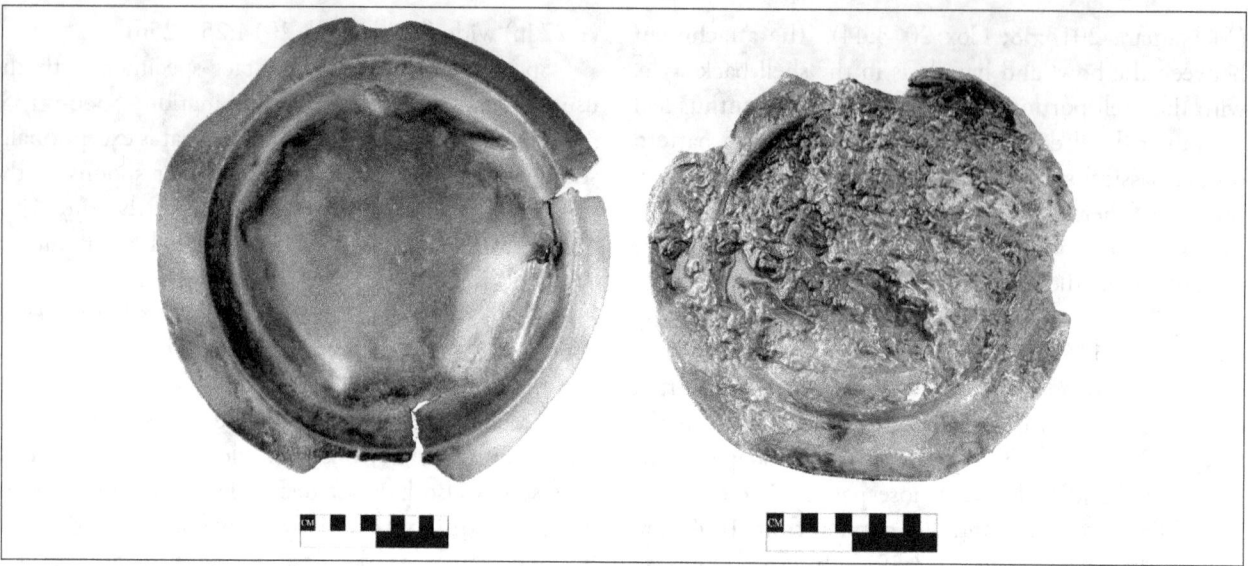

Figure 2. Two Pewter Plates. 11S-134.1, the charger, on the left and 11S-153.1, the trencher, on the right. Image courtesy of LAMP.

is missing. Either a drip pan would have been attached to the base, or the candlestick would have been attached to a larger lighting fixture. The candle socket is in the shape of a floral pattern. A similar pattern is presented in Neumann's study of colonial furnishings and is dated to 1740-1755 (Neumann 1984:66). In the 18th and 19th century, brass candlesticks were increasingly popular because iron and tin were not considered suitable for ornamentation (Hayward 1927:90). Candlesticks were also the most common source of lighting at the time. Since brass examples could be highly polished and molded into complex shapes easily, they are the most common contemporary candlestick material (Hayward 1927:90). This example appears to be cast, since there is no evidence suggesting it was soldered (Meide et al. 2014: 258). In the late 17th century, a two-piece mold was developed which enabled seams to be cast in two vertical halves and then joined. This technique continued until the close of the 18th century, when single-cast molds became the norm (Noël Hume 1969: 94).

Clothing Irons

Heated irons were used in Europe for smoothing clothes as early as the medieval period (Glissman 1970). The name "flat iron" was the general name for the hand-held iron by the 17th century and simply consisted of a handle with a solid, flat, triangular metal base. Flat irons were also sometimes referred to as "sad irons," with "sad" meaning solid or heavy; this may suggest that these irons were heavier versions of the standard flat iron. The term "smoothing iron" was also used. It was typical during the time to use two irons in tandem while ironing clothes. One of the irons would be left on the fire to heat while the other one was in use. A cloth or rag would often be necessary to hold the heated iron since the handle would have been too hot to touch, though sometimes handles were made of wood. By the late 19th century, removable handles were produced which could be attached to a pre-heated iron (Meide et al: 2014: 260).

While varied in style, the Storm Wreck irons are all simple designs featuring a wrought iron handle attached to a cast iron base. The spatial distribution of the irons recovered between 2010 and 2012 is of some interest. Four out of the five irons were seemingly recovered in pairs, with two from Unit 8 and another two from Unit 15. This is noteworthy because, as mentioned above, irons were typically used in pairs. The distribution of these irons suggests that archaeologists may have recovered two sets of irons owned by two individual families. They were probably packed along with other personal possessions in boxes or similar containers on board the ship and, due to their weight and shape, did not move very far from the location of their original deposition after the wrecking process (Meide et al. 2014: 260-262).

Brass Pins

Numerous brass straight pins were recovered from the Storm Wreck between the 2012 and 2013 field seasons. Seven of these pins are uncovered, while at least another 19 examples remain in concretions. The recovered pins range in size between 1.2 cm and 4.26 cm in length, indicating a broad spectrum of uses. Brass pins were used not only for sewing, but also for holding blanket folds, making lace, holding wigs on, and as clothing fasteners. Pins with lengths of just over 2.5 cm and 1.5 mm in diameter were most commonly used for sewing, although it was not uncommon for families to have a variety of sizes for other tasks (Beaudry 2006: 10-43; Cox 2013: 238-39). Brass pins similar to the pins recovered from the Storm Wreck were constructed from the 16th century onwards by cutting and filing one end of a brass wire to a sharp point, and wrapping a second thinner wire at least twice around it and stamping it with a machine to form a head (Franklin 2005:149-151; Noël Hume 1969:254; Bruseth and Turner 2005:88; Smith 2005:11). This was a very labor-intensive process. Brass pins were relatively expensive until the early 19th century, when brass pin manufacture was fully mechanized. Brass pins are common finds on terrestrial archaeological sites and shipwrecks, including the 1554 Spanish shipwrecks at Padre Island, the 1686 French shipwreck La Belle, the 1760 French shipwreck Machault, and the 1764 British shipwreck *Industry* (Arnold and Weddle 1978:287-289; Bruseth and Turner 2005:88-89; Franklin 2005:149-151; Noël Hume 1969:254-255; Sullivan 1986:92). Pins of this type were used to hold garments during tailoring, as well as in everyday life when a button was considered too bulky (Cox 2013: 46).

Fireplace Tools

As mentioned above, the hearth was the heart of the colonial home. From the hearth itself comes a collection of artifacts recovered from the Storm Wreck. 12S-234.1 is a pair of fire tongs that resemble the basic form for hearth tongs from 1700-1820. The tongs measure 36 cm from the base of the handle to their longest point, 8 cm wide, and 1.3 cm thick. 13S-350.6 is an andiron recovered from the wreck. Andirons, or firedogs, were meant to hold logs for the fireplace and to allow air circulation under them. The earliest American versions were stones or bricks, although cast and wrought-iron forms had long been established in Europe and were imported or made in the Americas by the mid-1600s (Neumann 1984: 156). The recovered specimen most likely resembles a two-piece "scrolled-top" form that would have been mortised into an arched base which, if the form is correct, is currently missing (Neumann 1984: 158). The full length of the andiron is 39 cm with a height of 25.2 cm. The andiron is 2.4 cm thick and 18 cm from the "scrolled-top" to the supposedly missing base.

Brass Drawer Handle

A brass drawer handle was recovered from the Storm Wreck that resembles an everted-ended bail handle with balusters and central knop, a style commonly used with a "batwing" or "angel's-wing" plate from about 1720 to 1750 (Noël Hume 1969: 278-79).

Glassware

Glassware from the Storm Wreck includes a wine glass foot; the broken remains of a few bottles; and a leaded glass stopper with a decorated edge. The wine glass foot, 10S-035.1, was located in the northwest quadrant of Unit 4 underneath a plank and consists of a colorless glass base, or "foot." A pontil scar exists on the underside of the foot, and swirl marks are evident throughout the glass fabric. None of the original outer foot rim remains, likely due to the fragile nature of the artifact. Wineglass bases are often the most substantial component of the vessel and can reveal much about the manufacture technique, decorative elements, and chemical composition of the glass metal (McNamara 2013:42). This foot appears to have a common design,

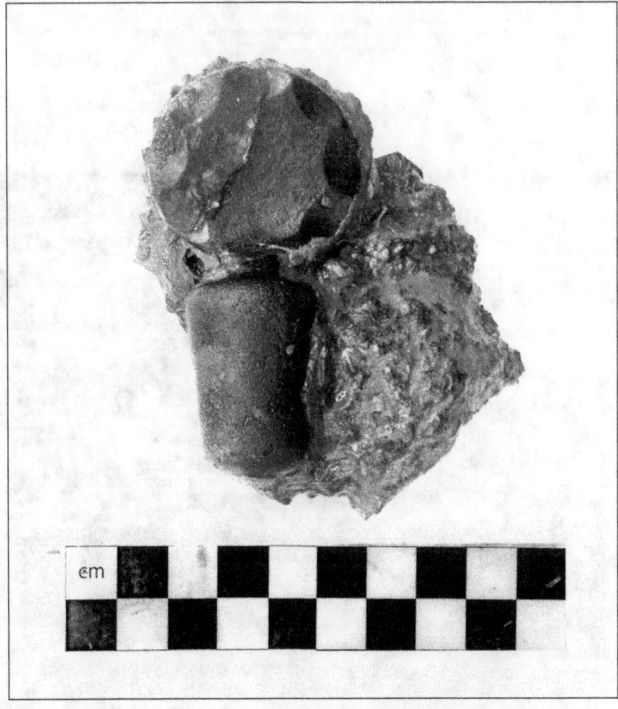

Figure 3. Specimen 13S-343.2, the leaded glass stopper. Image courtesy of LAMP.

referred to as a 'plain conical' foot formed into a narrow stem (Jones and Sullivan 1989:140). There is no finished edge on the foot to determine finishing treatment. Based on the shape of the foot and slender nature of what remains of the base of the stem, it is likely that this wine glass dates to between 1780-1805 (McNamara 2013: 42).

A dark brown glass bottle base was found, designated 13S-350.3, which seems to fit Noël Hume's descriptions of glass bottles from around 1770. It has a small bulb shape that is more common in the late 18th century and is significantly smaller than most earlier versions. In addition, a green bottle neck was recovered from a musket concretion that seems to fit the late 18th century description. The neck itself is longer and thins towards the mouth of the bottle much less dramatically than the more bulbous glass bottles used earlier, potentially putting it between 1761-1772 (Noël Hume 1969: 60-69). The glass stopper (Figure 3) found during the 2013 field season, 13S-343.2, would have been a common decoration for the late 18th century. Up until 1841, stoppers were manufactured individually to fit a specific bottle and would have been relatively expensive. This example resembles a "disc stopper" decorated with cut facets whose finial is a vertical, flat circle, also known as a "wheel" (Jones and Sullivan 1989: 155).

Keg Tap and Key

Artifacts related to kegs and dispensing liquids from them were found as well, including a copper alloy keg tap and keg key (13S-327.1 and 13S-310.3 respectively). It remains unclear whether these items were part of the colonial household or the ship's cargo.

Locks and Padlocks

When colonial Loyalists evacuated their homes, it would have been common practice to strip the house of useful hardware. Many evacuees disassembled their entire homes and transported them for eventual reassembly. One documented example was William Curtis, who decided to "pull down" his recently built home in Charleston and take it with him to his new home in Saint Augustine. His house and effects were lost, however, when his ship wrecked on the Saint Augustine bar (Meide 2015: 381). The Storm Wreck contained artifacts of similar origin. Inside concretion 12S-200.1, a padlock has completely eroded but left a "ghost image" in x-ray. Measuring 9.7 cm by 7.2 cm, the padlock was purse shaped and a typical design for padlocks in the 18th century (Noël Hume 1969: 250). Another lock is 13S-321.1 (Figure 4), an 18th century rim lock with the iron key contained inside and wrapped in cloth for

Figure 4. Specimen 13S-321.1, an open faced rim lock. Note the resin-filled hollow of the key on the left side of the image. Image courtesy of LAMP.

transport. The iron key has completely eroded away, but conservators were able to make a cast using the remaining hollow. In the last quarter of the 17th century, rim locks began to be made in brass cases that were attached to a door by three or four screws; by the 18th century, they featured a slide on the underside of the box. Early brass rim locks were expensive and were used on better American doors throughout the century (Noël Hume 1969: 246).

Conclusion

The domestic artifacts recovered from the Storm Wreck reveal much about the day-to-day lives of the colonial peoples aboard the vessel. The domestic assemblage represents a number of things, such as the need to provide for basic human needs like food and shelter, and varying socioeconomic statuses. These are represented by items and materials of varying costs, and by what appears to be a diverse group of passengers, including soldiers, sailors, and civilians. As the research on these specimens continues, archaeologists continue to gain better insight into the world that these particular Loyalists occupied, and of the things they deemed most important for survival and for creating a sense of normalcy as they attempted to start a new life during the final years of the Revolutionary War.

References

ARNOLD, J. BARTO III AND ROBERT S. WEDDLE
1978 *The Nautical Archaeology of Padre Island: the Spanish Shipwrecks of 1554*. Academic Press, New York.

BEAUDRY, MARY CAROLYN
2006 *Findings: The Material Culture of Needlework and Sewing*. Yale University Press, New Haven.

BRUSETH, JAMES E. AND TONI S. TURNER
2005 *From a Watery Grave: the Discovery and Excavation of La Salle's Shipwreck, La Belle*, Texas A&M University Press, College Station.

BROADWATER, JOHN (EDITOR)
1996 Final Report on the Yorktown Shipwreck Archaeological Project. 5 Vols. Report to National Endowment for the Humanities, Washington, DC.

COX, STARR
2013 ACUA 2012 Proceedings: *Personal Items Recovered from the Storm Wreck, a Late Eighteenth Century Shipwreck off the Coast of St. Augustine, Florida.*

FRANKLIN, MARIANNE
2005 Blood and Water; The Archaeological Excavation and Historical Analysis of the Wreck of the *Industry*, a North-American Transport Sloop Chartered by the British Army at the End of the Seven Years War: British Colonial Navigation and Trade to Supply Spanish Florida in the Eighteenth Century. Ph.D. dissertation, Nautical Archaeology Program, Texas A&M University, College Station, Texas.

GLISSMAN, A.H.
1970 *The Evolution of the Sad-Iron*. Self Published.

HAYWARD, ARTHUR H.
1927 *Colonial Lighting*. 2nd ed. Dover Publications, New York.

JONES, OLIVE AND CATHERINE SULLIVAN
1989 *The Parks Canada Glass Glossary for the Description of Containers, Tableware, Flat Glass, and Closures*, revised edition. Studies in Archaeology, Architecture, and History. Parks Canada, Ottawa.

JONES, THOMAS,
1879 *History of New York During the Revolutionary War*, 2 vols. (New York: New York Historical Society, 1879), 2: 235-236.

MCNAMARA, BRIAN
2013 ACUA 2012 Proceedings: *Cooking with Fire: What Cookware and Tableware Can Tell Us About an Unidentified Eighteenth Century Shipwreck.*

MEIDE, CHUCK
2015 "Cast Away off the Bar": The Archaeological Investigation of British Period Shipwrecks in St. Augustine. 500 Years of Florida History—The Eighteenth Century. Florida Historical Quarterly. Vol 93, Number 3.

MEIDE, CHUCK, P. BRENDAN BURKE, OLIVIA MCDANIEL, SAMUEL P. TURNER, EDEN ANDES, HUNTER BRENDEL, STARR COX, AND BRIAN MCNAMARA
2014 First Coast Maritime Archaeology Project 2011-2012: Report on Archaeological Investigations. Lighthouse Archaeological Maritime Program, St. Augustine Lighthouse & Maritime Museum, St. Augustine, Florida.

Neumann, George C.
1984 *Early American Antique Country Furnishings: Northeastern America, 1650-1800.* McGraw-Hill, New York, NY.

Noël Hume, Ivor
1969 *A Guide to Artifacts of Colonial America.* University of Pennsylvania Press, Philadelphia.

Sheridan, Terrence E.
2009 The Use of Pewter Spoons in America from 1650 to 1850. *Past Masters News* 12(3):1-5

Smith, Adam
2005 *An Inquiry into the Nature and Causes of the Wealth of Nations.* Pennsylvania State University, University Park.

Smith, Sheli O.
2008 *The 1779 Shipwreck Defence: An American Revolutionary War Privateer.* PAST Foundation. Lulu, Raleigh, NC.

Sullivan, Catherine
1986 Legacy of the Machault: A Collection of 18th-century Artifacts. *Studies in Archaeology, Architecture, and History.* Parks Canada, Ottawa.

Christopher McCarron
Southeastern Archaeological Research Inc.
12443 San Jose Blvd., Suite 204
Jacksonville, Florida 32223
Phone: (205) 937-7694
Email: mccarron.det012@gmail.com

An Archaeological Examination of Cookware from the Storm Wreck, 8SJ5459

Annie Carter

The Storm Wreck is an 18th century Loyalist shipwreck located off the coast of St. Augustine, FL. The shipwreck has been an ongoing focus of the Lighthouse Archaeological Maritime Program (LAMP) since 2009, and is still the object of field excavations for the organization. The examination of the site's cookware offers an entryway for the analysis and interpretation of Loyalist intentions. This cookware was once part of a colonial, capitalistic society, and a key toolkit in an intermediary and inconclusive time for a refugee population. These features allow a view of the cookware as both economic and social factors in Loyalist lifestyles; on one end, as objects that defined a sort of comfort and familiarity in the process of creating a home, and on the other as objects of profitability. Assessing the Storm Wreck cookware contributes to a narrative about a people largely forgotten by popular history.

Introduction

In August 2009, archaeologists at the Lighthouse Archaeological Maritime Program (LAMP) discovered the first piece of cookware from the Storm Wreck, an 18th century Loyalist shipwreck off the coast of St. Augustine, FL. After noting the various magnetic anomalies in the area, LAMP director Chuck Meide began target-testing the site with a hydroprobe. The site yielded a large, cast iron cauldron during this initial exploration, and this was the first of many artifacts discovered on the Storm Wreck.

As of 2015, nine cauldrons have been raised from the site, as well as a tea kettle and a cooking gridiron. By assessing the cookware present on the site, there is room for contribution to a narrative about a people largely forgotten by popular history. In this analysis, there will be an exploration of the typological data and history of the Storm Wreck's cookware, as well as an interpretation of the artifacts from an anthropological standpoint.

2010 Cookware

10S 0036.1: "Big Cauldron"

10S 0036.1, or "Big Cauldron" is the largest cauldron from the Storm Wreck to date. It helped LAMP archaeologists date the wreck to the colonial era, when it was discovered and almost immediately identified by its contours during the 2009 survey. Due to its size in comparison to other cauldrons, it is possible that 10S 0036.1 may have served as galleyware.

10S 0063.1 and 10S 0063.2

10S 0063.1 and 10S 0063.2 are a pair of nested cast iron cauldrons. A CT scan taken of the concreted cauldrons revealed 10S 0063.2 to be the smaller, inner example, with a visible lip distinguishing the two. Unfortunately, there were too many destructive difficulties anticipated in separating these cauldrons, so they were re-deposited on site.

10S 0038.1: "Baby Cauldron"

Affectionately known as "Baby Cauldron" to those at LAMP, 10S 0038.1 is the smallest cauldron from Storm Wreck. Unlike the other cauldrons, filled with mud and sand, this artifact had a solid, rock hard substance inside prior to deconcretion. This observed substance required very delicate airscribing, which revealed bits of wood and fabric.

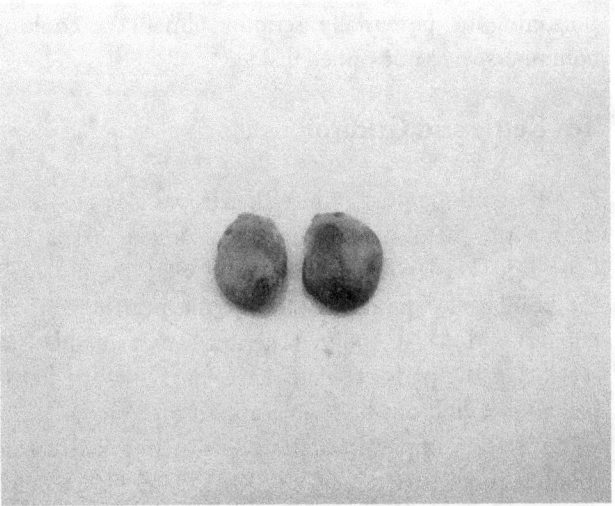

Figure 1. The remains of a pea (split in half), which were found in 10S 0038.1 during the cleaning process.

Additionally, the remains of a pea (Figure 1) were recovered during conservation of 10S 0038.1. This tiny remnant – about the size of a modern lentil – was mechanically removed from the concretion during its cleaning. As this cauldron was too small for galley cookware, it likely belonged to one of the families onboard. The pea may be food remains from a last meal cooked in 10S 0038.1 before the Storm Wreck sank.

2011 Cookware

11S 0106.1 and 11S 0156.1

The first cauldron discovered in 2011 (11S 0106.1) is similar in both shape and form to 10S 0036.1 and 10S 0038.1. A brick was found inside of this cauldron during cleaning. Additionally, a pair of copper nesting pots were discovered during the 2011 field season (Figure 2). The tripod-legged copper cauldron was manufactured into the 17th century, but by this time the cast iron cauldron

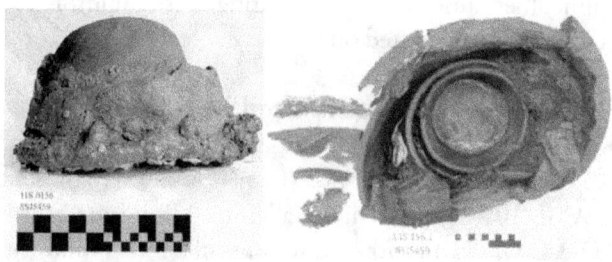

Figure 2. 11S 0156.1, a pair of nested copper pots. Left: in its concretion. Right: after deconcretion.

was prevalent in most homes (1969: 176). This could have been the result of the increasing awareness of copper poisoning, a potentially serious ailment if cooking containers were not tinned inside.

Tea Kettle and Gridiron

A traditional cast iron tea kettle was also recovered during the 2011 field season (McNamara 2013a:41). Cast iron kettles during this time were mainly used for boiling and pouring water at the hearth, whereas copper and brass spouted kettles were suitable for serving in the parlor (Neumann 1984:174). The kettle has a more bulbous body in comparison to later, high-shouldered examples; it appears similar to a kettle type manufactured between ca. 1720 and 1780 (1984:174). Casting seams became visible upon the cleaning of 11S 0125.5, indicating that the body of the kettle was cast in two pieces, and subsequently assembled with a spout. The kettle is shown in Figure 3 before and after cleaning.

The final piece of the 2011 cookware assemblage was a rounded cooking iron (McNamara 2013a: 42) as revealed in an x-ray of 11S 113.1 (Figure 4, left), showing wrought iron grating, rather than a solid disc of metal. Gridirons were used in the hearth for light cooking and as warming plates (Neumann 1984:192-193). The cooking iron or gridiron has been airscribed, though some remnants still obscure surface details prior to electrolysis (2011:249).

2012 Cookware

12S 0196.1 and 12S 0205.1

Two cauldrons were discovered during the 2012 field season, both of the same form as the cast iron cauldrons previously described. 12S 0196.1 was in very fragmented condition, as was 12S 0205.1; post-conservation, an attempt will be made to piece these fragments together. A tankard was discovered within 12S 205.1 during the cleaning process. There was concretion inside, so a cast was made from the outside. This tankard has since deteriorated; fortunately, the cast is available for further research and documentation.

2013 Cookware

Another cast iron cauldron, 13S 0308.1 was the only piece of cookware discovered during the 2013 field season. This cauldron was considered for redeposition, but upon further inspection, a pin flathead was observed near its rim. A more recent examination of the contents of 13S 0308.1 has yielded further cultural remains: a cooked fish vertebra (Shidner, this volume).

Typology and a History of Cookware

The cauldrons from the Storm Wreck "appear to be of identical form, that of the classic pot or cauldron" (Meide et al. 2011:118). This assessment is in concordance with the findings of George Neumann (1984:176), whose work *Early American Antique Country Furnishings: Northeastern America, 1650-1800* provides detailed examples, images, and descriptions of everyday, colonial-era items. According to Neumann's study, the cauldrons fall within the range of those manufactured between 1740 and 1780, with a rounded form rather than the more elongated, oval-shaped form (1984:176).

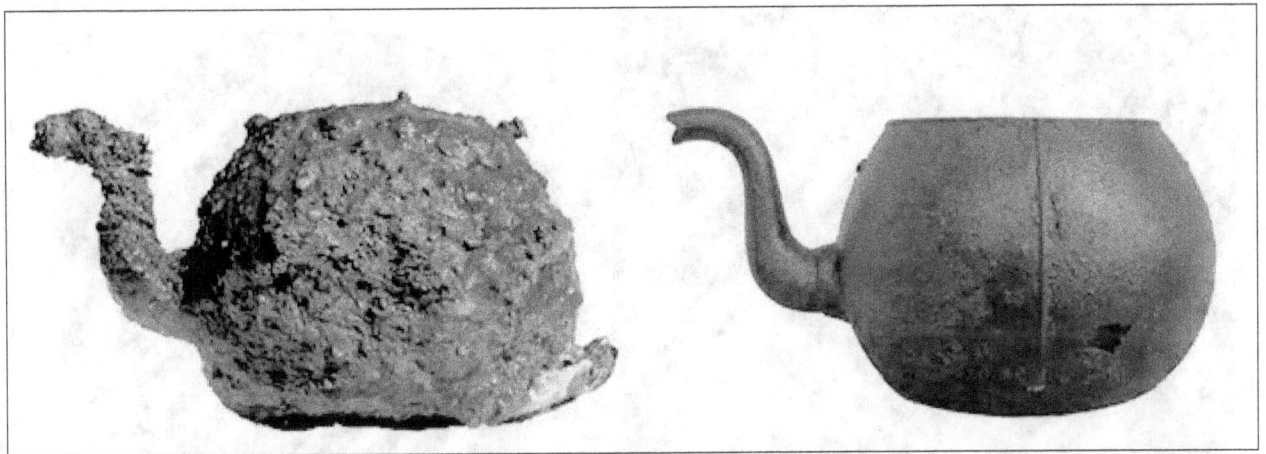

Figure 3. A traditional cast iron tea kettle, shown pre and post-conservation. Casting seams are evident on the kettle in the image on the right.

This type of cauldron would have been utilized up until the 19th century, especially in rural areas (McNamara 2013a:43).

As the data show, almost all of the cookware recovered from the Storm Wreck was made of cast iron. Vertical and horizontal seams on the cauldrons indicate that they were cast in multi-component molds. All of the iron cauldrons had three legs, or markings on their bellies indicating where legs once were. This was a common feature from the Middle Ages until the 19th century (David Eveleigh 1997:17). The legs were characterized by a taper that spanned downward before expanding into a foot in the beginning of the 18th century (Ivor Noël Hume 1969:176). Subsequently, cauldron legs merely tapered down until they came to a plain terminal, rather than branching out into a foot-shape. It appears that the cauldrons recovered by LAMP reflect this later style, lacking any sort of outward protrusion upon their legs.

All of the cauldrons' "ears" appear to be quite acute, rather than the more rounded style, which was introduced during the following century (Neumann 1984:176). With one attached near the rim on either opposing side, these ears would have once held a handle (most likely wrought iron), enabling one to set the cauldron above a fire. Unfortunately, there was no indication of these handles in the archaeological record, though both Neumann (1984: 176) and Eveleigh (1997: 17) mention this style as typical of the era in their typological analyses.

Noël Hume (1969: 176) refers to the history of the cauldron, citing the predecessor of both the iron cauldron and related copper skillet – "both types had a common ancestor in the fourteenth century, a tripod-legged bronze pot, having a flaring collar neck and with two earlike handles projecting from it and anchored to a shoulder. Such pots were suspended over the fire by means of a pair of hinged iron hooks." Noël Hume continues this history of cauldrons with the evolution of the skillet, which was partially fashioned in the image of the cauldron.

How Cookware Can Help Identify the Storm Wreck

The variety of domestic material from this site seems to indicate that the Storm Wreck was a refugee vessel with intentions of settling rather than one of a military nature. In one report, LAMP researcher Brian McNamara jokingly referred to the Storm Wreck as "the Martha Stewart Wreck" (McNamara 2013a: 43) due to the abundance of cookware present in the archaeological record.

It is important to evaluate the cookware's significance to the site. The Loyalist refugees would have depended on these objects to prepare their food on their quest for a new home. While some of the cauldrons may have been suitable for galley use, the quantity suggests that they were personal items intended for use in the home. These cauldrons did not reach their destination. During the time of the wreck itself, the cauldrons were transformed from mere objects; they became a livelihood lost. Among the many personal remains discovered on the wreck – spoons, belt buckles, flintlock pistols and many more – the cauldrons represent commodification, practical use and social relations.

The cookware present on the site offers an entryway for the analysis and interpretation of Loyalist intentions. This cookware was once part of a colonial, capitalistic society – key items in an intermediary and inconclusive time for a refugee population. By the time the Treaty of Paris was signed, Loyalists had already begun evacuating

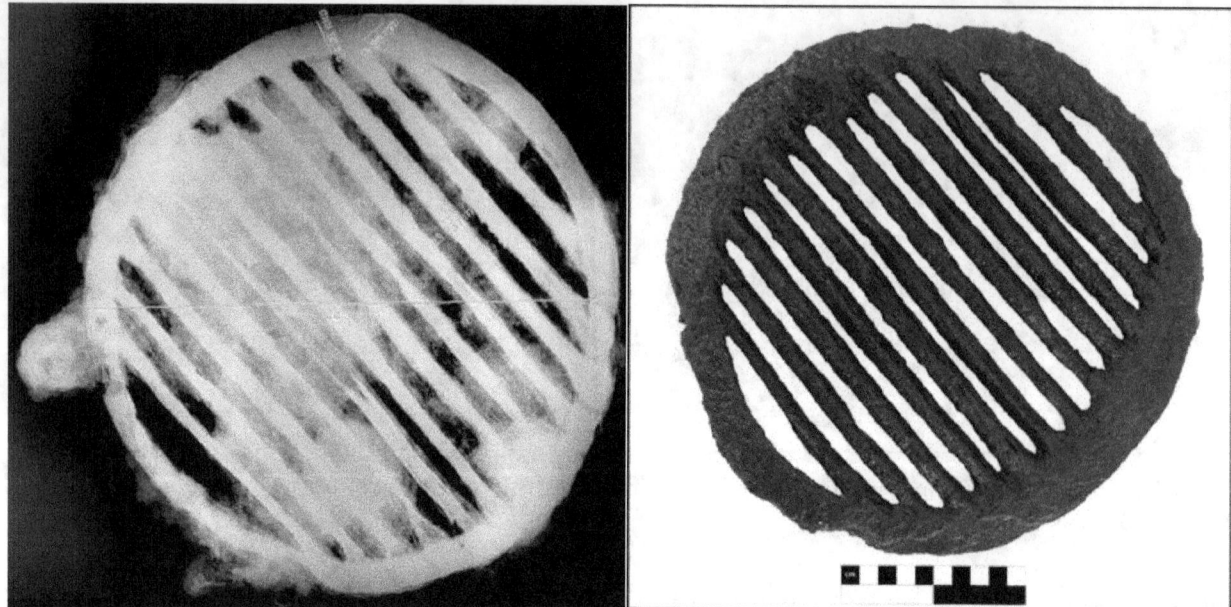

Figure 4. An x-ray image of the cooking gridiron (left), revealing the wrought iron grating. The gridiron has been deconcreted, but has not yet undergone electrolysis (right).

the southern colonies. The move southward was not a simple task – the once powerful Loyalist population had become the minority, desperately in need of money, resources, and a home base. Cast iron pots were used on an everyday basis throughout the Colonial period, and were not manufactured locally; therefore, they were an essential import to St. Augustine. Recent analysis of British port records indicate that iron pots were commonly listed on incoming cargo manifests. In a recently published slave narrative that takes place in St. Augustine, the autobiographer describes the unloading of iron cauldrons from ships in the harbor between 1815 and 1825, and notes that these items were so valuable that they were often stolen before they could be sold (Sitiki and Griffin 2009). If iron cookware was in great demand in the early 19th century, then one can imagine how scarce it would have been during the Loyalist influx, when tens of thousands of refugees flooded the city, many having lost their possessions due to the shipwreck. The cookware became a livelihood lost with the Storm Wreck.

Acknowledgements

I would like to thank my academic adviser during my time at New College of Florida, Uzi Baram, who guided me through the early stages of this research while I was writing my undergraduate thesis. Uzi has been a wonderful inspiration and an incredible mentor to me. I would also like to thank all of my friends and colleagues at the Lighthouse Archaeological Maritime Program. It has been a dream being a part of this project and an honor to work alongside such fantastic archaeologists and conservators.

References

annie.carter0392@gmail.com

EVELEIGH, DAVID J.
1997 *Old Cooking Utensils*. Shire Album No. 177. Shire Publications Ltd, Buckinghamshire. 1997. Print.

HUME, IVOR NOEL.
1969 *A guide to artifacts of colonial America*. 1st ed. New York: Knopf, 1969.

JASANOFF, MAYA.
2011 *Liberty's exiles: American loyalists in the revolutionary world*. New York: Alfred A. Knopf, 2011. Print.

MCNAMARA, BRIAN
2013a Cooking with Fire: What Cookware and Tableware Can Tell Us About an Unidentified 18th Century Shipwreck. In *ACUA Underwater Archaeology Proceedings 2012*, edited by Brian Jordan and Troy J. Nowak, pp. 38-43. Advisory Council on Underwater Archaeology, Baltimore, MD.

MEIDE, CHUCK, TURNER, SAMUEL P., BURKE, P. BRENDAN, & COX, STARR.
2011. *First Coast Maritime Archaeology Project 2010: Report on Archaeological Investigations*. Lighthouse Archaeological Maritime Program, St. Augustine Lighthouse & Museum, First Light Maritime Society, St. Augustine, FL. Print.

NEUMANN, GEORGE C..
1984 *Early American Antique Country Furnishings: Northeastern America, 1650-1800*. New York: McGraw-Hill, 1984. Print.

ORSER, CHARLES E..
"Beneath the Material Surface of Things: Commodities, Artifacts, and Slave Plantations. *Historical Archaeology* 26.3 (1992): 95-104. Print.

SEIBERT, WILLBUR H.
Loyalists in East Florida: The Narrative, vol. 1. *Publications of the Florida State Historical Society No. 9*, Deland, Florida. 1929. Print.

SITIKI, & GRIFFIN, PATRICIA C..
"The Odyssey of an African Slave." *The Florida Historical Quarterly* 88.3 (2009): 408-410. Print.

WILLIAMS, LINDA K. .
"East Florida as a Loyalist Haven." *The Florida Historical Quarterly* 54 (1976): 465-478. Print.

Annie E. Carter
732 Niagara St,
Buffalo, NY 14213
(352) 634-0229

Tools of the Trade: An Examination of the Tool Assemblage from the Storm Wreck

Sam Turner

This paper examines the collection of tools recovered from the Storm Wreck, a late 18th-century Loyalist evacuation transport lost in December of 1782 at the end of the American Revolutionary War on the St. Augustine Bar, in present-day St. Johns County, Florida. A variety of hand tools, many with their wooden handles intact, have been recovered and are currently undergoing conservation. While many of these tools were likely intended for general use in the home or farmstead, some represent those used in the shipbuilding or boat carpentry trade and other specialized professions such as that of the shoe maker.

In late December 1782, a large fleet of British government chartered and privately owned civilian transports departed the port of Charleston, SC. This was the second of three ports being evacuated by the British government, as its military power crumbled in its former 13 colonies in North America. A new Republic had been born from these colonial ruins and the remaining loyal colonies to the north in Canada and to the south in Florida became some of the refuges of last resort to loyal British citizens who did not want to, or could not, remain behind. Over a two-day period in the last days of 1782, 16 of these vessels, carrying British military and civilians alike, were cast away on the St. Augustine bar within sight of safety and a new beginning. This paper examines the collection of tools found on one of these wrecks (Meide et al, 2011:104).

When examining the tool assemblage from the loyalist refugee transport known as the Storm Wreck, it was decided to view the tool collection from the perspective of traditional occupational trades. These trades include the following: First, that of general timber work. This is the process of taking a tree and turning it into something that can be used in any form of construction ranging from shipbuilding to house, barn, furniture, and cabinet making. Some of these tools also have domestic applications, such as that of making firewood. Other trades include the cooper's trade, or barrel making; the upholsterer's trade; the cordwainer or cobbler's trade; that of the shoe maker and shoe repairman; the leather worker's trade; the general carpenter's trade; and the

Figure 1: Photograph of the croze blade found on the Storm Wreck.

caulker's trade—this last being intimately involved with the marine industries.

The cooper's, or barrel maker's trade is represented by a single tool (13S 310.9), or rather part of a tool, called a croze blade (Figure 1). The blade is the cutting part of the croze, a tool used to carve the grooves at either end of a barrel where the edges of the head pieces fit. While ships were dependent on casks for supplies ranging from water to salt pork, these were typically procured from coopers or chandlers who purchased them with or without contents. Casks were the predominant container for packing and shipping just about all comestibles. They were widely purchased and then packed with contents which were sold together with the casks that contained them. Casks and barrels therefore came from many sources and may have been sold and resold any number of times before arriving on board ship. While it is possible that a croze tool might be on board a vessel for repairing or maintaining ship's casks, it is more likely that this tool belonged to a professional cooper who was relocating from the Carolinas as a result of his political support for the British Crown.

Three hammers have been found on the Storm Wreck, two of which are representative of distinct trades (Figure 2). The third could be representative of any number of trades, so we will place this tool in the category of the general carpenter. This hammer is a typical claw hammer (10S 39.1), identical to one you could buy at any hardware store today. It is amazing to note that this tool has undergone no typological change since 1782, and no doubt even earlier. It illustrates beautifully that some things reach a form of perfection and utility that seemingly cannot be improved upon and truly stand the test of time.

The first of the hammers associated with a distinct trade is one particular to the upholsterer. This tradesman specialized in covering furniture such as chairs and couches with textile or leather and finishing them to a presentably high standard. One of the upholsterer's principal tools was a specialized tack hammer with which he drove the brass tacks that held both textile and leather coverings in place. Among the tools found on the Storm Wreck is a single example of such a hammer (Figure 2). It (12S 242) was first identified through x-ray; when mechanically cleaned, it was in a delicate condition with the wooden handle deteriorated and broken in places. Considering its burial in the relatively warm waters of northeast Florida, it could be in considerably worse shape. It must have eventually been covered by sand sealing it from oxygen and biological attack, permitting concretion to cover the entire head and handle.

An intact specialist cobbler or cordwainer's hammer also was found on the Storm Wreck (12s 200). This hammer is in much better shape than the upholsterer's, having closely associated iron material next to its handle which covered it with concretion before marine organisms could devour it. This particular hammer is emblematic of the cordwainer and cobbler's trade, having a unique look with a broad striking surface (Figure 2). There is a distinct difference between cobblers and

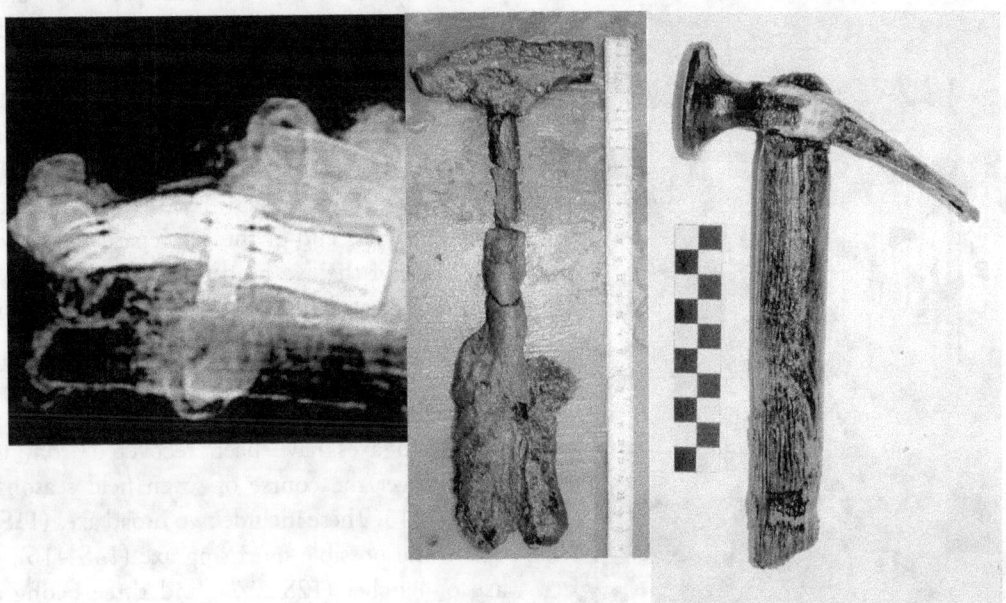

Figure 2: Image showing the three hammers found on the Storm Wreck. From left to right, they are a common claw hammer, an upholsterer's tack hammer, and a cordwainer's or cobbler's hammer.

cordwainers. The cordwainer was a shoe manufacturer, often making his wares from imported cordovan leather from Spain. The cobbler was a tradesman who repaired and maintained footware. Indeed the distinction was upheld by point of law and strictly enforced in England and the North American colonies as well, where cobblers were prevented from making shoes by proclamation. They were separated by a degree of skill that amounted to an extra five years training on the part of the cordwainer.

Two objects are indicative of the leather worker's trade (Figure 3). Two lead palms found on the site were used to protect the hands, specifically the palms, of leather workers as they forced large needles through leather which required a good deal of strength and force (14S 404.1, 14S 413.2). Other trades that use heavy gauge needles to sew leather or heavy canvas include cordwainers, cobblers, and mariners. None of these latter tradesmen used anything like the leather workers' type of large and distinctive palm guards. One surface is flat and the other is convex so as to conveniently fit in the palm of one's hand. The guard would have been wrapped in cloth or held in a pouch, and used to push needles through tough material, while protecting the user's palm. These objects likely indicate the presence of such a tradesman on board the vessel wrecked on the St. Augustine bar.

The only tool that we can definitively tie to the maritime construction or maintenance trade is a reef hook, also known as a rake hook. Two examples of this tool have been found on the site to date (14S 420.4 and 12S 252). These instruments were used to extract old and failing oakum caulking from the seams between planks. The seams between planks in a ship's hull and deck were always moving and flexing with changing sea states and through the drying effects of the sun and soaking effects of the sea. Periodically, the caulking had to be replaced. This was especially true of decks in southern climates, where the effects of the sun were harsher than more moderate climates.

The first example of a reef hook (Figure 3, 14S 420.4) from the Storm Wreck is similar in appearance to that of one pictured in an 18th century Spanish text. There they are called *mahujos* and described as irons for loosening or removing caulking from the seams (Lunwerg Editores, S.A. 1996:101). It was simply a forged piece of bar stock worked into a suitably curved shape and finished at both ends to pull out caulking. There was apparently no grip for this tool besides the iron itself. The second example of this tool, 12S 252, is still encased in concretion and has only undergone x-ray examination at this point. However, the x-ray shows that it is slightly different in shape and has a wooden handle. These tools are very likely part of the ship's equipment, though we cannot rule out the possibility that they represent the working tools of a caulker who practiced his trade in the Carolinas.

The most frequently found tool on the Storm Wreck is the axe, a variety of which was recovered (Figure 4). There is perhaps no tool more associated with the founding of America and the ever moving frontier than the axe. These come in all shapes and sizes, and vary from general use to very specialized. The Storm Wreck has yielded both sorts. The axe has a number of features that bare distinct names. The blade, known as the bit, is the business end of the axe regardless of size or type. The back of the axe head opposite the bit is called the poll. The top of the cutting edge, or bit, is known as the toe of the axe and its opposite at the bottom of the bit is called the heel. The two sides of the axe are known as its cheeks.

Seven axes have been recovered from the Storm Wreck over the course of seven field seasons between 2009-2015. These include two broad axes (11S 122, 13S 330); one possible mortising axe (14S 416); one hand axe or hatchet (12S 232); and three felling axes (09S 002, 13S 319, 15S 447). Five of the seven were hafted, with handles attached to them. This indicates that they

Figure 3: Image showing a reef hook, or seam rake (top), and a leather workers palm (bottom).

were in general use at the time of the sinking of the vessel. This is illustrated by an archaeological example of axe heads being imported into the colony of East Florida during the British Period. These were shipped in three wooden cases of twenty each and found on the wreck of the *Industry*, a coastal sloop lost on the St. Augustine bar in 1763 (Franklin 2005:112). Therefore, we can safely assume that these axes were not cargo but rather tools that had been in use and were being brought along by loyalist refugees for the purpose of starting anew in East Florida.

These axes include examples that appear to have been made in colonial America as well as England. These two types are distinguished by the size of their "ears", or pointed lugs on the bottom of the axe head. The Anglo-American colonial variety had much larger "ears," which helped keep the axe head attached to its wooden handle (09S 002, 11S 122, 12S 232, 13S 330.1). Those with considerably smaller "ears" (13S 319.1, 14S 416, 15S 447.1) are very likely English imports (Franklin 2005:116).

The broad axes are a typical frontier tool, used to square up logs once felled. The broad axe was instrumental in processing timber used in many applications, but it was critical to house and barn building where a certain standard of finished and squared timber was desired. One side or cheek of the axe was flat, while the other had a regular sloped shape beginning at the poll and running to the bit. The flat side of the axe was used to hew the rounded side of the log and give a flat finish to the cut. In addition to this, the handle of the broad axe was offset so that the craftsman wielding the axe could get his hand and blade right up against the log without scraping the back of his hand and knuckles against the log as he cut.

The flat side, or cheek, of the broad axe was often left unsharpened like a chisel. This feature is described as chisel-edged sharpening. Some broad axes however, including the two examples from the Strom Wreck, were knife-edged sharpened, or sharpened on both sides of the blade like a knife. The broad axe also had applications in the shipbuilding industry where it was known as the shipwrights axe (Horsley 1978:105). This was for much the same purpose as in house and barn building, in taking round and rough logs delivered to the shipyard and shaping them before going to the adzmen.

Another axe, a possible mortising axe, was a specialized tool for cutting mortises into timbers to accept tenons worked into the ends of other timbers. Fashioning the tenon was often done with the same mortising axe, since the mortise and tenon were usually both fashioned at the same time. This axe head had an unusual look to it since it had a relatively long body with a short or narrow bit, or cutting edge, in order to penetrate deeply into timbers while shaping the mortises. This axe pairs very well with the broad axe, as both would be very useful to someone planning to build a new home or barn in the loyal colony of British East Florida. This hafted axe is still concreted and awaits mechanical cleaning and conservation. Analysis is based on x-ray examination.

This brings us to the next category of axe. The

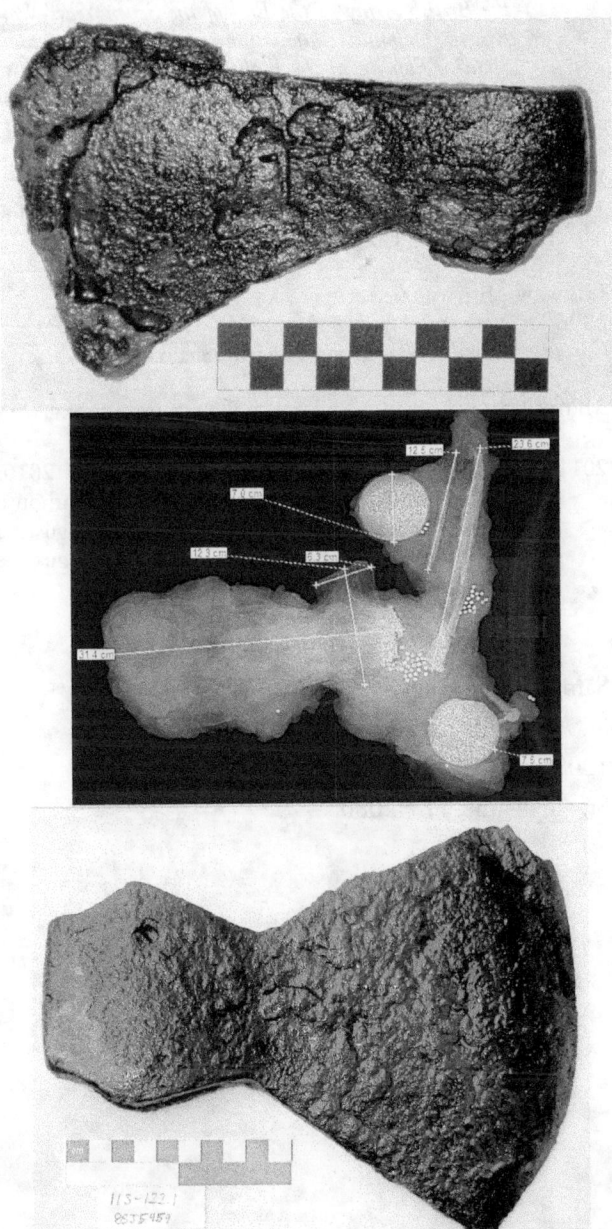

Figure 4: Image showing the three principal types of axes found on board. From top to bottom a felling axe, a mortising axe, and a broad axe.

felling axe is the typical axe that everyone pictures in their mind when they hear the word axe. As its name implies, the primary purpose of this axe is to chop down, or fell, trees. After the tree has fallen to the ground, the felling axe is then used to trim the tree branches and prepare the log for further work. The felling axe was also used to make spaced cuts into the trunk across its grain to a constant depth to prepare the log for squaring with the broad axe. The depth of the cross grain cuts determined what would then be the face of the flat surface. The broad axe would then be used between the spaced cuts going with the grain of the wood at 90^0 to the spaced cuts. Felling axes could also be used to cut branches and split wood into firewood, but had many other general cutting applications as well. A single example of a small hand axe or hatchet (12S 232) has also been found on the site. This tool, like the felling axes just discussed, was also very likely used in making firewood for cooking.

In conclusion, though the tools discussed above would have been used to produce many items used by the British military and loyalist militias believed to have been traveling on the vessel lost on the St. Augustine bar, the military did not typically manufacture their supplies but rather purchased them. It would seem therefore that much of the tool collection from this shipwreck may represent the presence of tradesmen on board who were moving themselves and their professions to a new land where they intended to set up shop and make a living to support themselves and their families. Unfortunately, the tools of their trades were lost when the Storm Wreck was lost on the bar.

The one category of tool that perhaps does not necessarily reflect the presence of a specific tradesman on board is that of the axe. Though all the assorted types found including the broad axe, mortising axe, and felling axe could have been found in the possession of a qualified house carpenter, it is equally, if not more likely, that they would have been owned by an average man living on the Carolina frontier intending to start over. The author does not suggest that these axes, or any of the tools under discussion for that matter, belonged to a single individual who had traveled on that lost vessel. Rather, as a collection, they would have served someone who had to begin anew by clearing a patch of woods and build a house out of its timber.

The last point to consider is the high proportion of felling axes and the hand axe (total of four out of 7) in this collection. This suggests that its utility was considered greater than that of other, more specialized, axes. One possibility is that they were preferred for their usefulness in making firewood which would have been necessary for the preparation of food for soldiers as well as for civilians and their families. This particular activity is represented by the multiple three-footed cooking cauldrons found on the site.

References

FRANKLIN, MARIANNE
2005 *Blood and Water; The Archaeological Excavation and Historical Analysis of the Wreck of the Industry, a North-American Transport Sloop Chartered by the British Army at the End of the Seven Years' War: British Colonial Navigation and Trade to Supply Spanish Florida in the Eighteenth Century.* Doctoral dissertation, Department of Anthropology, Texas A&M University, College Station, TX.

HORSLEY, JOHN H.
1978 *Tools of the Maritime Trades.* International Marine Publishing Company, Camden, ME.

LUNWERG, EDITORIAL S.A.
1996 *Navegantes y Náufragos; Galeones en la Ruta del Mercurio.* Barcelona, Madrid, Spain.

MEIDE, CHUCK, SAMUEL P. TURNER, P. BRENDAN BURKE, AND STARR COX
2011 First Coast Maritime Archaeology Project 2010: Report on Archaeological Investigations. Lighthouse Archaeological Maritime Program, St. Augustine Lighthouse and Maritime Museum, St. Augustine Fl.

Sam Turner
St. Augustine Lighthouse & Maritime Museum
100 Red Cox Road
St. Augustine, FL 32080

Personal Items from the Storm Wreck

Hunter Brendel

The Storm Wreck, a Loyalist refugee vessel fleeing Charleston near the end of the American Revolution in 1782, was discovered by the Lighthouse Archaeological Maritime Program (LAMP) in 2009. Since 2010, systematic excavations of the shipwreck have aimed at documenting, recovering, and conserving diagnostic artifacts to further understand this shipwreck and its role in Florida's Loyalist influx. This was a time of civil conflict and rapidly increasing population. This paper will review artifacts from the shipwreck categorized as personal items and effects, including spoons, straight pins, belt and shoe buckles, buttons, knives, a dirk sheath, pistols, coins, a lice comb, and a fausse montre or false watch. Most are undergoing conservation, although many have been deconcreted and physically examined. Some appear diagnostic, affirming the vessel's date, purpose, and cultural identity, while also providing a greater understanding of the social aspects of those on board forced to flee their homes.

Introduction

The Storm Wreck, designated 8SJ5459, is a maritime site located approximately one mile off the coast of Saint Augustine, FL. Discovered in 2009 through a remote sensing survey by the Lighthouse Archaeological Maritime Program (LAMP) during the First Coast Maritime Archaeology Project (Meide et al. 2010:184-186; Meide et al 2014:84), the Storm Wreck is a well preserved site protected by low visibility waters and dynamic sediment movement. From 2010-2015, LAMP conducted seasonal systematic excavations of the site, for which a detailed site plan has been established (Veilleux and Meide, this volume:Figure 1).

This paper focuses on diagnostic artifacts of a personal nature that have been recovered and conserved. Several were found in larger concretions that have since been x-rayed, carefully removed, and conserved at the LAMP conservation lab at the St. Augustine Lighthouse and Maritime Museum. Smaller artifacts, such as buttons and coins, are often found in dredge spoil from site excavation. Personal items from the Storm Wreck assemblage that are covered in this paper include modified spoons, a false watch, a lice comb, nine buttons, five coins, a dirk sheath, four buckles, and a pocket pistol. As of 2016, most of these items have been removed from concretions and conserved, allowing for subsequent physical examination and analysis.

Spoons

A number of spoons were found on the Storm Wreck site of which the typology and function are covered in this volume by Chris McCarron (McCarron, this volume). In particular, a few spoons were purposefully modified to suit personal needs. Spoon 12S-241.5 was truncated, or cut at the handle. Such practices were common amongst sailors because it allowed them to comfortably fit the spoons in their pockets (Broadwater 1996[1]:133; Smith 2008:88-90; Cox 2013:44).

Other examples of spoon modification on the Storm Wreck include marking by sailors to denote ownership (Marsden 1975:179; Smith 2008:88-89; Cox 2013:44). 13S-338.4 has what appears to be an *S* scratched into the handle at the tip. Other spoons such as 11S-104.1 and 11S-115.1 have *X* and asterisk marks, respectively, etched into them (Figure 1). These could possibly be

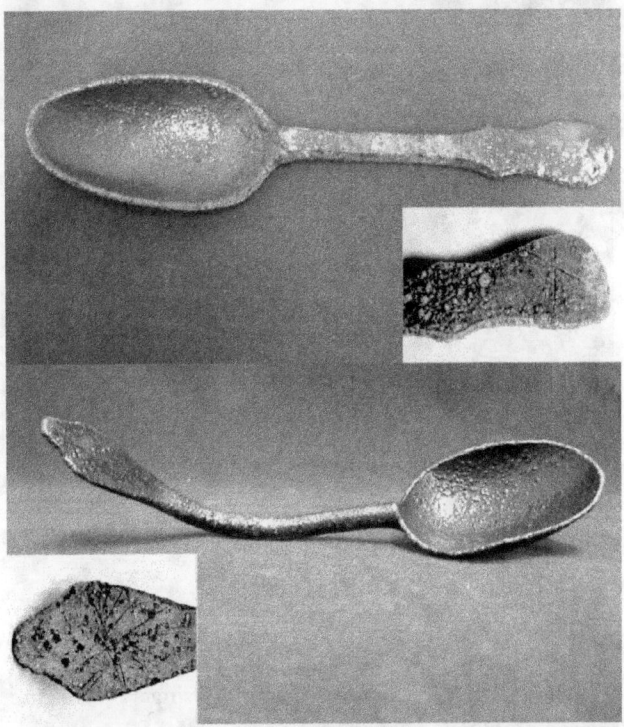

Figure 1. Top: Pewter spoon 11S-104.1 with a close up photo insert of an X scratched into the handle. Bottom: 11S-115.1 with a closeup photo insert of an asterisk scratched into the handle (St. Augustine Lighthouse & Maritime Museum).

indicative of more illiterate owners than the one of the *S* spoon. The presence of marked spoons on Revolutionary Era shipwreck sites is not an uncommon phenomenon. Such 18th century sites as *Defence* (1779) share similar rattail spoon designs with possible initials etched into the handles (Switzer 1998:190).

False Watch

A false watch was recovered from the Storm Wreck during 2013 excavations. It was located in concretion 13S-360.1 in the NW quadrant of Unit 18 and has since been removed, conserved, and catalogued as 13S-360.2. The false watch is made of cast pewter and measures 39.94 mm (1.57 in.) in diameter. Its dial measures 21.23 mm (0.84 in.) in diameter. The pewter watch dial has Roman numerals spanning clockwise with lozenges between the numerals indicating half hours. Like the marked spoons, the false watch also bears letters MAR etched on the obverse (Figure 2). A twisted rope

Figure 2. Top: False watch 13S-360.2 with measurements. Bottom: False watch 13S-360.2 illustrated for detail. Illustration courtesy of Loren Clark (St. Augustine Lighthouse & Maritime Museum).

border encloses the dial, very stylized in a rococo-like pattern. There is no evidence for a pendant that might have adorned the top of the facing. Using Forsyth and Egan's typology (Forsyth and Egan 2005:352-370), this is considered a Type 5 watch and falls into the late 17th and 18th centuries. Typology of this false watch cannot be easily dated, since the makers might have reused molds.

On the reverse are raised ridges displaying the number 14 and a pyramid-like icon that are most likely a product of the manufacturing process. More research is needed, however, since most English false watches produced in the 18th century were by William Hux and the Company, tentatively identified by a maker's mark of HUX/London (Forsyth and Egan 2005:342). Neither mark on the false watch indicates being manufactured by Hux or a competitor.

False watches were at the height of popularity in the 18th century, when carrying two watches suspended by leather straps from small pockets called fobs on their breeches was *en vogue* (Forsyth and Egan 2005:341). These were known as *fausse montre*, having origins in French fashion (Evans 1970:161-162; White 2005:132; Krivor et al. 2010:189). False watches have also been historically given to children as toys (Forsyth and Egan 2005:342). No other artifact in the collection indicates the possibility of children being present on board, so this particular watch was most likely used as a fashion piece. False watch cases have been located on other 18th century shipwreck sites, such as the Roosevelt Inlet Shipwreck (Krivor et al. 2010:189). The preservation of this false watch facing, however, is unique to the Storm Wreck.

Delousing Comb

A bone delousing comb (12S-200.4) was found in concretion 12S 200.1 from Unit 1. Delousing combs have been found on a number of maritime sites ranging throughout the second millennium. Examples of two-sided designs that have remained relatively unchanged on a number of shipwrecks spanning that time period include Serce Limani; *Mary Rose*; and *La Belle* (Bass et al 2004:283-284; Bruseth and Turner 2005:118). These were used to remove louse eggs and adult lice from heads and beards (Bass et al 2004:283).

Buttons

Out of the buttons in the Storm Wreck artifact assemblage, nine are without regimental numbers or a monarchial crown. Buttons denoting military presence are further covered in this volume by Brian McNamara (McNamara, this volume). A majority of buttons in the assemblage are pewter, excepting only two brass buttons and two blank wooden buttons. Buttons are the most commonly found personal item on historical sites, and can often tell through various designs and materials what people wore in the past and communicated through appearance (White 2005:50). The Storm Wreck button collection (Figure 3) displays a diverse assemblage of style, practicality, and social status.

11S-121.2 is a brass button of 1.65 cm (0.66 in.) removed from concretion 11S-121.1 that was recovered from Unit 14 in 2011. It features the motif of an eight-pointed flower or star in the center, encircled by a sun. The sun is surrounded by a circle of chevron-like points around the button face (Figure 3). The button appears to be stamped, with the shank no longer attached as it appears to have been soldered on.

11S-122.4, is another brass button removed from concretion 11S-122.1 in 2011 from Unit 14 in 2011. The button measures 1.75 cm (0.7 in.) in diameter. Its decoration is a thin wave pattern around the perimeter of the face, with a set of five rings etched around the center. It is the only button in the collection to have been silver-plated, as shown by a bluish tinge evident on the button face. The shank, similar to those on 11S-161.1 and 12S-291.1 discussed below, is intact with a wire eye loop inserted into a metal stem, then soldered over.

11S-161.1 is a pewter button found in dredge spoil in 2011 from Unit 13. It is an undecorated, larger button of 2.3cm (0.92in.) in diameter. The shank is still intact, though the loop is slightly bent. 12S-205.4 appears to be a wooden button blank or mold found in concretion 12S-205.1 from Unit 7 in 2012. It measures 2.0cm (0.8 in.) in diameter. It has a small hole at the center of the button measuring about 0.2 cm (0.08 in.) in diameter. The single hole suggests that the textile covered the button and gathered in the back to serve as a shank (White 2005:65-70; Meide et al 2014:232).

12S-259.1 is another undecorated pewter button. It measures 1.85 cm (0.75 in.) in diameter. It features a mold seam across its diameter, suggesting it was cast. The shank is partially intact. 12S-291.1 is a pewter button recovered from dredge spoil in 2012 from Unit 3. It is

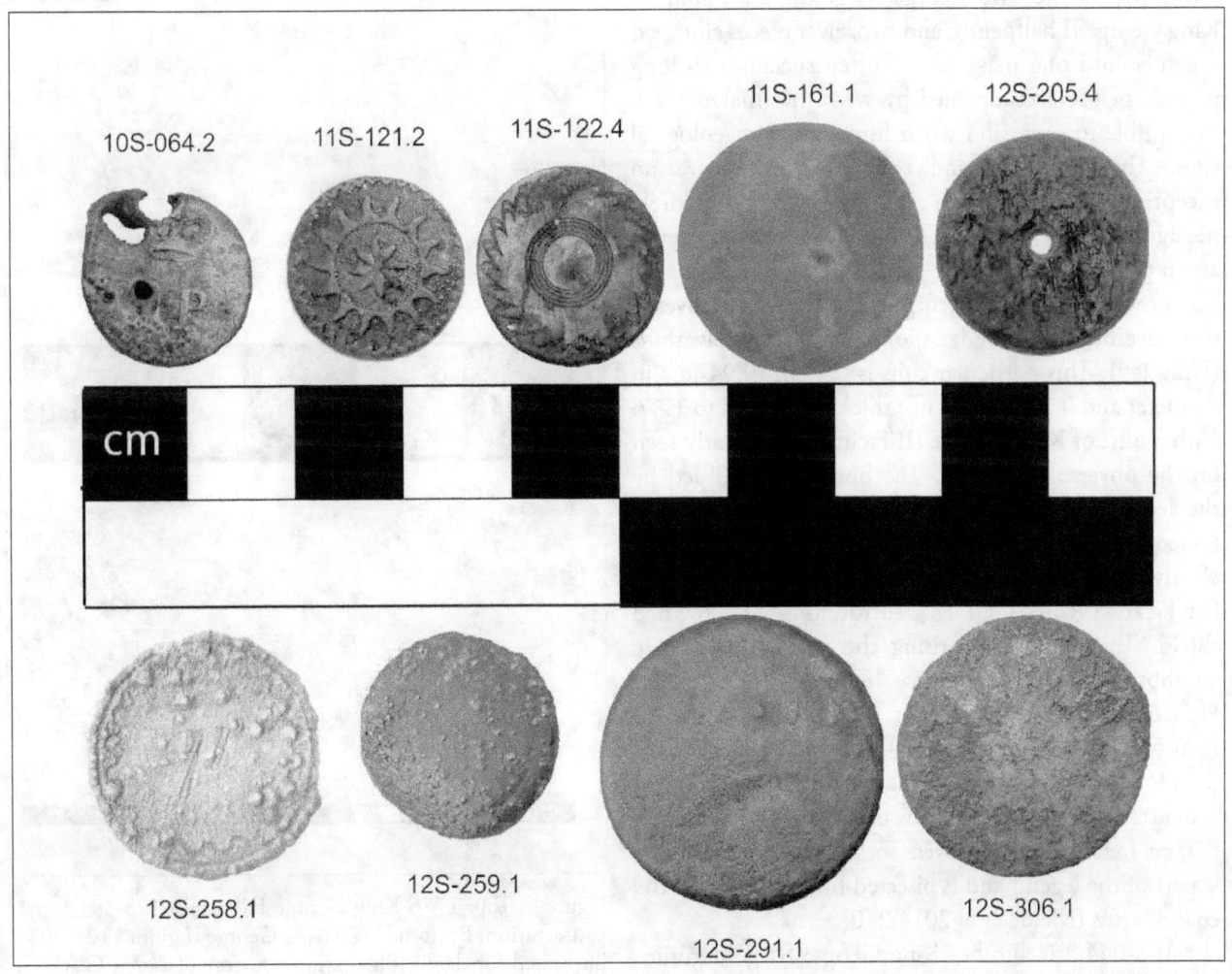

Figure 3. Examples of Storm Wreck buttons recovered through 2012 (St. Augustine Lighthouse & Maritime Museum).

the largest button in the collection, measuring 2.4 cm (0.96 in.) in diameter and 0.1 cm (0.04 in.) thick at the edge. The shank is fully intact with the stem a mound of metal apparently attached separately.

12S-306.1 is a pewter button also recovered from dredge spoil in 2012 from Unit 7. It measures 2.4 cm (0.96 in.) in diameter and 0.2 cm (0.08 in.) thick at the edge. The shank is fully intact, cast with the button, and drilled. A mold seam is visible across the back of the button. When the button began conservation, it had a Spirograph-like design visible on the face. 13S-336.3 is a pewter button and 13S-336.4 is another wooden button blank or mold. Both are currently undergoing conservation and do not have any visible decoration. Further analysis and research are required for these buttons.

Coins

Five different coins have been recovered from the Storm Wreck site: two George III gold guinea coins, a King George II halfpenny, and two silver pieces clumped together into one mass. Coins often succumb to long periods of use accompanied by wear that makes them susceptible to corrosion when found on archaeological sites. The halfpenny and two silver coins are no exception, having obverses and reserves that are barely negligible. The two King George III guineas, however, are in pristine condition.

12S-303.1 is a King George III gold guinea recovered from overburdened dredge spoil from 2010 excavations (Unit 1-5). This particular coin is 2.4 cm (0.94 in.) in diameter and 0.1 cm (0.04 in.) thick. It is dated to 1776 with a bust of King George III facing right, clearly seen on the obverse (Figure 4). The bust is surrounded by the legend, reading "GEORGIVS·III DEI·GRATIA·" ("George III by the grace of God"). The reverse type clearly denotes the legend "·M·B·F·ET·H·REX·F·D· B·ET·L·D·S·R·I·A·T·ET·E·" surrounding a crowned shield. The letters comprising the reverse legend are an abbreviation for the phrase "King of Great Britain, France and Ireland, Defender of the Faith, Duke of Brunswick and Lüneberg, Arch-Treasurer and Elector of the Holy Roman Empire" in Latin. The crowned shield is quartered, showing the arms of Britain and Scotland, France, Ireland, and Hanover. The coin's 1774 mint date is part of the legend and is bisected by the crown on the coat of arms (Meide et al 2014:240).

10S-044.2 is another King George III gold guinea of approximately the same dimensions as 12S-303.1. It was removed from concretion 10S-044.1 found in Unit 3 during the 2010 field season. The coin shares the same typing and legend on both obverse and reverse as 12S-303.1 with the exception of a mint date of 1774. Both coins belong to the fourth issue of the King George III guinea, which was in production for approximately ten years (Krause and Mishler 1993:500; Meide et al 2014:240).

Coins often see many years of use, and therefore can be worn and corroded when discovered on archaeological sites, making them difficult to identify. This is the case with both the copper coin and the clump of silver coins. The halfpenny 12S-257.1 was recovered from Unit 19 dredge spoil in 2012. It has a shape and orientation of a left-facing bust on the obverse that represents the "old-head" George II copper halfpenny. The "old-head" design was minted from 1740-1754 during the reign of King George II. Since no halfpennies were issued from 1775-1770, the coins saw long use that would wear

Figure 4. Top: 1776 King George III guinea 12S-303.1 after conservation. Bottom: 1776 King George II guinea 12S-303.1 illustrated for detail. Illustration courtesy of Loren Clark (St. Augustine Lighthouse & Maritime Museum).

down the surfaces (Krause and Mishler 1993:492; Noël Hume 1969:162; Meide et al 2014:240) 12S-257.1 measures 2.6 cm (1.02 in.) in diameter and 0.1 cm (0.04 in.) thick, which is slightly smaller than a typical George II halfpenny specimen. It is, however, reasonable to conclude that the reduction in size is linked to long-term wear on the coin.

Field specimen 12S-262.1 is a probable clump of two silver coins recovered from Unit 19 in 2012 that has survived poorly. Radiographs taken in 2012 suggest that little remains of the original metal. The coins are concreted together in an overlapping state, with the clump measuring 4.0 cm by 2.5 cm (0.98 by 1.57 in.) Using digital radiograph analytic software, the coins appear to be 2.5 cm by 1.4 cm (0.98 in. by 0.55 in.).

The variety of coinage recovered suggests they were for personal use rather than being transported in large amounts. A 9 January 1783 letter from Lieutenant Colonel Archibald McArthur, the military commander of East Florida, to Commander-in-Chief General Sir Guy Carleton, informed the general that while nine military vessels and hired Army transports in the convoy ran aground on the bar at St. Augustine, "all the cash arrived safe" (McArthur 1783:1). McArthur presumably was referencing coinage for military payment or official use, which would have taken precedence for recovery during the wrecking event (Meide et al 2014:243).

Dirk Sheath

Concretion 09S-003.1 was recovered in 2009 in the southeast quadrant of Unit 2. X-ray images of 09S-003.1 show a void area within the concretion that is in the shape of a dirk sheath or scabbard (Meide et al. 2011:158-160; Cox 2013:48). The sheath appears to have measured 24.1 cm (9.5 in.) long, and tapered in width from 3.6 to 1.7 cm (1.4 to 0.7 in.). It ended in a 2.7 cm (1.0 in.) wide round-tipped chape. The interior space of the sheath that would house the blade measures 0.5 cm (0.2 in.) (Cox 2013:48). The tapered shape of the blade indicated by the visible outline of the sheath resembles a dirk outline. Traditionally associated with the naval rank of midshipman, dirks were also regularly used as a tool and weapon by common sailors (Meide et al. 2011:160; Cox 2013:48).

Buckles

Two different shoe buckles were located and retrieved from the Storm Wreck site. 12S-237.1 is a copper alloy belt buckle found in Unit 19 during fieldwork in 2012. Measuring 4.5 cm (1.8 in.) wide and 6.0 cm (2.4 in.), 12S-237.1 has a substantial curve in the larger sides of the buckle to presumably fit over the upper part of a shoe.

18th century shoe buckles regularly consisted of four main parts: face, roll, tongue, and pin. The roll, tongue, and pin are often collectively referred to as the chape (White 2005:33; Meide et al 2014:234). The face and pin are what remains of 12S-237.1, which could be due to site formation processes. Often, the frame of the buckle was fashioned from a non-ferrous metal, while the chape was fashioned from iron or steel (Wróblewska 2008b:200). Since salt water has a corrosive effect on ferrous metals, the chapes of buckles made in this fashion deteriorate more quickly than their frames. Similar maritime sites to the Storm Wreck such as *Defence* (1779) and *General Carleton* (1785) exhibit more frames than whole buckles due to this process (Smith 2008:124; Wróblewska 2008b:200; Meide et al 2014:236). 12S-237.1, in regards to typology, is most similar in size and shape to buckles dating from 1730 to 1760, when shoe buckles were 5-6cm (2-2.5 in.) in length and rectangular or rectangular with rounded edges (Wróblewska 2008b:206-209; Meide et al 2014:236).

11S-112.1 is a buckle that is slightly larger than 12S-237.1 but exhibits similar structural features. Found in Unit 13 during the 2011 season, 11S-112.1 is 5.1cm (2.04 in.) in width and 7.5cm (3.0 in.) in length. This size is consistent with that of Artois buckles, those dating from 1760 to 1780. Although made of pewter, the buckle possesses stylized motifs with a beaded bow design flanked by small tulips on either side of the bows. Only the frame remains.

Noel Hume (1969:86) suggested that copper alloy buckles were normally worn by the middle class and could be intricately decorated and even plated with tin to display wealth. Cheaper were the pewter buckles that could be cast with elaborate designs to give an impression of greater social status. 11S-112.1 serves as an example of ornately casting pewter buckles to mimic increased fiscal and social value of the buckle. Another buckle, 10S-37.1, was recovered from Unit 0 during the 2010 excavations. Unlike the shoe buckles, 10S-37.1 is a copper alloy buckle that seems to serve more as a functional piece. Archaeologists believe it to be that of a belt buckle or for a shoulder strap (Meide et al 2014:238). Another shoe buckle visible with x-ray imagery is believed to be contained within concretion 12S-241.1. It is still in conservation.

Queen Anne's Pocket pistol

A pocket pistol was located within concretion (10S-44.1) retrieved from Unit 3 during 2010 field excavations. Starr Cox in this volume further elaborates on the function, make, and model of the pistol (Cox, this volume). Made of a brass frame, this field specimen is still in conservation. A ship's sailing master, mate, officer, captain, or wealthy passenger would have owned this pistol, since it was chiefly a civilian self-defense weapon made to fit inside a coat pocket (Meide et al. 2011:171-172, Hanks 2013:34-35, and Cox 2013:48-49).

Discussion

The personal artifact assemblage of the Storm Wreck serve as diagnostics to begin constructing more thematic theories like the socioeconomic status of those on board and the intended purpose of the voyage for those involved. When looking at the overall collection, one may notice the diversity of material and function of items from a societal point of view. Pewter is a metal predominately featured in the collection. However, as is the case with the decorated pewter shoe buckle, pewter items may be stylized in order to create an illusion of wealth. In the 18th century, pewter shoe buckles were considered a cheaper alternative to the copper alloy buckles. The pewter false watch, 13S-360.2, is another example of upper mobility aspirations, as its function is to facilitate a style that may not be affordable to the user. In contrast, the presence of a copper alloy shoe buckle, stylized brass buttons, King George III gold guineas, and a Queen Anne's pocket pistol suggest that those of higher status might have been on board.

Personal identification markings on the spoons also lead clues as to the status of those on board. Spoons that are marked with an *X* or asterisk may indicate those who are illiterate and/or uneducated. Truncation of spoons to fit in coat pockets also suggests the value of keeping the spoon safe and secure to prevent loss. Spoons marked with initials like the letter *S* also serve to show the presence of literate or and/or educated individuals on board.

The variety of material in the collection further reaffirms the working hypothesis of LAMP archaeologists that the Storm Wreck vessel was part of a larger fleet carrying Loyalist refugees fleeing from Charleston to East Florida towards the end of the Revolutionary War. These passengers would most likely be content with their lives and social status, resisting change and maintaining allegiance to the British Crown. While this working hypothesis has held through ongoing fieldwork, laboratory work, and research, more investigation is needed on the Storm Wreck and in the waters off the St. Augustine to further piece together the social dynamics of those affiliated with the Loyalist Influx.

References

Bass, G. F., S. D. Matthews, J.R. Steffy, and F.H. Van Doorninck
2004 *Serçe Limani: An Eleventh-century Shipwreck*, vol. 1: The Ship and Its Anchorage, Crew and Passengers. Texas A&M University Press, College Station.

British National Archives (BNA)
1783 Lt. Colonel Archibald McArthur to General Sir Guy Carleton, 9 January 1783. PRO30/55/60/6728:1-8, Headquarters Papers of the British Army in North America, The National Archives, Kew, United Kingdom.

Broadwater, John (Ed.)
1996 Final Report on the Yorktown Shipwreck. Archaeological Project. 5 Vols. Report to National Endowment for the Humanities, Washington, DC.

Bruseth, James E. and Toni S. Turner
2005 *From a Watery Grave: the Discovery and Excavation of La Salle's Shipwreck, La Belle*. Texas A&M University Press, College Station.

Cox, Starr
2013 Personal Items Recovered from the Storm Wreck, a Late 18th Century Shipwreck off the Coast of St. Augustine, Florida. In ACUA Underwater Archaeology Proceedings 2012, Brian Jordan and Troy Nowak, editors, pp. 44-49. Advisory Council on Underwater Archaeology, Baltimore, MD.

Evans, Joan
1970 *A History of Jewelry, 1100-1870*. Dover Publications, Inc., New York.

Forsyth, H and Geoff Egan
2005 *Toys, Trifles & Trinkets: Base-Metal Miniatures from London 1200 to 1800*. Unicorn Press, London.

Hanks, Matthew
2013 The Storm Wreck Concretions: A Look Beneath the Surface. In *ACUA Underwater Archaeology Proceedings 2012*, edited by Brian Jordan and Troy Nowak, pp. 32-37. Advisory Council on Underwater Archaeology, Baltimore, MD.

Krause, Chester L. and Clifford Mishler
1993 *Standard Catalog of World Coins, Eighteenth Century, 1701-1800.* Colin R. Bruce II, editor. Krause Publications, Iola, WI.

Krivor, Michael C., Nicholas J. Linville, Debra J. Wells, Jason M. Burns and Paul J. Sjordal
2010 Underwater Archaeological Investigation of the Roosevelt Inlet Shipwreck (7S-D-91A). Report prepared for the Delaware Department of State, Division of Historical and Cultural Affairs and the Federal Highway Administration and Delaware Department of Transportation by Southeastern Archaeological Research, Inc. (SEARCH), Dover, Delaware.

Marsden, Peter
1975 *The Wreck of the Amsterdam.* Stein and Day, Scarborough House, Briarcliff Manor, NY.

Meide, Chuck, Samuel P. Turner, and P. Brendan Burke
2010 First Coast Maritime Archaeology Project 2007-2009: Report on Archaeological and Historical Investigations and Other Project Activities. Report to Florida Division of Historical Resources, Tallahassee, from Lighthouse Archaeological Maritime Program, St. Augustine Lighthouse & Museum, St. Augustine, FL.

Meide, Chuck, P. Brendan Burke, Olivia McDaniel, Samuel P. Turner, Eden Andes, Hunter Brendel, Starr Cox, and Brian McNamara
2014 First Coast Maritime Archaeology Project 2011-2012: Report on Archaeological Investigations. Report to Florida Division of Historical Resources, Tallahassee, from Lighthouse Archaeological Maritime Program, St. Augustine Lighthouse & Museum, St. Augustine, FL.

Noël Hume, Ivor
1969 *A Guide to Artifacts of Colonial America.* University of Pennsylvania Press, Philadelphia.

Smith, Sheli O.
2008 *The 1779 Shipwreck Defence: An American Revolutionary War Privateer.* PAST Foundation. Lulu, Raleigh, NC.

Switzer, David
1998 *The Defence, 1779.* In *Excavating Ships of War,* M. Bound, editor, pp. 182-193. The International Maritime Archaeology Series, Vol. 2. Anthony Nelson, Oswestry, Shropshire, England.

White, Carolyn L.
2005 *American Artifacts of Personal Adornment, 1680-1820: A Guide to Identification and Interpretation.* AltaMira Press, Lanham, MD.

Wroblewska, Elżbieta
2008 *Buckles from Shoes and Clothing.* In *The General Carleton Shipwreck, 1785,* edited by Waldemar Ossowski, pp. 199-212. Polish Maritime Museum, Gdansk, Poland.

Hunter Brendel
St Augustine Lighthouse & Maritime Program
81 Lighthouse Avenue
St Augustine, FL 32080
361-947-9792
hunterbrendel@hotmail.com

Weight, Weight...Don't Tell Me: the Assemblage of Weights from the Storm Wreck

Andrew Thomson

The Storm Wreck is a British refugee shipwreck grounded off St. Augustine on 31 December 1782. Part of the evacuation fleet of Charleston, SC, it was responsible for transporting the Loyalists and their goods necessary to begin life again in East Florida. An assemblage of artifacts can help elucidate aspects of the refugees' lives, life aboard the ship, and the eventual wrecking event. A range of weights was recovered on the shipwreck, from merchant and fishing weights to a large livestock tether. This paper will discuss the identification, conservation and interpretation of the various weights found on the Storm Wreck site.

Introduction

The Storm Wreck, site 8SJ5459, was discovered by the archaeological research arm of the Saint Augustine Lighthouse & Maritime Museum. The Lighthouse Archaeological Maritime Program (LAMP) found the wreck in August 2009 following an earlier remote sensing survey conducted that summer (Meide et al. 2010:184—186). Diving operations and excavations started in June 2010 and have continued annually. Each summer LAMP conducts its field school, allowing students, staff and volunteers to perform underwater archaeology on site. The resulting fieldwork observations and excavated artifacts are being analyzed to help answer questions about the ship's voyage and its passengers.

Many of the artifacts need to undergo conservation and identification. There are a number of artifacts associated with the ship itself, including rigging equipment and fittings that one would expect from a wreck. Beyond those is a myriad of refugee cargo, including personal effects, cookware, housewares and construction equipment.

However, the assemblage of weights is unique. Several types have an interesting overlap of potential use by either the ship's crew or the evacuees onboard. Some were used for measurement; some for fishing; and others for the simple task of being a heavy object to hold its place. With limited time for evacuation and space onboard the departing ships, why would the refugees take these items? Despite literally weighing down the families and the vessels, it is apparent that those fleeing Charleston took everything they could to maintain a normal livelihood, both during the voyage and upon arrival at Saint Augustine.

The following will discuss the assemblage of weights excavated from the Storm Wreck. All artifacts from the 2013-2015 seasons will be discussed and published in forthcoming LAMP fieldwork reports. Site location and excavation units may be viewed in the most recent Storm Wreck site plan (Veilleaux and Meide, this volume; Figures 1-2).

Commercial Weights

The first group examined in the assemblage consists of measurement weights. They are most likely of commercial nature, used to determine the mass or volume of other items. It is difficult to say with any certainty what commercial use the weights from the Storm Wreck were for, but they are bigger and heavier than those typically used for coin or apothecary scales. Rather, the commercial weights look to be for larger hanging balance scales. A similar archaeological assemblage and interpretation can be seen on the 1760 French shipwreck *Machault* (Sullivan 1986:30).

The Storm Wreck collection consists of three conical pan weights, one flat disc-shaped trade weight, and one probable steelyard weight. They are described as follows.

13S 357.1

Artifact 13S 357.1 was found in Unit 18 during the 2013 LAMP field season. It was immediately recognizable upon excavation, as no concretion had built up on the surface of the lead. No x-rays were needed for further identification. Very little cleaning was necessary beyond a quick bath in hydrochloric acid, rinsing with reverse osmosis water, and sealing with molten microcrystalline wax (Hamilton 1998:84—87).

13S 357.1 is the smallest of the pan weights (Figure 1), with a diameter of 3.17 cm (1.25 in.) at the base tapering to 2.59 cm (1.02 in.) at the top and 1.63 cm (0.64 in.) high. It is made of lead poured into a mold and cooled, weighing 113.04 grams. The shape of the weight is conical, with a flat bottom and flat top containing one small circle and a central dot. There are no markings on the exterior to indicate the mass of the weight, unit of measurement, or if it belonged to a larger set.

13S 356.1

Artifact 13S 356.1 was found in Unit 18 during the 2013 LAMP field season, immediately adjacent to artifact 13S 357.1. It also was recognizable upon excavation, as the lead surface bore no concretion. No x-rays were needed for further identification. The artifact was placed in a quick bath in hydrochloric acid, rinsed with reverse osmosis water and sealed with molten microcrystalline wax.

The second pan weight of the group is of similar design as the smaller one described before (Figure 1), measuring 5.95 cm (2.34 in.) at the base narrowing to 4.97 cm (1.96 in.) on top and 2.9 cm (1.14 in.) high. The artifact is also made of cast lead and weighs 744.62 grams. The shape of the weight is conical, with a flat bottom and slightly concave top. In the top, there are three sets of identical markings around the center. There is a capital "P" above, with a numeral "2" underneath. The markings appear to be part of the casting mold, and not stamped in later, as the edges remain sharp show no signs of external force or wear. The "P2" should refer to the size of the individual weight. Either it may be the second in the series of a set, or it may mean it was two pounds.

13S 370.1

Artifact 13S 370.1 was found in Unit 18 during the 2013 LAMP field season, near the previous two weights. A slight covering of concretion had built up on the surface of the lead, but it was almost identifiable upon excavation. After an initial x-ray, no other material was found in the image. Concretion was removed by mechanically cleaning the surface using an air scribe. Afterwards, the weight was placed into a quick bath of hydrochloric acid, rinsed with reverse osmosis water and sealed with molten microcrystalline wax.

13S 370.1 is the largest of the first pan-scale type (Figure 1). It has a diameter of 7.46 cm (2.94 in.) at the base and 5.96 cm (2.35 in.) at the top and is 3.8 cm (1.50 in.) tall. It too is made of cast lead and weighs 1487.05 grams. The shape of the weight is conical, with a flat bottom and a slightly concave top. Like the artifact 13S 356.1, the top of the weight has three sets of identical

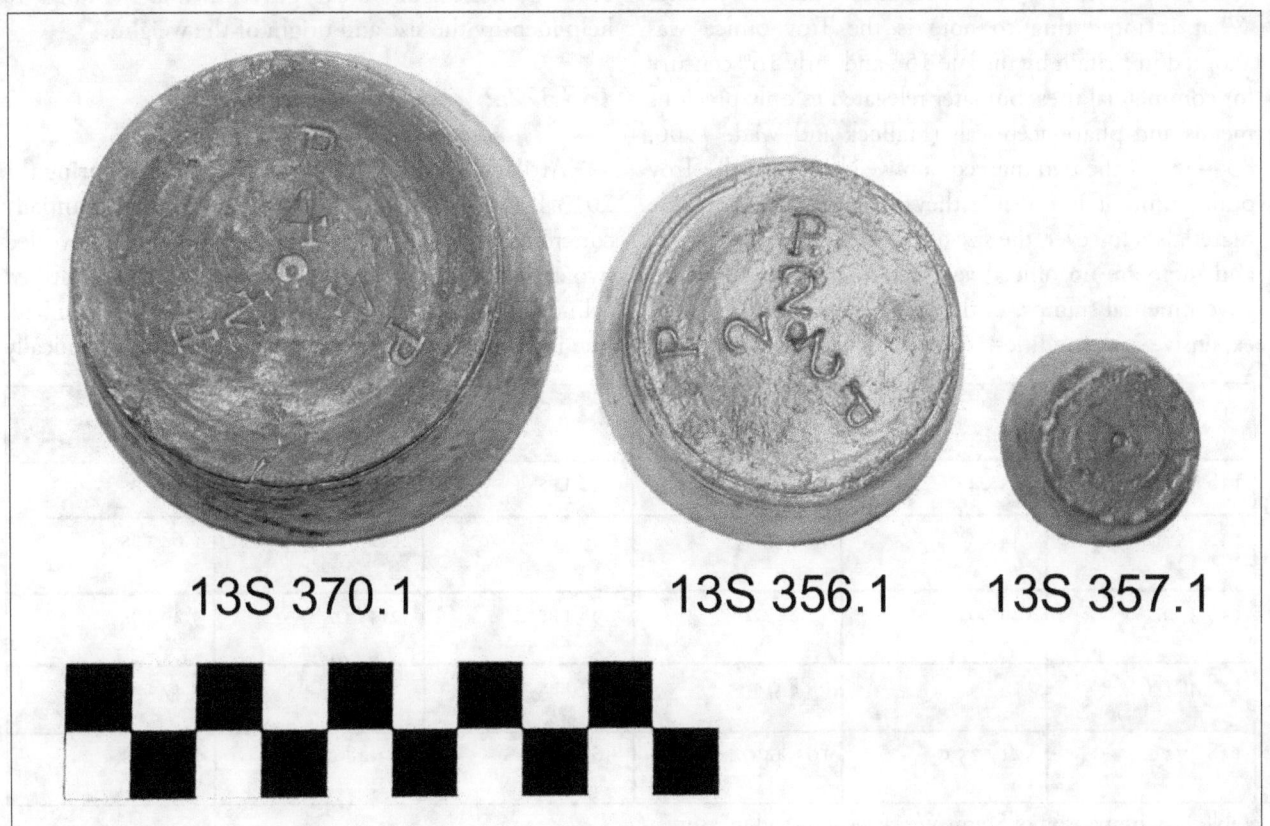

Figure 1. Three solid lead pan scale weights.

markings around the center. There is a capital "P" above, with a numeral "4" underneath. These markings also appear to be part of the casting mold, and not stamped in later. No signs of external force have been applied and the mark edges remain sharp. Either the "P4" on the top possibly refers to it being the fourth in a set of weights or to show the weight is four pounds.

While the "P2" and "P4" certainly seem to indicate pounds, it was uncertain what the exact unit of measurement for these weights is. Prior to the 18th century there was a confusing mess of weights and measures, as can be seen in the immense variety detailed in *A Dictionary of Weights and Measures for the British Isles: The Middle Ages to the Twentieth Century* (Zupko 1985). An effort to standardize units was undertaken to help simplify, regulate and control trade (Sheldon et al. 1996:25—26). Two likely candidates for a matching measurement system are the Troy ounce and the Avoirdupois ounce. Both were in use by the British during the late 18th century, but have a difference in standardization. The Troy ounce system only equates 31.10 grams per ounce and 12 ounces to a pound. The Avoirdupois ounce totals 28.35 grams per ounce and 16 ounces to a pound (Zupko 1985:24,30).

As seen in Table 1, both artifacts 13S 356.1 and 13S 370.1 come very close to matching the Troy pound. What is interesting to note is the Troy ounce was adopted in Britain by the late 15th and early 16th century for commercial uses, but later relegated to only precious metals and pharmaceuticals (Hallock and Wade 1906: 33—35). If the two marked pan weights are of the Troy ounce unit, it is possible they were used for valuable materials. However, the size of the weights is rather large and there are no official verification markings, such as governmental stamps, in the lead. If they were used for expensive commodities, these weights may not have been entirely legitimate.

14S 401.1

Artifact 14S 401.1 was found in Unit 35 during the 2014 LAMP field season. It was a small weight made of two different materials. No concretion had built up on the surface and no x-rays were needed. Very little cleaning was necessary beyond a quick bath in hydrochloric acid, rinsing with reverse osmosis water and sealing with molten microcrystalline wax.

This pan weight is much different than the previous three described. It is made of a cupreous alloy, likely brass, poured into a mold and weighs 214 grams. It is disc-shaped with a 5.29 cm (2.08 in.) diameter and 1.21 cm (0.48 in.) tall. The weight has a flat bottom and a slightly convex center on top. The exterior is clad in a few areas with a thin layering of lead. It is difficult to tell whether the whole weight was covered in lead, due to its condition. A capital "A" is stamped into one side of the top just off the center point. The "A" most likely refers to the avoirdupois weight system, in which artifact 14S 401.1 currently is just under a half pound (Table 1). The missing lead sheathing may have pushed the total weight up to a standard measure. Unfortunately, there are no other numerical or official governmental markings to help identify the size and origin of the weight.

13S 372.2

Artifact 13S 372.2 was found in Unit 18 during the 2013 LAMP field season. The object was substantially concreted and quite heavy for its size. X-rays revealed two artifacts within the image; one was an unidentified cylindrical object and the other a cast iron cannonball. The individual artifacts were separated by mechanically

Artifact	Measured Weight	Troy ounces	Troy pounds	Avoirdupois ounces	Avoirdupois pounds
13S 357.1	113.04 G	3.63 OZ	0.30 LBS	2.95 OZ	0.18 LBS
13S 356.1	744.62 G	23.94 OZ	1.99 LBS	26.27 OZ	1.64 LBS
13S 370.1	1487.05 G	47.81 OZ	3.98 LBS	52.45 OZ	3.29 LBS
14S 401.1	214 G	6.88 OZ	0.57 LBS	7.55 OZ	0.47 LBS
13S 372.2	3217.25 G	103.44 OZ	8.62 LBS	113.48 OZ	7.09 LBS

Table 1. Comparison of Storm Wreck weights and measures.

removing the concretion with an air scribe.

Upon cleaning, the cylindrical item was determined to be a distinct type of commercial weight, made for a different type of scale than the pan weights. Artifact 13S 372.2 was meant to hang from a steelyard. To use the weight, the product would hang from a short end of the steelyard and the weight would slide down the long arm as a counterbalance until equilibrium is achieved. Predetermined marks on the arm would show the measured weight.

The weight consists of three separate pieces (Figure 2) that together weigh 3217.25 grams (8.62 Troy pounds or 7.09 Avoirdupois pounds). The main piece is the lead weight at the center. There are also two pieces made of cupreous alloys, most likely brass, which covered the exterior sides and top of the lead weight.

The lead weight portion was first poured into a mold. It is cylindrical in shape with a flat bottom, a flat top and rounded edges. The base has a diameter of 7.42 cm (2.92 in.), narrowing to 5.59 cm (2.20 in.), and is 8.86 cm (3.49 in.) tall. The top portion appears to have once held an iron ring that has since corroded away. The ring allowed the weight to be suspended. There also appears to be lead added later to patch over the top of the hollowed area. On the side of the lead there are two markings opposite each other, stamped into the surface at a later time. The first is a small royal crown. The second is a series of numbers, "3426", stamped into the lead at a later time. The last number, "6", is especially hard to read due to a tack hole through the number.

Of the two small, thin pieces of brass covering the lead, the larger was held in place by small nails or tacks hammered into the side of the lead. The larger piece also overlapped the edge of the top, which held the smaller cap in place. A small hole would have allowed the iron ring to pass through. The larger piece covered the outside of the lead and had the same stamped markings as the weight.

The small royal crown and the numerals 342 were on opposing sides of the brass covering as well. However, the markings on the brass did not overlap with the markings on the lead underneath. The stamped figures on the brass were rotated 105° clockwise from the lead markings. Furthermore, the last numeral in the series "3426" in the lead was not in line with the numerals on the outside of the brass. Instead, it was stamped in the metal on the edge where the collar was nailed into the lead for unclear reasons. If the markings were stamped through the brass and into the lead, then the brass covering had to have been moved at some point during the process.

Although there are numbers stamped into the brass and lead, they are unclear. It should be safe to assume that they refer to the corresponding actual measurement of the weight. The total of the lead and brass pieces equals 3217.25 grams (8.62 Troy pounds or 7.09 Avoirdupois

Figure 2. Brass and lead steelyard weight separated after conservation, showing the exterior brass collar on the right, the lead weight in the center and the exterior brass cap on the left.

pounds), which is reasonably close to the figure "3426." It may be that a bottom brass section is missing, or the corroded iron ring at the top added to the overall weight.

Agricultural Weight

13S 362.1

Artifact 13S 362.1 was found in Unit 18 during the 2014 LAMP field season. It is one of the more interesting and initially confusing objects conserved thus far from the Storm Wreck. It was very heavy and dense in the initial x-rays. The image showed a large solid mass and a loop at the top of the artifact that had slightly corroded. Having to move the artifact for storage and x-rays, it was plainly a very heavy object and meant to be a weight of some kind.

After removing the concretion from the artifact, I found the large radio-dense section was made of cast iron and conical in shape with a flat bottom and rounded top (Figure 3). The base of the weight measures 16.11 cm (6.34 in.) in diameter, tapers to 14.61 cm (5.75 in.) and is 18.91 cm (7.44 in.) tall. With as much concretion cleaned off as possible before electrolytic reduction treatment, the overall weight is approximately 55 pounds. The underside of the weight was also cast iron, but had a central hole leading to a cavity inside the cast iron. This hollow was filled with molten lead. The rounded top also held a large, separate iron ring.

At that point fellow LAMP archaeologist Brendan Burke indicated it resembled a livestock tether (2015, pers. comm.). It could have been used to tie up horse or cattle, but would have also been mobile, possibly to move the animals through grazing pastures. Another possibility was a "buggy anchor." This would have served the same purpose as a naval anchor, but by tethering a carthorse in place instead of a ship.

Fishing Weights

The final set of weights let us take a glimpse into the voyage of the Storm Wreck. As can be expected from a long trip by sea, a certain amount of fishing would have taken place and we have found several weights that seem to corroborate this.

12S 285.1

Artifacts 12S 285.1 was found in Unit 11 during the 2012 LAMP field season (Meide et al. 2014:194-196). It consists of 12 individual pieces picked up with the underwater dredges while excavating the grid square. At the end of the field season, the dredge spoil was screened for potential artifacts. No concretion had built up on the surface of the lead and there was minimal damage from the dredge. Very little cleaning was necessary beyond a

Figure 3. Side and aerial view of cast iron and lead livestock tether.

quick bath in muriatic acid, rinsing with reverse osmosis water, and sealing with molten microcrystalline wax.

Upon initial inspection in the dredge spoil, they were thought to be solid musket shot. However, after rinsing, alterations of the shot were visible. Ten have small holes through each individual shot, one appears flattened with two small dimples and the final musket ball has no visible deformities (Figure 4). The methodology for making the holes is not definite. The casting seam is evident on most all of the shot, suggesting they were made with a bullet mold. The holes may have been drilled or pierced through the lead after the casting. Additionally, a foreign object may have been placed in the mold for the lead to cool around and later removed. The interpretation for these musket balls is that they were repurposed and turned into fishing weights. The holes would have allowed the lead to be placed on fishing lines or used to weight seine or casting nets (Meide et al. 2014:194—196).

13S 310.4

Artifact 13S 310.4 was found in Unit 25 during the 2013 LAMP field season. An x-ray revealed numerous different artifacts. Among them were musket shot; a brass tap key; pewter buttons; and a cooper's croze. The individual artifacts were separated using an air scribe. The lead weight was then placed in a quick bath in muriatic acid, rinsed with reverse osmosis water, and sealed with molten microcrystalline wax.

This is another lead weight likely for fishing. It is roughly cast and conical in shape, measuring 2.93 cm (1.15 in.) at the base, tapering to 1.5 cm (0.59 in.) at the top and 3.01 (1.19 in.) tall. There is a 0.66 cm (0.26 in.) hole running vertically through the center. While cleaning the hole, remains of cordage were found. This suggests the artifact could have been used on a fishing line or as a larger casting or seine net weight.

14S 422.2

Artifact 14S 422.2 was found in Unit 33 during the 2014 LAMP field season. It was part of a small, heavily concreted formation. An x-ray revealed a broken section of a cast iron cauldron and a very radio-dense oblong object. The items were separated using an air scribe. The lead object was further cleaned with a quick bath in muriatic acid, rinsing with reverse osmosis water and sealing with molten microcrystalline wax.

This looks to be another lead fishing weight. It is an oblong, ovoid shape measuring 11.47 cm (4.52 in.) long, 4.09 cm (1.61 in.), 2.71 cm (1.07 in.) tall, width tapering to 1.8 cm (0.71 in.) on each end, with two 0.62 cm (0.24 in.) holes in each end. The holes would have allowed a line to run through and hold the lead in place.

Miscellaneous Weights

12S 253.1

Artifact 12S 253.1 was found in Unit 15 during the 2012 LAMP field season (Meide et al. 2014:306,308—309). It was a lightly concreted, linear object. An x-ray revealed a slightly corroded cast-iron piece, with a tapered point on end and a loop on the other.

The remaining iron of the artifact measures 33.57 cm (13.22 in.) long and 3.70 cm (1.46 in.) at its widest point. The ring on the top has a diameter 4.73 cm (1.86 in.) wide with a 1.36 cm (0.54 in.) thick loop. The current hypothesis is it appears to be a window sash weight, due to the thin profile and ability to be tied and hanged.

13S 354.1

Artifact 13S 354.1 was excavated in Unit 18 during the 2013 LAMP field season, near the aforementioned pan weights. The final artifact is somewhat of a mystery (Figure 4). It is a rectangular lead object, measuring 11.47 cm long (4.52 in.) x 4.76 cm (1.87 in) wide x 2.71 cm (1.07 in.) tall. One end has a 0.94 x 5.49 cm (0.37 x 2.16 in.) separation between the lead and a 0.62 cm (0.24 in.) hole through each of the two resulting end pieces. It is unclear whether the lead was affixed to anything at the time of the wreck. The small, rectangular shape suggests it may be another window sash weight, but the holes are too small for robust cordage to hold it.

Another perplexing element of the artifact is the sign of later alteration. There are numerous cut marks and the "bottom" half is missing. Finally, there are what appear to be hammer marks on the end with the holes, with one of the flaps beaten in towards the other. The rough condition and signs of abuse may show that 13S 354.1 was being dismantled and used for scrap, possibly to be melted down and molded into other weights or objects. The cut marks may also be related to the interpretation of the wrecking event.

In the 2011 LAMP field season divers excavated a large lead deck pump (Meide et al. 2014:208—09). The pump showed signs of cut marks along the exterior of the main housing, as well as bent and broken sections of the

Figure 4. Left: Lead musket shot repurposed into fishing weights. Right: Unidentified cut lead weight.

lower pump tubes. The current hypothesis is the pump was hacked out and jettisoned after running aground, in order to lighten the load of the ship. The presence of cut marks on 13S 354.1 may be evidence of the desperate attempts to save the vessel.

Conclusion

The weight assemblage from the Storm Wreck, while small and diverse, is a unique collection that can assist with the interpretation on the nature of the crew, the passengers and the voyage. It is difficult to draw any concrete answers as to whom the weights belonged and their exact purposes, but they do offer insight on what was important to the Loyalists fleeing their homes.

The three separate types of trade weights suggest commercial activity onboard the ship or the presence of refugees with mercantile backgrounds. The fact that the small lead pan weights and the cupreous disc-shaped weight are of different measuring systems implies multiple different sets onboard. Additionally, the lead and brass steelyard weight would necessitate an entirely separate type of scale. These items could belong to one merchant fleeing Charleston or possibly multiple people all taking what they saw as necessary to continue life in St. Augustine. The large livestock tether gives a glimpse into the agricultural needs of the evacuation. Even a big, heavy piece of metal was important enough to pack up and ship, if it was useful. The various fishing weights show the ingenuity to create the tools as needed for fishing, either by the ship's crew while at sea or for evacuating anglers leaving South Carolina. A potential sash weight shows the lengths to which the evacuees would go to in dismantling their homes in order to bring all valuable and practical possessions with them. Finally, the unidentifiable cut lead weight gives an idea of the need for even basic materials that could be reused upon arrival.

References

Hallock, William and Herbert T. Wade
1906   *Outlines of the Evolution of Weights and Measures and The Metric System.* Macmillan and Co. London.

Hamilton, Donny L.
1998   Methods of Conserving Underwater Archaeological Material Culture. Conservation Files: ANTH 605, Conservation of Cultural Resources I. Nautical Archaeology Program, Texas A&M University, World Wide Web, http://nautarch.tamu.edu/class/ANTH605.

Meide, Chuck, P. Brendan Burke, Olivia McDaniel, Samuel P. Turner, Eden Andes, Hunter Brendel, Starr Cox and Brian McNamara
2014   First Coast Maritime Archaeology Project 2011-2012: Report on Archaeological Investigations. Lighthouse Archaeological Maritime Program, St. Augustine Lighthouse & Maritime Museum, St. Augustine, FL.

Meide, Chuck, Samuel P. Turner, and P. Brendan Burke
2010   First Coast Maritime Archaeology Project 2007-2009: Report on Archaeological and Historical Investigations and Other Project Activities. Report to Florida Division of Historical Resources, Tallahassee, from Lighthouse Archaeological Maritime Program, St. Augustine Lighthouse & Museum, St. Augustine, FL.

Sheldon, Richard, Adrian Randall, Andrew Charlesworth and David Walsh
1996   Popular Protest and the Persistance of Customary Corn Measures: Resistance to the Winchester Bushel in the English West. In *Markets, Market Culture and Popular Protest in Eighteenth-Century Britain and Ireland.* A. Randall and A. Charlesworth editors, pp.25-45. Liverpool University. Liverpool.

Sullivan, Catherine.
1986   *Legacy of the Machault: A Collection of 18th-century Artifacts.* Parks Canada. Ottawa.

Zupko, Ronald E.
1985   *A Dictionary of Weights and Measures for the British Isles: The Middle Ages to the Twentieth Century.* American Philosophical Society. Philadelphia.

Andrew Thomson
Lighthouse Archaeological Maritime Program
81 Lighthouse Avenue
St Augustine, FL 32080
904-829-0745
athomson@staugustinelighthouse.org

Life Among the Wind and Waves: Examining Living Conditions on Sailing Vessels Through the Use of Microscopic Remains

Jacob D. Shidner

Sediment samples collected during the 2015 Storm Wreck field season were compared to those previously analyzed from the Emanuel Point wrecks, which consisted of insect remains, animal bones, and botanical remains, and which painted a picture of living conditions aboard sailing vessels. Examined here is the methodology for the recovery and analysis of microscopic faunal remains with the hope that the methodology can be used on other sites. A preliminary examination of the Storm Wreck materials was conducted, and a comparison between the Storm Wreck and Emanuel Point sites will lead to an understanding of the living conditions in vessels of various nationalities, purposes and time periods.

Introduction

From 2008-2011, the author was a graduate student on the Emanuel Point II site excavations through the University of West Florida. The site was a 16th-century Spanish vessel wrecked as part of the Don Tristan de Luna expedition of 1559, which was attempting to establish a colony in Pensacola, FL (Worth 2009). As the second wreck of the fleet to be discovered, the site provided insight into the 'Age of Exploration' (Cook 2009). During excavations, the question arose whether or not cultural material was being missed through standard excavation techniques using an underwater dredge. Much like extracting flotation samples on terrestrial sites to look for remains missed using even the finest shaker screens, a new method was introduced to see if even smaller materials were being lost through dredging. Samples were collected from excavation units on Emanuel Point II and brought to the lab for analysis, where they were combined with samples previously taken from the first Emanuel Point wreck. Since these underwater samples were already waterlogged, flotation would be useless. It was decided that the best way to work through the samples would be simply to examine them under a microscope, literally one grain of sand at a time (Shidner 2011).

The outcome of that research question was something that had never been previously conducted on maritime sites. Therefore, when material was recovered, it was not readily clear how it could be used in an anthropological study. Materials such as the remains of at least 16 species of invertebrates were raised, along with the microscopic remains of some vertebrates. All of the microscopic materials had one thing in common: they are classified as pests in the modern world and would have had a significant impact on the daily lives of the people aboard the ship. While insect remains had been recovered previously on different maritime sites, there was never more than a simple identification and acknowledgement of their presence (Shidner 2011).

Current research looks to expand the previous analysis of microscopic remains from the Emanuel Point sites, and see if these materials can be recovered from other wrecks. If so, a comparison of the materials may lead to a better understanding of what life was like aboard ships in relation to the various insects and other animals that were also aboard. For example, does the nationality of the vessels change what is found? What about the size of the vessel, or its role? Are there more pests of a certain variety, or even in quantity, on a warship than on a cargo vessel?

The first site that became available for this comparison was the Storm Wreck, located off the coast of St. Augustine, FL. The Storm Wreck was a wartime refugee vessel that escaped Charleston, SC at the end of the American Revolution and was lost off the coast of St. Augustine on 31 December 1782. The site was excavated by the Lighthouse Archaeological Maritime Program over multiple field seasons.

While both wrecks are located in Florida, they could not be more different. The Storm Wreck is located in the Atlantic Ocean, in turbulent, dynamic waters that have uncovered and reburied the site numerous times over the course of fieldwork alone. The Emanuel Point wrecks are located in the protected waters of Pensacola Bay, where the sites have remained relatively undisturbed. The Storm Wreck was a vessel used to carry refugees from Charleston to St. Augustine, and while many of these refugees brought with them most of their belongings and those items they would likely be unable to easily replace, such as door locks and weapons, food items and livestock were not necessarily high on the list (Chuck Meide 2016 pers. comm.). However, as the colonization attempt in

Pensacola required starting from scratch, both livestock and dry goods such as grains and seeds were important inventory. These differences could lead to differences in the types of zooarchaeological specimens recovered on the ships. This could be due to what organisms were originally on the vessels, or to varying site formation processes.

Methodology

The methodology for the Storm Wreck materials analysis was nearly identical to that used in the earlier analysis of the Emanuel Point site, with some only minor equipment changes made to facilitate the screening (Shidner 2011).

During the screening of materials from the Emanuel Point sites, it was discovered that samples needed to be sorted by size before examination under the microscope. Therefore, the materials were water screened through a set of three stacking screens of 2mm, 1 mm, and 0.5 mm, or 500 micrometers (μm). The stacked screens were placed over a bucket to catch any material that might pass through the smallest screen. To facilitate the process, a hole was cut in the lid to the bucket to seat the screens. By tracing the bottom of the screen and using that as a guide, the hole allowed the stacked screens to sit perfectly in the lid of the bucket, eliminating the need for anyone to hold the screens (Figure 1). However, if the screen and hole are too perfect a fit, small holes will need to be placed in the lid around the screens in order to allow air to escape the bucket once the material is water screened.

The material was placed into the top screen using a large plastic spoon. The process generally was more efficient if only one or two large spoonfuls were placed into the screen at one time. Water was gently poured over the material in the screen, so that the sediment was slowly washed through. Even though only a small amount of material was screened at a time, the stacking screens still tended to clog with sediment. After every third or fourth spoonful, the screens would need to be separated, and the sorted material removed from each screen and placed into separate plastic containers. The process could then be repeated without the screens becoming clogged.

The largest 2 mm screen captured material large enough to be observed and identified with the naked eye. This was placed onto a large tray and sorted with the use of a tabletop magnifying glass with a built-in halogen light. This allowed the material to be examined quickly, and ensured that no material was overlooked, as some of the objects tended to adhere to one another.

The next two sizes, the 1 mm and 500 μm, which contained a large majority of the artifacts, was examined under the microscope to properly determine what was cultural material. Using a plastic spoon, one spoonful of the sorted sample was placed on a Petri dish and examined under a dissecting microscope. The material was slowly and methodically sorted with a dental pick or a bamboo skewer, and any artifacts were removed and sorted based on their visible type, such as bone, insect, plant or unidentified. If the artifact could be identified further, such as mammal or fish bone, or a specific part of an insect, it was then sorted further.

The final and smallest size sorted was the material that flowed through all three screens and collected in the bucket. This material was very fine-grain sand, and for the Emanuel Point material, was only a small fraction of the sediment sample. However, for the Storm Wreck, this fraction contained the most material of all four fractions.

As artifacts of this size and nature have rarely been recovered from a maritime site in this manner before, their long-term storage and conservation have not been addressed by maritime archaeologists. From previous

Figure 1. Stacked screens mounted onto bucket lid over bucket, creating 4 separate fractions (image by author).

work on the Emanuel Point sites, it was known that the materials could not be stored in small plastic bags since the weight of the bag alone was enough to damage some of the small, fragile remains. Also, while removing the artifact and the water from the bag in order to reexamine the artifact, the bag tends to compress, which also can damage the artifact. Storing the artifacts in small glass vials with leak-proof screw tops solved this problem.

Another problem was bacteria and algae growth. Normally, artifacts recovered from salt water are stored in constantly changed fresh water baths, to slowly remove the chlorides from the artifact. Bacteria and algae growth during this process can be controlled through various chemicals, with very little impact on the artifacts themselves. However, it was found that materials recovered from the sediment samples are so small that they are actually devoured by the bacteria and algae, and could be destroyed if either are allowed to grow.

Therefore, all of the faunal remains from the samples, such as bone and insect remains, were placed in 70% ethyl alcohol. However, plant remains and unidentified artifacts were stored in tap water, as alcohol would dry out the plant material, and might cause unknown damage to any unidentified artifacts. To further ensure that no algae growth would occur, the utmost care was taken to keep the samples out of the light whenever possible.

Materials Recovered

For the Emanuel Point sites, most of the material recovered from the 2 mm screen, such as olive jar fragments, brass pins, rodent bones, and wood, had been previously recovered during excavation. However, nearly all of the material found in the 1 mm and 500 μm fractions had not been encountered previously, and further added to our understanding of life aboard the ships. For the Storm Wreck, zero cultural material was found in the 2mm or 1mm fractions, with all of the recovered material found in the 500 μm fraction. For both sites the smallest sized fraction, the less than 500 μm material that passed through all three screens and was collected in the bucket, was devoid of any cultural material.

Emanuel Point

Over 6,600 invertebrate specimens were recovered from the Emanuel Point II sediment samples, representing at least 16 individual species. These include the American Cockroach (*Periplaneta americana*), skin beetles (family Dermestidae), weevils (Sitophilus sp.), darkling beetles (family Tenebrionidae), drugstore beetles (*Stegobium paniceum*), rove beetles (family Staphylinidae), grain beetles (*Oryzaephilus* sp.), ladybird beetle (Family Coccinellida), scuttle fly (Family Phoridae), fruit fly (*Drosophila* sp.), blowfly (Family Calliphoridae) or Flesh fly (Family Sarcophagidae), an intact Big Headed Ant (*Pheidole* sp.), and an unidentified spider *chelicerae*, or mouthpart and fang, from the Order Araneae (Figure 2) (Shidner 2011; Smith et al. 1995; Smith et al 1998).

At least 17 taxa were identified from the Emanuel Point II vertebrate remains, representing 5 classes: Mammalia (mammals), Aves (birds), Reptilia (reptiles), Osteichthyes (bony fishes), and Elasmobranchiomorphi (sharks) (Shidner 2011; Smith et al. 1995; Smith et al 1998). Thirteen different species were recognized, and 11 of those were positively identified. Most of these remains were recovered during dredging excavations; however, vertebrate remains were also recovered in the sediment samples from both Emanuel Point sites. The remains from the Emanuel Point sediment represent the smallest of the vertebrates on the ship, the rodents.

While a number of black rat (*Rattus rattus*) and two house mouse (*Mus musculus*) remains were found in the dredge excavations of Emanuel Point I, only

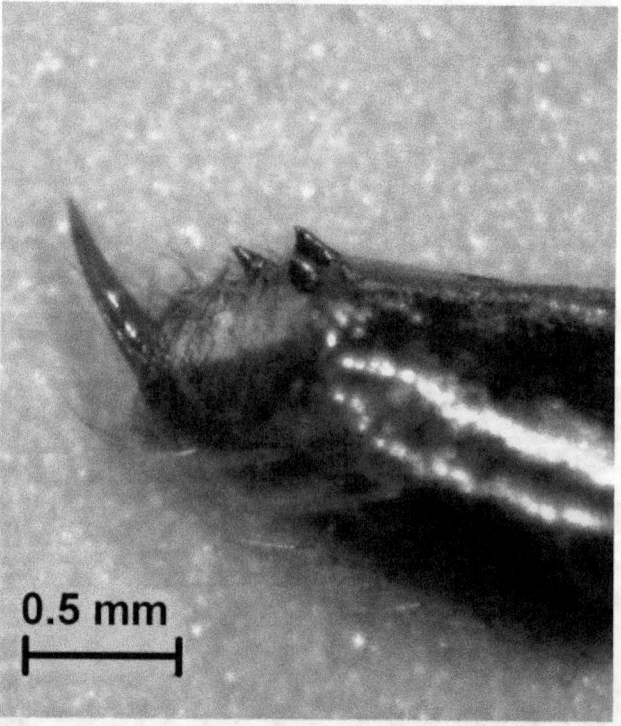

Figure 2. Spider chelicerae from an unidentified web-weaving spider, Order Araneae (image by author).

black rat specimens had been recovered from Emanuel Point II dredging. However, the sediment samples from Emanuel Point II greatly increased the rat remains, and produced 32 mouse specimens, of which none had been found with dredging. In fact, a number of the smaller skeletal elements that were missing from the dredging appeared in the sediment samples, including tail vertebra, tarsal bones, and teeth. It was these specimens that helped show the varied ages with the rodent population aboard the vessel, from infancy to advanced age. One exceptionally small intact rib was determined to be from a rat only a few weeks old, an age when it was still feeding from its mother. Juvenile remains also were recovered, including unfused bones, epiphyses, and unworn teeth. These features are indicative of animals that are self-sustaining, yet still growing. Other remains, such as fully-fused bones and well-worn teeth, are indicative of adult specimens. Evidence of scavenging and cannibalism are also present in the rat remains, as a few of the identified specimens showed evidence of gnawing. This indicated that the animal died and that its carcass became a meal for others within the colony before the ship sank. Without the materials recovered from the samples, this current understanding of just how infested with rodents the wreck was would not have been possible (Shidner 2011).

Among the most interesting finds from the Emanuel Point sediment samples were rodent feces. These were uniform in shape, with an oblong cylindrical form and varying only slightly in size. The destruction of a few samples revealed their contents to contain various insect parts, and a few contained what appeared to be seeds. As there is not much difference between the fecal size of rats and mice, it is impossible to determine exactly which species the excrement pellets are from. However, based on the size variance in the remains, it is likely that the remains represent both species as well as the various levels of growth represented in the skeletal remains (Shidner 2011).

Storm Wreck

Very little material culture was recovered from the sediment samples. Only 6 invertebrate specimens and

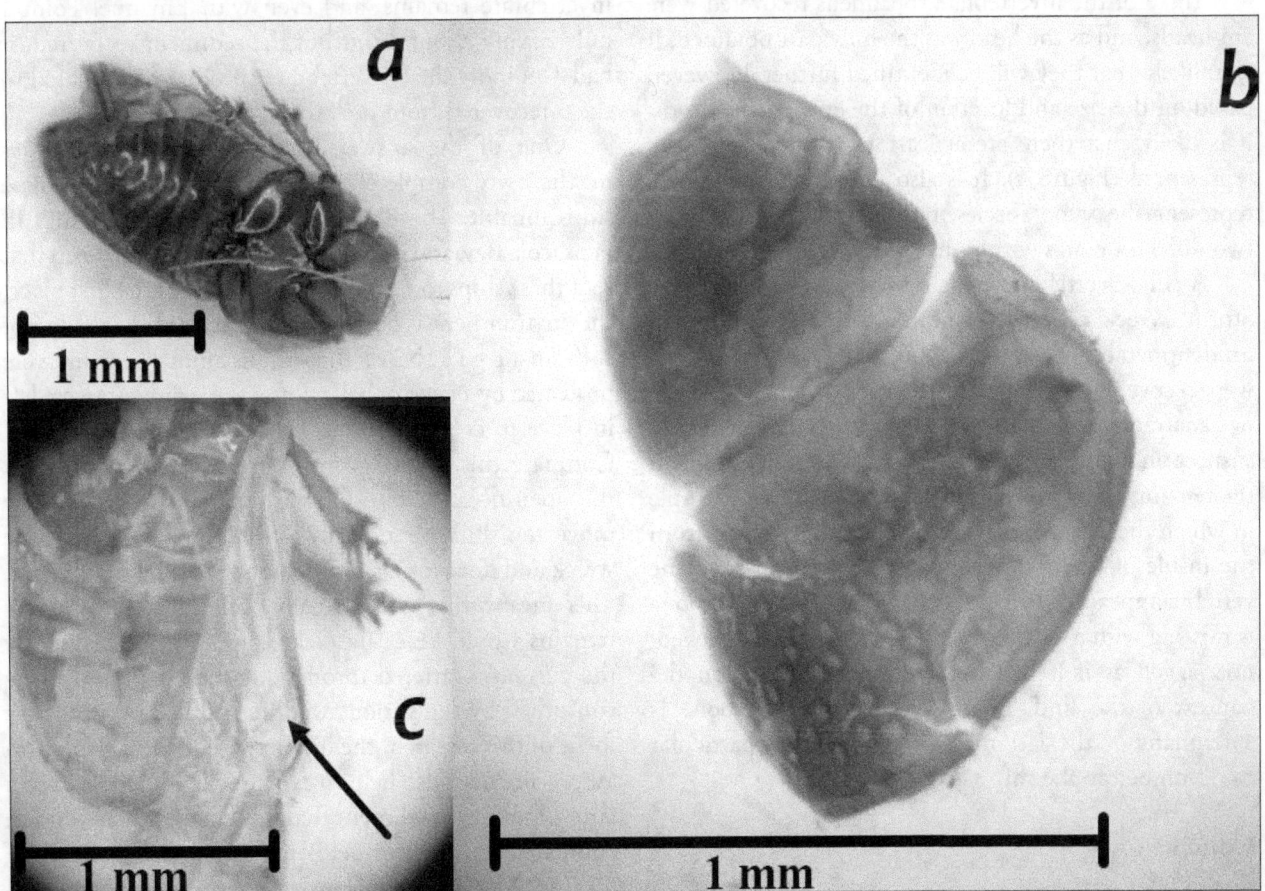

Figure 3. Stegobium paniceum, the drugstore beetle. 3a illustrates the ventral view of the abdomen, 3b the dorsal view of the thorax and head. 3c highlights the fragile flight wings (image by author).

1 vertebrate specimen were recovered from the 71.9 L of sediment. Other specimens were recovered, but they have yet to be identified and may not even be associated with the site.

Of the 6 invertebrate specimens, only one has been positively identified, the complete body of the drugstore beetle, Stegobium paniceum. The beetle was found intact, with only a small thread of exoskeleton still holding the head to the rest of the body, which was later severed during examination (Figure 3a-c). All of the legs were still present, along with both sets of wings, the protective outer wings that were also found on the Emanuel Point sites, and the delicate inner wings that actually allow the beetle to fly, as indicated by the arrow in Figure 3c. This specific beetle is less than 3 mm long fully mature. It feeds on just about anything, with one anonymous writer stating that it "eats anything but cast iron," from flours, breads, and cookies to wool, hair, and leather. Even though the beetle can fly, it usually only does when absolutely necessary, as it seems to prefer to live its life crawling on the surface of whatever it's consuming.

Three of the invertebrate specimens recovered were ant heads, and as the head was the only part obtained, it is unlikely that they will be identified further. However, based on the size and location of the eyes on the heads, it is likely that there are at least two different species represented (Figure 4). It is also possible that the ants represent the same species, but that they characterize two different castes within that species.

A single vertebrate remain was recovered from the Storm Wreck sediment samples: a vertebra from an unidentified bony fish (Class Actinopterygii). Fish bones were recovered from dredge excavations, but they were not analyzed for this study. Usually fish bones are highly suspect on maritime sites, as it is difficult to determine if the remains are intrusive. However, the sediment sample in which the vertebra was discovered was collected from the inside of one the cauldrons recovered on site. The vertebra appears to be cut, as a large portion of the bone is missing with a clean slice where it had been removed, not jagged as if it had been broken. Based upon the context of the find, it appears that the fish bone is a remnant of the last meal cooked in that particular cauldron before the ship sank.

Conclusions

The first question is whether or not these remains are intrusive. The answer is an unquestionable no. First, none of the recovered species utilizes the marine environment for any part of their lifecycle. For the Emanuel Point sites, it would be nearly impossible to have such a large number of individuals be intrusive to a site. For the Storm Wreck, about a mile offshore, any of the species would have a difficult time reaching the site. Of all the species recovered from the site, only the drugstore beetle can fly. However, as it's less than a few millimeters long and its lifestyle generally does not include flight, it is unlikely to have made the distance. Therefore, it is almost certain that all of these specimens are associated with the wrecked vessels, and that they were infesting the cargo when the ship slipped beneath the waves.

Next, why was so much more faunal material recovered from the Emanuel Point sites than the Storm Wreck? With about 94.6 L of sediment screened from the Emanuel Point sites (22.4 L from Emanuel Point I and 72.2 L from Emanuel Point II), and 71.9 L from the Storm Wreck, it is interesting how little material was recovered from the latter site compared to others. Either of the Emanuel Point sites had significantly more invertebrate remains, and even with Emanuel Point I only having about a third of the sediment recovered, it had 149 individual invertebrate specimens compared to the 6 recovered from the Storm Wreck.

One of the answers to this question likely lies in the two completely different environments these ships inhabit. The Emanuel Point wrecks are found in Pensacola Bay, and notwithstanding the major storm that sent these ships to the bottom of the bay in the first place, the environment is fairly calm and the sediments do not shift on a regular basis. The various animal remains were protected by a layer of ballast, and the sediments were left in place to create a protective, anaerobic environment. Compare this to the Storm Wreck, whose location in the open ocean allows for the sediments to constantly move and shift, periodically burying one portion of the wreck and uncovering another, often in a matter of days. This means that the virtually weightless invertebrate remains would be easily picked up and swept away by the current, scattered throughout the ocean and likely consumed by the various wildlife. While not a primary focus of this research, the high wave energy at the Storm Wreck site may also help to explain why the site had so a large amount of sediment that was smaller than 500 μm compared to the Emanuel Point sites. More than half of the 71.9 L of sediment from the Storm Wreck compared to about a third from the Emanuel Point sites.

One of the interesting details about the remains

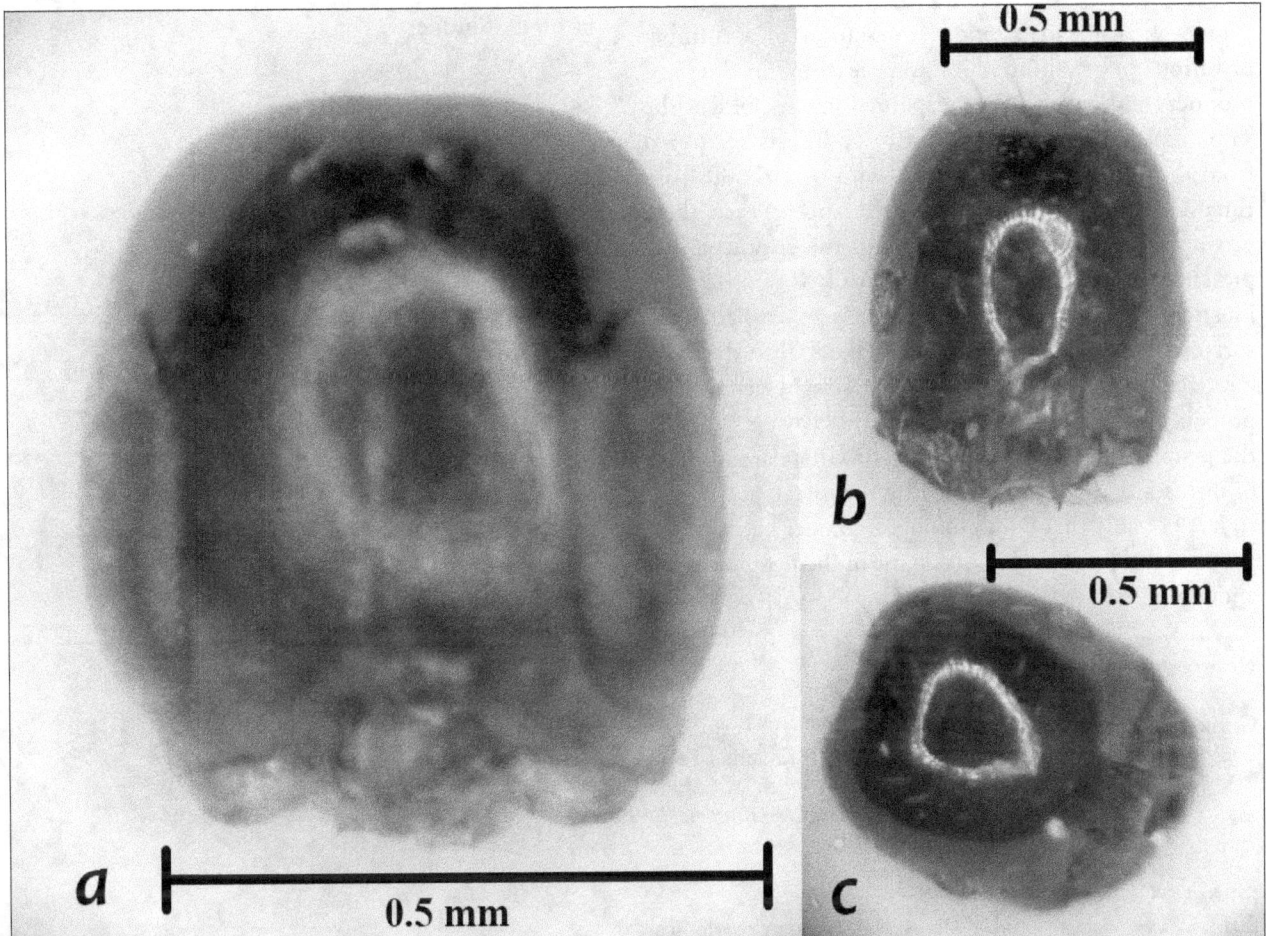

Figure 4: Ant heads recovered from the Storm Wreck. Notice the size and placement of the eyes of 3a compared to 3b and 3c, likely indicating two separate species (image by author).

recovered from the Storm Wreck is that they are remarkably well preserved. The drugstore beetle specimen is intact, and still has its very thin and fragile flight wings. While the ants are not intact and only their heads are available for study, the fact that their fragile compound eyes are unbroken is remarkable. This is due to the wave energy present at the site, which should have reduced these specimens to even smaller fragments. Of course, considering that they were some of the only specimens recovered from the site, it would seem it was only a matter of time before they were destroyed.

Another reason for explaining the difference in recovered material could have to do with the purpose of each vessel. The Emanuel Point wrecks were both much larger vessels than the Storm Wreck, and the purpose of their voyage was to start a colony. Therefore, they had all the food, livestock, and equipment necessary for the creation of a new settlement containing over a thousand people. These two vessels were also used as a storage facility for roughly a month, from the time that the fleet reached Pensacola until the hurricane hit. During this time, with most of the expedition ashore establishing the new town, it is likely that the pest populations exploded aboard the vessels, rapidly increasing up to the moment the ship sunk.

The *Storm Wreck*, on the other hand, was a ship whose cargo was gathered more quickly, as those loyal to England fled Charleston at the conclusion of the Revolutionary War. While there were most certainly some food and dry grains aboard the ship as it fled, the goal of those fleeing to St. Augustine was not to establish a new area, but rather to keep some semblance of normalcy in their lives. Therefore, they likely would have taken those goods that helped to make their transition easier, and hoped to find the everyday items in their new home. If this was the case, it would mean less food-invasive pests, and would likely lead to an increase in those that pervade other items, such as the wood from various house parts or crates.

What does this information tell us about life aboard sailing ships? The amount of material recovered from each of the Emanuel Point wrecks suggests that the people aboard had a serious infestation of a number of various pests, all of which were feasting on the food products and other dry goods stored in the hold of the ship. Based on the large quantity of insects recovered from the Emanuel Point wrecks, with over 6,600 from Emanuel Point II alone, it would appear that there was no escape from interaction with the creatures. The presence of insects on the Storm Wreck as well helps to illustrate the likelihood that all vessels at sea had some sort of pest or another, and that sailors aboard would have had to deal with these menaces to hygiene. They probably had a negative impact on every voyage, whether the people were used to them or not. There are number of diseases that are transmitted by the insects recovered, so it is possible that with prolonged contact between the humans and pests aboard that some of the people aboard ended up infected.

Jacob D. Shidner
4235 SW Birley Ave
Lake City, FL 32024
Cell: 352-598-2898
Email: jshidner@gmail.com

References

COOK, GREG
2009   Luna's Ships: Current Excavation on Emanuel Point II and Preliminary Comparisons with the First Emanuel Point Shipwreck. *The Florida Anthropologist* 62(3-4):93-99.

SHIDNER, JACOB D.
2011   A Macro- and Microscopic Zooarchaeological Examination of Living Conditions Aboard the Emanuel Point Wrecks. Master's Thesis, Department of Anthropology, University of West Florida, Pensacola, FL.

SMITH, ROGER C., JAMES SPIREK, JOHN BRATTEN, AND DELLA SCOTT-IRETON
1995   *The Emanuel Point Ship: Archaeological Investigations, 1992-1995.* Preliminary Report. Florida Department of State, Division of Historical Resources, Bureau of Archaeological Research, Tallahassee, Florida.

SMITH, ROGER C., JOHN R. BRATTEN, J. COZZI, AND KEITH PLASKETT
1998   *The Emanuel Point Ship. Archaeological Investigations 1997-1998.* Florida Department of State, Division of Historical Resources, Bureau of Archaeological Research, Tallahassee, Florida.

WORTH, JOHN E.
2009   Documenting Tristán de Luna's Fleet, and the Storm that Destroyed It. *The Florida Anthropologist* 62(3-4):83-92.

Gone for a Soldier: An Archaeological Signature of a Military Presence aboard the Storm Wreck

Brian McNamara

Six seasons of excavation yielded numerous artifacts from the Storm Wreck, site 8SJ 8459, a ship that wrecked off St. Augustine, FL on 31 December 1782 as part of the Loyalist evacuation fleet from Charlestown, SC. Many of these artifacts reflect the presence of military personnel among the ship's passengers, including Brown Bess muskets and diagnostic regimental uniform buttons. This paper will discuss a number of these artifacts and how they fit into the context of the Loyalist evacuation, ultimately leading to the identification of the Storm Wreck as one of 16 vessels reported lost during that event.

On December 14th, 1782 the last vestiges of the British armed forces began embarkation, leaving Charlestown SC, and England's northern 13 colonies to the American Patriots: victors of revolution and creators of a new nation. The participants in the Charlestown evacuation reflected all walks of life within colonial English society, including hardened veterans of the American war. On New Year's Eve, 1783 when 16 ships of Charlestown's evacuation fleet succumbed on the St. Augustine Bar to the effects of poor weather, poor navigation, and poor leadership, one of these ships sank beneath the waves, leaving us a veritable material-cultural library of the British colonial experience. The Lighthouse Archaeological Maritime Program (LAMP) has studied this wreck during six years of fieldwork and accompanying archival historical research, illuminating a forgotten chapter of the American Revolution. Among the artifacts recovered from the Storm Wreck during the 2011-2015 field seasons were several items that speak of a martial presence aboard the ship's crew and passengers. These were the archaeological signatures of British soldiers: those who had fought, endured and survived the rolling conflict across North America, now reduced to a small distillation of the grand army that once stood.

The first finds to indicate the presence of military personnel aboard the Storm Wreck were very small articles found in large concretions, or located in the particulate shell-hash dredge spoil painstakingly sifted and sorted by archaeologists and volunteers at the St. Augustine Lighthouse and Maritime Museum. The first and smallest military-diagnostic discovery was a small pewter button: 10S 064.2, which came out of the concretion that had formed on the ship's bell recovered in 2010. The button itself is of pewter, 1.6 cm in diameter; it is of the typical wire shanked construction common to buttons of the colonial period (White 2005: 63). When cleaned, the face of the button revealed the first markings to give a solid idea of the nationality and timeframe of the wrecked vessel. The unmistakable royal crown of England was boldly cast on its face, with the letters "RP". Further specimens of "RP" marked buttons also were found in concretions: buttons 13S 310.6 and 13s 345.2, measuring around 2.2 cm in diameter (Figure 1).

The inscription of a crown and "RP" is the representative badge of a British military unit comprised of Loyal American colonists who fought on the English side of the conflict as part of a regiment of "Royal Provincials". Political loyalties of the time were subject to pressures from both patriots and Loyalists. Family and friendship ties frequently crossed political boundaries, occasioning obligations that seemed to supersede the state. The effort to protect property during changing regimes complicated the picture even more (McCowen 1972: 43). Those who agreed to reaffirm their loyalty to the king and receive his protection were required to

Figure 1. Artifact drawing of a Royal Provincial regimental button recovered from the Storm Wreck. Drawing by Loren Clark. Image courtesy of LAMP.

sign an oath of allegiance; upon taking the oath, subjects were given the full rights of English citizens, and were guaranteed that they would not be taxed, except by their own representative assembly (McCowen 1972: 53). Loyalist units formed in America by the British were officially designated "Provincials" to distinguish them legally from units of the "Regular British Establishment". No fewer than 69 Provincial regiments were organized, and at least 21 took to the field with an average strength of several hundred men. Most of these would stand in battle against regulars, whereas others were suited only for ambushes, bushwhacking, and raiding (Boatner 1966: 899).

One button was recovered in 2013; button 13S 310.3 bearing a crown, the numeral "3", and the word "AMERICAN". This button represents a Provincial regiment known as the "3rd American Volunteers". This was a temporary corps of 175 officers and men drawn from volunteers of the Provincial units at New York City who otherwise would not be part of the Charlestown campaign. The corps providing the men included the 1st, 2nd, and 4th Battalion of New Jersey Volunteers, the 3rd Battalion Delancey's, The King's American Regiment, Loyal American Regiment, Prince of Wales American Volunteers and Nassau Blues. After the surrender of Charlestown, corps commander, Patrick Ferguson received permission to keep the unit in South Carolina, where they were invaluable in training Loyalist militia in light infantry tactics (Allen, Braisted 2011: 21-22).

Examples of uniform buttons representing Regular regiments of the British Establishment also were recovered; each one of pewter, boldly emblazoned with the numeral of regiments of English soldiers who had crossed the Atlantic to contest ownership of the crown's colonial territories. Artifact 12S 025.1 is a regimental button of the 71st Regiment of Foot, 12S 0223.2 is from the 63rd Regiment of Foot, and 13S 336.2 represents the 30th Regiment of Foot (Figure 2).

The 71st Regiment of Foot unquestionably saw more action than any other British regiment serving in North America during the Revolution. Most often employed at company level as light infantry, the two battalions were sometimes combined and used as shock troops. Patrick Ferguson commanded various temporary units composed largely or entirely of men from the 71st until his death at the Battle of Kings Mountain, on 7 October 1780 (Bailey 2009: 170). This unit was also recognized as "Frazier's Highlanders". Three battalions of this regiment were created. The third battalion of this regiment was moved from Savannah to Charlestown after Sir Henry Clinton campaigned to capture the town in 1780. The first battalion of the 71st bore the brunt of the fighting under Banastre Tarleton at the battle of Cowpens, January 17, 1781, and was captured after sustaining heavy casualties. The second battalion fought at the battle of Guilford Courthouse March 15, 1781 and conducted a limited pursuit after the battle. Remnants of this battalion were present at General Cornwallis's surrender at Yorktown on 19 October 1781. The third battalion the only group of this regiment not surrendering or killed in action, was present for the evacuation of Charlestown (McNamara 2014; 56).

The 63rd Regiment of Foot was part of the main British Establishment and saw active campaigning among the Carolinas; this regiment took part in Sir Henry Clinton's siege of Charlestown and became the garrison force for the town. Elements of the 63rds Light Infantry companies campaigned heavily as a detachment under the command of Banastre Tarleton, with his Provincial regiment The American Legion, thus becoming essentially mounted light infantry, also known as Dragoons (Bailey 2009: 169).

The 30th Regiment of Foot arrived in Charlestown in 1781 as part of an effort to bolster the troop numbers in the southern campaign. This regiment occupied Charlestown as a garrisoned unit until the evacuation in 1782. They appear on Sir Guy Carleton's "List of Transports for the Evacuation of Charlestown" penned

Figure 2. A collection of regimental buttons recovered from the Storm Wreck, each representing British Regiments present at Charlestown before and during the Loyalist Evacuation. Image courtesy of LAMP.

on 16 December 1782. After the evacuation, they were relocated to the islands of Antigua, St. Lucia and Dominica as a security force to quell slave insurrections troubling British sugar holdings within the islands (Riley 1983: 170). They would serve in this capacity for a further nine years beyond the end of the Revolution.

The madder-red regimental coat of the British soldier showed at a glance, who he was within the military hierarchy of the line of battle. Each unit was designated a specific color facing for the breast of the coat, while the size, number, and placement of buttons along these facings told of the soldier's placement within the line. A regimental button can tell us today the context of who the particular soldiers were within a military setting, but in this period, the manner of wearing these buttons also provided the "what" of self identification, confirming their role within the Georgian military machine. The buttons of officers were of gold, silver or brass but those of the rank and file were either brass or white metal depending on the regimental color. By 1768 the numbered buttons of officers and enlisted men changed to a cast flat pattern with a shank set into the rear of the button; made from pewter, this inexpensive button material was known as 'trifle', a pewter alloy of medium hardness consisting of 83 parts of tin to 17 parts of antimony. The objection to purer pewter was that it would not shine when polished. Sizes varied considerably due to different manufacturers. Jewelers usually made the silver or gilt buttons for the officers (Franklin 2012: 124).

The soldiers and officers of the regular line infantry companies wore their regimental buttons in evenly spaced rows of ten, down both facings of the double breasted coat. Each button hole was laced with a uniquely patterned cloth tape; for the 71st this was a white and red striped tape, sewn in a box pattern (Franklin 2012: 222). The flanking companies of Grenadiers and Light Infantry soldiers wore their buttons in doubled pairs, as well as epaulette "wings" on the coat's shoulders, marking them as the "elite" troops of their day. The grenadiers often wore the larger size button of 2.2 cm, while Light Infantrymen wore the smaller examples of 1.6 cm, although any number of combinations of the two sizes could occur depending on the particular regiment in question. Distinctions in dress were a conspicuous mark of rank or prestige in the army, as they were in civilian society (Frey 1981: 134).

The close-order tactics of the time reflected the state of technological development. The purpose of the line of battle was essentially to maximize the effectiveness of a units usage of the main battle weapon if the era, the smoothbore flintlock musket (Frey 1981: 96). Three examples of the British Land Pattern or "Brown Bess" musket were recovered by LAMP in 2012. Artifact 12S 197.1 is a 1769 Short Land Pattern musket. 12S 223.1 is a 1777 Short Land Pattern Musket, and 12S 236.1 is an older 1756 Long Land Pattern (McNamara 2014: 37-40). These muskets represent the most common firearm on the Revolutionary battlefields, carried by

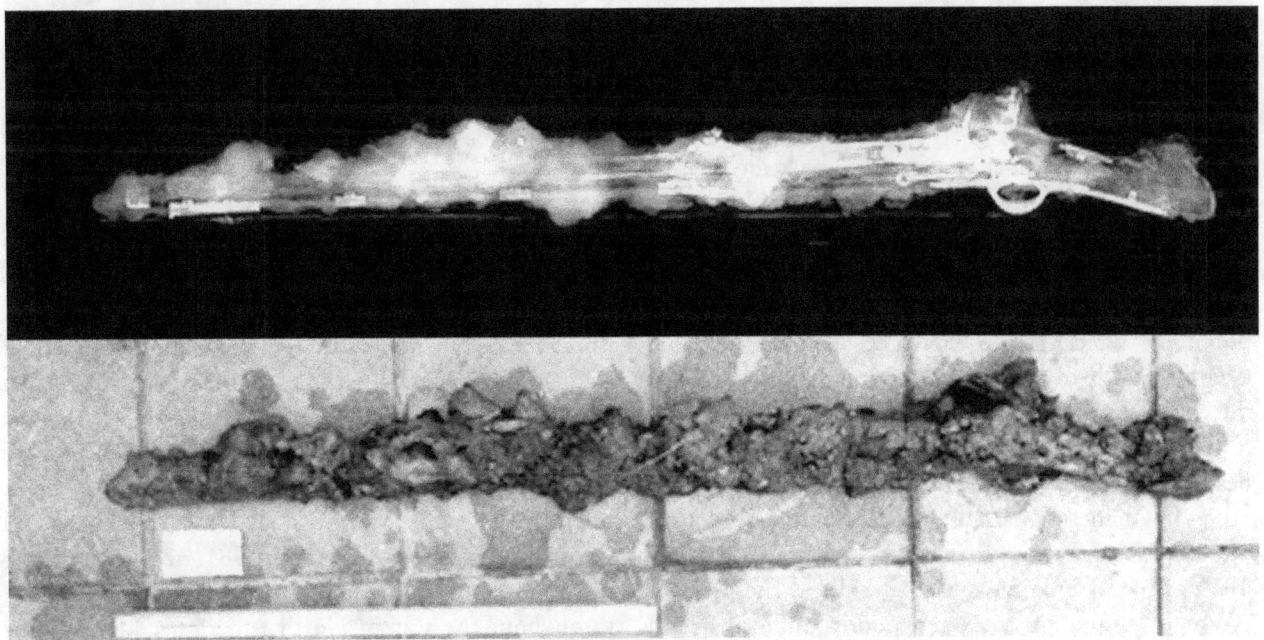

Figure 3. Artifact 12S 197.1: a 1769 Short Land Pattern musket. This musket is loaded with a cartridge of buck and ball, and its lock is in the half-cock position. Image courtesy of LAMP.

both Patriots and British. The Brown Bess was the most advanced infantry weapon of its time; its parts were built in lots by independent contractors throughout England and Ireland, and compiled by the Board of Ordnance in major arsenals such as the Tower of London or Dublin Castle into standardized, whole, functioning weapons. The Board of Ordnance in London usually supplied weapons to British soldiers and subjects everywhere but the Irish Establishment. The Irish Board of Ordnance was headquartered in Dublin Castle, and was responsible for procuring its own muskets and bayonets. The regiments serving in Ireland were thought of as a reserve, and when moved off the establishment, left their Irish made arms behind, to be replaced with British Ordnance weapons. Due to the urgent needs of the American Revolution a reversal of this policy occurred between 1774 and 1776, when many units heading to America were equipped with Irish Ordnance muskets and bayonets (Goldstein 2000: 40). On inspection, the three muskets recovered from the Storm Wreck show signs of being English in manufacture rather than Irish (McNamara 2014: 37-41).

The Land Pattern infantry musket enabled the companies of a line to stand in rigid formation, firing volley after volley of synchronized, aimed shots into the facing enemy's formations. Musket 12S 197.1 shows the effort put into maximizing the devastation a volley of fire can achieve, CT scanning of the artifact reveled that it was still loaded, and in the "half-cock" position. This musket had been loaded with a cartridge of buck and ball, which was developed to increase the damage inflicted by a unit's volley fire (Figure 3). Buck and ball consisted of the standard load of a .69 caliber musket ball accompanied by three or four .32 caliber buckshot acquired from the Royal Artillery stores (Bailey 2009: 250). Musket 12S 236.1 was found to be loaded with a shotgun-like load of Rupert shot, an atypical load for a military arm, but revealing for the mindset of evacuating soldiers, fleeing from the captured city of Charlestown.

The presence of the Land Pattern muskets aboard the Storm Wreck, a ship known to be outbound from Charlestown is of note. When a regiment departed at the end of a tour of duty, either at peace or in wartime, it was normally ordered to leave its small arms in the nearest Ordnance Stores (in this case the Ordnance Stores in Charlestown), and to receive a new set of arms upon arrival at their next posting (Bailey 2009: 148). The re-issue of used arms left behind was the primary means of equipping the often poorly uniformed and equipped Provincial regiments (McNamara 2014: 60). The existence of these weapons aboard an outbound ship, and in a loaded condition ready for use at a moment's notice, speaks of the duress under which the British were forced to leave Charlestown. Clearly these items were taken not only for defense and self preservation, but also to deny their usage by the Patriots after the British had left.

The overwhelming majority of the Storm Wreck's cargo is composed of personal belongings that passengers thought too important to leave behind. One particularly common item was a large number of small cast iron cauldrons (Figure 4). It has been speculated that these were either a cargo item or possibly the belongings of civilian passengers aboard the ship, as they were too small to serve as the communal cooking vessel aboard ship (McNamara 2012: 39-40). One alternate interpretation

Figure 4. One of several small cauldrons recovered from the Storm Wreck, a possible piece of military camp equipage. Image Courtesy of LAMP.

of these cauldrons is that they could represent the camp equipage of a Regiment. Soldiers were divided into groups of four to six for tenting and cooking together. This small group was called a "mess," and each mess of soldiers was issued with a single cooking vessel to use on the march, usually in the form of a tin camp-kettle (Frey 1981: 30). This kettle was frail and often did not survive the hard life of campaigning with a Regiment of Foot; often soldiers would acquire a replacement cooking vessel through purchase or theft (Frey 1981: 32). Considering the hard campaigning all of the British army endured throughout the war in North America, ending a tour of duty with the garrisoning of all units within the city of Charlestown, it would not be unreasonable to think these soldiers had plenty of time and opportunity to acquire cast iron cookware more suitable to their needs.

One further clue leading to this military-equipage interpretation of the Storm Wreck cauldrons was the British Army's usage of linen "kettle bags." Cooking with either a camp kettle or a cast iron pot on an open fire lead to the accumulation of soot on the cooking vessel concerned, and in order to keep the pot from soiling a soldier's uniform on the march, the pot was placed in a linen bag fitted with a draw string and carry handles specifically for this purpose. Several of the cauldrons recovered from the Storm Wreck were observed to have partial remnants of a linen bag or wrapping in the concretion while undergoing conservation. These cloth remnants could be what left of army-issued kettle bags, or they could be protective wrapping used during shipping. The former interpretation certainly fits with the narrative of a forced military evacuation.

Whether the passenger group aboard the Storm Wreck was a military regiment or a forlorn group of Loyalist civilians, the items they lost on St. Augustine's Bar represented the homes and lives they left behind, and the new lives which they hoped to make for themselves in the Colony of East Florida. The loss of life in the wrecking event of 31 December 1782 was negligible, but the loss of livelihood was surely tragic for the Loyalists who had already lost so much. Artifactual material recovered from the Storm Wreck unequivocally places the vessel within the narrative of the Charlestown evacuation at the Revolution's end, the signature of a British and Loyalist military presence is the principal marker, sealing this wreck in the history of St. Augustine, FL, and the greater nation.

References

ALLEN, T.B. AND BRAISTED T.W.
2011. *The Loyalist Corps, Americans in the Service of the King.* Fox Acre Press, Takoma Park, MD.

BAILEY, D.W.
2009. *Small Arms of the British Forces in America 1664-1815.* Mowbray Publishers, Canada.

BOATNER, M.M.
1966 *Encyclopedia of the American Revolution.* David McKay Company Inc. New York.

FRANKLIN, C.
2012 *British Army Uniforms from 1751 to 1783: Including the Seven Years War and the American War for Independence.* Pen & Sword, South Yorkshire.

FREY, S.R.
1981 *The British Soldier in America: A Social History of Military life in the Revolutionary Period.* University of Texas Press, Austin.

GOLDSTEIN, E.
2000 *The Socket Bayonet in the British Army 1687-1783.* Andrew Mowbray Publishers, Lincoln, RI.

WHITE, C.L.
2005 *American Artifacts of Personal Adornment, 1680-1820: A Guide to Identification and Interpretation.* AltaMira Press, Lanham, MD.

MCCOWEN, G.S., JR.
1972 *The British Occupation of Charleston, 1780-82.* University of South Carolina Press, Columbia.

MCNAMARA, B.
2012 *Cooking with Fire: What Cookware and Tableware Can Tell Us about an Unidentified 18th Century Shipwreck. Society for Historical Archaeology 2012 ACUA Proceedings.*

2014 *Out of Exile: Identifying the Storm Wreck, a Colonial Shipwreck off St. Augustine Florida; Finding Context through Artifactual and Archival Research.* Master Thesis for Flinder's University Department of Archaeology. Adelaide South Australia.

RILEY, S.
1983 *Homeward Bound, A History of the Bahama Islands to 1850, with a Definitive Study of Abaco in the American Loyalist Plantation Period.* Island Research, Miami Florida.

Brian McNamara
SEARCH - SEARCH2O
12443 San Jose Blvd., Suite 204
Jacksonville, Florida 32223
904-810-8942 cell 904-379-8338 phone
bmcnamara@searchinc.com

Archaeology for the Masses: Presenting the Storm Wreck through Public Archaeology

Olivia McDaniel, Brenda Swann, Jill Titcomb, and Paul Zielinski

The Lighthouse Archaeological Maritime Program's (LAMP) position as the research arm of the St. Augustine Lighthouse & Maritime Museum creates the perfect opportunity to present St. Augustine's underwater heritage to the public using a series of onsite public archaeology programs. Since the discovery of the Storm Wreck, a 1782 British Loyalist wreck, museum staff have developed a number of programs on the history, research, and conservation performed on the Storm Wreck artifact assemblage, and St. Augustine's broader maritime history and underwater archaeological resources. The purpose is to provide guests with an archaeological experience at the St. Augustine Lighthouse & Maritime Museum.

Introduction

In July 2009, LAMP began research on a site designated as the Storm Wreck (8SJ5459), since identified as a 1782 British Loyalist wreck located approximately one mile off St. Augustine, Florida (Meide et al. 2014: 311-321). Over the course of the project, LAMP's position as the research arm of the St. Augustine Lighthouse & Maritime Museum has created an opportunity to extend the Storm Wreck's story into the public eye through onsite public archaeology programs. Having LAMP's base of operations and an archaeological conservation facility on the same grounds as the exhibit space where the archaeological discoveries will eventually go on display allows the museum interpreters to present the archaeological process from beginning to end. The public archaeology programs developed at the St. Augustine Lighthouse & Maritime Museum are inspired by that process, and present not only the story of the Storm Wreck and its assemblage, but also St. Augustine's broader maritime connection and underwater archaeology as a whole.

Guided Tours

The most frequent programs, and the ones that feature the underwater archaeology program and the Storm Wreck most prominently, are daily guided tours throughout the lighthouse grounds. Over the six-year span of the project, different tour formats have been used and tour content has changed and evolved, due both to discoveries on the Storm Wreck and to a low percentage of annual visitors taking the tours.

Behind the Scenes and Lost Ships Tours

LAMP's research on the Storm Wreck was first incorporated into the museum's daily Behind the Scenes tour. Occurring twice daily most weekdays and three times daily Friday-Sunday, it was a popular addition to the museum's general admission. The tour included a guided walk through the exhibits housed in the historic keepers' house, and an in-depth look at all aspects of research at the Museum. This included lighthouse history and life as a keeper; the heritage boat works program; and the maritime archaeology program. The archaeology portion focused mostly on the historical context of the site, explaining how archaeologists used the artifact assemblage and historical research to identify the Storm Wreck as a 1782 British Loyalist ship. Docents presented the importance of conserving waterlogged artifacts in the museum courtyard, where two cannon from the wreck were undergoing electrolysis. Following the courtyard, docents led visitors through the outdoor conservation facility where they discussed the formation and removal of encrustation from artifacts, as visitors looked upon actual concretions from the Storm Wreck in wet storage.

In 2012, archaeologists developed the Lost Ships Tour, a 1.5-hour guided tour for visitors seeking an in-depth look at the underwater archaeology program. It was initially offered twice a day, three days a week, but was increased to twice daily, seven days a week in 2014. Led by staff archaeologists, the tour began with a multi-media presentation with PowerPoint and video components. All technical aspects of the project were discussed, including remote sensing survey and discovery, excavation, mapping and recovery, and conservation. The historical context and current research were presented here as well. In addition to visiting the same outdoor conservation area as the Behind the Scenes tour, guests were taken into the indoor conservation area, usually closed to the public. Here visitors could see many of the artifacts discussed in the presentation and those newly recovered or removed from concretion, thereby observing conservation in action and learning what those artifacts told archaeologists about the Storm Wreck.

Behind the Scenes: 2015 Format

Both the Behind the Scenes and Lost Ships Tours were well regarded, receiving mostly positive feedback from tour takers over the years. However, statistics showed that only 1.6% of the museum's nearly 200,000 annual visitors were taking the tour, and thus only 1.6% of our visitors were exposed to the Storm Wreck and archaeology program. To reach more people, the museum decided to re-format both tours into a single hour-long tour, offered free with admission and guided by museum staff or volunteer docents. It is offered five times a day, seven days a week. The new format created a streamlined hour long tour that discusses lighthouse history in the courtyard, the heritage boat works program in the boat building area, and the archaeology program in the outdoor conservation area. The streamlined format cuts considerable walking time out of the tour. New signage (Figure 1) in the outdoor conservation area provides visual aids on the technical and historical aspects of maritime archaeology and the Storm Wreck that were previously addressed in the multi-media presentation and visits to the indoor conservation space and archaeology office. Therefore, despite the shorter time frame and the removal of certain archaeology-related tour elements, the new tours still create opportunities to present and discuss all aspects of the Storm Wreck and underwater archaeology to visitors.

The new Behind the Scenes tours began December 1, 2015. At the time of writing, museum staff have compiled preliminary statistics for the first three months of this tour format using tour sizes reported by staff and volunteer docents. These show an increase in monthly tour attendance from 13.80 visitors per tour in December 2015, to 18.08 visitors per tour in February, 2016. These numbers are an approximation, as they rely on the tour guides' guest counts. Larger groups are often difficult to count with accuracy, and some tours are not reported at all. While it is too soon to know how these numbers compare to the percentage of visitors that participated in the previous tour format, so far the visitor response has been overwhelmingly positive. Tour attendance is visibly increasing and appears to be significantly increasing the number of visitors the Storm Wreck story reaches.

On-Site Conservation

Ongoing conservation is an important part of the public archaeology experience as well. It has been said that, "from a public perspective conserving, stabilizing, studying, and exhibiting those relics in a public environment is the stuff of a living museum (McCarthy 2011:1045)." The Storm Wreck conservation has played a significant role in onsite public archaeology, and it continues to do so. Due to limited conservation space at the museum, many conservation activities that are not always open to the public are extended into the public eye, creating a number of public archaeology opportunities. Conservators regularly clean and air scribe concretions at an outdoor workbench where visitors can watch and ask questions about the process (Figure 2). At this same workbench, dredge spoil is sorted after each field season, allowing visitors to watch as small discoveries are made by archaeologists and volunteers. The majority of

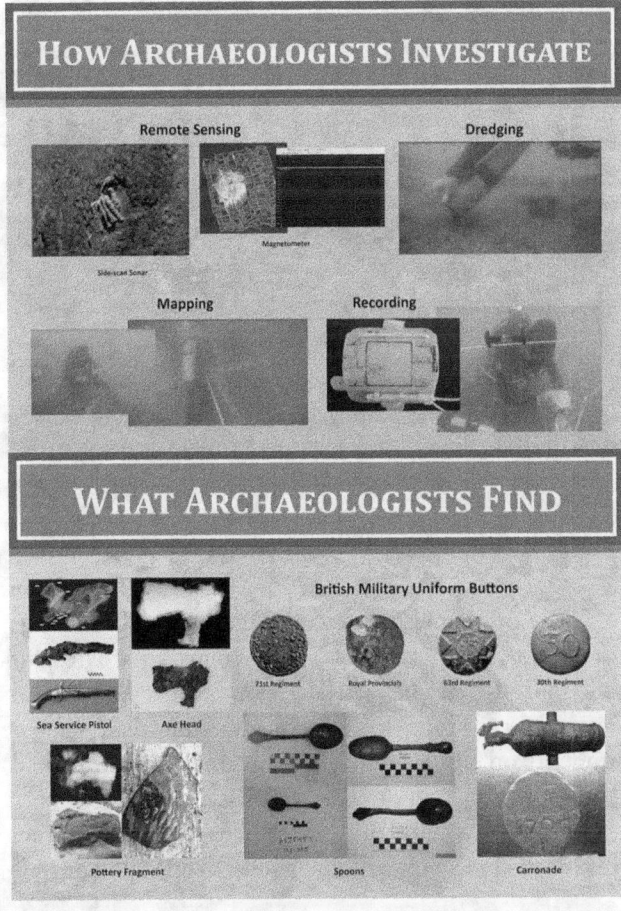

Figure 1. This interpretive signage now hangs in the outdoor conservation area that the new Behind the Scenes tour visits, giving docents visual aids to discuss all aspects of the wreck. Image courtesy of St. Augustine Lighthouse & Maritime Museum.

the cannon conservation took place in a corner of the museum courtyard, where their electrolysis vats created a constant conservation presence during their four and a half year treatment. For additional work the cannons needed (Figure 2), including electrolysis solution changes, air scribing, and weighing, a section of the museum courtyard was roped off, creating a makeshift workspace for conservators and simultaneously putting conservation efforts at the forefront of the visitor experience. As these activities occur, they are worked into the daily guided tours, creating more opportunities for a dialogue about archaeological conservation, the Storm Wreck, and maritime archaeology in general.

Figure 2. Shown here is one of the makeshift work spaces created while conservators work on the long gun in the museum courtyard, putting conservation and archaeology directly into the visitor experience. Image courtesy of St. Augustine Lighthouse & Maritime Museum.

Daily Archaeology Programs

The museum's five-year strategic plan (2013-2018) called for daily archaeology programs to excite our 200,000-plus annual visitors about the archaeological research program. In addition to the field school students on site every day during their month of field school, other year-round daily activities were developed. After several rounds of discussion, two programs were tested on site: Penny Cleaning and Dredge Spoil Sort.

Penny Cleaning

The Penny Cleaning activity is a demonstration designed to open a dialogue with museum guests about artifact conservation and the interdisciplinary nature of archaeology as a field that combines history, science, and conservation. The demonstration involves putting old, corroded pennies in a solution of salt and vinegar to show how chemicals clean objects. While cannon from the Storm Wreck were undergoing electrolysis in view of the public, this activity was conducted next to them in the courtyard to provide a segue into a discussion of electrolysis and the Storm Wreck.

Dredge Spoil Sort

The Dredge Spoil Sort program is a casual introduction to the methodologies of maritime archaeology through a short participatory activity. Mock dredge spoil made with purchased shells and salted with "artifacts" (buttons, bells, etc. from craft stores) is set on a table in the courtyard area between the lighthouse and keepers' house. Historic site interpreters invite visitors to sort through dredge spoil, which requires the interpreter to explain what dredge spoil is and why we collect it. Like the Penny Cleaning activity, the conversation naturally leads to a discussion of finding and excavating the Storm Wreck, including the fact that the military uniform button found in dredge spoil is one of the most definitive pieces of evidence that the wreck is a loyalist evacuee ship.

After a test period for both programs, it was determined that the Dredge Spoil Sort was the best received, particularly for families with young children—one of the museum's primary audiences. This activity was incorporated into our daily schedule, along with the new Behind the Scenes tour, as "Tiny Clues" offered twice daily.

Field School Public Archaeology

In addition to the programs mentioned above, LAMP's annual underwater archaeology field school includes student participation in daily public archaeology activities throughout the four-week course. The students split into groups, with one remaining at the lighthouse each day to engage the public about the Storm Wreck and underwater archaeology. On a table in the museum courtyard, artifacts in conservation are displayed. Among these are a concreted artifact with its laminated x-ray nearby, fully conserved artifacts now in dry storage, and some that are still in wet storage. Laminated photographs of fieldwork, historic documents, and other artifacts that played an integral part in the identification of the wreck are on hand to supplement the artifacts. The various items are intended to generate discussion with visitors about all aspects of the Storm Wreck project, from historical context to the modern investigation and conservation of the site. Museum visitors are able to speak with people who have worked on the site, and each group of future archaeologists is introduced to the importance of public archaeology while simultaneously solidifying the information they have been learning and presenting it to the public.

Maritime Archaeology Education Programs

Each year, hundreds of school groups of varying ages visit the museum. To cater to these large groups, museum staff designed maritime archaeology K–12 educational programs to introduce students to basic concepts and processes of archaeology as a means to address state curriculum standards in math, science, social studies, and language arts. The programs include Search for Shipwrecks, Shipwreck CSI, and Science of Conservation. Each leads the student through a different aspect of archaeology: discovery, research, and conservation practices.

Search for Shipwrecks

The Search for Shipwrecks program combines a presentation and hands-on activity to introduce students to underwater survey methods. Students are shown images of a sonar and magnetometer and what different readings from these remote sensing tools look like. They also learn about primary sources and that archaeologists also use historic documents to locate and identify sites. Students receive an aerial photograph of the St. Augustine coastline with a grid placed over the photograph. The educator calls out grid points for (pretend) positive magnetometer and sonar hits and places where historic documents indicate shipwrecks have happened. Students then plot the points on the grid over the aerial using "M", "S" and "D" to denote magnetometer, sonar and document locations respectively (Figure mcdaniel_Fig3). Once all the points are plotted, the educator leads a discussion about the best locations to target test and why.

Shipwreck CSI

Shipwreck CSI begins with a presentation designed to introduce students to the basic steps of underwater

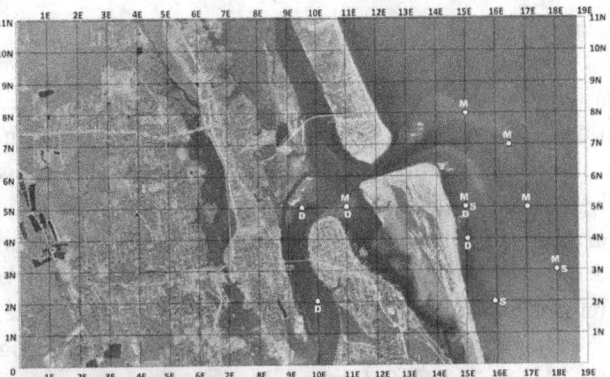

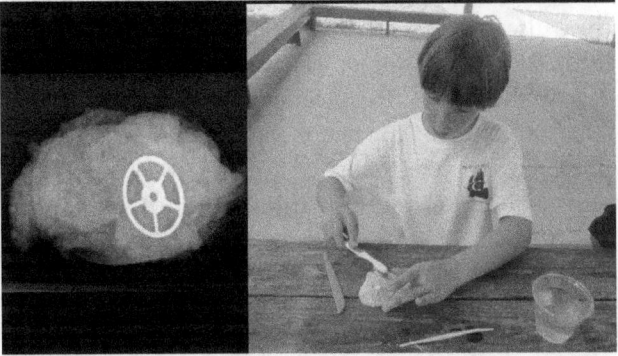

Figure 3. Shown at the top are the sonar, magnetometer, and documentary coordinates that students are asked to plot and analyze in the Search for Shipwrecks program. The bottom shows an x-ray of an "artifact" inside one of the plaster of paris concretions (left) used in the Science of Conservation program. A student uses the provided tools to carefully remove the "artifact" from the mock concretion surrounding it (right). Image courtesy of St. Augustine Lighthouse & Maritime Museum.

excavation with a primary focus on mapping large artifacts from a unit onto a grid. The students also learn why precise mapping is important and see a site plan of the excavation. Those artifacts safely brought to the surface for further study and conservation are the second focal point. Instruction is given to familiarize the students with concretions: what they are, how to determine their content, prioritization based upon x-ray analysis, and how they are processed and conserved.

The activity allows students to simulate the processes an archaeologist takes to identify the artifacts in their concretion. It is designed to be utilized with a hand-made quilt that represents the shape of a ship under the ocean with measuring tape guidelines gridded over the ship, but a large printout of the site plan map can also be used (Figure mcdaniel_Fig. 4). Students are formed into groups, each taking a small photograph of a concretion off the quilt. Each concretion has been mapped to scale to represent its location relative to other concretions on the site plan map. Once each group has a concretion, they go to a table and find the same concretion in a larger, 8" X 11.5" printout.

After studying the concretion, they write down on a worksheet what artifacts they believe are inside. Then they go to the table and find the x-ray of their concretion, subsequently writing down what artifacts they now believe are inside. The final step is to research what the artifacts are via a simplistic process of looking through a provided set of artifact cards. Careful observation is required to find the best possible match. For example, the x-ray should be examined so that the correct clothing iron is selected from five possible choices. Each group then discusses the artifacts to determine what can be learned about the ship or its passengers.

At the end of the program, the instructor reveals what is in each concretion and discusses the ideas proposed by the groups. Afterward, they map their artifacts back on the quilt using provided coordinates and everyone discusses what significance *in situ* artifacts may reveal.

Science of Conservation

The Science of Conservation program gives students an opportunity to further their understanding of conservation with a focus on maritime artifacts. Instruction leads the students through the definition of maritime, archaeology, and maritime archaeology. Next, a concretion is studied and its formation processes discussed. An x-ray of the concretion is shown with an explanation of what it potentially reveals: researchable details, decomposition, preservation, identifiable artifacts, etc. This leads to why care and patience are important when processing archaeological materials to ensure that any diagnostics remain.

A presentation is used to further explain underwater archaeological conservation methods (like electrolysis) and tools that are utilized (such as an air scribe). Finally, each student gets a plaster of paris concretion with a metal piece (jingle bell, wheel, chain piece, etc.) inside, a toothbrush, gloves, plastic clay working pick, and a glass of water (Figure 3). Here, they practice the careful patience of an archaeologist as they try to reveal what is inside their concretion.

Conclusion

In recent years, it is apparent that archaeology as a whole has become more publicly oriented (Merriman 2004: 100-101). This is especially evident in many museum-based archaeology programs, where "the museum-based archaeologist is clearly also a 'public archaeologist,' beholden not just to the site and the objects raised but also to the needs to the general populace..." (McCarthy 2011:1041). The programs presented here were designed to accommodate the general populace, with their varying types and levels of interests, from those who want an in-depth guided tour, to hands-on activities, to programs developed specifically for children. They help museum archaeologists and interpreters tell a side of American history that is not often told. Even as the Storm Wreck project progresses to the exhibition stage, these programs will continue as a supplement to the story, highlighting an unseen side of St. Augustine's history and underwater heritage.

Figure 4. Laminated photographs of concretions are placed on this quilt for the Shipwreck CSI program. Student groups choose a concretion, learning about site mapping and provenience while using the meter tape grid sewn into the quilt to record the location of each concretion. Image courtesy of St. Augustine Lighthouse & Maritime Museum.

References

McCarthy, Michael
2011   Museums and Maritime Archaeology. In *The Oxford Handbook of Maritime Archaeology*, Alexis Catsambis, Ben Ford, and Donny L. Hamilton, editors, pp. 1032-1054. Oxford University Press, New York, NY.

Meide, Chuck, P. Brendan Burke, Olivia McDaniel, Samuel P. Turner, Eden Andes, Hunter Brendel, Starr Cox, and Brian McNamara
2014   First Coast Maritime Archaeology Project 2011-2012: Report on Archaeological Investigations. Lighthouse Archaeological Maritime Program, St. Augustine Lighthouse & Maritime Museum, St. Augustine, Florida.

Merriman, Nick (editor)
2004   *Public Archaeology*. Routledge, New York, NY.

Olivia McDaniel
Lighthouse Archaeological Maritime Program
St. Augustine Lighthouse & Maritime Museum
81 Lighthouse Ave.
St. Augustine, FL 32080
Work Phone: (904) 829-0745
Home Phone: (208) 469-0985
Email: lamp@staugustinelighthouse.org

Brenda Swann
St. Augustine Lighthouse & Maritime Museum
81 Lighthouse Ave.
St. Augustine, FL 32080
Work Phone: (904)829-0745
Home Phone: (904) 599-8663
Email: bswann@staugustinelighthouse.org

Jill Titcomb
St. Augustine Lighthouse & Maritime Museum
81 Lighthouse Ave.
St. Augustine, FL 32080
Work Phone: (904)829-0745
Home Phone: (386) 225-1763
Email: jtitcomb@staugustinelighthouse.org

Paul Zielinski
St. Augustine Lighthouse & Maritime Museum
81 Lighthouse Ave.
St. Augustine, FL 32080
Work Phone: (904)829-0745
Home Phone: (904) 332-8563
Email: pzielinski@staugustinelighthouse.org

WRECKED! An Interactive Exhibition on a Revolutionary War Shipwreck in St. Augustine, Florida

Brenda Swann and Olivia McDaniel

The exhibition of the Storm Wreck, a Revolutionary War Shipwreck in St. Augustine, FL, has two components. As with traditional archaeology exhibits, it will share how historical documents and artifacts from the shipwreck tell the story of British Loyalists who, after evacuating Charleston, SC, arrived in St. Augustine only to run aground and lose many of their possessions on the ocean floor. The Discovery Lab part of the exhibit will allow visitors to participate in the methods and processes of archaeological discovery through hands-on stations, including the Navigation Station, X-ray Station, Survey Station, Maritime Archaeology Station, and more.

Introduction

Since the founding of the St. Augustine Lighthouse Archaeological Maritime Program (LAMP) as the archaeological research arm of the St. Augustine Lighthouse & Maritime Museum in 1999, the museum has supported LAMP's research as a means to uphold its mission to share the stories of the nation's oldest port with museum visitors through programs and exhibits. One such story is that of the Storm Wreck (8SJ5459), which research has identified as a Revolutionary War era vessel that carried British Loyalists evacuating from Charleston, SC in December of 1782. The ship ran aground and was lost on a sandbar about a mile off St. Augustine's shores on or around December 31 of the same year (Meide et al. 2014:311-321). The museum interpretive team chose two approaches to the story of the Storm Wreck in a new exhibit, titled WRECKED. One will address the underwater archaeological methods used by the archaeology team, and the second will focus on the story of the Revolutionary War period loyalist shipwreck as told by historical documents and artifacts. Combining these approaches will engage the visitor in both the modern investigation of the Storm Wreck and the history behind it.

The exhibit has been funded by a combination of museum donors and historic preservation grant assistance provided by the Bureau of Historic Preservation, Division of Historical Resources, Florida Department of State, assisted by the Florida Historical Commission. Using this, museum conservation staff have conserved and continue to conserve Storm Wreck artifacts for display. The museum interpretive team has contracted with Architecture is Fun, a design team out of Chicago, to help design and fabricate the new exhibit. It will be housed in the south half and basement of the historic lightkeepers' house on the museum grounds.

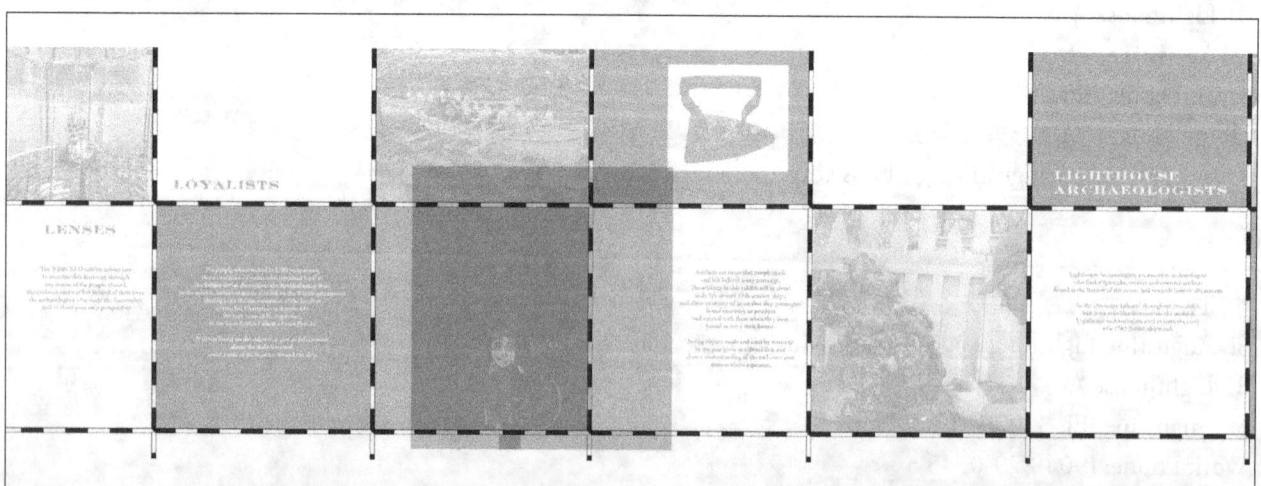

Figure 1. The square grid design element shown in this image is used throughout the WRECKED exhibit, subtly reminding visitors of how professional archaeologists record and learn about shipwrecks. Image courtesy of St. Augustine Lighthouse & Maritime Museum.

Entry Hallway

A square grid system will be used as a graphic element throughout the exhibit, as a subtle reminder of how professional archaeologists record and learn about shipwrecks (Figure 1). Visitors will begin in the entry hallway of the keepers' house, where they will find a general introduction to the final loyalist evacuation of Charleston, and a quote from Lieutenant Colonel Archibald McArthur, in a letter he wrote to the British Commander in Chief, Sir Guy Carleton, describing the wrecking event that declares,

> "Sir, I have the honour to inform Your Excellency that the fleet under convoy of the Bellisaurius, with Refugees and Provisions, arrived off this Bar on the 31st Ult. But in coming over it, the Rattlesnake Galley and two Provision Vessels with six others (private property) were lost; the Eighteen pounder and Rigging of the Galley were saved; four lives from the private Vessels were lost; the Cash arrived safe. (BNA 1783:PRO 30/55/60/6728)."

The surrounding text will inform the visitor that the Storm Wreck could be one of 16 vessels that ran aground on St. Augustine's notorious sandbar that day, and that they remained there until 2009, when Lighthouse archaeologists discovered the site and began to uncover its story. Entry hallway content also will introduce the four main "characters" of the exhibit: artifacts, archaeologists, loyalists, and the visitor themselves. Visitors then will be invited to join archaeologists in uncovering this story in the archaeology lab and on the sandbar itself in the exhibit.

Discovery Lab

From the entry hallway, visitors will go into the Discovery Lab, where several hands-on interactive exhibits will allow visitors to participate in archaeological research methods. The Discovery Lab will feature several different stations addressing various aspects of maritime archaeological research (Figure 2). These will include a Survey Station, X-ray Station, Navigation Station, and Maritime Archaeology Station.

Survey Station

At the Survey Station, museumgoers will be introduced to magnetometer and side-scan sonar survey principles, and an interactive display will enable them to complete their own sonar survey. This will be accomplished through the use of framed and laminated magnetic viewing film and a series of magnets of different shapes and sizes, flush-mounted underneath the ocean graphic grid. As visitors pass the viewing film over a magnet, a dark outline will appear that simulates sonar imagery.

Figure 2. The design layout for the first floor Discovery Lab is shown here. The Survey Station sits at the forefront, the X-ray Station hangs on the wall at the right, and the Maritime Archaeology and Navigation Stations are located near the windows at the back of the room. Note the square grid design

X-ray Station

No maritime archaeology discovery lab would be complete without x-rays of concretions. This station will allow visitors to put a replica of Storm Wreck concretion 10S-064.1 on a mock x-ray machine to reveal its x-ray image. Participants will be asked to identify artifacts within the x-ray and choose from a list of artifacts within the x-ray, which includes a pistol, iron hooks and a fastener, lead shot, a coin or button, and hollows of an iron hank and ring. Hints in the interpretive text will explain how the brighter areas in x-rays indicate metal remaining in the concretion, and the brighter the reflection, the more metal remains. They also will point out that dull outlines in the x-ray can indicate hollow spaces where metal artifacts have rusted completely away. The hints will help visitors figure out what the objects are, while providing additional information about archaeological methods.

Maritime Archaeology Station

At the Maritime Archaeology Station, the visitor will join the separate parts of a maritime archaeological investigation. Three iPads will play a video game that takes users through all phases of shipwreck archaeology, from survey to excavation to conservation.

Navigation Station

This station will turn away from the modern technologies used by maritime archaeologists, and will instead highlight navigational technology contemporary to the Storm Wreck. The octant pinnula, or peep sight, and the brass sector rule will be on display nearby (Burkett, this volume: Figures 1 and 3). Located near the west windows of the keepers' house, this station will provide an opportunity to practice 18th-century navigation skills. Visitors will use a replica octant to site a graphic representation of the North Star placed on the window. By reading the resultant angle shown on the octant, visitors will determine their latitude. In the case of this exhibit experience, the geometry of both the octant and the North Star image will result in a reading of about 30 degrees, which is the approximate latitude of St. Augustine.

Interpretive Wall: Loyalists Evacuating Charleston

One wall of the Discovery Lab will explain how archaeologists also use documentary and archival resources in conjunction with the technological tools presented at the various stations to provide a more complete site history. The wall will present documents concerning the loyalist evacuation of Charleston and some of the trials the convoys faced during the voyage to St. Augustine.

Sandbar

Above the spiral staircase leading down to the second level of the exhibit in the keepers' house basement, a video of Lighthouse archaeologists working underwater will prepare visitors to enter the basement, where they will descend into a partial recreation of the sandbar and the shipwreck within it. The basement is separated into two parts by a large cistern, so that when visitors come down the staircase, they will see just the southern side of the basement and must walk through a short hallway to access the northern side of the space. This feature, as well as structural supports along the walls, creates natural alcoves in the space where a combination of conserved artifacts from the site, interpretive text, and design elements and props will come together to tell the various sides of the Storm Wreck's history.

British Soldiers and Sailors

In the southeast portion of the basement, the sandbar will be recreated on the floor using a composite wood deck. Imbedded within the sandbar is a gridiron recovered from the site and a simulated wooden plank, representing the only possible hull remains found on the shipwreck. Around this area, ship related artifacts, such as hooks, hanks, rigging, rope, and a piece of canvas or sail cloth will be displayed, and people will be invited to interact with the exhibit by turning a ship's wheel in one of the architectural nooks near the sandbar. Nearby, Brown Bess muskets (Cox, this volume) and their associated shot, uniform buttons (McNamara, this volume: Fig. 2), spoons, plates, a keg tap (McCarron, this volume: Figures 1, 2, and 4), and fishing weights (Thomson, this volume: Figure 4) will tell the story of the soldiers and sailors aboard the ship.

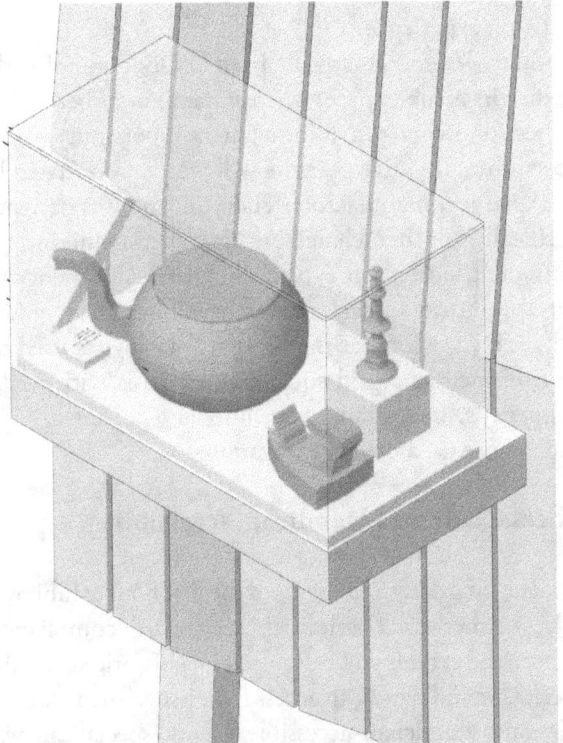

Figure 3. The downstairs exhibit space uses a combination of artifacts, interpretive text, and props to put visitors on board the ship and in the lives of the Loyalists on board. In the Daily Life and Social Status area, easily recognizable artifacts, such as the iron tea kettle, clothing iron, and candle stick holder pictured here, creates an easy link between visitors and daily life for a Loyalist. Image courtesy of St. Augustine Lighthouse & Maritime Museum.

Daily Life and Social Status

In the southwest area, the story of private loyalist citizens will come to life through personal and household items. Belt and shoe buckles, a pocket pistol, and a faux pocket watch will show that there were people aboard ship from the upper social strata and that the war affected everyone, regardless of wealth or social status. Various household items, including a kettle (Carter, this volume: Figure 3), flat irons and clothing pins, and a door lock and key (McCarron, this volume; Figure 3), will present daily life with easily recognizable objects that have similar form and function today, creating an easy link between visitors and the past (Figure 3). This area also will feature a small table and chairs with period teakettles, plates, and flatware props for younger guests to engage in play.

Two Sides of the Coin

In a large alcove across from the cisterns, a replica of one of the two gold guineas recovered from the shipwreck will be displayed (Brendel, this volume.). This British coin is useful for discussing the two sides of the American Revolution, which some have called America's first civil war. On one side, the coin is emblazoned with the bust of King George III, while on the reverse it is dated 1776, the year synonymous with American independence. Today, students in the United States learn the story of the colonists who wanted independence from King George III and England. This exhibit will bring the other side of the coin to the forefront, telling the story of those colonists who remained loyal to the Crown throughout the conflict. Near the coin display, guests will be invited to share the new perspectives they have gained throughout the exhibit.

Perils of the Sea

The northeastern side of the basement will present seven units from the northern part of the site plan. This area held many heavy objects, including cannons, cauldrons, tools, casks of nails, and the lead deck pump, which archaeologists believe indicate an attempt to save the grounded vessel by jettisoning heavy materials in order to lighten and refloat the ship. A large cauldron, a 4-pounder long gun (Meide, this volume: Figure 2), and the lead deck pump (Andes, this volume), complete with chop marks showing how it was cut away from the ship in order to be thrown overboard, will be on display to help bring the wrecking event to life. These artifacts and the recreated site plan will demonstrate the "Perils of the Sea" that ocean-going travelers faced, as well as give visitors a feel for what is was like to jettison these items when the ship ran aground.

Ship's Bell

Nearby, the ship's bell (Andes, this volume), also found among the heavy artifacts in the northern part of the site, will be displayed. The purpose of the bell display is twofold. First, it will provide visitors aboard the ship with an explanation of how sailors rang and heard the ship's bell to mark the hours of their watches. Secondly, it will explain to visitors how the unmarked bell most likely indicates a privately-owned vessel. Private vessel owners maximized their profits by declining to pay the higher price for a custom bell when outfitting their ship (Andes, this volume).

Interpretive Wall: Loyalists Arriving in St. Augustine

The northwestern corner of the basement will feature excerpts from documents concerning the loyalists from Charleston, similar to the interpretive wall in the Discovery Lab. However, where the Discovery Lab wall will show documents describing the loyalists' evacuation from Charleston, this area will show documents describing the arrival of the loyalists in St. Augustine and the dire situation they faced there, as the flood of incoming loyalists put a strain on the town's ability to feed and house the increased population (Meide et al 2012: 316-318).

A Kid's Perspective

In addition to the main narrative of the exhibit, the interpretive team has created the character Star Waters to engage young visitors (Figure 4). Star is an aspiring maritime archaeologist who will pose questions throughout the exhibit and then provide the answers she finds in a kid-friendly way. She will ask questions regarding different aspects of the wreck and its story, some of which include:

- How do concretions form on artifacts?
- How long does it take to conserve artifacts?
- What can you learn from a completely rusted artifact?
- How did archaeologists find a small item like an octant eyepiece on a shipwreck?
- Why are the spoon handles bent or broken?
- Where is the ship?
- How do archaeologists draw and take notes underwater?

Before she answers each question, she will describe where she looked for the answer. In some cases she will speak with archaeologists and conservators at the museum; visit the local library; or consult the internet to do her own research. In others, she will pursue her junior diver certification to join archaeologists on site, and learn how sites are excavated and recorded through hands-on experience.

Star Waters also will have a spotlight in the downstairs exhibit space, where a manikin of her will be dressed for diving, providing a photo opportunity within the exhibit. The dive gear she will wear was donated by local dive gear manufacturer Halcyon, and was designed specifically for her character. Near her manikin, her equipment locker will explain SCUBA equipment and gear specific to underwater archaeology. Here, guests will get a close look at the tools archaeologists used on the site, such as a grid square, clip boards with Mylar and pencils, meter tape reels, line, and sections of the dredge hose used during excavation.

Wheel Chair and Handicap Accessibility

The final design elements of the first floor exhibit will address American Disabilities Act (ADA) compliance. Because the exhibit will be housed in a historic structure, wheelchair and handicap access is an issue. The first floor is the only wheelchair-accessible level, so special care was taken designing the exhibit layout to ensure wheelchairs could easily access all areas and activities within the entry hallway and Discovery Lab. The downstairs exhibit space is only accessible by a spiral staircase from the first floor. To provide access to this area, eleven video cameras installed around the downstairs will play in a loop on a

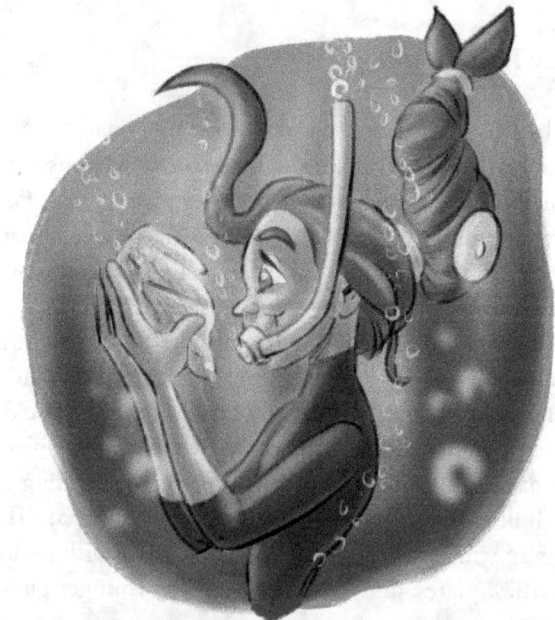

Figure 4. To engage young visitors, the interpretive team created the character Star Waters, an aspiring maritime archaeologist, who posed questions throughout the exhibit and provides the answers in a kid-friendly way. Image courtesy of St. Augustine Lighthouse & Maritime Museum.

monitor installed on the first floor. Directly below the monitor, a digital flipbook with graphics, interpretive text, and photographs of the downstairs exhibits also will be available on a large wall-mounted tablet. These measures will ensure that all visitors can experience the Storm Wreck story presented in the downstairs exhibit space.

Conclusion

The WRECKED exhibit, opening in May 2016, will allow for engagement in archaeological practices that turns visitors into participants actively discovering the Storm Wreck story through artifacts and historic documents. Demonstrating and engaging in archaeological practices in the Discovery Lab will help visitors take away a better understanding of how professional underwater archaeologists work, and what they value from shipwrecks and other archaeological resources. The story of the evacuation of Charleston at the end of the Revolutionary War and the arrival of loyalists in the loyal British colony of St. Augustine will be told by putting participants in the story itself, both through modern research and by recreating the very sandbar that caused the wrecking event over two centuries ago. Encouraging active participation in the exhibit will increase the likelihood that participants will remember their experience and what they have learned, taking away new perspectives on a side of American history rarely discussed.

References

BRITISH NATIONAL ARCHIVES (BNA)
1783   Lt. Colonel Archibald McArthur to General Sir Guy Carleton, 9 January 1783. PRO30/55/60/6728:1-8, Headquarters Papers of the British Army in North America, The National Archives, Kew, United Kingdom.

MEIDE, CHUCK, P. BRENDAN BURKE, OLIVIA MCDANIEL, SAMUEL P. TURNER, EDEN ANDES, HUNTER BRENDEL, STARR COX, AND BRIAN MCNAMARA
2014   First Coast Maritime Archaeology Project 2011 – 2012: Report on Archaeological Investigations. Lighthouse Archaeological Maritime Program, St. Augustine Lighthouse & Maritime Museum, St. Augustine, Florida.

Brenda Swann
St. Augustine Lighthouse & Maritime Museum
81 Lighthouse Ave.
St. Augustine, FL 32080
Work Phone: (904)829-0745
Home Phone: (904) 599-8663
Email: bswann@staugustinelightouse.org

Olivia McDaniel
St. Augustine Lighthouse & Maritime Museum
81 Lighthouse Ave.
St. Augustine, FL 32080
Work Phone: (904) 829-0745
Home Phone: (208) 469-0985
Email: lamp@staugustinelightouse.org

www.ingramcontent.com/pod-product-compliance
Lightning Source LLC
Chambersburg PA
CBHW081443070526
44586CB00019B/2211

EXCEL STILL MORE

2 Peter & Jude

DENNY PETRILLO

JOE WELLS

GARRETT BERNETHY

BILLY CLABAUGH

MICHAEL HITE

An In-Depth Exegetical Study *with* **Practical Application** | The *Excel Still More* Workshop

KAIO PUBLICATIONS, INC.

Excel Still More: 2 Peter and Jude
Copyright © 2024 by Kaio Publications
http://www.kaiopublications.org

All rights reserved. No part of this publication may be reproduced, stored in a retrieval system, or transmitted in any form by any means, electronic, mechanical, photocopy, recording, or otherwise, without the prior permission of the author, except as provided for by USA copyright law.

First printing 2024
Printed in the United States of America

Scripture quotations taken from the New American Standard Bible® (NASB),
Copyright © 1960, 1962, 1963, 1968, 1971, 1972, 1973,
1975, 1977, 1995 by The Lockman Foundation
Used by permission. www.Lockman.org.

The Holy Bible, English Standard Version® (ESV®)
Copyright © 2001 by Crossway,
a publishing ministry of Good News Publishers.
All rights reserved.
ESV Text Edition: 2016

ISBN: 978-1-952955-46-4

Grammar edited by Tonja McRady
Graphic Designer: Kristin Arbuckle